TRAFALGAR

ALSO BY PAUL O'KEEFFE

Some Sort of Genius:
A Life of Wyndham Lewis

Gaudier-Brzeska:
An Absolute Case of Genius

A Genius for Failure:
The Life of Benjamin Robert Haydon

Waterloo:
The Aftermath

Culloden:
Battle & Aftermath

TRAFALGAR
Battle & Aftermath

PAUL O'KEEFFE

THE BODLEY HEAD
LONDON

3 5 7 9 10 8 6 4

The Bodley Head, an imprint of Vintage, is part of the
Penguin Random House group of companies

Vintage, Penguin Random House UK, One Embassy Gardens,
8 Viaduct Gardens, London SW11 7BW

penguin.co.uk/vintage
global.penguinrandomhouse.com

First published by The Bodley Head in 2026

Copyright © Paul O'Keeffe 2026

The moral right of the author has been asserted

Penguin Random House values and supports copyright. Copyright fuels creativity, encourages diverse voices, promotes freedom of expression and supports a vibrant culture. Thank you for purchasing an authorised edition of this book and for respecting intellectual property laws by not reproducing, scanning or distributing any part of it by any means without permission. You are supporting authors and enabling Penguin Random House to continue to publish books for everyone. No part of this book may be used or reproduced in any manner for the purpose of training artificial intelligence technologies or systems. In accordance with Article 4(3) of the DSM Directive 2019/790, Penguin Random House expressly reserves this work from the text and data mining exception.

Typeset in 11.5/15.2pt Sabon LT Std by Six Red Marbles UK, Thetford, Norfolk
Printed and bound in Great Britain by Clays Ltd, Elcograf S.p.A.

The authorised representative in the EEA is Penguin Random House Ireland,
Morrison Chambers, 32 Nassau Street, Dublin D02 YH68

A CIP catalogue record for this book is available from the British Library

ISBN 9781847921833

Penguin Random House is committed to a sustainable future
for our business, our readers and our planet. This book is made
from Forest Stewardship Council® certified paper.

For Siobhan and Steve, Caitlin and Lewis, Grace and Will,
and for Amy, Jon and Betsy: the extended
family inherited from my much-loved brother
Stephen O'Keeffe (1941–2018)

CONTENTS

PRELUDE: ROCK & MENACE . . . 1

PART I: BATTLE & BUTCHER'S BILL . . . 25

PART II: AFTERSHOCKS . . . 99

PART III: TRIUMPH & OBSEQUY . . . 165

PART IV: MONUMENTS . . . 241

CODA: CONSEQUENCES . . . 283

Notes . . . 301
Bibliography . . . 315
Acknowledgements . . . 327
List of Illustrations . . . 329
Index . . . 331

PRELUDE
ROCK & MENACE

STRIKING a Union flag from HMS *Diamond Rock* on 2 June 1805, and hoisting the tricolour in its place, marked Vice Admiral Pierre-Charles Villeneuve's first notable success – his first and his last – in the execution of Napoleon Bonaparte's complicated strategy to invade the kingdom of Great Britain and settle a grudge he imagined predated the Crécy débacle of 1346: 'We have six centuries of insults to avenge.'[1]

The Emperor's 'Grand Design' had called for two French squadrons, under British naval blockade in the ports of Toulon and Rochefort – squadrons commanded by Villeneuve and Rear Admiral Édouard Burgues de Missiessy respectively – to break out from their confinement and sail for the West Indies, rendezvousing at Fort Royal, Martinique. From there they were to plunder Britain's merchant shipping and Caribbean possessions, inviting pursuit and retaliation by the Royal Navy. With England's naval defences distracted and weakened, the squadrons were to sail back across the Atlantic and join a Spanish fleet from Cadiz in support of the vast invasion force that had been amassing along the French coast since May 1803.

Bonaparte was a soldier, his training and expertise in field artillery, his genius in the rapid outflanking tactics of a land army. And on land the strategy of feint and decoy might have succeeded. But the uncertainties of wind, swell and weather across three thousand nautical miles made a successful outcome to his far-fetched naval plans unlikely. However, were this maritime gamble to pay off, and grant him a modicum of short-term success over a superior naval power in the Channel, Bonaparte's preferred mode of warfare would have a chance to prevail on British soil. 'Let us be masters of the straits for six hours,' he declared, 'and we shall be masters of the World!'[2]

*

Villeneuve attempted to escape from Toulon – with eleven sail of the line, seven frigates, two brigs, and 3,500 troops – on 17 January, during a gale that had scattered the blockade. But the storm that facilitated the squadron's escape made further headway impossible. Villeneuve reported that although his ships 'looked well in harbour [they] were helpless at sea', and within three days they had returned to Toulon. However, eight days earlier, on 11 January, Missiessy had succeeded in evading the blockade of Rochefort during a snowstorm. His squadron comprised the 120-gun flagship *Majestueux*, four 74s – *Magnanime*, *Jemappes*, *Suffren* and *Lion* – and three 40-gun frigates: *Armide*, *Gloire* and *Thétis*. By 20 February they were approaching Martinique and the crew of HMS *Diamond Rock* prepared for action – but the French stayed out of range and reached Fort Royal without interference two days later.

During the next three weeks, Missiessy's ships captured thirty-three British merchant vessels, as well as attacking His Majesty's possessions of Dominica, St Kitts, Nevis and Montserrat. But on 12 March he received orders from the French Minister of Marine, Admiral Decrès, to return to France, the joint operation having been cancelled due to Villeneuve's failure to leave Toulon. Missiessy lost no time in re-crossing the Atlantic and by 20 May had anchored back in Rochefort. There, despite his Caribbean successes, he found himself in disgrace because he had failed in one particular objective. 'I was choked with indignation to read that he has not taken the Diamond,' wrote Bonaparte. 'I should have

PRELUDE: ROCK & MENACE

preferred to lose a warship, if it meant that Martinique was rid of that hump.'[3]

Like a colossal decayed molar, rising six hundred feet from the sea and less than half a mile in circumference, the volcanic plug of basalt off the southern tip of Martinique was known to sailors as Diamond Rock because 'when the sun struck its salt-coated surface from a certain angle, the whole rock sparkled like a fine-cut gem against the blue backcloth of the sky and sea.' The Rock's strategic importance to the Royal Navy lay in its effective control of the Fours Passage, a mile-wide stretch of sea separating it from the main island, a route invariably taken by ships approaching Fort Royal. The British occupation, manning and arming of the Rock in January 1804 had enabled Commodore Samuel Hood, Commander-in-Chief of His Majesty's Ships and Vessels in the Windward and Leeward Islands, to maintain a tight blockade over the French military and naval base. To Bonaparte this was a double affront: not only an insult to French national pride, but a stain on the Caribbean birthplace of his own wife, the Empress Josephine.*,[4]

*

First Lieutenant James Wilkes Maurice, of Hood's flagship *Centaur*, had been assigned the task of converting the Rock into a fort and signal station, commanding from its summit an area of surveillance forty miles in every direction with guns capable of blowing blockade runners attempting to negotiate the Fours Passage out of the water. Maurice was promoted Master and Commander, a naval rank between his former lieutenancy and that of post captain. This intermediate status entitled him to command a ship of war mounting fewer than eighteen guns, or in this case, 'the vessel attached to the service of the Diamond Rock ... registered by the name of the *Diamond Rock* sloop', armed with

---

* Marie-Josèphe-Rose Tascher de La Pagerie was born at Trois-Îlets, Martinique on 24 June 1763, the day a treaty was signed by Britain restoring the island to France.

sixteen, mainly small-calibre, 6-pounders. The precise wording of Maurice's commission, however, named the vessel 'His Majesty's Ship *Fort Diamond*', while Commodore Hood's report to the Admiralty referred to 'the present establishment of the *Fort Diamond* as a sloop-of-war, including the Rock'. Thenceforth, sloop and Rock were synonymous, a conflation referred to for administrative and provisioning purposes as His Majesty's Sloop *Diamond Rock*. Land-based Royal Naval establishments with the prefix HMS bear the playful designation of 'Stone Frigates', and in keeping with its anomalous definition, the same naval customs were followed on the Rock as on a vessel made of oak, hemp and canvas. Three 'watches' divided and governed the men's lives and activities through twelve hours: four on duty, eight 'below'. A sand glass was turned and brass bell struck, to mark each half-hour passage of the day and night. Five strokes signified that two-and-a-half hours of a watch had elapsed, 'eight bells' that it was at an end. Divine service was performed every Sunday and observed by the entire company, and once a month on that occasion, the Articles of War were read to remind them of penalties for the most serious infractions of naval discipline.

Hammocks were slung in caves that penetrated the Diamond's eastern face, serving an incidental purpose of keeping the sleeping men clear of the ground and the lethal *fer-de-lance* vipers that infested the place. Thought to have been introduced onto the main island of Martinique by French planters to deter their slaves from absconding, how the reptiles later made their way across the intervening channel to flourish on the Rock was a mystery.

The command structure below James Maurice comprised two naval lieutenants – the senior appointed 'First of the Rock', the junior commanding the sloop – and one Lieutenant of Marines. There were two midshipmen, a purser, surgeon, and five warrant officers: boatswain, gunner, carpenter, cooper and cook. The full complement of crew comprised 121, including seamen, boys and twenty Marines.

The armament consisted of two long 18-pounder guns, laboriously hoisted by jackstay hawser from the deck of HMS *Centaur* to the 'Fort Diamond Battery' on the Rock's summit. A deep cave, 230 feet up in the north-facing cliff, housed the 'Hood Battery', a single 24-pounder carronade. This was 'a cannon of peculiar construction, being much shorter and lighter than the common cannon, ... generally of a large calibre'. Deriving its name from the Carron Iron Company in Falkirk, Scotland, where it was invented and manufactured, the short-range but devastating gun was known affectionately to British crews as a 'Smasher'. At sea level, connected by a 400-yard-long covered way, there were two gun emplacements – a 32-pounder cannon to each – the 'Queen's Battery' trained north across the Fours Passage, the 'Centaur Battery' commanding the seaward western approach. Later, a 9-pounder carronade was installed halfway between, and named 'Maurice's Battery' in honour of the Rock's commander. On the north-east side was a large cave, and when the bats had been smoked out and guano cleared, it served as the crew's living quarters and hospital. At the foot of the north-west face, the stalactite-festooned 'Vulcan's Cave' housed the smith's two forges, the cook's galley and coppers, and the purser's, gunner's, boatswain's and carpenter's stores. A nearby concrete cistern contained 3,000 gallons – or fifty tons – of fresh water, supplemented by infrequent rainfall. By May 1805 the Hood Battery's 24-pounder carronade had been replaced by a 32-pounder and Centaur's and Queen's 32-pounder guns by longer-range 18-pounders.[5]

When HMS *Diamond Rock* was first commissioned in early 1804, Commodore Hood described it as 'a perfect naval post [that] thirty riflemen could hold ... against ten thousand'. But despite superior offensive and defensive capabilities, it would be shortage of water that ultimately forced its surrender.[6]

*

The second French sortie from Toulon, on 30 March, met with greater success than the first. By 9 April Villeneuve's 80-gun flagship *Bucentaure*, leading ten more sail of the line and six frigates, had passed the Gibraltar straits and was approaching Cadiz, while the Royal Navy's Mediterranean fleet, believing Napoleon's objective was an attack on Naples, Egypt or the Peloponnese in southern Greece, searched for them in vain. At Cadiz, Villeneuve instructed Admiral Don Federico Gravina to follow with six Spanish line-of-battle ships and two French 74s under his command, and the combined fleet – embryo of that which would meet its destiny in the same waters seven months later – set sail for the West Indies, carrying 3,000 French troops and 1,500 Spanish. They reached Martinique on 14 May, six days before Missiessy's squadron arrived back at Rochefort, having inadvertently passed one another mid Atlantic. Unlike his predecessor, Villeneuve – carrying new orders from the Emperor – was fully cognisant of his primary objective. Before putting into the harbour of Fort Royal and staying out of range of Diamond Rock's guns, he reconnoitred the rugged stronghold from *Bucentaure*'s quarterdeck, as three of his 74s fired testing shots at the impervious basalt cliffs, while equally ineffective fire was returned from the summit.

Two days later the Spanish 80-gun *San Rafael*, a belated straggler from the combined fleet, approached from the east and – deceived by the Rock's French colours 'hoisted as a decoy' – ventured to within three-quarters of a mile, at which Maurice ordered the colours shifted and 'opened a well-directed fire of round and grape' from the two long 18-pounders of the Diamond Battery. Retaliating with but 'one feeble shot', the Spaniard sustained little serious hurt before reaching the safety of Fort Royal. Later that day a French brig-of-war began cruising to windward of the Rock. Always out of range of the British guns, and reinforced by frigates, schooners and sloops, for the next two weeks it provided an effective blockade, ensuring no much-needed supplies reached Maurice's increasingly beleaguered crew. The French could have no knowledge of how desperate their situation was. On 16 May Maurice was informed that a full month's supply of fresh water had been lost. Recent earth tremors had opened a crack at the base of the concrete cistern outside Vulcan's Cave and – it was thought – the vibrations of gunfire directed at the *San Rafael* that morning had widened the fissure causing 3,000 gallons to drain away in minutes. Even though it was severely rationed, only two weeks' water remained in barrels and some of that was polluted. Any further hope of replenishing supplies vanished nine days later on the 26th when Maurice and his men watched, helplessly, as Second Lieutenant Roger Woolocombe and Mortley Riordan the purser – returning by sloop from St Lucia with ten barrels of fresh water, as many half-barrels of gunpowder, and 'between ten and twelve cwt of soft bread', were intercepted and captured by the relentless French brig despite 'a spirited fire' from Centaur's, Maurice's and the Diamond Batteries. It was scant comfort that the two officers were able to cast overboard the gunpowder before being taken, but from then on it would be only a matter of time before further defence of the Rock became impossible.

Villeneuve's attack began on the last day of May, coordinated by Commodore Julien Marie Cosmao-Kerjulien, of the 74-gun *Pluton*. He was supported by *Berwick*, another 74 – formerly HMS *Berwick*, captured by the French ten years earlier – and by the 44-gun frigate *Sirène*. A 16-gun brig, *Argus*, and 14-gun schooner *Fine* brought up the rear. Under the command of Major Eugène-Edmond Boyer, two hundred men of the 82ème Régiment d'Infanterie de Ligne had embarked at Fort Royal aboard *Pluton* and *Berwick*, for passage to the Rock. The first landing parties were transferred into longboats with small brass cannon mounted at the bows, to be towed into position by *Argus* and begin the assault.

'Seeing the impossibility of defending the lower works against such a force,' and calculating that the defenders would, any later, be prevented from retreating higher 'without considerable loss', Maurice decided to abandon the sea level batteries and concentrate his defence of the Rock at the level of the Hood Battery and the summit. Final discharges were fired at the enemy from Centaur's and Queen's guns, the scant remaining powder 'drowned', and by ten minutes to eight the lower works were deserted, 'excepting the cook, who was [subsequently] made a prisoner'. At ten minutes to eight *Berwick* opened fire and by eight o'clock 'the whole of the enemy's squadron of ships and gun-boats were in action . . . the troops in the boats keeping up a heavy fire of musketry.' The decision to evacuate his men from the sea-level emplacements proved a wise one as 'stones hove down [from the rock face] by the enemy's shot would have killed and wounded the whole of [them].' The seaward bombardment would continue for three days until the defenders capitulated.

Under covering fire from the ships, Cosmao's gunboats 'crowded with troops' were rowed ashore between nine and ten in the morning, and the first landing effected 'much sooner, and with less difficulty, than ... expected'. Even so, Maurice reported 'that the execution done [by his men] was considerable'. Once disembarked, Boyer's troops were faced by 'immense precipices, perpendicular rocks, [and] a threatening enemy entrenched in a number of cavities, which nature had formed at different heights, ... impossible to reach but by ladders 40 feet high.' While the ordnance of the Hood and Diamond Batteries were unable to deploy against an enemy directly below them at the foot of the cliffs, Maurice's men were able to harass the French very effectively from their caves with 'a galling volley of musketry, large fragments of rock, [dropped] cannon ball[s], and casks filled with stones, which they poured down' on their assailants, in the manner of medieval siege defenders. The attackers found refuge and shelter to tend their wounded 'in two cavities in the Rock', one of them Vulcan's Cave. The gunboats had been forced by 'tremendous fire' to withdraw hurriedly after disembarking their troops, and were unable to land the supplies of food, water or ammunition that they carried. 'Our situation', wrote Boyer, 'was truly dreadful; we were exhausted with fatigue, and the want of nourishment was the more severely felt by the troops, who had been prevented by the sea sickness from taking any for the two preceding days that they were on the ships ... In short ... we had nothing to offer our wounded, of whom some were in a most deplorable state.' Later in the day a few casks of water were discovered that Maurice's men had abandoned. The contents, 'though perfectly putrid', brought doubtful benefit to the wounded and 'endeavoured to assuage the thirst that devoured [the rest]'. The situation was considerably improved, however, at the end of the first day, by the arrival of a boat under cover of darkness with a reinforcement of sixty grenadiers and – in the course of the following night – another carrying provisions, ammunition and the remainder of the two hundred troops of the 82ème who had originally embarked. Later, sixty scaling ladders were landed from the schooner *Fine*, preparations watched anxiously from the Diamond Battery.

The defenders' plight – their fresh water exhausted and deprived of supplies by the two weeks' blockade – was desperate. Although only two had been killed and one wounded 'their fatigue and hardships [were] beyond description,' Maurice reported, 'having only a pint of water [per man] during 24 hours under a vertical sun, and not a moment's rest day or night'. Many fainted from dehydration 'and some of them [were] obliged to drink their own water'. At four in the afternoon of 2 June, Maurice inspected his garrison's ammunition. 'I found we had but little powder left, and not a sufficient quantity of ball cartridges to last until dark.' Short of throwing stones at an enemy 'endeavouring to carry the heights by assault that night', his defensive capability was negligible. Half an hour after, he 'threw out a flag of truce', and at five o'clock it was returned.[7]

The Rock was occupied and French colours hoisted on the summit. Maurice and his men were given refreshments and, at sunrise on the 3rd, he led the garrison to the Queen's Battery, where they laid down their arms. Maurice and his officers surrendered their swords to Major Boyer which he, 'to treat a vanquished enemy with respect [and] following ... the rules of French generosity', allowed them to retain. The following day the prisoners were taken to the British island of Barbados in a cartel – 'a ship commissioned to exchange prisoners ... for this reason she has only one gun on board for the purpose of firing signals'. Of the 107 prisoners captured, Maurice claimed that fourteen had been 'forcibly detained ... getting men to swear they were French' and enter the service of the Emperor.[8]

The two 18-pounder guns of the Diamond Battery were tipped into the sea, along with the platform, powder and shot. Boyer had one of the flagstaffs cut down, 'leaving only that on which the French colours were flying'.

Editorial comment in the *Naval Chronicle*, which published a translation of Boyer's report,* questioned the accuracy of the military strength – '200 men of the 82nd regiment' – employed to subdue the Rock, favouring instead Maurice's highly inflated estimate of 'from the nearest calculation, 1,500 troops'. The *Chronicle* also disparaged the French casualty figures, 'instead of 50 killed and wounded; as stated by Boyer, [they] are known, by persons who were on the spot, to have lost nearly 600', emphasising the assertion with two exclamation marks.[9]

*

Meanwhile, ten Royal Navy ships, led by HMS *Victory*, and including *Belleisle*, *Conqueror*, *Leviathan* and *Swiftsure*, together with three frigates, had belatedly abandoned their search of the eastern Mediterranean for the escaped Toulon squadron, and rapidly crossed the Atlantic in just twenty-four days, hoping to bring the French to an action. They arrived in Carlisle Bay, Barbados, on the afternoon of 4 June. The following day, receiving word that their quarry had left Martinique and was threatening His Majesty's possessions of Trinidad and Tobago, the British fleet sailed south in pursuit. The intelligence proved groundless, however. The French squadron was in fact active five hundred miles to the north, where it captured a convoy of fourteen British sugar ships out of Antigua on 8 June. It was then that Villeneuve learned from his prisoners of the recent arrival at Barbados of a formidable enemy fleet. His own ships in need of repair, and with yellow fever – endemic in that latitude and time of year – spreading among his crews, he was unwilling to risk doing battle. Instead, he set sail for Europe, ostensibly in accordance with the Emperor's most recent orders. He was

---

* Published first in the *Martinique Gazette*, then, translated, in the *Barbados Gazette*.

to proceed to El Ferrol and rendezvous with five French and nine Spanish ships, then join Vice Admiral Ganteaume's squadron at Brest, whose twenty-one ships, added to his own and those from El Ferrol, would comprise 'a strength greater than any the enemy could bring against him'. This Combined Fleet was then to sail for Boulogne in support of the long-awaited invasion, and 'with the help of God, ... put an end to the future ... existence of England'. By the end of the crossing, *Achille* numbered 200 men sick, *Indomptable*, *Intrépide* and *Aigle* 150 each, and from 60 to 120 in every one of the rest.[10]

*

In the late morning of 22 July Vice Admiral Sir Robert Calder, with fifteen ships of the line, two frigates and two cutters, met Villeneuve's returning fleet in a fog 'so thick that it was impossible to see any thing, and each ship could scarcely see the vessel next to it'. Calder had been blockading the approaches to El Ferrol and Coruña since February but when the Admiralty received news that the enemy force was returning to Europe from the Caribbean, he was ordered to 'proceed 40 leagues* north-west of Cape Finisterre, and cruise six or eight days in order to intercept'. The enemy fleet – 'twenty sail of the line, seven frigates and two armed brigs' – was larger than Calder had been led to expect: 'only 16 sail' according to his most recent intelligence. The ensuing action – made chaotic by the fog and further obscured by gun smoke – continued for about nine and a half hours, '[ships firing] by the light of the enemy's fire almost always without seeing them' – until nightfall when the firing ceased. It was not until daylight the following morning that Villeneuve discovered he had lost two Spanish ships as prizes to the British. The 74-gun *Firme* and the sluggish 80-gun *San Rafael* had struck their colours in the closing stages of the battle, both 'dreadfully disabled', having

---

* 'LEAGUE, a measure of 3 miles, much used in estimating sea distances' (*The British Mariner's Vocabulary; or Universal Dictionary of Technical Terms and Sea Phrases*, 1801).

borne the brunt of the fighting, their masts demolished, *San Rafael* 'nearly a perfect wreck'. The 476 men killed and wounded comprised three-quarters of the Combined Fleet's entire casualties. Spanish prisoners claimed that the French 74-gun *Scipion* had also struck 'but escaped owing to the thickness of the fog and darkness of night'. The total Spanish and French losses came to six hundred and forty-seven, those of their opponents to one hundred and ninety-eight.[11]

By the morning of the 23rd the combatants had drifted seventeen miles apart but were still in sight of one another. However, with little or no wind, hostilities were not resumed by nightfall, nor on the morning of the 24th, and by that evening Villeneuve's squadron had disappeared into the mist and distance.

Calder would later defend his decision not to resume the action. Still outnumbered, and burdened with two crippled prizes to retain, or at the least prevent from falling back into enemy hands, he was aware also of a threat from nine French ships that had sailed from Rochefort five days earlier, on 17 July, and had already begun a campaign of plunder against merchant shipping in the same area. There was an additional possibility that a change in wind direction might have enabled another sixteen vessels to escape from the now unblockaded port of El Ferrol. Had the additional twenty-five men-of-war joined forces with Villeneuve, his own squadron would have been overwhelmed. Nevertheless, Calder's reputation suffered in the London newspapers. The *Morning Post* reported that the outcome of the engagement 'furnish[es] almost the only topics upon which turn the general conversation of the town' and although 'the Public entertain a high enthusiastic opinion of the skill of our Naval Commanders, and of the discipline and intrepidity of our honest tars ... on the present occasion, there certainly appear more symptoms of disappointment than of applause; and were we to follow the stream as it now seems to run, we should be carried rather into censure than into praise.' Opinion was stoked by criticism from within Calder's own squadron. An officer on HMS *Malta*, in a private letter – which, notwithstanding, found its way into public print – wrote of his 'surprise and mortification, after losing a glorious opportunity of completely destroying the Combined Squadron, and adding additional honour to the British Flag, [that] we have let them completely escape from us'. Acidly disingenuous, he asserted that 'it is not for me to attach blame to a superior Officer, much less to a Commander in Chief,' while at the same time musing on the 'reasons, private reasons, and, indeed, orders of such a peculiar nature, that govern his conduct, and tye up his hands'.[12]

*

An early report from Brussels, in the summer of 1803, claimed that 'the number of troops which are destined for the landing in England is now estimated at 200,000.' Camps were to be established 'at Cherbourg of 60,000 men; at St Omers, of 50,000; at Compiegne, of 50,000; and in the Batavian Republic [or Netherlands] of 40,000'. Flotillas of landing craft were to be assembled at Dunkirk, Boulogne and Calais. 'The attack, for which a great quantity of artillery is already prepared, will be made from every side at once.' 8,000 gun boats were reportedly under construction, and if its readers might doubt the practicability of landing artillery and horses as well as men, the *Morning Post* pointed out that 'they may throw many thousands of their hordes on our shores with muskets and bayonets in their hands, ammunition and provisions on their backs, who may do the most serious mischief', regardless. And there was to be no doubt of what that mischief might entail. 'The promise of ... plunder ... will animate French soldiers to any enterprise, however desperate, and that promise is made to them in every way that can inflame their passions.'[13]

By early August, rumour was sharpening to include more detailed descriptions of the proposed operation. At Saint-Malo and other ports, 400 large flat-bottomed boats were described by the *Sun*. 'They row thirty-six oars each, are very light, [and] capable of holding a great number of troops.' And in case the threat of attendant rapine be entirely forgotten: 'The soldiery are mad for the attempt, in the hopes of plunder.' Just a day later, the rumoured statistics had increased, the *Morning Post* reporting that 'gun vessels ready for sea are said to be nearly one hundred, and the number of flat-bottomed boats is calculated at nine hundred and twenty-nine.' The latter craft, it was claimed, were each capable of carrying 150 men. Even allowing for exaggeration – and that the capacity of each flat-bottomed boat was just one hundred – Britain was potentially threatened by an 'immense force of ninety-two thousand troops'. The *Star* reported information received of several locations – Boulogne, Calais, Dunkirk, Ostend and Holland – where embarkation of the invading armies was planned. 'Twenty thousand men, on board a fleet consisting of gun-boats and other vessels, of various denominations' were to sail for the Sussex Coast and 'land, if possible, near Brighton'. Other landings were planned in Kent and Essex. 'Such of the armies as are fortunate enough to get footing on the English shores [were] to make a junction with every possible dispatch and afterwards fight their way to the British metropolis.'[14]

Concerned that the invasion might come by way of Holland, the daughters of a Norfolk banker prepared to leave their home in Earlham. 'I think we shall be in a very unprotected state if the French should land while my father is away, without a single man, or even boy, to take care of us', Priscilla Gurney wrote to her married sister Elizabeth Fry, the future prison reformer: 'As soon as ever we hear the news of their arrival, we six [unmarried sisters], Danny [twelve-year-old brother] and the Nurse and, if we can manage it, Molly and Anne [the maids], are immediately to set off in the coach-and-four for Ely [forty-five miles away], as my father thinks it is a very safe place, being so completely surrounded by marshes ... Mrs Freeman is to stay to take care of the house, as it will be necessary for somebody to be here. My father intends to write down directions for every individual of the family, so that there may be no confusion or bustle whenever the moment of danger arrives.' Priscilla was just one of many correspondents across the country for whom the war seemed a growing threat to their formerly settled existence. Robert Howard, a chemist in Sun Street, Shoreditch, was 'seriously apprehensive of the Invasion being soon and suddenly attempted'. His daughter, Elizabeth, was at Ramsgate, and he imagined her in the very path of a French incursion. 'If you do not return soon,' he warned her, 'it is not at all unlikely you may be put to some inconvenience if not to Suffering ... It would be a sad thing to be on the Coast if any great bustle should happen.'[15]

*

The East Indiaman clipper *Admiral Aplin*, under Captain John Rogers' command, sailed from Portsmouth for Madras on 28 August 1803. Four months later, west of Sumatra, she encountered the 32-gun French privateer *Psyche*, and after a six-day chase was brought to action and forced to surrender by the predator's 'superiority of metal' over her own '16 small guns'. As was customary in the event of capture, Rogers threw overboard 'the [East India] Company's dispatches, and all letters which he considered to be of any consequence', to prevent their falling into enemy hands. However, he neglected to drown a large consignment of private letters sent from home to friends, relatives and business associates in India. By 16 September, over eighty of these 'Intercepted Letters' had been translated, edited and published in Paris across eleven pages of *Le Moniteur universel* – the French government's official journal of record – as encapsulating England's low state of morale in face of the invasion threat.[16]

Opinion in the letters was divided as to how well prepared the country was to meet the crisis. 'Bonaparte threatens ... to land 100,000 men', a Berkshire gentleman told his brother. 'We, at Newbery, have three hundred infantry and one hundred cavalry to resist him.' Twenty-four miles away Mr Taylor, of King's Somborne in Hampshire, was more bullish as to the capacity for both local and national resistance: 'We have actually more men than arms', he declared. 'Nearly 800 men are enrolled in the parish of Kensington, and 150 in [our] little village ... London and Westminster will furnish not less than 40,000, and all the country together ... will produce a force of at least a million of men; perhaps it will reach to two millions.' That confidence was not shared by Mr Hammond, who wrote in apocalyptic terms to Mr Middleton: 'This letter will, perhaps, be the last you will receive from me; perhaps even before you receive it this country will be annihilated, and he that wrote it, as well as all that belong to him, will have bitten the dust! Perhaps, what is worse, we shall be wretches, without fires, or homes, without a stone to lay our heads upon.' A recurring complaint concerned the economic impact of the war with France. 'Money is scarce beyond all expression', an unnamed gentleman confided to Alfred Tufton, a civil servant in Bengal; 'commerce experiences a very great stagnation, since we are in a manner excluded from the Continent of Europe [and] taxes are augmented to excess.' Another gentleman pointed out that 'a man of £1200 a year pays £600 in taxes [and] duties.' Mrs Seton, writing to her son, was also preoccupied by 'new taxes [and] new subscriptions for the aid of the country' and pronounced the period as 'truly detestable'. Ten days later she was bemoaning inflation, 'all articles of the first necessity ... at a higher price than ever'. She even 'fear[ed] the people, in their discontent, would join the French if they should ... come.' Miss Lydia Macdonald, writing to her sister, also feared the social consequences, and contrasted 'the ruin of the most opulent commercial houses' with 'the situation of those possessing less brilliant resources'.[17]

A fortnight after publication in *Le Moniteur*, and professing 'reluctance and regret' at what he was doing, Mr John Ginger of Piccadilly – bookseller to the Prince of Wales – had the French re-translated into English and offered for sale at two shillings and sixpence. He suspected – and hoped – that some unpatriotic and discreditable sentiments expressed in the letters were not typical of national feeling, and 'that ... interpolations ha[d] been made [to the originals and] many passages ... altered' by the French for propaganda purposes. Mr Ginger's tortuous justification for his catchpenny production was 'that an opportunity might be afforded to the British Public, of vindicating themselves from ... erroneous interpretations of their feelings, and of repelling ... unfounded charges against their principles ... made in some parts of the Correspondence.' Whether or not his publication succeeded in its stated aim, the opportunity of reading other people's private letters was submitted 'to the curiosity of the Public'.

Excerpts were printed in the popular press, with commentary on the most noteworthy. The outspoken, radical views of Mr Stuart Hall were particularly disparaged. Two letters from this gentleman were included in the collection, the first, evoking an England divided by class, was deemed 'too bad even for a Jacobin', by the *General Evening Post*. 'Our great men ... press the people to submit to heavy taxes', wrote Hall, 'and preach up the necessity of leaving one's family ... to encounter the enemy and die for one's King and Country ... whilst the titled and the opulent loll[ing] in their carriages, with from three to thirty idle fellows in livery to add to their luxury and swell their pomp ... contribute the least to the defence of the country.' The *Evening Mail* questioned the authenticity of this document and declared that 'no Englishman could possibly have written it.' Hall's second letter, last in the collection, cast doubt not only on the conduct of the war, but its prospects of success. 'Without fixed plan or definite object,' he claimed, 'we have plunged, like madmen, into the most expensive and destructive war that ever afflicted this country.' And as for combatting the expected invasion, he had scant faith in his countrymen, *en masse*, answering a defensive call to arms, arguing that 'the measure was tried in the case of Hanover, and the inhabitants positively refused to come forward.' Meanwhile, Ireland was 'ripe for rebellion' again – five years after the insurrection of '98 – and in the event of the French landing, he had no doubt they 'would be received with open arms by the people'. In short, he feared 'that some terrible explosion is about to take place, and that it will be attended with terrible consequences'. The *Morning Post* asserted these views 'by no means creditable to the author, either as a man of sense, [or] a patriot', while the *Weekly Dispatch* derived some consolation 'that those who have maintained such sentiments, and drawn such conclusions, stand singular and isolated from all the rest of their countrymen'. The shining example of a Miss E. Tomson, writing to her brother in the 6th Regiment of Native Cavalry at Madras, was held up by the *Dispatch* as 'one of the most *manly* and courageous letters in the whole Correspondence'. Like Mr Hall, she referred to Bonaparte's recent occupation of Hanover and confessed that thoughts of what took place there 'freeze every drop of blood in my veins'. She was told, 'not a woman ha[d] been spared ... neither youth nor age; all were indifferently abandoned to the brutality of the soldiers.' And yet despite such threatened horrors, she had no doubt that before her brother received the letter, 'the enemy will have perished' or the invasion been repelled. 'The spirit of unanimity and courage which manifests itself here in all classes, is truly extraordinary ... Can a conquest be so easily effected over a nation thus united, who respect their King, idolise their constitution, and detest their enemy? I hope not.'[18]

*

By mid 1805, according to the testimony of a French prisoner of war, there were about 30,000 vessels at Boulogne, eight hundred of which were armed, the rest being transports for troops and stores. There were, he claimed, nearly 1,000 more at Étaples, and about six hundred at Vimereux, and four hundred at Dunkirk, at Ostend and at Calais. Troops were bivouacked in small camps, about 80,000 at Boulogne, and the same number around Calais, Vimereux, Étaples and places inland. The prisoner seemed confident the attempt would be made that summer, and that a combined French and Spanish fleet of sixty sail would fight a Royal Navy force while large frigates would make their way up the Channel and convoy the invasion flotilla across what Bonaparte contemptuously referred to as 'the ditch'. The troops were reported to be 'very eager ... and entertain[ed] the most sanguine hopes of success ... and great reliance [was] place[d] on the genius of Buonaparte'. The prisoner's testimony was greatly exaggerated. Even the most optimistic official report given to the Emperor in August put the invasion flotilla at only 1,016 'war vessels', in addition to 1,058 transports, and the entire fleet capable of carrying 167,500 men and 9,149 horses. Nevertheless, on 22 August Bonaparte wrote to Villeneuve, ordering him not to lose a moment in leaving the port of Brest and entering the Channel with his combined squadrons. 'England is ours,' he declared. 'We are all prepared, everything is embarked. Come within twenty-four hours and all will be finished.' But Villeneuve was not in Brest. Following the action with Calder a month earlier, his damaged and depleted squadron had put into the Spanish port of Vigo, before sailing a further hundred or so miles to El Ferrol. Despite reiterated orders from the Emperor, he had not then continued north to the Breton port of Brest, where Vice Admiral Ganteaume's squadron of twenty-one ships of the line was waiting to join him. He did not leave El Ferrol until 10 August, when he sailed southwards instead.[19]

*

The London papers printed rumours in late August that 'Bonaparte had suddenly quitted Boulogne ... in consequence of dispatches received by him from Paris, and that orders had been received in Holland to suspend the further embarkation of troops in the ports of that country.' *Johnson's Sunday Monitor* added that 'the present aspect of Continental affairs renders this statement by no means improbable.' This referred to the armies of Francis II, Emperor of Austria, and Tsar Alexander of Russia mobilising on the Bavarian and Polish borders respectively. A cutter arrived at Dover on 6 September and reported that 'being off Boulogne, they saw a body of troops, which they suppose amounted to 5,000 men, marching off ... with waggons and their baggage, camp equipage, &c.' The following day a telegraph from Deal stated 'that the camps near Boulogne were all breaking up, and that the troops have been marched into the interior – most probably to the Rhine'. This intelligence, the *London Chronicle* suggested, 'almost needless to say, is decisive of a Continental War'. It was equally unnecessary to observe 'that the menaces of the invasion of England are also done away by this sudden ... movement'. The *Morning Post* summed up the cause for national relief with a laborious play on words. 'The army of Boulogne have at length *struck* their tents. Two years of proud menace to *strike* a desperate *blow* against this country have been consumed in *feints*, and terminated in *striking* their own encampment.' The threat having receded, one young lady observed of the invasion that, if nothing else, it had long been a useful 'topick' to fill any uncomfortable lull in the conversation.*,[20]

Over 170,000 of Bonaparte's troops, divided into seven corps numbering twenty, thirty or forty thousand each, marched eastwards from Ambleteuse, Boulogne and Étaples, across a seventy-mile front, crossing the Rhine on 25 September, a distance of some 325 miles in less than a month. They reached the Danube three weeks later, where the siege, capitulation and capture of an Austrian army at Ulm was followed by the French occupation of Munich and Vienna. It culminated, on 2 December, in the defeat of Russian and Austrian forces at the 'battle of the Three Emperors' – Bonaparte's blood-soaked tactical masterpiece, Austerlitz – and the British Prime Minister, William Pitt's remark that the redundant map of Europe should be rolled up and put away for the next decade.

Meanwhile, on 20 August, Vice Admiral Cuthbert Collingwood, on board HMS *Dreadnought*, was cruising with a small blockading squadron off the Spanish port of Cadiz when 'thirty-six sail of men-of-war' approached from the north. 'We were

---

* Marianne Spencer-Stanhope: see Stirling, *The Letter Bag of Lady Elizabeth Spencer-Stanhope*, vol. 1, pp. 68-9.

only three poor things, with a frigate and a bomb',* he told his wife, 'not very ambitious ... to try our strength against such odds', and they retired a short distance, followed by sixteen of the enemy, while the rest entered the harbour. The sixteen then 'joined their friends in Cadiz, where they are fitting and replenishing their provisions'. Collingwood resumed his blockade. It would only be a matter of time before the congested Spanish anchorage, 'now as thick as a wood' with ships, would have to disgorge the Combined Fleet and it could be brought to an action.[21]

---

* 'BOMB *vessel*, a small vessel particularly calculated to throw bombs into a fortress, being built remarkably strong, in order to sustain the violent shocks produced by the discharge of their mortars' (*The British Mariner's Vocabulary; or Universal Dictionary of Technical Terms and Sea Phrases*, 1801).

PART I
BATTLE & BUTCHER'S BILL

I

AT approximately quarter past one in the afternoon, unheard in the din of battle, a French musket discharged a 22-gramme, 15-millimetre ball from the mizen top of *Redoutable* – a distance of 'a mere 70 feet' – down to the larboard* side of HMS *Victory*'s quarterdeck where it struck Horatio, Lord Viscount Nelson, Duke of Bronte, Vice Admiral of the White.[1]

Little damage was visible. Other wounds received in the last decade of a thirty-five-year naval career had bled more abundantly, disfigured more conspicuously, disabled more radically. During an assault on the Corsican stronghold at Calvi in 1794, a round shot struck a nearby sandbag dashing gravel into his face and ripping off part of the right eyebrow. It also lost him the sight of that otherwise unblemished eye. A musket round three years later at Santa Cruz de Tenerife had shattered the bone above his right elbow and cut his brachial artery, the gushing haemorrhage shielded from him by his companion's hat. Trauma of wound, surgical amputation of the arm and convalescent pain alleviated by opium had turned his hair temporarily white. And at the battle of the Nile in 1798 a fragment of jagged iron, or 'langrage', had glanced across his forehead, leaving 'the cranium bared for more

---

* 'The old term for the left-hand side of a ship when facing forward, now known as port ... To avoid confusion with the similar sounding starboard ... the change was made official in 1844' (*Oxford Companion to Ships and the Sea*).

than an inch, the wound 3" long' and ripping free a flap of skin wide enough to hang down and obscure his sighted eye.[2]

The outward effects of *Redoutable*'s bullet were unspectacular by comparison and most of the blood subsequently found on Nelson's clothing was not his own. The projectile had nicked the edge of his epaulette, passing through the material of his coat into the left shoulder. But internal devastation increased along its downward diagonal path. A curving spur of bone – the acromion – at the topmost corner of the shoulder blade or scapula was fractured, followed by the second, then third rib. Piercing the left lung, and cutting a branch of the pulmonary artery, the bullet severed the spine, splintering the sixth and seventh vertebrae as it crashed between. The soft lead ball – deformed by collisions with bone – ended its flight embedded in muscle 'about two inches below the inferior angle of the right scapula'. It was still wrapped in the scrap of blue woollen cloth punched from the Admiral's coat, together with a small quantity of gold fibres and a fragment of yellow silk from the epaulette's lining, dragged into the wound at the instant of its penetration and passage. Some strands of bullion thread were so firmly attached as to seem 'inserted ... while in a state of fusion' to the base metal of the bullet. The ruptured silk – as Dr William Beatty, *Victory*'s surgeon, remarked – was a clear refutation, if such were needed, of 'an opinion entertained by some, that silk possesses in an eminent degree the power of resisting the force, or arresting the velocity, of a musket or pistol ball'.[3]

Given the slightness of Nelson's frame and the narrowness of the target he presented to a musket fired from above, it is possible that the bullet was not aimed but found him by chance in the dense cannon smoke that intermittently shrouded *Victory*'s quarterdeck at the height of battle. Poor visibility, and the motion of both ships grinding together in the swell, magnifying the sway of *Redoutable*'s mizen top, would certainly have made it more difficult for the Frenchman who fired it doing so with any degree of accuracy from a smooth-bored weapon and a moving vantage platform. It may even have been deflected by a ricochet in the rigging and its momentum nearly spent when it struck. This would account for its failure to force an exit from Nelson's body, lodging instead within the tissue of the latissimus dorsi muscle.

*

Nearly eight hours earlier – and a more obscure calamity – the first death recorded in the British fleet that day had occurred at half past five, thirty minutes before dawn, when twenty-year-old Aaron Crocan of Bridgwater, Somerset fell from the 74-gun *Conqueror* and drowned. He was described in the ship's muster roll as a landsman – 'the distinctive appellation of [one] on board a ship who [has] never before been at sea'.[4]

On the morning of the battle several ships' logs noted 'a heavy swell from the westward', a powerful surface turbulence originating from high winds perhaps hundreds of miles out in the Atlantic and presaging the violent storm which was to reach them from that direction in the days following. Despite the localised 'Light airs, inclinable to calm' also logged, and what Midshipman Hercules Robinson, aboard the 36-gun frigate *Euryalus*, remembered as 'a beautiful misty sun-shiny morning ... the sea like a mill-pond', that 'ominous ground-swell' would nonetheless have generated a pitching and rolling of vessels, sufficient to tip an inexperienced sailor overboard in the darkness. However, even had Landsman Crocan been otherwise there is no more likelihood he could have saved himself, given that a high proportion of even experienced able seamen in the Georgian navy were unable to swim. Any sailor who could was untypical, and if capable of rescuing men who could not, he would be a notable hero to his messmates. James 'Jack' Spratt of HMS *Defiance* boasted of having 'save[d] five ... from a watery grave at the great risk of my own [life] one in particular from between two sharks'. But for the majority of seamen it was a skill deliberately unlearned. Better a swift drowning than futile exertion prolonging the inevitability of certain death.[5]

Sunrise was at 6.52, but a little before 6.00 the eastern horizon was lightening. Twelve or fifteen miles off Cape Trafalgar, a lookout at the topmast head of *Revenge* sighted 'a sail on the starboard bow'. Then minutes later, 'more than one sail'; and, as the day strengthened, plainly seen even from the deck, 'a forest of masts rising from the ocean'. Midshipman William Stanhope Badcock also saw them from the forecastle of *Neptune*, 'strange masts ... to leeward.' It was described more effusively by Able Seaman James Martin in the same vessel, particularly awestruck by the occasion: 'perhaps the Grandest Sight of Hosteil Fleets ever Behild ... maned with the Flowr of their Respective Nations and Comanded By the most Celibrated Admirals of the Nations the Enemy had'. Such a spectacle would not be seen again in anyone's lifetime. Nevertheless, a comforting rumour went around *Neptune*'s decks that all was not as well with their adversaries' morale as might appear. Having cast his glass across the distant rigging, a lieutenant told Martin's gun crew that 'theair was a Mutiney in the Enemys Fleet [and] thay have two [men] Hangen at the yard Arms'. Neither Spanish nor French records lend any credence to this speculation.[6]

Royal Marine Second Lieutenant Paul Harris Nicholas on board *Belleisle* was woken by cheering and a scrambling of the men to get their first view of the combined French and Spanish fleet. 'The horizon appeared covered with ships' about nine miles away to the south-east. Another marine, Lieutenant Lawrence Halloran, discerned the enemy's composition in more detail from *Britannia*, 'laying to in a fine semicircle, alternate French and Spanish, decorated with their respective flags, ensigns, etc.' Lieutenant Nicholas remembered that 'the delight manifested exceeded anything I ever witnessed, surpassing even those gratulations when our native cliffs are descried after a long period of distant service.' Able Seaman John Brown on *Victory* wrote that the sight of the distant enemy fleet 'like a great wood on our lee bow ... cheered the hearts of every british tar ... like lions Anxious to be at it.' On *Swiftsure*, Alexander Barker waxed purple in his confident superlatives. 'Our Seamen display'd that nautical skill which ranks them superior to every Nation in the Universe, while they navigate the Wooden Walls, which protect old Albion, and compel the world to own them the favorites of Neptune.' Excitement at the prospect of imminent battle was fuelled partly by belligerence and patriotism, and partly by the likelihood of profit. It moved James Martin to verse:

> The British Hearts did Lift for Joy
>   The Sight for to Behold
> We Sone prepaird to fight them
>   For Honnor and for Gold.[7]

While the rank and file of a victorious land army on campaign would be expected to supplement their meagre pay by pillaging conquered territory and plundering battlefield dead, the Navy had its own longstanding and official tradition of incentivising its crews, dating back to the mid fifteenth century. The prize system – whereby captors of an enemy ship were given shares of her value when sold – was a potent inducement to fight. Following any successful action, the flag officer – of rear admiral's rank or above – in overall command would receive an entire eighth of the proceeds, the captains below him sharing a quarter, and sea lieutenants and masters, another eighth. A further eighth would be equally divided between warrant officers below master's rank – boatswains, gunners, carpenters, pursers, surgeons, chaplains and lieutenants of marines – while midshipmen, warrant officers' assistants and skilled tradesmen such as caulkers, sail- and rope-makers, received equal shares of another eighth. The final quarter of spoils was divided equally between the remaining, and largest, category of each ship's company: 'Trumpeters, Quarter Gunners, Carpenters' Crew, Stewards' Mates, Cooks' Mates, Gunsmiths, Coopers, Swabbers, Ordinary Trumpeters, Barbers, Able Seamen, Ordinary Seamen, and Marines and other Soldiers, and all other persons doing duty and assisting on board'.[8]

An additional sum, divided in the same proportions, was payable to the victors, amounting to 'Five pounds for every man who was living on board any [enemy ship] taken, sunk, burnt or otherwise destroyed at the Beginning of the Attack or Engagement'. This figure – computed from muster rolls – included those no longer living at the *end* of the said attack or engagement. The bounty was known as 'head money'.⁹

On the gun decks of *Bellerophon* they were already 'fixing the number of their prizes, and pitching upon that which should fall to the lot of each of our ships'. It was generally agreed, 'by the calculation of the oldest sailors on board', that the 136-gun Spanish flagship *Santísima Trinidad* was the most desirable. Reputed to be the most formidable and certainly biggest vessel then in existence, the head money alone payable on her prodigious complement of crew promised £5,550. However, *Bellerophon* was 'far from being the only ship in the fleet that fixed upon her'. On board *Victory*, the commander-in-chief himself had encouraged the crew with the scale of prize money they might expect: 'This will be a glorious day for England whoever lives to see it,' he told them. 'I shan't be satisfied with 12 ships this day as I took at the Nile.' Seven years earlier, Nelson had been awarded £3,090 as his share from that engagement although there was a stark disparity between his and the crew's. Each seaman, landsman, marine and boy who fought under him at Aboukir Bay was enriched by just £7 18s.¹⁰

*

At seven o'clock, *Victory*'s signals officer, Lieutenant John Pasco, had general signal number thirteen hoisted, a horizontal blue cross on a white ground above a yellow saltire on blue: 'PREPARE FOR BATTLE'. And throughout the fleet, drummers 'beat to quarters', the rattling staccato rhythm known as 'Hearts of Oak' sending ships' companies to their fighting stations. 'Now they cannot escape us,' Nelson was reported to have remarked to his officers. 'I think we shall make sure of twenty of them. I shall probably lose a leg, but that will be purchasing a victory cheaply.'¹¹

As crews 'cleared for action', carpenters' mallets hammered down partitions and bulkheads, 'breaking away the captain's and officer's cabins and sending all lumber below', permitting unobstructed passage of powder and ammunition to guns the entire length of the ship. No area was sacrosanct, no quarters exempt from this orderly sweep. Lord Nelson 'gave particular directions for taking down from his cabin the different fixtures', ordering that especial care be taken with the portrait of his 'Guardian Angel', Lady Hamilton. His sleeping cabin was soon furnished with nothing but a pair of long 12-pounder cannon, his dining cabin with four more, while his day cabin, although lacking ordnance, had been stripped of furniture. When Lieutenant Pasco delivered a message to the admiral he found him kneeling on the floor – writing his final thoughts, instructions, and a codicil to his will favouring Emma and their daughter Horatia – as all the chairs had been stowed.[12]

Vessels left a trail of jetsam in their wake as quantities of stores that might otherwise clutter the gun decks and hamper the destructive endeavours of the ship were hove into the sea. *Belleisle* was particularly wasteful in this regard and 'threw overboard unavoidably, in clearing for action', two tubs of halyard rope, sixty iron coopering hoops in parcels of ten, and ninety empty biscuit bags. Also ejected was 'Some Beef & Pork in Harness Tubs' – the containers so called because their notoriously tough preserved contents were known to seamen as 'salted horse' – and seven empty butts, or half barrels, together with two containing rum and water 'cut for Grog'. The cut of a man's daily ration was four to one, a quart of water to a half pint of rum,* and was named after its originator Admiral Edward Vernon, nicknamed 'Old Grogram' for his distinctive boat cloak of grogram cloth, a coarse blend of silk and mohair. *Conqueror*'s log was less explicit as to wastage, mentioning only five butts, contents unspecified, and 'sundry other articles' jettisoned as 'being in the way of the guns'. One such article, although 'by misadventure', was an officer's pet dog – a Sardinian Pointer – thrown through one of the main-deck gun ports, and its fate, along with that of Landsman Aaron Crocan, forgotten in the excitement.[13]

What was neither stowed nor thrown into the sea might be hoisted aloft. When *Tonnant* cleared for action, the wardroom Windsor chairs were suspended on a rope stretched – clothesline

---

* Half that quantity for a boy.

fashion – between the main- and mizenmasts. One was later claimed and kept as a souvenir of the battle by Mr Chevers, the ship's surgeon, as exemplifying the power of musket fire. Part of a leg had been shot away, 'and another bullet had passed completely through its thick oaken seat'.[14]

Apart from clearing the decks there was a further preparation. The General Order Book of HMS *Mars* stated that officers commanding at their different quarters were 'directed to see the Decks wetted, and sand or ashes strewed upon them, whenever the Ship is going into Action'. It can be assumed that the same procedure was followed in other ships of the British fleet. It certainly applied in the Spanish navy, and when the naïve protagonist of Pérez Galdós's account of the battle asks a more experienced hand on board *Santísima Trinidad* why sand was being spread, he receives the curt reply: 'Es para la sangre' – for the blood.[15]

Gun crews prepared themselves. 'Some were stripped to the waist,' observed Lieutenant Nicholas on *Belleisle*, 'some had bared their necks and arms, others had tied a handkerchief round their heads.' Samuel Burdon Ellis, second lieutenant of Marines on the *Ajax*, going below decks found 'the majority ... stripped to the waist; a handkerchief ... tightly bound round their heads and over the ears, to deaden the noise of the cannon, many men being deaf for days after an action'. William Robinson, on *Revenge*, wrote of gun crews in action following orders by dumb show: 'the noise of the guns ... so completely made us deaf, that we were obliged to look only to the motions that were made,' instead of hearing commands. On *Victory*, another lieutenant of marines similarly recorded that 'Lips might move, but orders and hearing were out of the question: everything was done by signs.' The more permanent infirmity of *Bellerophon*'s Signals Midshipman John Franklin cannot have been uncommon. He survived the battle without injury, to die in sub-zero temperatures four decades later while searching for the fabled North-West Passage. But 'after Trafalgar', a relative recalled, 'he was always a little deaf.'[16]

*

Below the impending pandemonium of the gun decks, preparations were made at the rear of the orlop to receive the wounded. In 1770 William Northcote, 'many years in His Majesty's service', had given 'brief directions to be observed by the sea-surgeon in an engagement'. Carpenters were to be employed constructing a platform. 'On top of a smooth and even tire [of] cask[s], let there be deals or planks laid close together, over them an old sail and upon that some seamen's bedding . . . ready made up . . . to place your wounded men . . . after they are drest.' Beds in the surgeon's and purser's cabins were to be made up 'to receive the captain, or any of his commission officers, who may chance to be wounded'.

Directly under the lowest gun deck, the cockpit was separated from the thunderous discharges of the ship's biggest ordnance – the 32-pounders – by just a six-inch thickness of oak timber. 'Oh *Victory, Victory*', the dying Nelson is said to have murmured during one devastating concussion, 'how you distract my poor brain.' And if it was a disturbance to the injured, it was more so for those requiring a steady hand treating them. Edward Ives complained after first conducting an amputation during a naval action in 1741 that 'the very shaking of the lower gun-deck, owing to the recoil of the large cannon . . . just over his head, is of itself sufficient to incommode a surgeon, and . . . prevent the skilful performance of his duty.'[17]

Visibility was another factor. The orlop deck was 'utterly dark, half of its depth being below the water line' and hanging lanterns offering scantest illumination. Northcote, in his manual on *The Marine Practice of Physic and Surgery*, recommended that 'a number of large candles should be immediately lighted, as soon as the engagement begins.' At Trafalgar, Mr Forbes McBean Chevers instructed his two assistants on HMS *Tonnant* to hold the candles 'torch-like' for him to operate by. 'If you look straight into the wound', he told them, 'and see all that I do, I shall see perfectly.' Most of the injuries he tended were 'huge splinter wounds . . . more formidable than those inflicted by shot [and] terrible, even to a surgeon'. Bending closely over his work between the two glimmering candle flames he found, when he came later to wash his face, 'that his eyebrows had been burnt off'.[18]

Wherever possible a triage system of treatment was adopted, the surgeon being advised to 'always first take care of him who is in the most immediate danger'. However, 'if any is brought down with a limb off, or a violent haemorrhage, and you happen to be in the midst of an amputation, ... and cannot that instant attend, order your mate or assistant ... immediately to fix a tourniquet on the part, to restrain the flux of blood from being fatal to the patient ... till you have finished the operation you were about.' But when there was little or no difference in the severity of injury, he was to 'dress them as they come, without distinction'. Many accounts of the action on 21 October refer to this democratic system of wounded men stoically awaiting their turn, but some forecastle hands believed that timely assistance was often withheld on the basis of a too strictly applied rule of rotation, with the result that 'in many instances some have bled to death'. An additional consideration was the distance wounded men had to be carried to the cockpit, down several stairways and levels, the farthest being from the most exposed positions of poop and quarterdeck. In 1782, William Bayne, commanding HMS *Alfred*, 'had his knee so shattered with a round shot, that it was necessary to amputate the limb [but he] expired under the operation, in consequence of the weakness induced by the loss of blood in carrying him so far'. For this reason, the surgeon Gilbert Blane always 'carried in [his] pocket several tourniquets of a simple construction in case accidents to any person on the quarter deck should have required their use'. He even suggested that every man on board 'carry about him a garter or piece of rope-yarn in order to bind up a limb in case of profuse bleeding'. And if it was thought such a responsibility 'apt to intimidate common men', then at least officers should be encouraged in the practice, 'especially as many of them, and those of the highest rank, are stationed on the quarter deck ... and far removed from ... where the surgeon and his assistants are placed'.[19]

William Northcote recommended a space of between eight and twelve feet square for the surgeon to operate in and, should there 'be not height enough for [him] to stand upright', a chest of a proper height on which to sit, and another nearby on which to lay out his apparatus.

Capital knives – the very term denoting their importance and the gravity of their purpose – were employed for the rapid circular slice through skin and fat, then through muscle to bone - during amputation. Speed was of paramount importance if the suffering of the still-conscious patient was not to be prolonged, and advantage taken of the limited anaesthetic effects of shock and adrenalin. 'The Heat and Surprize in Action makes it the properest Time for amputating,' remarked John Atkins in his 1732 handbook *The Navy Surgeon*, 'Men meeting their Misfortunes with greater Strength and Resolution than when they have spent a Night under thought and Reflection.' Their steel honed to razor sharpness, several capital knives might be required during the course of a costly naval engagement as edges chipped and blunted with use.[20]

Smaller double-edged 'catlin' knives were designed for trimming muscle fibre from the narrow space between bones of the forearm or below the knee, allowing a clean passage of the tenon saw – another essential capital instrument – without its teeth clogging with raw flesh. Tourniquets were to lie in readiness. The model invented by Jean Louis Petit in the previous century was favoured because it could be tightened or relaxed by a simple screw mechanism, controlling the flow of blood like a tap. Northcote pointed out that Petit's design was particularly convenient in the post-operative period because 'the patient can easily manage it himself after it is fixed'. Crooked needles were to be at hand, ready threaded with ligatures for sewing up arteries and veins. Other essentials included rolls of bandage 'of all breadths and lengths', together with an array of materials for staunching and cleaning: a large quantity of lint, 'some mixed with flour in a bowl' for absorbency, and pads of tow spread with yellow basilicon ointment, supposed to prevent gangrene. There were to be at least two buckets: one of water 'to put your spunges in', the other empty 'to receive the blood in your operations'. Blood, that is, and severed body parts.[21]

Northcote advised the surgeon 'to have . . . mates and assistants properly instructed in what part they were to act, that every one may know his station, and what he has to do, to prevent confusion in time of action'. Besides the surgeon himself, three men were deemed necessary to assist at an amputation. To take off a hand, for instance, one was required to stand behind the patient holding him round the body, another at the elbow, and a third grasping the extremity to be amputated. After applying a tourniquet to the upper arm for compression of the brachial artery, the second assistant was to draw back taut the skin of the forearm and apply a length of tape around it 'to guide [the] knife'. On the pitching deck of a man-of-war, shaken at close proximity by heavy cannon, a naval surgeon needed every aid available to steady his hand. Atkins recommended two lengths of tape 'leaving only Room between them for the Knife to go round', their purpose being both 'to swell the Flesh to the Knife, and guide it for . . . a compleat circular Cision'. Following an initial, shallow cut – the *coup de main* – the same assistant was to draw the divided skin up as far as possible, as he might a tight shirt cuff, enabling a deeper stroke – the *coup de force* – 'through the flesh to the bones . . . close to the edge of the retracted skin'. The assistant would then sling a slit piece of linen into the incision, pulling on its two ends and dragging skin and raw flesh back even further to expose the maximum length of bone to the saw. After trimming the interstitial tissue with a catlin knife, radius and ulna were to be 'divided at the same time without splintering them' and 'a little higher than the incision, . . . that the flesh may afterwards wrap over them'. This was to ensure a comfortable covering across the bone ends when skin was closed over stump. The same procedure of alternate incision and retraction was necessary to achieve that desired outcome, whatever the thickness of limb, although drawing back the mass of meat from bone at the thigh might test the strength of the assistant concerned, more than at the forearm. When severed hand, arm, leg or foot was tossed into the bucket a surgeon's most delicate task remained still to do. 'Removal of a limb should not occupy two minutes,' remarked the army surgeon George Guthrie, 'but ... securing the blood vessels should be done without reference to time.' By the simple expedient of slightly loosening the Petit tourniquet and allowing the first ooze or spurt of blood, severed veins and arteries could be located in the spongy mass of raw flesh and swiftly 'secured by ligature with a crooked needle and waxed thread'.[22]

On board *Victory* there was an additional requirement, by standing order of the commander-in-chief himself. Nelson's abiding memory of the ordeal suffered during amputation of his arm at Tenerife was the imagined 'coldness of the knife'. William Beatty's predecessor, Sir George Magrath, had humoured this phobia and at the admiral's insistence provided a plentiful supply of hot water in which to immerse the blades 'whenever there was a prospect of coming to Action ... in the event of his being the subject of operation, on which he always calculated'.[23]

*

On the quarterdeck, naval officers wore blue frock coats, hats, swords, knee breeches, silver buckled shoes and white silk stockings. This last article was not for any spurious protective efficacy of the material, but for practicality in the likely event of injury. 'You had better put on silk stockings, as I have done,' Vice Admiral Collingwood told a booted lieutenant, 'for if one should get a shot in the leg, they would be so much more manageable for the surgeon.' When Nelson toured the decks before the battle he is said to have given practical sartorial advice to a lowlier member of *Victory*'s crew who he noticed was still wearing a shirt. 'Take that off, my boy,' he told one of the powder monkeys, 'or you'll be in trouble later in the day.' It is assumed that this was to save the lad from sparks igniting his clothing but might equally have applied to the dangers of infection from dirty cloth fragments embedding themselves in splinter or gunshot wounds.[24]

The commander-in-chief himself wore his customary '"undress

coat", somewhat threadbare in places'. His stockings were a cotton-and-wool blend, not silk. He carried no sword on this occasion having, by an apparent oversight, left it behind in his cabin and neglected to send for it. Ominous in retrospect, it was pointed out afterwards that 'this was the only action in which he ever appeared without a sword.' A more immediate cause of anxiety, marking him out as a blatant target for small-arms fire, was the ostentation of decorations – albeit salt-tarnished, sequinned replicas – encrusting his chest: orders of the Bath, of St Ferdinand and of Merit, of St Joachim, and, in recognition of his action at the Nile, the highest honour the Sultan of Turkey could bestow upon a non-Muslim, the Order of the Crescent. Dr Beatty voiced what a number of officers were thinking, that he should be persuaded to cover them with a handkerchief, but was told by Mr Scott, the admiral's secretary: 'Take care, Doctor, what you are about; I would not be the man to mention such a matter to him.' On board *Royal Sovereign* someone venturing to advise Captain Rotherham that his very large hat made him a similarly conspicuous figure on the quarterdeck was turned away with, 'Let me alone! I've always fought in a cocked-hat, and I always will.' Rotherham and his hat survived the battle entirely undamaged.[25]

*

By eight o'clock the British fleet, numbering twenty-seven ships of the line, was sailing east-south-east in two columns towards the enemy fleet of thirty-three. The 'Weather' or northernmost column of twelve vessels was led by *Victory* and, a mile and a half to the south, the flagship of Nelson's second-in-command, Vice Admiral Collingwood, led the 'Lee' column of fifteen. *Royal Sovereign* bore on her prow 'a gigantic full-length carving of King George III in the battle-day dress of a Roman Imperator, with sword at his side and red war-cloak on his shoulders', winged figures of Fortune and Fame blowing gilded trumpets to right and left.[26]

In addition to the Weather and Lee column warships, the British fleet included six smaller craft – the frigates *Euryalus, Sirius, Naiad* and *Phoebe*, the schooner *Pickle*, and *Entreprenante*, a cutter. These served as observation and communication vessels and were regarded as non-combatants, it being 'an honourable agreement between two contending fleets, that they never fire on frigates, nor on any cutter or boat, unless they make a part of the opposing force'.[27]

Ships moved with all canvas set on fore-, main- and mizen-masts, studdingsails* extended either side effectively doubling the breadth of wind capture so as to take maximum advantage of the 'light airs'. Progress, notwithstanding, was snail-slow, and they moved at no more than one and a half knots, or under two miles per hour.

In the absence of speed, ships' bands played during the long approach to engagement keeping adrenalin at high pitch. A popular quickstep called 'Downfall of Paris', and Thomas Arne's 'Rule Britannia',[†] were rousing staples for fife, drum and whatever other instruments could be mustered. On board *Belleisle* – behind *Royal Sovereign* in the Lee column – Paul Nicholas remembered 'our consort was playing "Britons, Strike Home"'. Purcell's march had originally been composed for a 1695 revival of John Fletcher's *Bonduca, or the British Heroine*, loosely based on Queen Boudica's struggle against Roman tyranny. The song had been given five new verses in 1803, stoking patriotic resistance to another, more pressing, threat of invasion:

> Should Frenchmen e'er pollute Britannia's strand,
> Or press with hostile hoof this sacred land;
> The daring deed should every Briton arm,
> To save his land from dire alarm,
> Her free-born Sons should instant take the field,
> The Altar and the Throne at once to shield.[28]

---

* Pronounced 'stunsails'.

† Originally composed for the masque *The Distresses of Alfred the Great, King of England, with his Conquest of the Danes* and first performed in 1740.

The sixth line was a reminder that Protestant Britain's traditional enemy had not only guillotined their own King a decade earlier but, after a period of revolutionary iconoclasm, France was once again, following the 1801 Concordat with Rome, nominally a detested Catholic country.

On board the *Ajax* 'three or four [men], as if in mere bravado, were dancing a hornpipe' to undisclosed accompaniment, while those of *Britannia*, fifth in Nelson's Weather column, 'amus[ed] themselves with nautical jokes' and scraps of dramatic recitation. This ship, like many others, had maintained a tradition of amateur theatricals to relieve the boredom of blockade duty outside Cadiz. During the previous two months Lieutenant Halloran and his fellow officers participated in no fewer than ten different dramatic productions, including one – *The Village* – of his own composition. David Garrick's *Miss in her Teens* had been 'very well done', and Thomas Morton's *Columbus, or a World Discovered*, featured, as a climax, 'the Destruction of the Temple by an Earthquake accompanied by Thunder, Lightning, and Hail-Storm with the rescue of Cora from the Ruins by Alonzo'. Preparations for a further, sadly unspecified, play – scheduled to be staged that day – had been interrupted by news 'that the enemy were at sea'. As *Britannia* sailed into action Halloran was gratified to hear his men declaiming lines from a Prologue he himself had recently performed:

We have great guns of Tragedy loaded so well,
If they do but go off, they will certainly tell.[29]

Behind *Belleisle* in Collingwood's Lee column sailed *Mars*, the war god as figurehead frozen in the act of unsheathing his sword. That morning Captain George Duff had penned a hasty note to his wife Sophia, informing her they were going into action, trusting in God 'that we shall all behave as becomes us' and hoping to take her and their children in his arms when it was done. He reassured her that their eldest son – a midshipman under his command – was 'quite well and happy' but that he had been 'ordered . . . off the quarter-deck'. Thirteen-year-old Norwich Duff remained below throughout the battle and did not witness his father's terrible death.[30]

Meanwhile the martial tune played aboard *Belleisle* had been taken up astern of *Mars* by the bassoons, hautboys, fifes, drums and triangles of *Tonnant*'s ensemble, Captain Charles Tyler's pride and joy: not good enough for a band, according to a wag in the midshipmen's berth, but bad enough for banditti.

> Britons, strike home! Avenge your Country's cause,
> Protect your KING, your LIBERTIES, and LAWS!

They would play – well or badly – until interrupted by a shot that killed two of their number.[31]

*

Crews were piped to dinner, the food differing from ship to ship. On the *Tonnant* every man was given 'bread and cheese and butter and beer', and John Cash told his brother, 'we ate and drank, and were as cheerful as ever we had been over a pot of beer.' John Brown and his mates on *Victory* 'ate a bit of raw pork and half a pint of Wine'. Piped to a dinner of unspecified fare on *Defiance*, Colin Campbell and his mates enjoyed a 'good glass of grog'. On board *Achille* – namesake of the French 74 whose destruction would mark the end of the day's hostilities – they had boiled rice and when it was noticed that a surplus remained there was a scramble for second helpings. One man, towards the rear of the press grew impatient and 'made use of such dreadful curses and bad wishes towards those who had the good fortune to be nearest the copper, as to stagger even sailors'. He was said to be *Achille*'s first casualty of enemy fire when the ship came within range of the Combined Fleet's guns. A round shot struck the side of his head, smashing it to pieces, one of which – his tongue – was 'dashed against the still hot copper to which it stuck, and so remained for some hours'. The macabre poetry of this supposed judgement on profanity-laced greed would be talked of by the crew 'for many a day afterwards'.³²

*

At noon Nelson instructed his signals officer to inform the fleet: 'ENGLAND CONFIDES THAT EVERY MAN WILL DO HIS DUTY.' Lieutenant Pasco suggested that transmission might be expedited by changing the second word of the message to 'EXPECTS', this being 'in the vocabulary' of Popham's signal code, whereas 'CONFIDES' – that is, 'has confidence' – would require spelling out and hoisting letter by letter. The amended version was accordingly telegraphed, taking twelve separate hoists and four minutes to complete, but only the word 'DUTY' having to be spelt. It was greeted with cheers from each ship when repeated by officers to their gun crews. On the decks of *Bellerophon*, there was 'a general shout of "No fear o' that!"' Marine Lieutenant Ellis heard an *Ajax* crewman muttering, 'Do our duty! Of course we'll do our duty. I've always done mine, haven't you? Let us come alongside of 'em and we will show whether we will do our duty!' Collingwood's response was less forthright, but of similar tenor: 'he wished Nelson would make no more signals, for they all understood what they were to do.' Other commanders may have felt the same. Captain George Johnstone Hope 'did not make [the signal] publicly known on board *Defence*', believing that 'no stimulus of the kind was required'. Even so, Midshipman Thomas Huskisson believed that 'the message could have done no harm and ought ... to have been promulgated amongst the men.'³³

Nelson appeared, for a time, to concede that his flagship's leading position in the order of battle would attract a concentration of enemy fire and signalled *Téméraire* and *Leviathan* to take the lead instead. But it was a half-hearted concession, and, when it was represented to Captain Hardy that *Victory* would have to lessen sail to allow the other two vessels to overtake, he declined doing so, 'as he conceived His Lordship's ardour to get into battle would on no account suffer such a measure'.³⁴

11

THE term point-blank range derives from the French *point blanc* – the white centre of a target – and signifies the distance within which a piece of ordnance throws its shot 'in a supposed direct line: the gun being laid at no elevation, but levelled parallel to the horizon' – the distance, that is, before the projectile begins a gradual downward parabola as its momentum decreases. Point-blank range was not an absolute term but dependent on the weight of shot and the strength of explosive charge used to propel it.

An article in the *Naval Chronicle* of 1800 was concerned with 'The Advantages of Close Action'. At point-blank range, its author declared, 'the velocity of cannon balls is so great, that in penetrating a Ship's side, few or no splinters are torn off,' and consequently fewer injuries inflicted on men close to the point of impact. The anonymous authority pointed out the seeming paradox that at close range 'a quick-flying ball makes an aperture less than its own diameter'. This was due to the timber's natural elasticity contracting following the shot's passage. The obverse was that at longer range and towards the end of its flight, 'a spent [round] produces innumerable deadly splinters, ... shivering the object it strikes, and making wide and extensive rents in it [thereby increasing] the proportion of the wounded to the killed.' The variable effects were cited of a spent cannon round that killed Captain John Nott in his cabin on *Centaur* during an action off Fort Royal, Martinique, on 29 April 1781. After tearing away 'an whole plank of the ships side', producing splinters that killed 'a young gentleman, the only person near him', it struck [Nott] in the groin, and . . . was so far spent that it stuck in his body' lacking the momentum to pass entirely through.[35]

*

Royal Sovereign had come 'within musket-shot' – a 300-yard range – of the Combined Fleet when *Fougueux* signalled her readiness to fight by hoisting the French colours and pendant. At the same moment the thirty-seven guns of her larboard broadside opened the battle.

French and Spanish gunners were trained to aim high with specialised shot – bar, chain and expanding, as well as round shot – which could splinter and topple masts, smash spars and shred the sails and rigging of opposing ships. Canister shot, filled with langrage or with musket balls, was equally effective for killing and maiming personnel. As was grapeshot: a bundle of three-and-a-half-ounce lead balls, tightly wrapped in canvas, it derived the name from its knobbly resemblance to a bunch of fruit. Clearing the cannon's muzzle the canvas ripped apart spreading the missiles shotgun-fashion across an enemy deck.

Five years earlier, an article in *Le Moniteur* had challenged the prevailing ballistic orthodoxy, arguing that 'when the guns are pointed principally against the rigging, the hull of the Ship cannot be struck, the [enemy's] guns cannot be dismounted, nor any considerable number of men killed and wounded: from which it follows that the crew of the enemy being so little injured, his valour, his force, and consequently the briskness of his fire, cannot be much enfeebled.' It was argued further that because English gunners directed their shot against a vessel's hull, they succeeded 'in striking between wind and water' – at or below the line of immersion – 'in dismounting guns, and in killing . . . a [greater] number of the crew'. And therein, the author declared, 'the whole superiority of the British Navy' consists. In addition, by holing a ship below the water line 'they force their enemy to take away a number of men from the management of the guns for the service of the pumps, and nothing is so fatiguing or dispiriting as this. When a fear of sinking is induced, men are not much disposed to contend for victory.' Finally, 'the carnage which is produced among the crew ... spreads terror and alarm among the survivors to such a degree that their courage, their force, and consequently the briskness of their fire must abate.'[36]

The contrasting results of these opposing policies were described by a French admiral and naval historian of a later generation: 'picture ... the destructive effects from a mass of iron, whose total weight sometimes exceeds 3000 lbs, driven through space with a velocity of 500 metres per second, and suddenly meeting in the course of its flight a penetrable obstacle which tears and flies into splinters more murderous than the ball itself. Instead of wasting this irresistible force as we [French] used to then, in the hope of cutting some ropes ... or destroying some important rigging or wounding a mast, the better trained English concentrated it upon a more certain object, the enemy's batteries. They littered our decks with corpses while our shot passed over their ships.'[37]

Efficacy of shot was equally dependent on anticipating the movement of the ship itself as upon aiming her guns, and if the elevation and firing of the French and Spanish ordnance was not precisely coordinated, with the 'ships rolling heavily from the effect of the sea which was taking [them] on the beam,' as was frequently the case at Trafalgar, then the disparately shaped lumps of iron categorised as dismantling shot flew lower: harmlessly into the sea, into the English hulls or sweeping their open decks, leaving spars and rigging untouched but with catastrophic mutilation to flesh and bone. Ironically, the anonymous *Moniteur* contributor might have been more gratified by some of the deadlier effects of poor gunnery practice on the British fleet than of good.[38]

Auguste Gicquel, a lieutenant on *Intrepide*, identified another detrimental feature in French ordnance. 'We still used slow matches which fired the shot with a desperate slowness [sending] whole broadsides ... over the masts without causing the least damage.' The smouldering match, or linstock, made accurate shooting impossible because it often failed to ignite the powder charge on the instant it was applied to the touch hole, an essential requirement when timing the fire to a vessel's rise and fall. The gunner also had to stand to the side when firing, to avoid the recoil. Gicquel explained that 'the English had flint gunlocks, fairly clumsy but much superior to our slow matches.' The mechanism, modified from the flintlock musket, had important benefits. It was fired by tugging a lanyard, the gunner standing at a safe distance in the rear and therefore able to sight along the barrel. A British gun could not only be more accurately aimed, but its firing co-ordinated with the ship's roll, the struck spark precisely timed to the second, like pulling the trigger of a pistol.[39]

But of equal advantage to elevation and technology was the superior rate of fire achieved by British gun crews, whose broadsides 'succeeded each other without relaxation', Gicquel remarked. This would be reflected in the disparity of casualties inflicted on either side before firing ceased at the end of the day.

*

What had appeared at dawn as a straight line of ships fringing the horizon was deceptive. 'The structure of [the enemy] line,' according to Collingwood, 'formed a crescent convexing to leeward; so that in leading down to their centre, [*Royal Sovereign*] had both their van and rear abaft the beam.' It was the maritime equivalent of entering a salient in a land battle: vulnerable to fire from the front and from either side. As they came within range of the enemy's guns, *Royal Sovereign*'s marines and the quarterdeck gun crews were ordered to lie down at their stations until it was time to engage. Captain Hargood on *Belleisle*, astern of *Royal Sovereign*, instructed his people to do the same. The band had stopped playing and the silence was broken only by the captain's terse instructions, echoed by the ship's master, William Hudson, to his quartermasters at the helm:

'Steady! Starboard a little! Steady so!'

An officer's peremptory bark – 'Lie down there, you sir!' – kept nervous or impatient men in order. Nevertheless, stray projectiles, ricochets and razor-sharp splinters from the material damage aloft still wrought their havoc below: 'a shriek ... a cry of agony ... the loss of the head of a poor recruit', prematurely raised. Despite precautions, casualties mounted and Lieutenant Nicholas stood appalled 'at the bloody corpses ... and the moans of the dying'. His senior officer, First Lieutenant John Owen, ventured to suggest that a broadside be fired to mask the ship in a cloud of smoke. But Hargood ignored the suggestion, choosing even to wilfully misunderstand it. 'No, we are ordered to go through the line, and go through she shall, by God!' Between twenty and thirty men were killed and wounded on her decks during the final approach – and before a single one of her own guns was fired for camouflage or in aggression. Hargood himself was hit by a broken lump of wood, leaving 'an extensive bruise reaching from the throat nearly to the waist.' Owen was hit by a splinter 'which tore away a small portion of muscle from the left thigh,' an injury he did not notice until after the battle.[40]

Before reaching the enemy line an unnamed midshipman aboard *Bellerophon* is said to have inadvertently opened British hostilities when he trod on a lanyard attached to one of the gun locks, firing its charge prematurely. Mistaking this for a signal shot, and 'conceiv[ing] that she was the [English] flag-ship', the Spanish *Monarca* and *Bahama*, the French *Aigle*, and *Swiftsure* – captured from the Royal Navy four years earlier – concentrated their fire on *Bellerophon* in return. First Lieutenant William Cumby made no mention of the midshipman's clumsiness, however, claiming instead that, because 'we were losing men as we approached their ships from the effect of their fire, and also suffering in our masts and rigging,' Captain John Cooke gave the order Hargood had refused – to open fire earlier than intended 'from the double motive of giving our men employment and at the same time of rendering the ship a less ostensible mark to be shot at by covering her with smoke'.[41]

*

At the stern of Vice Admiral Álava's 112-gun flagship *Santa Ana* – as at that of every Spanish vessel going into battle – a large wooden cross hung from the spanker boom where it projected over the taffrail. All crosses would have been solemnly blessed by the priests on board 'and meant as *fetiças* to ward off disaster'.[42]

In a prominent position on every French vessel – at the foot of the main mast – was the no less revered fetish of a gilded eagle. Presented by Napoleon at the time of his coronation the previous December and consecrated as the principal icon of his new Empire, 'these eagles will always be your rallying point,' their custodians had been told; 'they will go everywhere the Emperor deems it necessary for the defence of his throne and his people.' The quasi-sacred obligation imposed on each ship's company to 'defend [their eagle] with courage and conduct themselves like Frenchmen fighting bravely for the honour of the flag' would have been the same as that on an army regiment, as embodied in the oath demanded, and enthusiastically sworn, when the eagles were first presented: 'to sacrifice your lives in their defence and to maintain them constantly on the road to victory'. The loss of one would be 'an affront to regimental honour for which neither victory nor the glory acquired on a hundred battlefields can make amends'. This unconscionable disgrace would besmirch the reputation of the 4ème Régiment de Ligne when its eagle was captured by Russian cavalry at the battle of Austerlitz. The Emperor's furious tirade at those responsible would reduce even a guiltless onlooker to tears, gooseflesh and a cold sweat.[43]

But six weeks earlier, as the time of battle approached, Commander-in-Chief Vice Admiral Villeneuve toured the gun decks of *Bucentaure* with his staff, their eagle standard carried ahead by the two *aspirants de marine* – or midshipmen – charged with guarding it. '*Vive l'Empereur!*', the crew roared as they passed, '*Vive l'Amiral Villeneuve!*'

*

From the onset of action, the timing of events as recorded by participants varied radically from ship to ship.* This is understandable in the confusion of battle when men have more pressing concerns than keeping an accurate chronological record. Most accounts were compiled retrospectively, logs and journals across the English fleet being discrepant by as much as an hour and eight minutes between the earliest and latest estimate of the time *Royal Sovereign* broke through the enemy line: *Africa* recording the action as beginning at 11.32 and *Dreadnought* at 12.40. *Belleisle*, however, immediately astern of Collingwood's flagship, offers 12.04. On board *Sovereign* herself, Lieutenant Joseph Simmonds' journal reads '11.50, began to engage', whereas Collingwood records the moment as a quarter past twelve.[44]

Santa Ana's wooden cross proved no protection against *Royal Sovereign*'s guns as she passed slowly astern of the Spanish vessel. Shot fired into this most vulnerable elevation of a ship – its timbers thinner than at any other part of the hull, encrusted in delicately carved ornament, and much of its surface occupied by windows of the commander's quarters and wardroom – was intended to 'scour the whole length of her decks' accompanied by a blast of sharded glass and wooden splinters. The tactic was known as 'raking fore and aft ... one of the most dangerous incidents that can happen in a naval action'. A Plymouth schoolboy – the future historical painter Benjamin Robert Haydon – would remember for the rest of his life being taken aboard a ship docked for repairs, and being shown the effects of just such a rake: 'the trace of a shot which had passed fore and aft, taking off the heads of the captains of several guns, scattering blood and brains along the beams'.[45]

---

* For an analysis of such anomalies see John Terraine, *Trafalgar*, Appendix B, pp. 204–5.

Each barrel loaded with a single shot, *Royal Sovereign*'s fifty larboard guns were capable of firing a broadside weighing 1,048 lbs. But her guns had instead been double-, and in some cases treble-shotted – a loading so heavy as to be effective only at point-blank range in anticipation of close-quarters combat – and they raked the *Santa Ana*, every piece of ordnance detonating in succession, timed to the English ship's leisurely passage across her stern, with a combined heft of nearly one and a half tons. Collingwood's biographer claimed it was 'a broadside and a half', an indication of the length of time the English ship took to pass with little or no wind in her sails – given that a good gun crew could fire, load and fire again in under two minutes.

At the same time as she demolished the Spaniard's stern with her larboard guns, her starboard batteries fired a broadside of round shot 'big and small', and canisters packed with musket balls into the almost equally vulnerable bows of the French 74-gun *Fougueux* to *Santa Ana*'s rear. 'The storm of projectiles that hurled themselves against and through [our] hull', Master-at-Arms Pierre Servaux recalled, 'made the ship heel to starboard. Most of the sails and rigging were cut to pieces.' With her three gun decks to *Fougueux*'s two, Collingwood's ship had the advantage of height and was able to fire, not only into the hull, and the masts and canvas, but also in between, so that her 'upper deck was swept clear of the greater number of the seamen working there, and of the soldier sharpshooters' in the tops. Looking out from one of *Royal Sovereign*'s stern gunports, fifteen-year-old Midshipman George Castle glimpsed a spectacle of carnage that might have been *Fougueux* and that he did not scruple describing to his sister in Durham: 'shocking to see the many brave seamen mangled so, some with their heads half shot away, others with their entrails mashed lying panting on the deck, the greatest slaughter was on the quarter deck and Poop'. From his lower gun-deck station such a view of the French vessel was unlikely, however, and the scene could well have been witnessed on board his own ship later in the day, juxtaposed impressions still excitedly being processed in the memory for his sister's dubious benefit a fortnight later.

In fact, Midshipman Castle by his own admission saw little with any clarity in the confusion of battle: 'nothing but French and Spaniards round firing at us in all directions ... the smoak was so thick ... we cou'd hardly make out the French from the English.' At a later stage of the battle, while engaged with *Santísima Trinidad*, Captain Eliab Harvey ordered his gunners on *Téméraire* to cease fire for a time, 'fearing [we] might from the thickness of the smoke be firing into the *Victory*'. *Royal Sovereign* would also come under accidental fire from *Belleisle* until Collingwood signalled her to desist, while his own ship poured friendly fire into Nelson's flagship. William Robinson, aboard *Revenge*, suggested that these cannot have been isolated incidents: 'Often ... we could not see for the smoke, whether we were firing at a foe or friend.'[46]

For George Castle there was no difficulty either finding or distinguishing a target for his own 32-pounder – 'heaviest guns in the Ship' – after coming alongside *Santa Ana*. 'It was glorious work,' he told his sister, revelling in his adolescent virility, 'you would have liked to have seen me thump it into her quarter ... I stuck close to one gun and poured it into her, she was so close, it was impossible to miss her.' Understandably, some of the Spanish crew found a comparatively safe place to avoid the barrage, 'hiding themselves outside the[ir] ship on the opposite side to the enemy'.[47]

Meanwhile – her quarterdeck and poop a shambles – *Fougueux*'s lower gun decks had 'suffered less severely', according to the master-at-arms, and with 'not more than thirty men in all put *hors de combat* ... a well-maintained fire showed the Englishmen that we too had guns and could use them.' With these the French crew were able to deliver a broadside to *Royal Sovereign*'s stern which, fortunately for Miss Castle's brother, fell on the opposite quarter to where he was thumping his 32-pounder into *Santa Ana*. The English ship's bow was also coming under fire from the smallest vessel of the Combined Fleet, the Spanish 64-gun *San Leandro*, while her starboard beam was pounded by two 74s, the French *Indomptable* and *San Justo*, another Spaniard. And, despite the ruin wrought by Collingwood's first raking broadside into her stern and by George Castle's continued vigorous attentions, *Santa Ana* was yet able to retaliate with a starboard broadside, powerful enough at the closest range, gunports nearly touching, to rock the *Sovereign* two strakes – or horizontal lines of planking – out of the water. Apart from Captain Rotherham and the Vice Admiral's secretary Mr Cosway, 'nearly all were killed or wounded on the quarter-deck and poop.' Collingwood's precautionary forethought of wearing silk stockings seemed justified by 'a splinter – a pretty severe blow', that did not, however, require a surgeon's attention, although 'bleeding and swelled, and tied up with a handkerchief'. He also received 'a good many bumps', one of them in the back that he took to be a powerful buffet of air from the close passage of a shot, as he did not see what had caused it.[48]

Royal Sovereign had made such good time in advancing on the enemy that for fully ten or fifteen minutes she fought alone before *Belleisle* arrived to deliver another fore-and-aft rake for good measure into the ruins of *Santa Ana*'s stern, as well as one to the larboard bow of *Fougueux*. Captain Hargood's ship had suffered considerably in the approach, 'our masts and yards and sails [were] hanging in the utmost confusion above our heads,' recalled Lieutenant Nicholas, 'numbers lay dead upon the decks, and eleven wounded were already in the surgeon's care'. Undaunted, Hargood pointed at the 80-gun *Indomptable* ahead.[49]

'There's your ship, sir!', he shouted to the master, William Hudson. 'Place me close alongside her!'

But after pouring 'a most galling raking fire upon us', the larger Frenchman avoided any closer confrontation and, 'quitt[ing] the fighting-line very early, having had her rudder damaged,' drifted off around one in the afternoon to take no further part in the battle. Instead, *Belleisle* fell alongside a far more truculent opponent, *Fougueux*, and for some twenty minutes they pounded broadsides into one another to their mutual devastation.[50]

Of all the ships in the British fleet, *Belleisle* would incur the most damage by the end of the day. '[She] was the only [vessel] totally dismasted. Her hull was literally knocked to pieces: scarcely a spot in her sides, bows, or stern, appeared untouched: – all her ports, port-timbers, chain-plates, channels, &c., were cut to pieces; and she was exceedingly leaky from shot holes.' As well as from *Fougueux*, she came under 'a most awful fire' from the 74-gun *San Juan Nepomuceno*, *San Justo*, *San Leandro*, the 112-gun *Príncipe de Asturias*, from two French 74s, *Achille* and *Aigle*, and the 84-gun *Neptune*. In addition to losing her masts, reported George Sievers, *Belleisle*'s master-at-arms, 'they cut our Bowsprit in Pieces and dismounted a number of our Guns [and] left us a compleat Wreck ... All our Boats were ... Shot Cut in Pieces.' With most of her gunports covered and rendered inoperable by fallen canvas, she 'lay a mere hulk covered in wreck and rolling with the swell'. With the detritus of yards, sails, ropes, blood and mangled remains on her upper decks, and the profusion of splinters from the smashed timbers, *Belleisle* was likened by Lieutenant Nicholas to 'a shipwright's yard strewed with gore'.[51]

Mars had broken through soon after *Royal Sovereign* and *Belleisle*. 'The wind, which had been light, then became more uncertain, and prevented the rest of the ships [of Collingwood's Lee column] from closing immediately with the enemy; so that the few who were engaged, were in a manner surrounded.' *Mars* was under fire from *Santa Ana* to the fore, *Monarca*, the French *Pluton* and *Algésiras* astern. 'In a few minutes our poop was totally cleared,' recalled Midshipman James Robinson, 'the quarter-deck and foc's'le nearly the same, and only the Boatswain and myself and three men left alive.'[52]

Captain Duff was taking full advantage of his impressive stature – 'strong and well made, above six feet in height' – to lean out from the end of the quarterdeck, peering through smoke, to ascertain whether his guns could be brought to bear against the *Fougueux*. By then the Frenchman had disengaged from *Belleisle* and was threatening *Mars*'s starboard quarter. Before Duff's order could be passed to the lower batteries for the guns 'to be pointed more aft', *Fougueux* had drifted into range and fired her larboard broadside. George Duff was struck high in the chest by a round shot that ripped his head off and killed the two men standing immediately behind him. Robinson claimed that crew members lifted their captain's raggedly decapitated corpse up to the rail, flourishing it at the enemies opposite, 'and gave three cheers to show they were not discouraged by it', before returning to their guns. This gruesome mark of respect and defiance was not communicated to the captain's widow, only that 'his fate was instantaneous, and ... without a moment's pain.'[53]

The ship's log, completed by Acting Commander Lieutenant William Hennah the following day, stated that 'the poop & Quarterdeck [were] nearly cleard of officers & Men & all [our] running rigging shot away, in that the Ship was entirely unserviceable & was frequently raked by the Enemys Ships.' According to Hennah's reckoning, Duff fell at a quarter past one, the same time as Nelson sustained his death wound, and within five minutes of Captain John Cooke's fatal receipt of two simultaneous musket rounds to the chest on board *Bellerophon*.[54]

Meanwhile, the *Fougueux*, after firing on *Mars*, and with a casualty rate from her exchanges with *Belleisle* already approaching eighty-four per cent of her crew — the highest in any ship of either fleet that day — drifted from the vicinity of the Lee column to that of the Weather, and received an additional mauling from *Téméraire*.

Revenge's log estimated it was ten minutes after *Royal Sovereign* broke through the centre of the enemy line that she reached the rear, passing between the French *Achille* and *San Ildefonso*, raking the Spaniard's stern and being raked in turn by the Frenchman. Later, Captain Moorson recorded 'the men firing with all expedition and spirit, having upon us four French ships and a Spanish three-decker'. Admiral Gravina's flagship *Príncipe de Asturias* had earlier engaged *Defiance* although, according to Midshipman Colin Campbell, to little effect. 'She only killed one man on board of us; the whole of her shot went through our rigging and over our mastheads. They fired so high that they shot away our main-top-gallant-truck.'* He estimated that 'the slaughter on board [the Spaniard] must have been great ... Every one of our shot told upon her and made the splinters fly.' But when she turned her guns on to *Revenge*, the Spaniard claimed a heavy toll of both men and superstructure. 'Our yards, rigging and sails [were] cut to pieces', Moorson reported, 'and lower masts very much wounded.' The most destructive type of shot was what William Robinson called 'deafeners' – eighteen-inch-long double-headed iron bars weighing thirty pounds. 'Two of these ... we observed to be sticking in our main-mast, which, miraculously and fortunately for us, was not carried away.' Another of these deadly projectiles – its tumbling, end-over-end flight designed to shred canvas and cordage – left a freak trail of destruction through the *Revenge*. Fired from *Príncipe de Asturias* it entered the lower deck through the third gunport from forward on the starboard side, and struck the barrel of a 32-pounder gun 'in which it made a large dint' then glanced off into the between-decks section of the foremast, scooping out a large proportion of its timber. It then ricocheted, taking the head off a young midshipman named Grier, killed seven men of the forwardmost gun crew 'by severing them nearly in two' before embedding itself low down in the ship's side where 'it was scarcely perceptible ... from the force with which it was buried in the wood.' So eccentric was its career that the bar shot was cut out as a curiosity at Captain Moorson's request and subsequently served as the iron pedestal for a sundial in the garden of Airy Hill, his home in Whitby.[55]

Apart from Grier and the gun crew, no other men were killed or injured on the lower deck. Grier's fellow midshipman, Edward Freeman Brooke, was the only other officer killed on *Revenge*. An obituary in the *Leeds Intelligencer* described this coroner's son from Wakefield, as 'a very spirited and promising youth, in the 12th year of his age'. He was less favourably remembered by those who shipped with him. William Robinson described a sadistic

---

* The circular block of wood fixed to the highest point on the main mast. Also known as the acorn.

martinet, feared and loathed by the crew and an example of 'the danger of giving too much power into the hands of young officers'. Hit by a blast of grapeshot from *Príncipe de Asturias*, his fate was unlamented and recounted with relish in the forecastle, 'body greatly mutilated, his entrails being driven and scattered against the larboard side [of the quarterdeck]'.[56]

*

As the vessels of Collingwood's Lee column engaged the enemy, with little wind to propel them, ship came 'on board' ship as though drifting together by mutual attraction. *Royal Sovereign* came on board *Santa Ana*, following that first destructive salute to her stern, and *Belleisle* came on board *Fougueux*. *Colossus* ripped off four of her own lower deck starboard gunport lids as she ran alongside *Argonaute*, while *Bellerophon* came so close on board *Aigle* that she was able to elevate her gun barrels to fire upwards through the French ship's interior 'so as to tear [her] decks and sides to pieces'.[57]

Tonnant had broken through the line, raking the Spanish *Monarca* and French *Algésiras* as she passed between, so close, Lieutenant Hoffman wrote, that 'a biscuit might have been thrown on the decks of either of them'. Then the French ship manoeuvred, 'and poured a raking broadside into [*Tonnant*'s] stern, which killed or wounded forty petty officers and men, nearly cut the rudder in two, and shattered the whole of the stern, with the quarter galleries'. It was such 'well-sustained fire', Captain Laurent Le Tourneur claimed, 'as soon reduced her to the same state as ours'. Her own rigging stripped by British grapeshot, *Algésiras* rammed *Tonnant* amidships, fouling her bowsprit in the other's shrouds. Musket fire from the Frenchman's tops cleared the English poop and wounded Captain Tyler in the thigh, but a French boarding party was repelled with great losses. For more than half an hour the two ships fought, 'sides grinding so much against each other that [they] were obliged to fire the lower deck guns without running them out'. Inevitably, at such close range, blazing wadding from the gun barrels caused fires, first in the French boatswain's storeroom killing three men, then rapidly spreading to *Tonnant*, whose crew 'got the [fire] engine and played it on both ships, and finally extinguished the flames, although two of them were severely wounded in doing so'.[58]

*

Royal Sovereign and Álava's flagship *Santa Ana* were near wrecks: the Spaniard with her starboard side 'almost entirely beat in', her stern shot to pieces, while her principal opponent was 'perfectly unmanageable', main mast brought down, and mizen with it. *Santa Ana* struck her colours. The admiral was seriously wounded, and so it was the Spanish captain, José de Gardoqui, who went on board *Royal Sovereign* to surrender his sword. He asked the name of the ship and when told, patted one of the still warm English guns gingerly and observed, 'I think she should be called the Royal Devil.' *Royal Sovereign* was, however rolling so violently following the loss of her main- and mizenmasts that George Castle found he 'could scarcely fight the lower deck, the water was almost knee deep'. And ever eager to impart the compelling detail, he informed his sister that 'it served to wash away the Blood'.[59]

Between 2.30 and three o'clock, 'an officer from the *Victory* came on board, and informed [Collingwood] of Lord Nelson being severely wounded and near expiring.' An hour later Captain Hardy came across 'and acquainted [him] of the death of the Commander-in-Chief'.[60]

III

SHORTLY before his flagship and the succeeding craft of the Lee column broke through the enemy line, Admiral Collingwood, flushed with exhilaration and shouting to be heard above the roar of cannon fire, turned to *Royal Sovereign*'s captain:

'Rotherham! What would not Nelson give to be here!'

At about the same moment, a mile or so to the north-west and a quarter of an hour before his own flagship arrived at the same critical point of engagement, Nelson lowered his Dollond glass and shouted to Captain Hardy:

'See, see how that noble fellow Collingwood carries his ship into action!'

Then, as *Belleisle* followed *Royal Sovereign* amongst the enemy, firing larboard and starboard broadsides into *Santa Ana* and *Fougueux*:

'Nobly done, Hargood!'[61]

White plumes of water had been spouting in front of *Victory* for half an hour, as the Combined Fleet's gun crews endeavoured to find their range.

Captain Jean-Jacques-Étienne Lucas, astern of the French flagship *Bucentaure*, saw the opportunity of giving his men on *Redoutable* an object lesson in ballistics. 'I ordered on deck a large number of the captains of guns in order to point out to them how badly our ships were firing: every shot was aimed too low and fell in the sea; I urged them to fire at the masts.'

Then a single shot from *Bucentaure* made the first rent in *Victory*'s main topgallant sail, and there was a cry of '*Vive l'Empereur!*' from the French. Captain Lucas later claimed that his own guns 'carried away the fore-topsail yard' of *Victory* with their first broadside, '[and] in less than ten minutes ... her mizen mast, her fore top-mast and her main topgallant mast'. Whether the entirety of that damage was due to his gunnery tutorial is doubtful, because by a quarter past twelve Nelson's flagship was under heavy fire, not only from *Redoutable* and *Bucentaure*, but also from *Héros*, *Mont Blanc*, *Duguay-Trouin*, and from three Spaniards, *San Francisco de Asis*, *San Agustín*, and the gigantic *Santísima Trinidad*. Nor was the destruction confined to timber, ropes and canvas. During her slow approach and before firing a shot in return, *Victory* 'lost about twenty men killed, and had about thirty wounded'. Nelson's secretary, John Scott, was among the first to die, 'killed by a chain-shot which cut him asunder,' according to *The Times*.[62]

'Is that Scott who has gone?' Nelson asked, as the remains were manhandled overboard by marines. 'Poor fellow.'

Another ink-and-paper man was Thomas Whipple, Captain Hardy's clerk. Eighteen years old, he might have passed a long, steady and safe life in a Plymouth office, but instead was said to have perished by the 'wind of a ball', the shot passing within an inch of his head. This mysterious phenomenon was cited by naval surgeon William Turnbull as 'most dangerous when it approaches the stomach, and has often, in such cases, proved instantaneously fatal, without the least visible mark of injury'. Turnbull's additional assertion, that 'the wind of a ball has never been fatal on the head' was, admittedly, contradicted in Whipple's case, but for the rest not a single blemish, graze or contusion was to be found upon the young man's lifeless body when he was carried below. It was as though he had died at his desk. Owing to the loss, early in the battle, of 'the two persons whose places ... it was to take minutes', the log entries of HMS *Victory* for that day are particularly unreliable.⁶³

The vicious reel of a double-headed bar shot fired from *Santísima Trinidad* carved a channel through Captain Adair's forty-strong company of marines assembled on *Victory*'s poop, killing a single file of eight outright. Before leaving Swansea to take up his post, Second Lieutenant Lewis Rotely, a Welsh marine who survived this bloodbath, had been comforted with fatalistic advice from his father, a veteran of the American War of Independence: 'Whatever you do, be sure to keep your head erect in battle. Never bow to a Frenchman's shot; it is folly, for when you hear the balls whistle you are safe, the ball has passed harmless before you can hear it.' Nevertheless, his son believed that had Nelson ordered the marines to lie down at their quarters until wanted, as had been the practice on other ships, 'many a life would have been saved'. Instead, 'we had 20 Marines, the two Senior Lieutenants Peake and Reeves, several Naval officers and several seamen hors de combat from the poop alone before we fired a shot.' By contrast, *Conqueror*, three ships astern of *Victory*, suffered comparatively lightly with only three killed and nine wounded throughout the day, in part because 'all the men from poop, forecastle & quarterdeck were ordered below thro' the great quantity of small shot that was fired from the Enemy coming on those decks.' No such order having been given by Nelson, Rotely declared, 'no man went down until knocked down' and among the marines, erect in their scarlet coats, 'not a man was hit below the waist'. On board *Neptune*, ahead of *Conqueror*, Midshipman Badcock observed, 'the whole of the crew, with the exception of the officers, were made to lie flat on the deck, to secure them from the raking shots, some of which came in at the bows and went out at the stern.' She suffered fifty-four casualties in the action: ten killed and forty-four wounded. However, despite their greater vulnerability during the approach, no officers were injured.⁶⁴

Following the passage of *Santísima Trinidad*'s bar shot through his contingent of marines, Captain Adair was instructed by Nelson to disperse his people at broader intervals about the ship.

This belated attempt to reduce casualties among vulnerable concentrations of scarlet-coated men was a measure believed to have hastened the commander-in-chief's own death, because marines firing from their elevated position on the poop would have been best placed to eliminate French marksmen in *Redoutable*'s tops.

'There was no longer more than the merest stirring of wind,' and with her studdingsail booms shot away, every other sail fretted, and her fore topgallant brought down – even if this was not quite the comprehensive damage claimed by Captain Lucas – *Victory* ghosted towards the Combined Fleet, driven 'onward by the swell and the remains of her previous impetus'. Then more shots from *Bucentaure* – about two and a half cables' length, or 500 yards, away – brought down her mizen topmast and smashed the wheel so that her quartermasters, miraculously uninjured in the blast of splintered timber, were unable to move the rudder and steer. Ship's master, Mr Atkinson, hurried below to arrange alternative means of control.[65]

Sometime between 12.25 and 1.00, *Victory* was approaching a section of the Combined Fleet occupied by three possible enemy prizes: *Santísima Trinidad* on the larboard bow, *Bucentaure* directly ahead, and *Redoutable* close astern of the French flagship. Hardy was uncertain as to which he should engage.

'I cannot help it,' Nelson replied, 'it does not signify which we run on board of.'

His strategy had been to sever the Combined Fleet's line in two places – separating van from rear – and bring forward what he called 'a pell-mell Battle' between. Chaos and confusion were essential to his plan. 'Something must be left to chance,' he had declared, 'nothing is sure in a Sea Fight beyond all others.' And in the smoking turmoil of battle, when 'signals can neither be seen or plainly understood,' a considerable degree of autonomy among commanders was to be assumed and even encouraged. When in doubt, therefore, 'no Captain can do very wrong if he Places his Ship alongside that of an Enemy.' The last signal Lieutenant Pasco hoisted, and which remained at *Victory*'s mizen throughout the action until shot away, was number 16 in Popham's code – 'a flag quartered red and white over a Dutch ensign reversed'. It served to reinforce Nelson's instruction and define the very nature of his battle: 'ENGAGE THE ENEMY MORE CLOSELY.'[66]

*

As the head of the Weather column approached, from *Bucentaure*'s quarterdeck Admiral Villeneuve estimated *Victory* to be 'almost within half pistol-shot' – some fifteen to twenty feet away – 'while we, for our part, prepared to board and had our grappling-irons ready for throwing'. It was the moment for a grand gesture. He strode to the mainmast and seized the ship's prized eagle, brandishing it above his head. 'My friends,' he shouted, 'I am going to throw this on board the English ship. We will go and fetch it back or die!'[67]

Then the oncoming vessel altered course.

'Go on board which you please', Nelson had shouted to Hardy. 'Take your choice.'

Hardy took it, gave the order, and the quartermaster repeated it, bellowing through a copper speaking tube.* Three decks down, the forty men working a laborious secondary steering tackle in *Victory*'s gun room hauled her massive spare tiller 'hard to larboard', moving rudder then ship ponderously towards the bows of *Redoutable* and across *Bucentaure*'s unprotected stern, into which she delivered a rake of 12-, 24-, and 32-pounder guns as she passed. The first piece discharged was the snub-muzzled carronade on her forecastle. Boatswain William Willmot had loaded the 'Smasher' with a keg of 477 assorted four- and eight-ounce musket balls, backed by a 68-pound round shot, 'to give it force'.

This monstrous discharge raised a dense cloud of dust from *Bucentaure*'s disintegrating stern, thickly covering the clothes of Nelson, Hardy and others on the quarterdeck, while seconds later smoke, draughting back through the ports as each larboard gun

---

* 'Recent research has revealed that ships refitted in 1803 were being furnished with such devices and there is every reason for *Victory* to have been so fitted' (Peter Goodwin, *Nelson's Ships*, p. 259).

fired in succession, blinded and suffocated the deafened crews who were already reloading preparatory to firing again. The weight of iron commanded by Mr Willmot – and the double- and treble-shotted loads hurled by the rest of the ordnance in that opening broadside – could be effective only at close quarters, and this was to be the closest maritime conflict imaginable.

Having raked *Bucentaure*'s stern with her larboard batteries, *Victory*'s starboard guns fired as she crashed beam to beam with *Redoutable*. Captain Lucas is said to have remarked that 'what ever fired from [the English ship's] forecastle ... he was sure it killed or wounded between 4 and 5 hundred of his men as he had them all on deck with small arms.' If this were so, then the single carronade, packed like its larboard fellow with more than two hundredweight of disparately calibred shot, accounted for a majority of *Redoutable*'s 522 casualties – three hundred dead, the rest grievously wounded – out of a total crew numbering 643. Admittedly, Lucas' comment was reported by William Rivers, *Victory*'s gunner, who might be expected to extol the effectiveness of his own ordnance.[68]

Ravaged by her catastrophic encounter with *Victory*, the demolished stern of *Bucentaure* received a further broadside from *Neptune* – next in the Weather column to break the line – and then 'a most severe dressing by raking of her fore and aft' from *Téméraire* before she in turn fell alongside *Redoutable*. The resulting close engagement gave rise to what Dr Beatty would call an 'extraordinary and unprecedented circumstance'. *Victory* lay to larboard of *Redoutable*, *Téméraire* to starboard, and then *Fougueux* – crippled from her encounters with *Royal Sovereign* and *Belleisle* – to starboard of *Téméraire*: 'four ships of the line ... scrubbing sides in the heat of the fight with their heads all lying the same way as if moored in harbour'.[69]

French grappling irons tightening their embrace in a deadly intimacy, the attrition of *Victory* and *Redoutable* was ferocious. 'Our broadsides were fired muzzle to muzzle,' wrote Captain Lucas, '[and] there resulted a horrible carnage.' So close were the gunports that the likelihood, with each blast, of burning cartridge wadding setting the opposite timbers on fire made English crews especially attentive to the French ship's welfare, if only because such a conflagration would have engulfed not only *Victory* but *Téméraire* on the French ship's starboard side as well. 'Here then was seen the astonishing spectacle of the firemen of each gun standing ready with a bucket full of water, which as soon as his gun was discharged he dashed into the Enemy through the holes made in her side by the shot.' Precaution was also taken to depress each of the English guns on the middle and lower decks – by hammering the wooden quoins or wedges forward to their fullest extent under the breeches to point their muzzles down – then firing with 'a diminished charge of powder, and three shots each . . . to obviate the risk of *Téméraire*'s suffering from their shot passing through the *Redoutable*'.

Following *Téméraire* into action, *Conqueror* engaged the riddled *Bucentaure*, firing broadside after broadside into her starboard beam. 'Our men,' recalled Lieutenant Humphrey Senhouse, 'who from constant practice had gained great quickness in the use of their guns, aimed with deliberate precision, as if they had only been firing at a mark, and tore their opponent to pieces.' Not that great precision of aim was necessary as '[the] cannonading [was] at so short a distance that every shot winged with death and destruction.' After ten minutes the 'main and mizen masts [of *Bucentaure*] went by the board'.[70]

*

Santísima Trinidad's single bar shot had left *Victory*'s poop deck 'a slaughter house', and with the additional wounding of two Marine lieutenants and a number of private men, the forty Royal Marines originally posted there was reduced by half, when Captain Adair sent his remaining lieutenant below for reinforcements.

'A man should witness a battle in a three decker from the middle deck,' Lewis Rotely would tell a rapt audience of his fellow townsfolk at the Shades Tavern, Swansea, forty years later. 'It beggars description. It bewilders the senses of sight and hearing. There with the fire from above, the fire from below, besides the fire from the deck I was upon. The Guns recoiling with violence. Reports louder than thunder. The decks heaving and the sides straining I fancied myself in the infernal regions where every man appeared a devil.' Returning to the poop with thirty-five men taken from the guns, Rotely found that a stand of one hundred muskets had been smashed by another bar shot, leaving all but thirty useless. It was while these were being distributed that Captain Adair gave his last order:

'Rotely! Fire away as fast as you can.'

Then he fell dead, with a musket round from the mizen top of *Redoutable* through the back of his neck.[71]

*

Captain Lucas' men had been well trained for a battle at close quarters. 'I had 100 carbines fitted with long bayonets on board [and] the men to whom these were served out were so well accustomed to their use that they climbed halfway up the shrouds to open a musketry fire.' It was a tactic that Nelson would not countenance aboard his own ships on account of the danger of sparks setting sails aflame. But the mariner's traditional dread of fire was not, it seemed, shared by Lucas who, in addition to carbines, had brass coehorn mortars in the tops which rained down langrage onto *Victory*'s quarterdeck. He had also taken great pains to drill his men in the use of grenades – first throwing cardboard mock-ups at sea, then practising ashore 'to have them explode [live] iron grenades'. By the time *Redoutable*'s crew came to action, 'they had so acquired the habit of hurling them that on the day of the battle our topmen were throwing two at a time.' A hollow cast-iron ball four inches in diameter, the grenade's shape recalled a pomegranate, from which the word derived. It was filled with a three-ounce charge of powder and fitted with a short fuse timed to burn through in approximately six seconds. 'The case flies into many shatters,' Samuel Johnson's definition noted, 'much to the damage of all that stand near.' It was certainly powerful enough to blow a man's foot off, and Lucas claimed that more than two hundred of these vicious, but not entirely reliable, devices were thrown onto *Victory* during the course of the battle.[72]

The lower of *Redoutable*'s two gun decks had been effectively put out of action when its ports were shut to prevent her from being boarded through them by the enemy's crew. So the shot that mutilated Lieutenant William Ram came most probably from the one above. Fired upwards from a gun barrel elevated by removing the quoin from under its breech, the 18-pound ball erupted through *Victory*'s quarterdeck at Ram's feet in a shower of splinters that left him shredded below the waist. Carried down to Mr Beatty's care, when he realised the extent of his terrible injuries, the twenty-one-year-old officer 'tore off with his own hand the ligatures that were being applied and bled to death'.[73]

The Revd Dr Alexander Scott's 'natural tenderness of feeling ... quite disqualified him from being a calm spectator of death and pain ... in their most appalling shapes'. But as *Victory*'s chaplain, 'he suppressed his aversion as well as he could' to assist and console among the wounded in the cockpit. Scott was spared the sight of his unfortunate namesake's mangled body because the remains of Nelson's secretary were hurriedly jettisoned overboard close to where he was killed. But the chaplain saw Lieutenant Ram's desperate end and it was a horror too far. He fled from the screaming abattoir of the orlop, up the blood-slimed companion ladder to the 'noise, confusion, and smoke' above. He was in time to see Nelson fall.[74]

Pacing the quarterdeck with Captain Hardy to his right, the admiral had just turned about, facing *Victory*'s poop, to begin the return – Hardy a step or two ahead – when he was suddenly thumped downwards by a powerful blow to the left shoulder and at the same instant felt his spine snap. With the instantaneous loss of sensation and strength to his lower body, he dropped to his knees in secretary John Scott's blood, supporting himself for a moment with his one arm, then forwards onto his face.

*

'The first order I gave was to clear [*Redoutable*'s] Mizen top,' recalled Lieutenant Rotely, who took command of the marines following Captain Adair's death. 'Every musket was levelled at that top and in five minutes not a man was left alive in it.' Because Adair had been shot shortly before the commander-in-chief received his fatal wound, and from the same vantage point, Rotely was convinced the volley of musket fire he ordered had settled both scores at once and that the killer himself was dead 'five minutes after Nelson fell'. The Welshman's title of avenger was contested, however, by two midshipmen – John Pollard and Edward Collingwood – who concentrated their fire on the last two marksmen left alive in the top. One was shot in the back by Pollard as he tried to escape down the rigging. The other, wearing 'a glazed cocked-hat and a white frock', had been identified as the principal assassin by John King, *Victory*'s signals quartermaster. 'That's he, that's he!', shouted King, before a bullet to the mouth silenced him. Pollard and Collingwood fired simultaneously and the Frenchman was later found 'with one ball through his head, and another through his breast'. Half a century after the battle – and with Edward Collingwood dead – this account was disputed by Pollard who claimed sole credit for shooting the man who shot Nelson.[75]

IV

HMS *Victory*'s figurehead comprised an oval shield containing the king's arms, surmounted by a crown and supported either side by a naked boy. The starboard figure was adorned with a sash painted blue, to represent the men of the Royal Navy, that to larboard with a scarlet sash representing those of the Royal Marines. After the fighting, as the ship's carpenter, Mr Bunce, surveyed the damage suffered, it was noted that the blue-sashed figure had lost one of its legs, while the one with the red sash had lost an arm. It was 'a strange Coincidence', gunner William Rivers remarked, that although 'Sailors lost Legs and the Marines Arms, we had not one Seaman that lost an Arm or a Marine a Leg'.[76]

In the dark and cramped cockpit astern of *Victory*'s orlop deck William Beatty and his small surgical team* had amputated legs from eight seamen and arms from two marines.

Among the seamen's legs amputated was that of Midshipman William Rivers, the gunner's seventeen-year-old son and namesake. His foot 'hung by a Piece of Skin' having been all but detached by an exploding grenade thrown from *Redoutable*. Awaiting the surgeon's attention in the cockpit, he is said to have grown impatient and called for James Cosgrove, the purser's steward – nicknamed

---

* Assistant Surgeon Neil Smith, Surgeon's Mate William Westburgh, two loblolly boys and, after the battle, Simon Gage Britton, assistant surgeon of the schooner *Pickle*.

'Old Putty Nose' – to bring him a knife 'to Cutt the foot off' himself. He was persuaded at length to leave the procedure to a more expert hand, but refused to lie on the operating table, choosing instead to sit during the subsequent surgery as Beatty first cut through skin and muscle, then sawed short tibia and fibula four inches below the kneecap. The irrepressible Rivers rallied the wounded men waiting their turn behind him: 'It is nothing to have a Limb off,' he told them. 'You will find Pleasure when you come here Men, to git rid of your Shattered limb.' And when Beatty had finished sawing through the bones, he hoped he had been 'left ... with some Marrow'. He had, however, been left with a requisite length of stump in keeping with standard surgical procedure. 'The leg must be taken off a little below the knee,' William Northcote stipulated, 'even though the disorder extends no farther than the foot, to avoid a long and useless stump, which can be only an encumbrance and deformity to the patient.' There was another consideration: 'after a loss of the foot, a long stump cannot be commodiously adapted to a wooden leg, which must be fastened to the knee.'

Conversely, amputation at the thigh was to be done, if at all practicable, 'within two fingers breadth' above the knee, 'or else as low as possible'. This was among the most dangerous of capital procedures, not least because of its proximity to the 'extremely large' femoral artery, as 'an error in this respect may occasion a fatal haemorrhage in a minute's time.' Besides, a sizeable proportion of such amputations were attended by deadly post-operative complications because the higher up the thigh it was performed the greater the expanse of raw tissue exposed to infection. Ordinary Seaman Joseph Gordon 'Died of Sudden Spasm' – a primary symptom of lockjaw, or tetanus – six days after losing his leg above the knee, and William Smith contracted the same condition after being transferred to the Naval Hospital in Gibraltar. A visiting surgeon, touring the wards, took an especial interest in Smith's case. Dr James Fellowes wrote that the patient had been 'seized ... with locked jaw' and that while mercury ointment 'answered' for a time, 'what struck [him] as curious, was th[at] rubbing gently with the hand the upper part of the stump, kept off the Spasms – so much so that whilst his shipmate who was also wounded & lay next to him gently rubbed his thigh he was easy but the spasms came on when he left off.' Regardless of that relief, cause of death a fortnight after the procedure was recorded as 'Tenasmus' – an unproductive straining at stool – presumably rupturing an insecurely ligatured blood vessel.*,77

Richard Jewell 'had lost a great deal of blood before he was brought to the Cockpit,' and the required amputation was conducted so high into the region of his pelvis that his death shortly after was attributed to 'the great violence done' to his constitution and from his having 'sustained the removal of so large a portion of the body'.

After undergoing an 'Amputated Thigh high up', Able Seaman Thomas Smith appears to have survived, as did landsman William Jones, and Joseph Burgin, the ship's poulterer, a role earning him the nickname 'Coxhead'. Burgin lived long enough to receive his Naval General Service Medal with Trafalgar clasp, issued to survivors of the battle in 1848. Four years earlier he had acquired national celebrity of a kind when his engraved likeness – plump and with a turned wooden peg-leg protruding from the left trouser of his Chelsea Pensioner uniform – featured in the *Illustrated London News*.78

Along with the two Royal Marines enduring upper limb surgical amputation – Corporal William Taft, high 'at the neck of the Humerus' near the shoulder, and Private William Wells 'just below the Cubit', or elbow – Private James Burgess, his leg shattered and amputated below the knee, proved a solitary exception to the pattern of mutilation set by the red-sashed boy on *Victory*'s figurehead. Marine Lieutenant Rotely's remark that among his people on the poop deck 'not a man was hit below the waist' was further contradicted by Private Isaac Harris, his leg contused 'by a Splinter', by two others with 'Lacerated Wound[s] on the Thigh',

---

* Sir James Watt in 'Surgery at Trafalgar', *Mariner's Mirror*, vol. 91, no. 2 (2005) refers to this as a case of tetanus but the MS of 'Surgeon's Journal of *Victory*', TNA, Adm 101/125/1 clearly reads 'Tenasmus'.

and by Privates William Knight and Thomas Rayner, both with compound fractures to the lower leg, and both later 'Discharged Dead' from the hospital at Gibraltar.

A number of men posted on *Victory*'s poop deck had never come to Mr Beatty's attention. When the wreckage of yards and masts toppled in the battle was cleared, a Marine was found who appeared as though presenting arms when crushed by the falling debris, 'with his Musquet Close to his Brest with his Arm Round the But and his Musquet Bent over his Shoulder, Dead.' Another had been transfixed by his own weapon, musket likewise bent but 'with his Bayonat Fixt and in his Back'. Others 'lay on the Forecastle dead with their Musquet[s] to their Brest as if they were going to fire'. And one musket was found 'with the hand Grasp'd fast to it, the Body gone'.[79]

*

The five pages of William Beatty's journal pertaining to the action on 21 October contain a list of wounded numbering just over a hundred. Each man's name is given with his 'Quality' – whether landsman, ordinary or able seaman, boy, marine, or rank if an officer – along with the nature of his wound and the date on which he was pronounced either 'Cured on board, Sent to an Hospital, or Died'. Mr Beatty's written concern for his patients did not extend beyond those sparse particulars.

Twelve casualties were specifically ascribed to splinters although some multiple injuries involving lacerations and contusions, not so specified, might also be included in that category. Able Seaman John Bush had been struck by splinters 'in many parts of the Body', while Jeremiah Sullivan was literally scalped by a large one and his wound logged as a 'Denuded Cranium'. Grape, canister shot and in one instance 'a piece of Iron' accounted for other wounds, while at least nine were caused by musket rounds, presumably fired from the tops of *Redoutable* after the two ships engaged. The son of a cutler in St James's Street, Midshipman Palmer was shot through the thigh, and although the ball's passage left 'Bone and large Vessels untouched', his death was reported in the *London Gazette* of 27 November, sending his grieving family into deep mourning. However, on the following Sunday they received a letter from him explaining 'that another of the same name had been unfortunately killed, but that he had escaped with a wound in the thigh'. His namesake was Marine Private John Palmer of Bedfordshire. But jubilation in the cutler's household was brief. Midshipman Alex Palmer's reassuring letter had been written and dispatched during the seven-day interval between the infliction of his wound and his death from tetanus on 28 October, the 'Cold affusion and ... Digitalis with large Doses of Opium' prescribed by Mr Beatty counting for nought.[80]

Shot through the abdomen, eighteen-year-old Colin Turner later died of 'mortification', and Henry Cramwell, having suffered 'a simple fracture' below the knee and 'several severely contused wounds on different parts of the body', succumbed to gangrene within a week. By contrast, boatswain's mate William Castle, despite being 'Dangerously wounded in the Groin and [sustaining] several other bad Wounds', was received into the Gibraltar Hospital and discharged for active duty back on board *Victory* in early November.

Only patients undergoing treatment were listed in Beatty's journal. Those killed instantly or dead on arrival in the cockpit numbered around fifty. The roll made no mention of *Victory*'s most notable casualty, carried below with a handkerchief concealing his face – and belatedly his honours – to avoid disheartening the crew. The injured men on the orlop deck awaiting treatment were not deceived by the disguise, however.

'Mr Beatty, Lord Nelson is here; Mr Beatty, the Admiral is wounded.' And, having just examined, and pronounced dead, the bodies of Lieutenant Ram and Thomas Whipple, Beatty turned and saw the handkerchief fall away.

'Ah, Mr Beatty! You can do nothing for me. I have but a short time to live; my back is shot through.'

He had said the same to Captain Hardy on the quarterdeck, moments after he fell, and during the two hours and forty-five minutes it took for him to die he repeated several times that 'he was confident his back was shot through'. Asked by Beatty to describe his sensations he replied that 'he felt a gush of blood every minute within his breast; that he had no feeling in the lower part of his body; and that his breathing was difficult, and attended with very severe pain about that part of the spine where ... the ball had struck.' And he said again, 'I felt it break my back.' The rhythmic 'gush' he described came from the damaged left pulmonary artery, the respiratory difficulty from his punctured left lung and the accumulating blood rising in that side of the chest cavity. This would be among the most precisely documented deaths in battle ever recorded. It must surely also be one of the most self-conscious. He had lost 'all power of motion and feeling' below his breast, he told Beatty again, and added, '*You* very well *know* I can live but a short time.' The emphasis he placed on the two words indicated he was comparing his own case with that of another of the surgeon's patients, a thirty-six-year-old American, native to South Carolina, pressed into service from Sheerness in 1803 and lost during the *Victory*'s voyage back from the West Indies earlier in the year. Beatty had logged James Bush's injury 'from a fall', off the island of St Mary in the Azores, as a 'Contused Head & Spine', attended by 'slow pulse', a 'loss of motion & sensibility of the inferior extremities', and inevitably in cases of paraplegia, 'involuntary stools and evacuations of Urine'. Damage to the '1st Dorsal [or thoracic] Vertebra' appeared to be the cause. He lingered for almost a fortnight, Beatty noting on each of his morning rounds that he 'continues as yesterday', until 13 July when he died at one in the afternoon.

Bush's paralysed plight and symptoms had left a strong impression on Nelson and, three months later, 'he now appeared to apply the situation and fate of this man to himself,' although in his case the additional internal haemorrhage would make an end much sooner. While the surgeon tested his extremities for sensation – just as the Revd Scott and Mr Burke, the purser, had already done – the patient said with the same emphasis, '*You know* I am gone.' And Beatty concurred: 'My Lord, unhappily for our Country, nothing can be done for you,' then turned away to conceal his emotion. Nelson put a hand to his left side and said that he felt something rising in his chest.

Beatty's *Authentic Narrative of the Death of Lord Nelson*, published two years later, purportedly contained every word spoken in his last hours: the repeated assurances that he was 'done for' and 'a dead man'; reiterated instructions for the care of Lady Hamilton and Horatia left as a 'legacy' to his country; the gasped monosyllables – calling for Scott's lemonade, or for the cooling motion of a piece of paper agitated by Mr Burke – 'Drink, drink,' and 'Fan, fan.' Gentle massaging of his chest also seemed to offer relief, and a third breathless instruction was addressed to Scott and to Burke, performing that office by turns: 'Rub, rub.'

Mr Beatty told a visiting surgeon at Gibraltar that 'upwards of forty men were brought [below] about the time Lord Nelson was carried down the ladder.' However, his *Authentic Narrative* of the admiral's last hours conveys no impression of the resulting congestion, nor of the sights, sounds and smells on the orlop deck. Scott spoke of it only once. Pressed on the subject by a friend shortly after his return to England, 'it was like a butcher's shambles,' he replied, and would say no more.[81]

Marine Lieutenant Nicholas believed that what he witnessed in the cockpit of *Belleisle* was unusual, 'a scene of suffering and carnage which rarely occurs'. It was however all too typical. 'So many bodies in such a confined place, and under such distressing circumstances ... Even the dangers of the battle did not seem more terrific ... On a long table lay several anxiously looking for their turn to receive the surgeon's care yet dreading the fate which he might pronounce. One subject was undergoing amputation, and every part was heaped with sufferers. Their piercing shrieks and expiring groans were echoed through this vault of misery; and ... the heart-sickening picture is [still] alive in my memory.'[82]

While there were no peaceful places anywhere aboard a man-of-war in time of action, the orlop deck was among the safest, its situation offering protection from all but indirect enemy fire. Northcote wrote that sometimes those who were slightly injured were unwilling to leave its comparative security and encouraged his colleagues to 'insist on their going again to their quarters, otherwise threaten to report them when the engagement is over'. Robert Young, a surgeon aboard HMS *Ardent* at the battle of Camperdown in 1797, also had occasion to observe less than noble behaviour among the common seamen. 'Some with wounds, bad indeed and painful, but slight in comparison with the dreadful condition of others, were most vociferous for my assistance. These I was obliged to reprimand with severity, as their voices disturbed the last moments of the dying.' Northcote was even more scathing. 'I have many times known cowardly lubbers come tumbling down the ladder with most violent groans and complaints, though at the same time they have received little or no hurt; and all I could do or say would not prevail on them to make a second trial of their courage, nor go up again till the action was over.'[83]

Of the thirty-six Articles of War established for the Royal Navy in 1749, number twelve carried a penalty of death for 'every person ... who through cowardice, negligence, or disaffection, shall in time of action withdraw or keep back, or not come into the fight or engagement'. Common seamen, eager and motivated by the promise of prize money and often shielded from direct enemy fire on the lower gun decks were rarely accused or court-martialled under Article XII. Such charges might more readily be brought among the upper echelons of ship's masters, commanders and admirals, those most exposed to danger on the quarterdeck and whose orders could 'withdraw or keep back' an entire ship, squadron or fleet from engaging. While specific imputations of cowardice, weakness or of any conduct falling short of selfless devotion to duty among lower ranks were uncommon, not everyone can have been a hero, nor can allegations made by Northcote of desperately self-inflicted wounds have been entirely unwarranted. 'Dastardly fellows have actually put their feet, or stood in the way of the [recoiling gun] carriage, on purpose to be hurt, that they might have a plausible pretence for going down to the doctor.'[84]

Towards the end of Dr Beatty's journal, eight men are listed as being 'wounded Slightly'. It is open to question how far William Terrant with his 'Slightly Wounded Face', Will Bond with 'wounded Back and Shoulder Slightly', Sam Hampton with a 'Slightly Wounded Hand', and the rest, fell within Northcote's definition of 'cowardly lubbers'. However, while understandable faint-heartedness under fire can at best be inferred, anecdotes of bravery abound. If the severity of *Royal Sovereign*'s master, William Chalmers' wound is to be credited, for example, his grit was remarkable – hit by 'a great shot [which] almost divided his body ... he lay in the cockpit until the Santa Ana struck [her colours]; and, joining in the cheer which they gave her, expired with it on his lips'. There was a similar case on *Tonnant*. A man named Smith, after his leg had been amputated, cheered as *Algésiras* struck. The exertion 'burst the blood vessels, and before they could be taken up he died'. Another was carried to Mr Chevers, 'with all his bowels hanging out, encouraging his gunmates, and huzzaing along the decks as he passed below'. Chevers liked to recall a less drastic case as illustrative of 'how these men ... bear pain in all its various forms'. Shot through the big toe, 'which hung by a fragment of skin', a seaman refused to leave his post 'for this trifle' and resisted his companion's advice to go below to have it dressed. While they were disputing the point, a carronade 'took a cant accidentally, from a roll of the Ship', and settled the argument by crushing the whole of his foot. He was forthwith carried to the cockpit, said Chevers, and 'is now ... doing well'.[85]

*

The orlop deck did not always offer a safe haven. Edward Ives, writing in 1773, cited 'several instances of surgeons or their mates being wounded ... by cannon balls' and recommended they conduct their operations even further below decks, in the unsanitary realm of the hold. The cockpit, he argued 'cannot be a proper station for men upon whose personal security the lives of so many brave seamen entirely depend'. At Trafalgar, *Revenge* was holed eight times below the waterline through her copper-cladding, and a 42-pound shot 'entirely shattered a beam' on the orlop within six inches of Revd John Greenly, wounding him 'in twenty places by splinters'. Although they were 'mere scratches' and 'so slight that [he] would not be put in the list of wounded,' he admitted it to be 'rather an unusual thing for a Chaplain to be wounded in Action', given his pastoral role so far below among the injured and dying. William McDonald, surgeon on *Colossus*, also had a lucky escape. 'He had just performed an operation, when a cannon shot passed thro' the Cockpit – knocked down his table, wounded his assistant who was taking him some dressing' and sending 'the unhappy brave fellows who were laying down on the deck after being amputated roll[ing] over one another'. No Royal Navy surgeon is known to have been injured during the battle, but ten of the French fleet's eighty-eight were killed, including two aboard *Redoutable*. The *Victory* crews' tactic of lowering their gun muzzles and firing downwards caused the carnage described by Captain Lucas: '[Our] decks were shot through and riddled, in such a manner that numbers of the wounded below on the orlop, and as they lay in the cockpit, were ... killed helplessly.'[86]

Cosmao-Kerjulien's recently built 74-gun *Pluton*, launched early that year at Toulon, sustained a 'large number of shot-holes between wind and water' losing 180 men killed and wounded, although an injured infantry officer put the casualties at more than twice that number. Captain Charles Pernot lay on a mattress in the crowded cockpit, fortunate to have no bones broken. He had a wound to the left eye which he thought lost but would be out of danger in four days, another injury to the left hand which would take longer to heal, and also a painfully swollen contusion from one shoulder to the other, the result of a blow to his chest close to the collar bone. He must have thought his part in the battle was over. Then a round shot crashed through the orlop timbers, wounding the chief medical officer, René-Marie Fournier, and killing Jean Barof, a surgeon. The near-blinded Pernot was injured twice more in the head by flying splinters and buried underneath twenty other wounded men – but survived. He later attributed *Pluton*'s extensive structural damage to 'the poor quality of the ship although new', rather than to the skill of English gunners.[87]

*

With 127 men badly wounded, forty slightly, besides twenty-eight killed, *Bellerophon*'s surgeon was overwhelmed. During a lull in the firing William White reported that 'the cockpit was so crowded with wounded that it was quite impossible for him to attempt some operations which were highly requisite, and begg[ed] to bring some subjects up into the late captain's cabin for amputation if the fire was not likely to be renewed for a quarter of an hour.' First Lieutenant Cumby – having taken command following the deaths of Captain Cooke and ship's master Edward Overton – gave permission on the understanding 'that [White] must be prepared to go down again' to the orlop should the two 18-pounder guns occupying the captain's cabin require further employment. One of the injured operated on in the more spacious accommodation was Marine Captain James Wemyss, 'badly wounded by splinters' and necessitating amputation of his right arm. ''Tis only a mere scratch,' he had told Cumby while waiting, 'and I shall have to apologise to you by and by for having left the deck on so trifling occasion.'[88]

More horrific injuries treated by Mr White included a number inflicted by a type of incendiary weapon called by the French *pots à feu* and by the English 'stink pots'. Similar in principle to the grenades favoured by *Redoutable*'s topmen – and confused with them in some accounts – they were earthenware containers 'charged with powder, mixed with other inflammable and suffocating materials [such as sulphur] with a lighted fuze at the aperture'. Thrown into an enemy ship, 'they burst and catch fire, producing an intolerable stench and smoke, and filling the deck with tumult and distraction.' Quantities of this 'infernal apparatus' were thrown onto the forecastle, gangway, and through the gunports of *Bellerophon* from *Aigle* during their extended attrition. Upwards of twenty-five men were injured, 'many ...

dreadfully scorched'. Maddened with pain, one individual 'ran aft and threw himself out of one of the stern ports'. Destruction of the entire vessel was avoided only by purest chance when a stink pot rolled close to the open door of the powder magazine. 'A sudden motion of the ship shut to the door – and it blew up a gunner who stood near it & wounded him most dreadfully.' Of the fifty-one most seriously wounded from this ship transferred to the hospital at Gibraltar, fourteen were registered in the admissions book as 'Blown Up'. Of these, three died, one a Royal Marine expiring between ship and shore and 'Landed Dead'. Dr Fellowes, touring the wards, described *Bellerophon*'s men as 'dreadfully cut up & [several] totally disfigured'. Twenty-three of the ship's wounded would be dead within a month.[89]

If British surgeons like White had difficulty coping with the mangled numbers brought bleeding and screaming to their overcrowded workstations, French and Spanish surgeons were hard pressed also, and with considerably more casualties requiring attention. On board *Swiftsure*, Jean-Baptiste Delivet informed Captain Villemadrin that it was impossible 'to make room for any more wounded, that the space cleared in the hold and the orlop-deck were thronged'. The captain could not say precisely how many were *hors de combat* but believed that 'it must have amounted to nearly 260 to 300 killed and wounded'. A more accurate number, however, was closer to two thirds that upper figure: sixty-eight killed and a hundred and twenty-three wounded.[90]

*

Sixth in the Weather column, the slow but heavily armed 100-gun *Britannia* – the oldest ship of either fleet – bore the flag of the third-in-command, Rear Admiral Lord Northesk. She entered the fray firing a double-shotted broadside into the crippled *Bucentaure* – still being battered into submission by *Conqueror* – before engaging *Santísima Trinidad*, with another into her stern, 'shatter[ing] the rich display of sculpture, figures, ornaments and inscriptions with which she was adorned'. Marine Lieutenant

Lawrence Halloran, commanding the aftermost larboard 32-pounder gun on the lower deck, had a fleeting impression of the magnificent Spanish craft he was helping to disfigure. 'I never saw so beautiful a ship.' And as an amateur painter, he particularly appreciated the 'imposing effect' presented by her four-decked starboard elevation, 'of a rich lake colour'. Later only Halloran and a midshipman named Tompkins were left uninjured when the muzzle of his gun was struck by a large enemy shot that split into several pieces 'each of which took its victim'. The mangled body of Marine Private John Jolley – 'his stomach being shot away' – was thrown out of the gun port, while the rest were 'left to be examined' by the surgeon. An Italian known as Pilgrim had both his arms ripped off in the same strike. He later received a naval pension which he supplemented by travelling the country with his wife, 'who turn[ed] a hand organ'.[91]

The devastating punishment of *Bucentaure* by *Conqueror* approached its merciful conclusion around two o'clock. Twenty minutes after the fall of her main- and mizenmast, her foremast collapsed. 'The upper works and the 24-pounder gun-deck being deserted and strewn with dead and wounded; the lower deck guns dismounted or masked by the fallen masts and rigging,' she was unable to retaliate or protect herself. 'Lying motionless, and ... impossible to make any movement,' wrote Villeneuve, 'I was obliged to yield to my fate and put an end to a slaughter already vast, which was from henceforth useless.' She was among the first of the Combined Fleet to surrender. According to Lieutenant Senhouse 'it was at half-past two she struck to the CONQUEROR', although Joseph Seymour, *Conqueror*'s master, recorded that she struck at five past. Whatever the precise time, it was not a literal token of capitulation, there being no mast left erect to strike her colours from. Instead, Midshipman William Hicks reported, 'officers of the French ship wav[ed] their handkerchiefs in sign of surrender'.[92]

Bucentaure's eagle never reached *Victory*'s quarterdeck as Villeneuve had promised. It was retrieved from the foot of the truncated mainmast by one of its guardians. The young *aspirant de marine*, Antoine Donadieu, was commended for his bravery when 'at the time ... the upper works were deserted and under a deadly fire, the ship being totally dismasted and no longer showing any colours ... he fastened the Eagle of the Empire about his body.' To prevent the revered relic providing a trophy of conquest for the enemy, at the moment *Conqueror*'s boarding party took possession of the ship, it was broken in pieces by Lieutenant Fulcran Fournier and the fragments thrown into the sea, along with a lead box containing the ship's signal book and secret papers. The same procedure must have been followed aboard every other captured French ship because no imperial eagles fell into British hands at Trafalgar.[93]

V

WHEN Nelson's Weather column broke through the enemy's line, the leading vessels of the Combined Fleet were divided from its centre, and the seven-ship squadron commanded by Rear Admiral Pierre Dumanoir le Pelley – together with *San Agustín*, *Héros* and *Intrépide* – continued sailing northwards away from the ensuing fight. At the same time, Villeneuve had signalled the fleet from *Bucentaure*'s mizen- and foremasts, ordering 'every ship, which by her present position was not engaging, to take any such [position] as would bring her as promptly as possible into action'. This being a general signal, Dumanoir had seemingly disregarded it, perhaps awaiting more specific instructions relevant to his squadron alone. The most favourable gloss to be placed on his non-compliance was that he had been unable to see the signal for cannon smoke. However, that the signal had to be made at all was to be interpreted as an accusation of dishonourable conduct of those 'to whom it was addressed'. In his prior instructions to the Combined Fleet, Villeneuve, like Nelson, had encouraged autonomy of individual command in battle before reliance on centralised control. 'A captain,' he declared, 'must consult his own daring and love of honour far more than the signals of the Admiral, who being perhaps engaged himself and shrouded in smoke, may no longer have the power of making any.' From this followed the blunt, unequivocal and uncompromising pronouncement, that 'any captain ... who is not under fire will not be at his post ... and a signal recalling him to his post will be a reflection on his honour.'[94]

At about 1.45, an hour and a quarter after sending his general signal – during which time *Bucentaure* had been battered into ruin by the British guns – and shortly before her main-, mizen- and foremasts collapsed, Villeneuve ordered his final signal to be hoisted, while a mast survived to receive it. This time the instruction to Dumanoir's squadron was specific, to alter their northerly course and engage: 'THE AVANT-GARDE TO WEAR TOGETHER.'

Wearing a ship of the line – turning through 180 degrees with her stern to windward – was easier ordered than accomplished with 'a swell running, the wind very faint and almost a calm, the ships barely answer[ing] to the helm'. Dumanoir's 80-gun flagship *Formidable* and the 74-gun *Scipion* had to lower long-boats, to allow their toiling oarsmen to tow them into the wind. *Mont-Blanc* collided with another 74, *Intrépide*, splintering her own jib-boom and ripping the other's fore-sail. These four French ships, together with the 74-gun *Duguay-Trouin* and the Spanish *Neptuno*, accomplished the manoeuvre, albeit slowly. The 80-gun *Neptuno* then engaged in a protracted fight with two English 74s, *Spartiate* and *Minotaur*, leaving her, after an hour and a half, 'very much disabled'. She would be one of the last two vessels of the Combined Fleet to surrender, submitting 'a few minutes before sunset' to the *Minotaur*. Meanwhile, *Intrépide* had sailed eastward into the roaring smoke-shrouded *mêlée*, and would battle to the finish, pounded by the 74s *Africa*, *Orion* and the 100-gun *Britannia* into inevitable capitulation, within half an hour of *Neptuno*. The other three French vessels – *Scipion*, *Duguay-Trouin* and *Mont Blanc* – led by *Formidable*, 'pass[ed] to windward of the enemy instead of standing boldly into the thick of the fight ... exchanging some shots, for the most part at a great distance' – for which the Rear Admiral would later face a court of enquiry.[95]

Bucentaure had surrendered soon after the vanguard belatedly responded to Villeneuve's final signal, rendering any possibility of assistance from that quarter futile. Seeing his commander-in-chief's flagship dismasted and already in enemy hands, Dumanoir would later blame his tardiness and inability to assist on Captain Valdés of the beleaguered *Neptuno* for the 'greatest indecision in his manoeuvres' and on 'the failure of the [other] van ships ... to comply with the order to go about'. Four of these – the French *Héros* and the Spaniards *Rayo*, *San Francisco de Asis*, and *San Agustín* – finding it impossible to wear, had tacked instead, an opposite procedure, bringing their bows into the wind, but achieving the same general end and direction of sail. *Héros*, *Rayo* and *San Francisco de Asis* then 'bore away' to the east and would take no further part in the fighting before eventually reaching the safety of Cadiz. *San Agustín*, however, was engaged by *Leviathan* and so efficiently mauled with round shot and grape in the encounter – before being grappled and boarded – as to sustain the loss of 201 wounded and 184 dead, to her adversary's four killed and twenty-five wounded. *San Agustín* suffered the highest number of casualties in the Spanish fleet, amounting to fifty-four per cent of her crew.[96]

*

On the larboard side of *Victory*'s orlop deck, Nelson lay propped against one of the immense sloping timbers, lung slowly filling with blood. His final hours were shaken by the detonation and recoil of the ship's heaviest cannon a few inches' thickness of oak overhead; pierced by the screams of wounded undergoing surgery in the adjacent cockpit; heartened by the bursts of cheering from above as French and Spanish ships struck their colours.

'I hope none of our ships have struck, Hardy,' he said at one point.

'No, my Lord,' came the reply, 'there is no fear of that.'[97]

*

By 2.15, Richard Burstal, the master of *Dreadnought*, 'observed several of the enemy's ships dismasted and strike their colours'. Burstal's log appeared to claim the distinction of capturing the first enemy prize of the action as early as two o'clock when the Spanish 78-gun *San Juan Nepomuceno* struck to *Dreadnought*'s ninety-eight. The Spaniard's report, however, claimed that she held out until after four o'clock.[98]

After *Redoutable* had struck to *Victory* she was boarded by a prize crew from *Téméraire*, Eliab Harvey's ship having also taken possession of her own battered prize, the *Fougueux*. Captain Lucas later submitted an inventory of catastrophic damage to the Ministère de la Marine, justifying *Redoutable*'s surrender, while François Marie Bazin, second-in-command of *Fougueux*, would inform the same authority of a captain mortally wounded, first lieutenant dead, second in seniority nearly so, and the next shot in the leg; of one battery nearly silenced, the guns of another entirely dismounted, only fifteen gunners left alive, and 'all the people that [he] had on deck or in the tops . . . killed or wounded'. Earlier in the battle Bazin himself had been wounded several times but was still capable of limping below to retrieve and drown 'the leaden box containing confidential papers' from the captain's cabin. Returning to the quarterdeck he found the *Fougueux* overrun. 'The colours were then hauled down and gradually the slaughter ceased.'[99]

Although *Bucentaure* had struck to *Conqueror*, the English ship – being thenceforward heavily engaged with *Santísima Trinidad* – was unable to observe the due formalities of capitulation and Admiral Villeneuve was instead rowed with his senior officers to the *Mars*. There, on the quarterdeck, he relinquished his sword to Lieutenant Hennah, in sole command following the death of Captain Duff. An incident was witnessed by Midshipman James Robinson and recounted to his father as 'display[ing] the soul of a British sailor'. As he passed Duff's headless corpse, the French commander-in-chief remarked something to one of his attendants. He may also have been seen to smile and this slight – real, coincidental or imagined – provoked a crew member to lay violent hands on the Frenchman. 'When my Captain lived he was able to revenge an insult,' he growled. 'Now he is dead it is my duty to revenge it for him.' So saying he threw the startled admiral aside and covered his captain's body 'with a spare colour, an union jack'.[100]

Algésiras struck and was 'taken in possession' by *Tonnant* with 160 men dead, her captain wounded and Rear Admiral Magon – already splinter-wounded and shot through the arm – killed instantly by a musket round to the chest. An alternative account has him nearly cut in two by a round shot, while according to another he was hit in the stomach by grape.[101]

Newly promoted to commodore on *Bahama*, Dionisio Alcalá Galiano had the Spanish flag nailed to her main mast and instructed Alonso Butrón – a *guardiamarina* or midshipman – not to take it down even if ordered to do so, 'because no Galiano surrenders and no Butrón should either'. His ship under fire to starboard from *Colossus*, and to larboard from *Bellerophon*, Commodore Galiano had already received a splinter wound to the face, when the wind of a ball knocked the telescope from his hand. His coxswain ran forward to retrieve it and was passing the instrument back when a round shot ripped him in two, drenching the Commodore in blood and viscera. Moments later another ball took away the top of Galiano's head. Young Alonso Butrón was absolved from his obligation to keep the flag aloft by his commander's death, as well as by dint of being injured himself. The colours had, besides, by this time been shot down along with the mast. The severely wounded senior lieutenant Don Roque Guruceta gave the order to surrender and British flags were displayed to *Bellerophon* and *Colossus* who immediately ceased their fire, *Colossus* taking possession of *Bahama* and *Bellerophon* of *Monarca*.[102]

Raked by *Neptune* and *Conqueror*, *Santísima Trinidad* was also under fire from *Leviathan* and *Britannia*. Rear Admiral Baltasar de Cisneros 'gave orders to crowd on all sail possible in the crippled condition of [her] rigging' in order to get clear. The resulting profusion of canvas made the collapse of first her main- and then mizenmast a particularly awe-inspiring spectacle for her antagonists. 'Her immense topsails had every reef out, her royals were sheeted home but lowered,' recalled an officer on *Conqueror*, 'and the falling of the mass of spars, sails, and rigging, plunging into the water at the muzzles of our guns, was one of the most magnificent sights I ever beheld.' The Spanish flagship 'was unmanageable, ... a large part of the guns out of action and the rest unable to fire on account of the decks being encumbered with masts, rigging and sails, with many shot-holes between wind and water and the decks strewn with dead and wounded.' With no colours left aloft to strike, she signalled her capitulation by an officer 'waving [a British] flag by hand having no place to fly it'.[103]

Of *Conqueror*'s remarkably light toll of casualties – three fatalities and nine wounded – the only two officers killed fell during her fight with the giant Spaniard, and at the same instant. Seventeen-year-old Midshipman William Hicks had just delivered a message to First Lieutenant Robert Lloyd when he stooped to pick up a souvenir piece of grapeshot from the quarterdeck and put it in his pocket. It was an impulse that saved his life as he narrowly avoided the trajectory of a round shot. Straightening up he saw behind him Lieutenants Lloyd and William Molyneux St George lying side by side. He ran to them and said he hoped they were not seriously hurt. When he raised Lloyd's head, blood from the severed neck gushed into his shoes. Hicks himself was one of the nine wounded, albeit not seriously enough to merit mention in his own memoir of the battle.[104]

'At 4.30 in the afternoon precisely' – Lieutenant Don Anselmo de Gomendio must have consulted his pocket watch to be so particular – *San Ildefonso* struck to *Defence*. Captain José Ramón de Vargas being severely wounded, his first lieutenant went aboard the English ship, where he impressed Midshipman William Huskisson with his nonchalance. Having surrendered the Spanish captain's sword, Don Anselmo 'very cooly took a [smouldering] match out of one of the match-tubs on the quarterdeck, lighted his *segar* and smoked it unconcernedly as if nothing particular had occurred'.[105]

*

Late in the afternoon, aboard *Tonnant*, Lieutenant John Salmon counted seventeen enemy ships that had struck, 'the best part dismasted'. His journal entry also reported that around 5.40, 'the [rest of the] combined fleet ... made off in all directions – that is to say, 4 stood to the southward and 12 for Cadiz.' British ships' logs were in general agreement regarding the disposition of enemy vessels remaining at liberty as the battle neared its end, although the times of sightings varied. At six o'clock – his ship lying further to the north-east than *Tonnant* – Richard Burstal aboard *Dreadnought* reported a clearer view of the vessels making sail to the Spanish port and was able to distinguish an additional six smaller craft accompanying them: four frigates and two brigs. However disparate as to timing, references to the other four – French ships, 'one with a Rear-Admiral's flag' – were precise and consistent: 'to windward, standing to the southward with all sail set'. *Colossus* reported 'receiv[ing] a fire from the enemy's van passing to windward', as did Eliab Harvey, writing of the 'French ships ... about ¾ of a mile to windward [who] opened their guns upon *Téméraire*, and her prizes'. *Redoutable* and *Fougueux* were lashed either side of Harvey's ship, and Rear Admiral Dumanoir later admitted that, firing on *Téméraire*, 'in spite of all the precautions we took ... the *Fougueux* received some of our shots.' Captain Lucas testified that *Redoutable* also came under friendly fire from the same direction. Midshipman William Pitts, one of the English boarding crew, was hit by a round shot, dying in the care of the French surgeon after the amputation of his shattered leg. The two prizes hampered for a time deployment of *Téméraire*'s guns, but when 'those [guns] we could fight with were brought to bear upon the enemy,' Harvey boasted, 'the gentlemen thought proper to haul to a more respectable distance'. An allegation of fire directed at Spanish ships – following their surrender – would occasion further animosity regarding Dumanoir's conduct from friend and foe alike.[106]

It might have been argued that the ship of an ally that had struck her colours to the enemy, became *de facto* an enemy vessel herself and thereby a legitimate target regardless of the nationality or allegiance of those left on board. The argument would have been strengthened if the colours she was flying in token of surrender were those of her captors, as was the case in several recorded instances at Trafalgar, when French or Spanish colours had earlier been shot away. And in any case the hoisting of their own colours would have been among the first actions of a British boarding party on taking possession. However, no such argument or justification was used at the time.

Dumanoir claimed in defence of his squadron's departure from the battle, that *Formidable* had herself suffered 'considerable damage' from an encounter with two English craft 'at the distance of pistol shot', and later that four three-deckers had 'handled [her] very severely', leaving her with sixty-five men killed and wounded, 'her masts severely damaged, all her tackling, and the greater part of her shrouds cut to pieces, . . . sails entirely crippled, [and making] besides four feet water in an hour, by reason of the shots she had received below the water-mark'. The other three vessels under his command, moreover, 'were nearly in the same state'. *Duguay-Trouin* had thirty-five men disabled in the action, *Scipion* fourteen killed, '19 wounded, most of them seriously [of whom] 3 died of their wounds shortly afterwards,' and 'the loss in men [on *Mont Blanc*] was very nearly the same.' Dumanoir's negative assessment of the fighting capability of the ships remaining under his command as he withdrew to windward was contradicted by Captain Harvey, who described them, admittedly from a distance, as 'apparently in good order', and by Lucas, who reported them as 'retir[ing] from the battle-field – without appearing to have their rigging damaged'.[107]

Had he been better supported, Dumanoir claimed in justification of his actions, and 'if I had had with me ten ships [instead of four], however desperate our position, I should have been able to bear down on the scene of action and to fight the enemy to a finish . . . and perhaps it would have been reserved for me to have made the day glorious for the Allied Fleet.' Instead, he argued, 'on account of the depletion of my division, I could not have done much damage. It was therefore my duty in this painful situation to endeavour to effect the repairs of my division in the hope of more favourable chances on the morrow.' He would get another chance a fortnight later.[108]

*

Prisoners brought on board *Victory* remarked to their gratified captors that 'the Devel loded the [English] guns for it was impossible for men to load and fire so Quick as we did.' Royal Navy gun crews – through exhaustive and regular practice during the longueurs of blockade duty – could fire three shots in five minutes. Collingwood had told the men of his former flagship, *Dreadnought*, that if they achieved this rate of fire 'no vessel could resist them'. It was said that they had even achieved a rate of three shots in three and a half minutes. Their opponents by contrast might take anything from four to eight minutes to load and fire once: an average of three shots in seventeen minutes. There was a remarkable correlation at Trafalgar between the two average rates of fire and the roughly three-to-one ratio of casualties in the Combined and British fleets: 5,230 dead and wounded to 1,666. 'The superiority of artillery among our adversaries was such that in a few moments our crews were decimated,' Auguste Gicquel observed, 'while theirs only suffered relatively slight losses.'[109]

The efficiency of British gunnery was apparent, when the firing stopped, to crews taking possession of the mauled prizes. Revd John Greenly was unclear as to the exact scale of fatalities found on *Santísima Trinidad*, only that numbers of 'the killed ... must have been dreadful', because her captors were 'employed all the morning in throwing their dead bodies over board'. Midshipman Badcock had seen the gore-spattered effects of fore-and-aft rakes on the Spanish flagship, as had *Conqueror*'s Captain of Marines James Atcherley on *Bucentaure*, where the mutilation of bodies had continued even after the killing. 'The dead, thrown back as they fell, lay along the middle of the decks in heaps and [more] shot, passing through these, had frightfully mangled the bodies ... an extraordinary proportion had lost their heads.' Atcherley was told by a French officer that one single raking shot to the lower deck 'through the thickest of the people had killed or disabled nearly forty men'. Lieutenant Senhouse counted two hundred corpses as they were later tossed into the sea and estimated a hundred and fifty wounded. *Bucentaur*'s was one of the largest number of battle losses suffered by the French fleet.[110]

A latecomer to close action from Dumanoir's vanguard, *Intrépide*'s casualties numbered eighty killed and 162 wounded, a quarter of her complement estimated at between 550 and 600. But while the English rate of firing may have decisively accounted for the degree of slaughter in this case, the 74-gun *Intrépide* was at times under attack from as many as six Royal Navy vessels, including *Neptune* with ninety-eight guns and *Britannia* with a hundred. The combined casualties of those six line-of-battle ships amounted to only thirty-three killed and 170 wounded.

A naval historian writing forty years later suggested that the near fanatical zeal of Napoleon's fighters was an additional determinant in their higher toll of death and injury. 'The resistance of French ships was . . . prolonged beyond the bounds of duty, and to the verge of desperation,' Commander Edward Plunkett declared. 'The captors often took possession of a slaughter-house rather than a ship of war.'[111]

Perhaps the most fanatical defence of French colours, as reflected in her dilapidation and the scale of her casualties, was aboard *Redoutable*. With 120 dead and 130 gravely wounded, she was 'so riddled with shot that she seemed to be no more than a mass of wreckage'. When *Téméraire* hailed her to surrender 'and not prolong a useless resistance', Captain Lucas responded by ordering the soldiers near him on the quarterdeck to continue firing their muskets regardless, 'which was performed with the greatest zeal'. Her stern completely stove in, guns dismounted or burst, the sides of the ship cut to pieces, decks torn open and covered with dead, buried beneath debris and splinters, with four out of her six pumps shattered and reports from below that water flooding her hold was so considerable it could not be long before she sank – only then did Lucas give the order to strike. But before the tricolour could be lowered, it came down of itself when the fractured mizenmast fell. Estimating the battle casualties in the Combined Fleet is complicated by the unknown numbers who would perish during the storm and shipwrecks that followed, in addition to prizes deliberately sunk or burnt on Collingwood's orders. By far the greatest loss of life – by drowning – was yet to come.

*

Fifty-seven of *Victory*'s company had been either killed during the battle or would later die of wounds, the highest rate of fatalities in the British fleet. *Téméraire* and *Royal Sovereign* lost forty-seven dead apiece. The combined death toll of the twelve vessels in Nelson's Weather column came to 161, but that of the fifteen in Collingwood's Lee column to nearly twice that number: 297. When wounded were added to the butcher's bill* the total losses of Nelson's squadron rose to 538, Collingwood's to 1,128. Ships in the vanguard of the fleet, engaging early and bearing the brunt of close-quarters fighting for longest, inevitably lost most. Nevertheless, only two of the Weather column – *Téméraire* and *Victory* – suffered more than a hundred dead and wounded each, while four of the leeward vessels passed that threshold: *Royal Sovereign*, *Belleisle*, *Bellerophon* and, with two hundred, *Colossus*. Those six – sharing a total of 889 dead and wounded – accounted for fifty-four per cent of British losses. Casualties aboard the majority of Royal Navy ships were in double figures. *Dreadnought* lost seven killed and twenty-nine wounded, *Orion* one dead and twenty-three wounded – 'not one officer killed or wounded ... except ... two mids, ... wounded slightly' – while *Polyphemus* suffered the fewest, just two dead and four wounded. *Conqueror*'s 'loss [was] very trifling' too: besides Lieutenants Lloyd and Molyneux St George, the only other man killed was

---

* The term's earliest appearance in print occurred in Captain Frederick Marryat's first novel, *The Naval Officer, or Scenes and Adventures in the Life of Frank Mildmay*, published in 1829: 'Having delivered his "butcher's bill", i.e. the list of killed and wounded, together with an account of our defects, they were sent up to the Admiralty' (chapter 5). The novel is regarded as substantially autobiographical and based on Marryat's naval career beginning in 1806.

a member of the carpenter's crew, appositely named Robert Mallett. The unfortunate Landsman Aaron Crocan, drowned before the battle began, did not appear among the day's losses. Fifteenth in the Lee column and last to engage, the 98-gun *Prince* could be omitted from the reckoning altogether, as suffering no casualties of any kind.[112]

Notwithstanding her negligible sacrifice to the British body count, *Prince* was responsible at the close of battle for delivering a *coup de grâce* into the French two-decker *Achille*, precipitating the single most devastating catastrophe of the Combined Fleet and the death of an estimated 480 men. Firing 'at pistol-range', the first broadside brought down the Frenchman's mainmast, 'and, as a result of several more, fire broke out in the fore-top, which immediately fell – as did the two others – amidships and lengthways of the ship'. Her fire engine and buckets crushed under the wreckage, the unchecked blaze 'spread ... with the greatest rapidity' down from the quarterdeck to the deck below where the 18-pounder battery was soon engulfed in flames, abandoned guns, left primed and shotted, detonating spontaneously in ragged volleys as the fire reached them. 'Nevertheless the crew ... still continued to serve the 36-pounders [on the lower deck] with a zeal and courage worthy of a happier ending.' *Prince*'s assistant surgeon, Joshua Horwood, recounted the efforts made to evacuate her. 'We could not save more than 250 men out of 850, and it was with the utmost difficulty we could save so many. Ten of our own men and one midshipman were unfortunately left in ... her. The scene was dreadful. Every part of the ship, which the flames did not reach, ... was crouded with the unfortunate sufferers, crying out for assistance. The captain of the *Achille* had both his legs shot off. The first lieutenant was cut in two by a double headed shot, and three other lieutenants were killed in the latter part of the action, so that there was only one lieutenant left.' Captain Deniéport did not long survive his injuries.[113]

An alternative account of the *Achille*'s destruction casts a less honourable light on *Prince*'s conduct. A twelve-year-old midshipman, Robert Coutart McCrea, serving on HMS *Swiftsure*, claimed that it was his own ship's firing that 'Cut away [the *Achille*'s] Main and Mizen Masts, Fore Yard, Bowsprit and Fore Top mast in the Course of seventy minutes, [and] set her on fire in several places, particularly in the Fore Top'. At this point the French ship ceased firing and struck her colours. And it was while *Swiftsure* was preparing to take possession of the prize, that *Prince* 'bore down and poured a whole broadside into her'. McCrea concluded: 'It was horrid murder and in a few minutes she was totally enveloped in flames. Had it not been for the Prince's cruel work we might have saved her and 500 men from being burnt to death.'[114]

It was generally agreed that the spectacular demise of *Achille* marked the battle's end. Consistent with other significant incidents on 21 October there is considerable variance in the times that eyewitnesses recorded the event, although a rough consensus might be hazarded at between five-fifteen and a quarter to six. Acting Lieutenant Casimir Quiot put it at 'very nearly 5.30'. His report stated that, 'seeing the absolute impossibility – in spite of all efforts and of all possible vigilance – of being able to arrest [the fire's] progress, orders were given to open the bilge-cocks' so as to flood the hold, and more importantly, the gunpowder magazine. According to testimony submitted to the Ministère de Marine by two other survivors, the strategy was successful. Perhaps in anticipation of the potentially scapegoating court martial attending the loss of any ship, they made light of the explosion that destroyed her: 'It was not very violent,' declared Lieutenants Clamart and Lachasse, 'seeing that we had taken the precaution of drowning the remainder of our powder.'[115]

Other eyewitnesses, having a more impartial stake in the disaster, could afford to view it in a detached, even aesthetically discriminating, manner. Lieutenant Senhouse, on *Conqueror*, called it 'one of the grandest spectacles to be met with in nature', as an aristocratic tourist of the previous century might have described an eruption of Etna or Vesuvius. Another lieutenant, Frederick Hoffman of *Tonnant*, described it as 'sublime and awful', Captain Harvey of *Téméraire* as 'extraordinary and magnificent', while for an onlooker on the *Defence*, 'it was a sight the most awful and grand that can be conceived.' The apocalyptic imagery of this man's account seems anachronistic a century and a half before the culmination of the Manhattan Project: 'A column of vivid flame shot up to an enormous height in the atmosphere and terminated by expanding into an immense globe, representing for a few seconds, a prodigious tree in flames, specked with many dark spots, which the pieces of timber and bodies of men occasioned while they were suspended in the clouds.'[116]

PART II
AFTERSHOCKS

I

THE battle had taken place '9 or 10 leagues' south-west of Cadiz. Nothing could be seen by anxious citizens crowding the ramparts, balconies, towers and every other available viewpoint, but their 'ears [were] assailed by the roaring of distant cannon'. Throughout that Monday the mood ashore had fluctuated as 'suspense . . . wound up the feelings of the people almost to a state of phrenzy . . . anxiety of the females border[ing] on insanity; but more of despair than of hope was visible in every countenance.' When the Combined Fleet had prepared to sail from port two days earlier, 'every man, at all accustomed to the water, was impressed to man the navy. The carnage of that day consequently fell principally on the population of Cadiz.' And not only those with seafaring experience had fallen prey to the indiscriminate, forced recruitment. An unfortunate actor was snatched from the stage, mid-performance, to serve on a French ship and was still wearing his Harlequin's costume when captured and taken on board HMS *Britannia*.[1]

At first Spanish rage was directed against the British perpetrators of as yet barely imagined slaughter, and anyone heard uttering their language was a target for vengeance. 'Two Americans, who had [previously] mixed with the people, fled, and hid themselves, to avoid this ebullition of popular fury.' Later, however, Spanish animosity was turned against their erstwhile allies and it was said that 'a Frenchman dare hardly land at Cadiz, for fear of being murdered.'

About fifteen minutes to six in the afternoon, with the faraway gunfire fading, 'a column of dark smoke' became visible, even at that great distance, and 'a sound, louder than any that had preceded it,' announced the obliteration of *Achille* and end of the battle. Antonio Alcalá Galiano – son of Commodore Galiano and yet to learn of his father's partial decapitation on the quarterdeck of *Bahama* – was watching from one of the tallest towers in the city, an eminence that commanded a particularly wide and distant vista. He saw – seconds before the sound of the explosion reached him – 'a tremendous flash on the horizon, the shape of a ship silhouetted against its fatal brilliance'.[2]

*

Out at sea, the victors took stock, seemingly unsure as to the magnitude of their success – the number of prizes captured differing from one witness account to another, and ships of both sides indistinguishable in their uniform dereliction. In *Euryalus*'s log there is a blank space where the number 'of the enemy's ships in our possession' should have been. Midshipman McCrea on *Swiftsure* wrote that 'it was impossible yet to ascertain how many Ships had struck to the British, the Ships were so much scattered and it soon became dark after the Action.' Collingwood wrote of 'eighteen hulks of the enemy lying amongst the British fleet without a stick standing, and the French *Achille* burning'. On board *Britannia*, Lieutenant Halloran put it at 'twenty-one or twenty-two sail of the Enemy's Line [made] Prizes and dismasted, one burning furiously, which soon after blew up'. Master's Mate Colin Campbell looked about him from the quarterdeck of *Defiance*: 'Nothing [was] to be seen, but wrecks of masts and yards floating about and some hundreds of dead bodies.' Lieutenant Senhouse observed the devastation from *Conqueror*, 'at a distance of about four miles around covered with about thirty ships dismasted, lying like logs on the water, the surface of which was strewed with wreck from various vessels and their hulks interspersed with the remaining part of the fleet in a most shattered state'. Halloran was particularly impressed by 'a strange contrast to the morning, the sky lowering in the distance, a heavy sea rising, and an awful kind of pause succeeding the crash of falling yards and masts and the roar of the guns. The evening was fine, though a storm seemed to be coming up, and around us as the darkness closed in the scattered and forlorn wrecks lay floating in disorder ... It was a scene of desolation, helpless prizes and dismantled victors rolling heavily, as the sea began to roughen with the breeze.' At the beginning of that terrible day, Midshipman Hercules Robinson on *Euryalus* had observed a calm sea and the sun shining through morning mist. And as the day of battle ended, he, like Halloran, remarked on the contrast of 'an angry sunset and the moaning of the wind [giving] an ill promise' of what was to come. By the afternoon of Tuesday the 22nd that wind had increased and logs across the battered fleet were brought up to date, recording variations of 'strong gales and squally, with heavy rain'.[3]

*

For the inhabitants of Cadiz, 'the storm that succeeded the battle tended only to keep alive, through the night, the horrors of the day, and to prepare them for the melancholy spectacle of the ensuing morning, when the wrecks of their [ships] were seen on the shore.' Ten days later an English traveller took a walk along the isthmus that connects the city to the Andalusian mainland, to see 'the terrible effects of the battle'. He found a portion of mast marked *Swiftsure* and stamped with three convergent strokes forming the arrowhead that denoted British Government property. He assumed it had come from William Rutherford's 74-gun vessel of that name, tenth in the line of Collingwood's Lee column, which had her mizen topmast shot away during the action. However, it could equally have come from her namesake in Villeneuve's fleet, formerly HM government property before her capture by the French off the Barbary coast on 24 June 1801. This vessel had lost all but her foremast in the battle and storm that followed. The Englishman climbed to the crosstrees of another piece of wreckage and as far as his eye could reach, the sandy, Atlantic-facing strand, Playa de Santa María, 'was covered with masts and yards, the wrecks of ships, and here and there bodies of the dead'. A Spanish witness described 'bloated corpses ... rendered doubly horrific by the mutilation of shot, and the passage of so many hours emersed in salt water'. Severed limbs and other body parts, thrown overboard by the bucketful, drifted ashore on every tide. Spanish mounted patrols coordinated burial parties, posted at intervals along the beach, disposing of the swollen battle carrion in hurriedly dug sandy graves. Some engaged in this grim work were British prisoners of war, among them a party taken from the merchant vessel *Barbara* out of Greenock, captured and sunk the previous August, and the crew in captivity ever since. One sea-battered carcase they found proved to be the blood-drained corpse of Lieutenant William Ram, thrown from *Victory* during the battle. After several days, only 'the Name being Mark[ed] on the Shirt made it known to be him'. The *Barbara*'s commander, Captain McTaggart, applied for, and was granted leave by the Marqués de la Solana, Governor of Cadiz, to lay him to rest inside the city walls and 'they Buried him in a[s] Dasent [a] Manner [as] they could.'[4]

Humanitarian gestures were made by both sides in the immediate aftermath of battle. 'To alleviate the miseries of the [enemy] wounded as much as in my power,' Collingwood wrote, 'I sent a [boat under flag of truce] to the Marquis Solana, to offer him his wounded.' Although guided by administrative interests and advantageous for hard-pressed surgeons to be relieved of caring for hundreds of enemy wounded, Collingwood's gesture was greatly appreciated, and 'all this part of Spain [was] in an uproar of praise and thankfulness to the English.' Solana sent him the present of a cask of wine in return, Collingwood returning the favour with porter. Relations were further enhanced by his release of most Spanish prisoners.[5]

In the harbour, 'ten days after the battle, they were still employed in bringing ashore the wounded, and spectacles were hourly displayed at the wharfs, and through the streets, sufficient to shock every heart not yet hardened to scenes of blood and human suffering.' The English traveller observed harrowing disembarkations, 'when, by the carelessness of the boatmen, and the surging of the sea, the boats struck against the stone piers, a horrid cry, which pierced the soul, arose from the mangled wretches on board'. And although he shuddered at the memory, the Englishman 'lent a willing hand to bear them up the steps to their litters ... the slightest false step [making] them shriek out ... [as they] were carried away to the hospitals in every shape of human misery, whilst crowds of Spaniards either assisted or looked on with ... horror'. Even the Spanish gentry assisted, their fine clothes having 'the appearance of ostentation, if there could be ostentation at such a moment'. Distraught women crouched 'with their heads between their knees' on piles of discarded weaponry and luggage. Sailors who had escaped the fighting unscathed 'walked up and down with folded arms and downcast eyes,' as though incapable of knowing where to go or what to do.[6]

*

After the fighting ceased, *Victory*'s gunner came below to enquire after his son. 'Here I am Father,' Midshipman Rivers called out. 'Nothing is the Matter with me; only lost my leg and that in a Good Cause.'

Later, around midnight, lying in a cot in the gunner's cabin, the young man heard activity on deck, it being 'customery, after dark, to throw Legs & Arms that [were] Cutt off overboard, and such as be Ded'.

He asked what the men were doing.

'Nothing Sir.'

'I suppose you are throwing Legs & Arms overboard?'

'Yes Sir.'

'Have you got mine?'

'I don't know Sir.'

Then:

'I understand Old Putty Nose [the Purser's Steward] was to have them for Fresh Meat for the Sick.'

From his father's notes, it is unclear whether this last remark came, by way of a dark pleasantry, from the stoical Midshipman Rivers himself or from the anonymous sailor reporting from the upper deck.[7]

The same routine was followed on other ships, although not necessarily under discreet cover of darkness. 'Orders were ... given to fetch the dead bodies from the after cock-pit,' wrote William Robinson, 'and throw them over-board ... bodies of men who were taken down to the doctor during the battle, badly wounded, and who by the time the engagement was ended were dead.' Of course, the remains of *Revenge*'s two midshipmen, Thomas Grier and the hated young tyrant Brooke, killed outright on the lower gun deck and quarterdeck respectively, had been summarily tossed overboard as and where they fell. But haste proved premature when a stunned survivor of Grier's slaughtered 32-pounder crew, presumed dead, was being manhandled out of the lower gun port and, regaining consciousness, began to struggle. He recovered quickly and 'fought the battle out'. There was another seemingly miraculous resurrection on the *Belleisle* as a seaman, shot in the head by a musket round and about to be thrown overboard, was seen to breathe. After a week in the hospital at Gibraltar, 'the ball which entered the temple came out of his mouth'.[8]

Only those surviving until a convenient opportunity presented itself for their disposal were granted the dignity of formal exequies. Francis Roskruge, *Britannia*'s signal lieutenant, was 'brought down senseless with a severe wound in his head'. He never regained consciousness but breathed until nine o'clock that evening, when he died. His body was 'committed to the deep' two days later after a short ceremony conducted by the chaplain, the Revd Laurence Hynes Halloran, Lieutenant Halloran's father. High rank afforded deferential treatment when a ship's captain fell in action. George Duff's headless corpse lay beneath its Union Jack on the *Mars* quarterdeck until late afternoon on the day after the battle when – lashed by 'Hard gales and squally, with heavy showers of rain' – it was sewn into a hammock and launched over the side with due solemnity, weighted with the customary brace of round shot. On the same evening, Lieutenant Cumby, acting commander of *Bellerophon*, read the funeral service over the bodies of his captain, James Cooke, and ship's master, Edward Overton, 'as they were committed to the deep amid the heartfelt regrets and unbought tears of their surviving shipmates'.[9]

While the rapid disposal of bodies during a battle was necessary to prevent their cluttering the gun decks and obstructing the deadly activities of the living, the inordinate haste to be rid of them even when the guns fell silent came from a deeper-seated cause. 'Sailors ... have a great objection to the body of any one who has died remaining amongst them,' an officer observed, 'a superstition easily accounted for amongst men whose whole lives are passed, as it were, on the very edge of the grave, and who have quite enough, as they suppose, to remind them of their mortality, without the actual presence of its effects. An idea prevails amongst them, that sharks will follow a ship for a whole voyage which has a corpse on board; and the loss of a mast, or the long duration of a foul wind, or any other inconvenience, is sure to be ascribed to the same influence. Accordingly, when a man dies on board ship, there is an obvious anxiety amongst the crew to get rid of their late shipmate as speedily as possible.' The same anxiety would be shared by men on board *Victory* regarding the continued proximity of their former chief's corpse, however revered he was in life. To this baleful posthumous presence some would ascribe not only the storm that followed the battle but the notoriously contrary winds further north in the Bay of Biscay which beset their homeward voyage.[10]

A precisely converse instinct and superstition prevailed among the crews of French ships, resulting in conditions observed with revulsion by Gilbert Blane, stepping below decks on a captured enemy vessel in 1782. 'The blood, the mangled limbs, and even whole bodies of men, [had been] cast into the ... hold, and lay there putrefying for some time. The common sailors among the French have a superstitious aversion to the throwing of bodies overboard immediately after they are killed, the friends of the deceased wishing to reserve their remains, in order to perform a religious ceremony over them when the hurry and danger of the day shall be over. When, therefore, the ballast, or other contents of the holds of these ships, came to be stirred, and the putrid effluvia thereby let loose there was then a visible increase of sickness [amongst the English prize crew].' When Lieutenant Fournier assumed command of *Bucentaure*, just prior to surrendering her, he admitted that 'the decks [were] encumbered with a great number of slain whom the crew in their zeal had neglected to remove.' And when *Aigle* surrendered to *Defiance*, Master's Mate Colin Campbell noted the distinction between the British and French traditions: 'The slaughter on board of her was horrid, the decks were covered with dead and wounded. They never heave their dead overboard in time of action as we do.'[11]

*

'Don't throw me overboard, Hardy', Nelson had said. 'You know what to do.'[12]

He had spoken before of the possibility, indeed likelihood, of his own death in battle, and Hardy knew that he wished his body conveyed back to England. In the event of his country's declining the cost of burial, he was to be laid next to the remains of his father in the Norfolk village of Burnham Thorpe, where Edmund Nelson had been rector and his famous son born. But if the funeral was to be at the State's expense, then the Burnham Thorpe parishioners were to be denied the honour of accommodating him and his place of interment was to be grander. 'Westminster Abbey! Or glorious victory!' he is said to have shouted at the battle of Cape St Vincent as he led a boarding party from HMS *Captain* onto the Spanish *San Nicolás*. However, he had subsequently told Hardy that he wished to be buried in St Paul's Cathedral, and that his monument was to be erected there. Eternal rest, he believed, could not be guaranteed at Westminster Abbey, that structure being 'built on a spot where once existed a deep morass, and he thought it likely that the lapse of time would reduce the ground on which it now stands to its primitive state of a swamp, without leaving a trace of the Abbey'. The final decision as to his resting place, however, would be taken by the King, on the government's recommendation.[13]

Other arrangements were made in compliance with the admiral's wishes. His hair was cut off by Captain Hardy, to be presented, with his bloodstained coat and waistcoat, to Lady Hamilton. As a result, on the morning after the battle, when Lieutenant Lewis Rotely came down to view the body and procure a memento for himself, he had to be content with a small tuft of hair remaining at the nape of the neck. The acquisitive Welshman had already laid claim to the hero's bloodied, soiled breeches and woollen stockings, in addition to the Spanish bar shot that had ripped through eight of his own men on the poop deck. As the most senior Marines officer left alive, Rotely was given charge of the corpse itself. An empty barrel of the largest size available – called a 'leaguer', its capacity 159 English imperial gallons, and customarily used for storing fresh water – was lashed upright to the capstan on the middle gun deck and the body, naked but for a shirt, placed in it 'head foremost'. The barrel was then filled to the brim with brandy, 'of which spirit there was plenty on board'. William Beatty believed brandy to be a superior preservative to rum, although better than either was purified alcohol, known as 'spirit of wine', but this was in shorter supply. The leaguer had 'a closed aperture at its top and another below; the object of which was, that as a frequent renewal of the spirit was thought necessary, the old could be drawn off below and a fresh quantity introduced above, without moving the cask, or occasioning the least agitation of the Body'. The spigot fitted to the base of the container and the periodic replenishment of the liquor gave rise to the legend that members of *Victory*'s crew took to siphoning off and drinking the brandy in which their chief lay steeped, a practice known as 'tapping the admiral'.* Just as supplies of alcohol were customarily stored securely under lock and key to prevent theft and drunkenness on a ship of the line, Rotely took the precaution of posting a Royal Marine sentry to guard the receptacle from any such interference.

Two days later, the early stages of decomposition caused 'a disengagement of air from the Body' and potentially explosive conditions inside the barrel. Summoned by the sentry 'in great consternation [who] said that there was something the matter with the Admiral,' Rotely found 'the head of the cask heaving and raised up ready to burst'. But with the aid of a gimlet a 'vent was given to the air and all was right'. The incident would have done nothing to ease the superstitious qualms of the crew about keeping a corpse on board, however eminent. During the following week, 'the spirit was drawn off once, and the cask filled again,' but no further 'collection of air took place' within. When *Victory* arrived at Gibraltar on 28 October, Mr Beatty was able to procure a supply of his preferred preservative, spirit of wine. The brandy was once again drained and it was found to be depleted, not by pilferage but by osmosis, 'the Body's absorbing a considerable quantity' to itself.

HMS *Victory* was already a shrine to Nelson's memory and visitors, then as now, had the exact spot at which he received his fatal wound pointed out to them. When Dr Fellowes came aboard on 1 November to dine with Captain Hardy, he 'trod with respect on the plank on which the Hero fell but a few days before'. Descending the companionway to the middle deck, then walking aft to the wardroom, he passed the tall barrel and its still vigilant sentry. 'I felt more than I can describe,' he told his father.[14]

During the five-week voyage to England the liquid was

---

* The phrase had appeared in print fifteen years earlier: 'Tapping the Admiral, is still a favourite practical joke with the Jolly Tars – particularly on board India ships – it first originated from the puncheon of rum in which the body of Admiral Lestock [1679–1746] was transported from Jamaica to England – the sailors soon made an end of the rum, of which, when the ship cast anchor, there was literally not any *remains*.' (*Caledonian Mercury*, 27 Mar. 1790). It is further defined as being 'opprobriously applied to those who would "drink anything"', by William Henry Smyth in his *Sailor's Word Book: An Alphabetical Digest of Nautical Terms* (1867).

replenished twice more, and 'on these occasions brandy was used in the proportion of two-thirds to one of spirit of wine.'

There was a suggestion that the frigate *Euryalus* – being the faster ship – would take the body back to England from Gibraltar. However, superstitious aversion to the prolonged presence of a corpse notwithstanding, *Victory*'s crew refused to part with him. 'We told Captain [Hardy] as we brought him out, so we would bring him home – so it was.' But inevitably, some among them attributed their 'stormy and protracted passage ... to a corpse being on board'. And it was further supposed 'that till the noble Admiral was buried (as they thought he ought to be) in his own empire, the Ocean, [the ship] would never pass the chops of the Channel'.[15]

II

THROUGH *Achille*'s floating debris English longboats plied their oars in search of survivors. One was a black pig, swimming frantically from the wreck and rescued by men from *Euryalus*, where it later provided 'a glorious supper of pork chops' in the midshipmen's berth. Another more fortunate individual was plucked from the water by a boat from the frigate *Naiad*: a naked Frenchwoman named Jeanette Caunant, found clinging to a six-foot plank, part of the *Achille*'s quarter bill board – designed to protect the ship's hull from damage by the 'bill' or fluke of the hoisted anchor. The wife of a main topman, Jeanette had escaped by climbing out of the blazing vessel's gunroom port and onto the rudder chains. There she stripped off her clothes but hesitated risking herself to the uncertain prospects of the sea until forced to abandon her perch by molten metal from the taffrail's lead sheeting pouring down onto her 'head, shoulders, legs and several parts of her body'. She swam to a floating spar but was kicked away by the men already clinging to it, eventually reaching another piece of flotsam which supported her until she was rescued and sent aboard *Pickle* and from there, the following morning, to *Revenge*, where she was reunited with her husband. 'We were not wanting in civility to the lady,' wrote Captain Moorson, 'I ordered her two Purser's shirts to make a Petticoat & most of the officers found something to clothe her; in a few hours Jeanette was perfectly happy & hard at work making her Petticoats.' There are variants of this widely told and greatly embellished story in which the contributions to her makeshift wardrobe included a pair of 'seaman's trowsers', a large cotton dressing gown, a pair of the Chaplain's old shoes, 'two pairs of white stockings and two silk handkerchiefs' and 'a length of blue sprigged muslin' originally purchased by an officer for his wife 'from which she made herself a jacket and dress in the Flemish fashion'.[16]

It was claimed that 'hundreds were in the *Achille* at the time [she blew up]' and that prior to the explosion 'many jumped overboard and were drowned'. The frigate *Naiad* rescued ninety-five afterwards, and *Prince* a hundred and forty more. The schooner *Pickle* – whose place in history was soon to be secured – saved 'one hundred and twenty or thirty men', while the cutter *Entreprenante* 'preserved [from *Achille* and] from different wrecks ... upwards of 169 men'.[17]

Elsewhere, another survivor of the battle was the Sardinian Pointer thrown out of an upper gunport while *Conqueror* was clearing for action. The dog did not fall into the sea but landed on a ledge supporting the larboard swing boom. Despite this precarious refuge being on the side of the ship most engaged during the fighting, the creature had cowered there throughout the day, British gun muzzles discharging right, left and above. French and Spanish shot, however – from *Bucentaure* and *Santísima Trinidad* – did most of their damage to the *Conqueror*'s rigging and little, if any, to the hull in the animal's immediate vicinity. After the battle he was found in a dazed and half stupefied condition, but otherwise unharmed. The ship's crew 'ever afterwards took so strong an affection to the dog that, when, later, they turned over to HMS *Barham* they took him with them'. He was still alive in 1820, fifteen years after his ordeal.[18]

*

Of the three principal signals hoisted to *Victory*'s mainmast in the late morning of 21 October, only two concerned the conduct of the coming battle: ENGAGE THE ENEMY MORE CLOSELY, and that more famous pronouncement destined to be carved, engraved or embossed across the world on each and every monument subsequently raised to its author. The third signal – number 62 in Popham's code – concerned the aftermath of battle alone: PREPARE TO ANCHOR AFTER THE CLOSE OF DAY. Nelson had anticipated the storm that was to follow – a storm presaged by the heavy swell from the west that had figured in ships' logs since morning – and the prospect and potential consequences of that storm occupied his dying thoughts.

'*Anchor*, Hardy, *anchor*!'

And when *Victory*'s captain voiced his assumption that 'Admiral Collingwood will now take upon himself the direction of affairs' –

'Not while I live, I hope, Hardy!' and, trying to raise his part-paralysed body from the orlop deck, 'No, do *you* anchor, Hardy.'

'Shall *we* make the signal, Sir?' The original 'preparative' hoist required confirmation to be effected.

'Yes, for if I live, I'll anchor.'

'If Lord Nelson had lived,' Lieutenant Senhouse wrote to his mother a week later, the fleet would have anchored immediately after the action, as we were only five leagues from land and in shoal [or shallow] water where our anchors would have rode the ships securely, and having nothing else to attend to, we could have employed ourselves in rigging jury-masts* and in securing the prizes; but this was neglected.[19]

William James would level the same criticism in his *Naval History of Great Britain* two decades later, prompting the editor of Collingwood's correspondence to call expert testimony from 'naval officers of much experience and skill' in his defence. 'Anchoring on a lee shore in a gale of wind . . . where the water shoals rapidly, as in the Bay of Cadiz . . . is a thing to which no sailor would resort but in the last extremity, and when every other expedient had been tried in vain . . . A fresh ship [anchored] may ride out a gale in safety . . . But to anchor a disabled ship would be, if her anchor parted, to ensure

---

* 'Jury-mast: It seems to be properly *durée* mast . . . a mast made to last for the present occasion.' (Johnson.) Another authority derives the term from '*journiere* mast: i.e. a mast for the day' (Grose, 2nd ed. 1788).

her destruction.' Nelson was below decks for much of the battle and unaware of the damage wrought to his own flagship and to the rest of the fleet. *Victory* had suffered both 'the starboard bower and spare anchors ... broke, and the stock of the sheet anchor damaged by shot'. *Belleisle* had 'her boats and anchors ... shot away', and others were 'in a very perilous situation, many dismasted, all shattered, in thirteen fathom water, off the [rocky] shoals of Trafalgar ... few ... had an anchor to let go, their cables being shot'. The prizes were in comparable, or worse condition. One consultant, 'a distinguished Admiral' opined that 'on a question of mere seamanship, it is no injustice to [Nelson's] fame to say that he was inferior to Lord Collingwood, who was considered by all the Navy to be a seaman of very uncommon experience and knowledge.'[20]

'Anchor the fleet?' Collingwood is said to have exclaimed, when Captain Hardy informed him of Nelson's dying instruction, 'Why, it is the last thing I should have thought of.' Nevertheless, at nine o'clock that night, he finally 'made the signal with a gun, prepare to anchor,' albeit after considerable indecision, 'now and then tugging at the waistband of his unmentionables* ... his only food a few biscuits, an apple and a glass of wine every four hours'.[21]

*

The least damaged British ships passed hawsers seven and a half inches in circumference to tow crippled prizes and Royal Navy vessels alike. Among the latter was *Royal Sovereign*. She had lost both mizen- and mainmast by the time the firing ceased and, with her foremast in need of securing, she was put in tow by *Euryalus*. The shattered *Belleisle*, 'quite dismasted', was towed by *Naiad*, while another frigate, *Sirius*, took charge of *Téméraire*. With two shot holes between wind and water, an injured bowsprit and foremast, and splintered main topmast, *Spartiate* was still able to tow the *Tonnant*. *Colossus* was towed by *Agamemnon*. Despite considerable damage – her mizenmast fallen 'about 10 feet above the

---

* A nineteenth-century euphemism for trousers, not – as later – underwear.

poop', lower masts, yards and bowsprit 'all crippled' and rigging and sails 'very much cut' – *Victory* did not submit to a tow.

Prizes too damaged to sail were divided between abler vessels. *Conqueror* had charge of her own hard-won prize, *Bucentaure*, while *Thunderer* was ordered to take *Santa Ana* in tow, and *Prince*, *Santísima Trinidad*. The *Minotaur* towed *Neptuno*, and *Dreadnought* the French *Swiftsure*. The frigate *Phoebe* was 'employed the whole night giving assistance to [other] ships in distress'. To co-ordinate the logistics of recovery, Collingwood had shifted his rear admiral's flag to *Euryalus* because *Royal Sovereign*, being without masts, was incapable of hoisting his signals.[22]

Despite her non-combatant status during the battle, the 36-gun frigate had sustained damage, not only from unintentional enemy shot but, after the firing stopped, from *Royal Sovereign*'s smashing into her starboard beam, 'there being a great swell'. Captain Blackwood wrote to his wife the day after the battle: 'Ever since last evening we have had a most dreadful gale of wind, and it is with difficulty the ships who tow [the prizes] keep off shore. Three, I fear, must be lost and with them many hundred souls each. What horrid scourge is war!'[23]

The shot-riddled *Fougueux* was the first prize lost, 'shattered from stem to stern, and with two enormous gaps forced in on the starboard side at the water line, through which the sea poured in a stream'. Thwarting *Phoebe*'s attempts to take her in tow on the morning of the 22nd, later in the day she was storm-driven along the coast south of Cadiz and battered to pieces on the Sancti Petri rocks. Before saving himself by jumping from a lower deck gunport, Master-at-Arms Pierre Servaux witnessed 'scenes of horror on board the ship ... the most awful and fearful that imagination can call up, ... the water ... risen almost to the orlop deck. Everywhere ... the cries of the wounded and dying.' One of about thirty men said to have survived the wreck, he managed to swim to one of *Orion*'s boats. *Phoebe* had evacuated around forty others, several of whom were wounded, but was unable 'to save all the people' before the vessel broke up. The thirty men of *Téméraire*'s prize crew perished with the rest. Commander Bazin's official report claimed that only 110 or 120 men remained alive 'out of a ship's company of 682 souls who were on board the day that we put to sea'. The assertion of *Orion*'s Captain Edward Codrington that 'of those on board the *Fougueux* only three were saved' was clearly wide of the mark.[24]

Within hours of the battle ending, HMS *Swiftsure* had taken *Redoutable* in tow, sending a lieutenant and an additional party of seamen on board the battered Frenchman to assist another prize crew from *Téméraire*. Every effort was being made to keep her afloat, Midshipman Robert McCrea reported, and all hands were employed at the remaining pumps, 'prisoners not excepted'. But according to her French commander, 'we had cause to fear that she might go down under our feet.' The following day, despite 'a most violent Gale of Wind', *Redoutable* had 'seemed to weather it tolerably well notwithstanding her shattered state'. Then, about three in the afternoon, 'from the violence of her rolling in a Heavy Sea she carried away her Fore-Mast, the only Mast she had standing.' By evening the prize crew repeatedly fired guns as a signal of distress. *Swiftsure* hoisted out her boats and 'although there was a tremendous Sea running, and ... fearful the boats would be swamped alongside, ... succeeded in bringing off the best part of [the prisoners] from the wreck as well as Lieutenant Thomas Read, part of the seamen, and 2 Midshipmen with some ... belonging to *Téméraire*.' McCrea reflected that 'if our situation was disagreeable ... what must not the Unfortunate Prisoners have suffered [left] on board. What added to the horror of the night was the inability of our saving them all as we could no longer risk our people in open boats at the Mercy of every sea and a most Violent Gale of Wind.' Lieutenant George L. Browne of *Victory* asserted, with puzzling precision, that '397 or 400 men who were wounded ... on the orlop deck, and the ship making water fast ... went down with her.' Captain Lucas wrote that, although some of the injured, 'seeing that the ship was about to sink, ... dragged themselves up to the quarter-deck' and were saved, a substantial number were left below. At seven o'clock in the evening – the sea gushing into the yawning cave of splintered timber that repeated rakes had left of her after-works, *Redoutable* sank, stern first, 'carrying ... with her the greater part of these hapless men, whose courage had made them worthy of a better fate'. As she went down, Robert Hilton, *Swiftsure*'s surgeon's mate, 'could distinctly hear the cries of the unhappy people we could no longer assist'; while with brutal austerity Mr George Forbes's log counted the economic cost: 'Cut the tow, and lost two cables of eight-an-a-half inches, and a cable of 5 inches, with the prize.'[25]

Only thirty-six of those left aboard survived, picked up from desperately crafted rafts at first light the following morning. But 'many of these unfortunate men were unable to get up the [*Swiftsure*'s] side, as most of them were not only fainting from fatigue but wounded in the most shocking manner. Some expired in the Boats before they could get on board, completely exhausted and worn out with struggling to preserve their lives, ... upon a few crazy planks exposed to every inclemency of the weather.'[26]

Winning the prizes in battle would prove more straightforward than keeping them in the days that followed. Three more French, and four Spanish, prizes would be destroyed by the storm alone. 'The battle after all,' Edward Codrington remarked, 'is nothing compared with the fatigue, the anxiety, the distress of mind which succeeds it [in] such horrible weather as we had to encounter ... It is not fighting ... which is the severest part of *our life*, it is having to contend with the sudden changes of the season, the war of elements, the dangers of a lee shore ... which produce *no food for honour or glory* [and are] passed by others unknown and unnoticed.' Only a mariner could fully comprehend the terrifying consequences a south-westerly gale presented, driving vessels to their destruction on the rocks of an eastward lee shore.[27]

The Spanish *Neptuno*, with a prize crew of twenty-five, commanded by Marine Second Lieutenant Thomas Reeves, broke loose from *Minotaur* in a powerful squall when two eight-inch hawsers came apart. Captain Mansfield sent another fifty men on board but made no further attempt to re-establish the tow. As the storm increased towards midnight, 'a severe pitch' caused the remains of *Neptuno*'s mainmast to fall, staving in the quarterdeck and poop, crushing, 'by the impact of so great a weight', the main cabin in which her Spanish officers were confined, killing a member of the English crew and the paymaster, Don Diego de Soto as he slept in his cot. The following three hours were spent shoring up broken beams to prevent the deck falling in, before having to drop anchor in only eighteen fathoms of water close to the shore.[28]

Lieutenant Thomas Colby, with a prize crew from *Thunderer*, had taken command of Admiral Álava's ruined flagship, *Santa Ana*, but as the weather worsened on the night of the 22nd, they had difficulty keeping control of her. 'Tried every possible means to get the Prize's head off shore, but in vain from her being so encumber'd with wreck.' When she broke adrift from the tow, *Thunderer* stayed as close as was safe, but 'the swell had been ... so very heavy from the Westw'd', wrote Colby, 'that we found it extremely dangerous to approach so near ... as to get hold of their Hawser.'[29]

That same night *Dreadnought* was 'taken aback', her sails blown hard against the masts by a sudden violent squall. Such an occurrence could drive a ship's stern under water or even bring her masts down, but in this instance the jarring shock tore away the hawser, cutting the French *Swiftsure* adrift from her tow. The useful frigate *Phoebe*, however, was able to retrieve her the following morning, and sent two carpenters on board 'to assist plugging up shot holes', thus preserving what would prove to be Collingwood's only French prize.

Algésiras was being crewed by sixty-six men from *Tonnant*, commanded by Lieutenant Charles Bennett and a captain of marines, Arthur Ball. While that number might have managed to sail a captured prize in fair weather, her condition on the night after the battle – fore-, main- and mizen-masts fully or partially lost, and borne by the wind and swell to within half a league of the Trafalgar shoals – they could only do so with the cooperation of their prisoners. Bennett and his men had occupied themselves thus far in 'clearing the deck [of wreckage] and firing signals of distress', signals that had brought no response from the scattered British fleet. Bennett therefore decided to open the hatches, freeing upwards of three hundred able-bodied Frenchmen. Captors and captives then worked together for their mutual preservation, 'rigging topgallant-masts on [the mast] stumps ... and ... the topgallant-sail serving as a foresail'. By the end of the night the ship was in a condition to get clear of danger. Meanwhile the French officers had come to a decision of their own. The prize master and two other officers were invited into the ship's council chamber, and Pierre François Feuillet, the late Admiral Magon's secretary, 'who spoke the best English', conducted negotiations. 'After the noble defence of our ship [during the battle],' he began, 'we have a right to expect assistance from the English fleet which you yourselves have vainly demanded. Feeling ourselves thereby released from the obligations that we had assumed when placing ourselves in your power, we have decided to retake our ship.' Bennett and his colleagues 'displayed a great deal of resistance and the greatest firmness', but they and their men being outnumbered five to one, Feuillet was negotiating from a position of strength. 'You can expect to be treated with consideration on our part,' he told them, 'provided you do not compel us to employ force ... after which you would still find yourselves obliged to yield.' Another version of the parley was that 'if [Bennett] and his men did not agree, they would be thrown overboard.' In fifteen minutes *Algésiras* was back in French hands. As cheering and shouts of '*Vive l'Empereur!*' resounded throughout the ship, the prize crew was disarmed and herded 'under a strong guard' into the council chamber – whatever comforts it boasted shared thinly between sixty-six men – while their officers were confined in a separate cabin.[30]

Repeated attempts had been made by *Defiance* to take *Aigle* in tow following the onset of the storm, but all had failed, and by the afternoon of the 22nd, Captain Durham decided that 'she ... be abandoned to the French' and his prize crew taken off. This evacuation was accomplished, with the exception of Lieutenant Purchase, a master's mate, and twelve seamen, 'which could not be got without risking the loss of their own ship, being so close on a lee shore'. However, the expatriate Netherlander Lieutenant

Asmus Classen, senior uninjured officer of *Aigle* when she surrendered, reported that the number of English left on board was nearer fifty, suggesting that some of a prize crew from *Britannia* must also have been left behind. Classen made the further claim that, before the ship was returned to him, her anchor cables were to be 'cut into fragments'. This instruction, Durham informed him, had been at the express insistence of Admiral Collingwood. It would have made a safe anchorage impossible in such weather, consigning the ship to near inevitable wreckage with all hands.[31]

Collingwood made no mention in his correspondence to issuing this order, although silence regarding such a discreditable, even criminal, measure would be understandable. It is possible that Durham was acting on his own initiative but assigning responsibility for it to a superior authority. It is also conceivable that Classen misunderstood Durham's purpose and that the sense of their spoken exchange had been lost in translation. Whatever the truth of the matter, Lieutenant Purchase – his own fate and that of the men under his command being entwined with *Aigle*'s French crew – was 'happily ... prevailed upon ... not to carry out this barbarous order'.

Rigging a makeshift conglomeration of studdingsails and topgallants to their truncated masts, they made for Cadiz but, 'the ship not answering to her helm in the least,' they were carried in the opposite direction and forced to anchor near the Sancti Petri rocks. For two days they were 'exposed to high winds and to the on-shore sea'. Battered by rollers, they tried to lighten the ship by throwing overboard the upper deck's 18-pounder guns and more 8-pounder ordnance from the forecastle and quarterdeck, as well as thirty tons of ballast from the lower deck. Classen estimated they were just 'three cables' length' – about six hundred yards – from the ill-fated *Fougueux*'s wreckage.[32]

*

Deeming it better to drown drunk than sober, some on board the stricken, storm-lashed prizes abandoned hope of preserving their vessels and broke open the liquor stores instead. When a prize crew of twenty from *Defiance* took possession of *Argonauta* they found her decks full of wounded, besides '600 Spaniards on board and most of them drunk'. Villeneuve's erstwhile chief of staff, Mathieu Prigny, left wounded aboard *Bucentaure* after the admiral's removal to *Revenge*, reported the same of his own countrymen. 'All our seamen were either drunk or disabled, and we, the officers, could not get any work out of them.' By contrast, the prize crew from *Conqueror*, led by Lieutenant Richard Spear and Marine Lieutenant John Fischer, who took control of the battered French flagship, when 'it came on to blow a gale of wind ... immediately set to work to shorten sail and reef the topsails, [behaving] with as much regularity and order as if [they] had not been [earlier] fighting a dreadful battle.' Prigny admitted to being 'all amazement, wondering what the English seamen could be made of'.[33]

But, as the storm worsened in the week following the battle, anarchy born of desperation spread to the prize crew on board *Intrépide*, where the pumps had been abandoned, 'the doors of the storeroom ... broken down, and ... everyone, English and French, had rushed there to get drunk'. Alerted by the stoppage of the pumps, Auguste Gicquel arrived below decks in time to avert disaster. He found the men – prisoner and guard alike – 'reduced to the state of brutes', and a broken cask of spirits spilling its contents around the foot of a lighted candle. Stamping out the flame, he plunged the storeroom into darkness and lashed out blindly 'with punches and kicks'. As threatening voices were raised against him, Gicquel succeeded in ejecting the rioters and barricaded the door. With the cooperation of the British officers order was restored.[34]

Discipline had also collapsed on board *Monarca*. Lieutenant Edmund Fanning Thomas, Midshipman Henry Walker and eight men from *Bellerophon* took charge of the Spanish ship and about 500 prisoners during the battle. The prize crew was later reinforced to fifty-five by a disparate company of sailors and marines from the frigate *Phoebe*, from *Prince*, *Achille* and *Dreadnought*, 'most of whom were in a constant state of intoxication'. Walker claimed to have felt no fear during the battle, but saw it in the faces of those around him as they surveyed the state of vessel and crew. 'The [*Monarca* was] very much injured in every respect [and] made three feet [of] water in ten minutes... our people were almost all lying drunk upon deck, [while] the Spaniards, completely worn out with fatigue, would no longer work at the only chain pump left serviceable.' As the dismasted hulk drifted inexorably towards destruction, the midshipman lost hope, shrouded himself in a Union Jack, lay down and waited for death.³⁵

*

At noon on the day after the battle, *Conqueror*'s log recorded that she had '*Bucentaur* in tow'. But at some time during the rest of that turbulent day and night of 'strong gales with heavy rain', a seven-and-a-half-inch hawser and a three-and-a-half-inch rope had failed and the prize was cast adrift. Twenty-four hours later the log of Ship's Master John Seymour stated that *Conqueror* was 'endeavouring to take the ship in tow'. But this minimal chronology is contradicted by a more detailed account from on board *Bucentaure* herself. Lieutenant Fournier, most senior of the French ship's officers still fit for service, observed that at 4.30 in the afternoon of the 22nd, the 'English ship which had several times attempted to pass us a tow without success, went about on the larboard tack and made off. Nevertheless, she remained within sight.' Mathieu Prigny believed that the British 'kept to the wind to look to their own safety'. From a distance and with visibility decreasing in the worsening storm, those observing from *Conqueror* would have no knowledge of what took place aboard their prize during the ensuing night.³⁶

Lieutenant Fournier, in consultation with Prigny – notwithstanding the latter's purported admiration for English discipline and seamanship – recognised 'circumstances... as urgent as the opportunity was favourable' and determined to take back their crippled ship from the outnumbered prize crew of forty-eight. The transfer of power seems to have been conducted with courtesy, Lieutenants Spear and Fischer being invited into Prigny's cabin and consenting to surrender, sparing their former prisoners 'the necessity of employing force'.[37]

After clearing away wreckage and the fallen foremast, the Anglo-French crew used the mast stump to rig a royal – the smallest of sails – and steered for Cadiz. Fournier was gratified to note that they 'made good as much as five miles per hour', firing shots at intervals to give notice of their approach so that the San Sebastián lighthouse might be lit to serve as a leading mark in the darkness. A Spaniard in the crew, who claimed to have 'fished in these waters for six years', had promised to pilot the ship past the Puercas, the Cochinas, Diamante and Galera rocks that fenced the harbour. But despite their pilot's professed expertise, at 8.15 in the evening they experienced 'a very severe shock' from a concealed shoal off the coastal fortress of Santa Catalina, 'which unshipped the rudder and carried away two planks' in her side. Dropping anchor in just seven and a half fathoms, they were obliged to clear away the now useless rudder which was crashing violently against their stern frame and threatening to smash it in. Next, they tried to lighten the ship by throwing overboard 'wood, spare spars, flour, salt provisions, [and emptying] the water casks, wine and brandy barrels'. Longboats, riddled with shot during the battle, were also jettisoned. But the reduction in weight was counteracted by a 'considerable leak which was overmastering the pumps'. In addition, the tide had begun to ebb and the depth, separating *Bucentaure*'s already holed and weakened hull from the rocks beneath, to decrease.

At two o'clock in the morning a boat from the French 80-gun *Indomptable* found them in the darkness and enquired as to their needs. Relatively unscathed from the battle, apart from a damaged rudder, she had since been anchored in the bay of Cadiz with other French and Spanish ships, thus far escaping destruction or capture. During the following hours more craft reached *Bucentaure* at Lieutenant Fournier's urgent request for 'as many boats as possible'. The Spanish pilot had advised that reaching a safer anchorage was impossible and 'all that could be hoped for was to save the people'. Five hundred, including all her wounded, are said to have been taken aboard *Indomptable* alone, but as the evacuation proceeded, so did the ebbing tide. At 5.15 *Bucentaure* 'began to touch ground' on the rocks, and by about eight o'clock was 'grounding heavily [and] suffer[ing] such violent shocks that the water began to enter the hold in such a manner as to do away with all hope of saving her,' if any yet remained. Her crew were clear by 1.30 in the afternoon, and in half an hour 'the water reached the orlop deck' as Prigny, Fournier, their officers and the men of HMS *Conqueror* were taken aboard a French frigate and into Cadiz. An hour later Villeneuve's flagship had sunk. Contrary to a lurid report in the *Gibraltar Chronicle* telling of 'utmost cruelty and ... every species of insult and inhumanity', Spear, Fischer and their people were well treated by their French captors.[38]

*

Earlier that morning – 23 October – as the rocks had begun to rip through *Bucentaure*'s timbers, a look-out on *Minotaur* reported activity in Cadiz harbour. At eleven o'clock signal 370 was hoisted: ENEMY ARE COMING OUT OF PORT. Then, about noon, thirteen ships were seen to emerge bearing east-north-east. 'The remains of the French and Spanish fleet have rallied,' wrote Captain Blackwood, 'and are at this moment but a few miles from us.'

Ship's Master John Seymour's log implied that until this unexpected development, *Conqueror* had been 'endeavouring to take the [*Bucentaure*] in tow' and that those endeavours only ceased 'in consequence ... of the enemy's ships ... making after us,' upon which we 'made all sail for the fleet'. Seymour was apparently unaware that they had already lost their prize to the French the night before and that by noon of the 23rd, she was past preserving for either side, grinding to destruction some ten miles to the north. It has been suggested that he may have mistaken *Aigle* – by then anchored off the island of Sancti

Petri – for *Bucentaure* and, given the distance, high seas and atmospheric conditions, such confusion was understandable, one dismasted hulk looking much like another. Lieutenant Senhouse, also observing from *Conqueror*'s quarterdeck, made no such mistake, but ascribed her withdrawal to the avoidance of a lee shore rather than the enemy incursion: 'On the morning of the 23rd, at daylight, we found ourselves within three miles of the beach, and the *Bucentaur* close in, with the lighthouse of Cadiz some little distance from us. With great exertion we got off the shore, but our prize struck on the rocks and is totally lost.' Neither Seymour's nor Senhouse's account suggests those on board *Conqueror* had any knowledge of *Bucentaure*'s recapture the previous day.

The squadron that emerged from Cadiz was led by Commodore Julien Cosmao-Kerjulien – captor of the Diamond Rock the previous June – his 74-gun *Pluton* bearing the injuries inflicted only two days earlier, 'leaking a great deal from the large number of shot-holes between wind and water, and [her] masts ... barely secure'. Other vessels included the Spanish 100-gun *Rayo*, her mainmast similarly insecure, the 74-gun *San Francisco de Asis*, the French *Héros*, and *Neptune*, of 74 and 84 guns respectively, and the congested *Indomptable*. Five frigates and two brigs sailed in support.[39]

Exhausted British crews beat to quarters once more, clearing for action, while a cordon formed of 'eight sail of the most perfect [vessels] to leeward of the British disabled ships and prizes'. The enemy's purpose, Captain Blackwood assumed, was 'to recover some captured ships, or take some of the disabled English; but they will be disappointed, for I think and hope we shall have another touch at them ere long.' He was astonished 'that they had exertion enough to come out again,' so soon after such a battle, showing 'they are no longer a navy to be despised as we used to do'. Nevertheless, he hoped this time 'they may persevere, and we shall then convince Mr Bonaparte, that even with his best discipline, we can give them such an overthrow as the annals of history cannot produce.' With *Euryalus* now nominally Collingwood's flagship,

Blackwood was gratified to be leading the fleet into action, and this time with the prospect of more than just an observer's and support role, 'which, you will believe,' he informed his wife, 'suits my taste'. With more ships 'ready to come to us if we want them,' he trusted that their opponents would 'fall an easy prey', adding that 'the Admiral has a strong desire to put a finisher to the affair.' Both would be disappointed.[40]

The enemy's sortie was audacious but neither foolhardy nor suicidal. Far from renewing hostilities with a greatly superior adversary, Cosmao's plan had been to pursue the more limited objective of recapturing two Spanish prizes – *Santa Ana* and *Neptuno* – isolated from the protection of the British fleet and closest to the shore.

Thunderer had been attempting to take Vice Admiral Álava's flagship in tow but without success until, at one o'clock in the afternoon, 'the Enemy's ships ... nearly within gunshot' decided the issue, wrote Lieutenant Thomas Colby. 'We reluctantly withdrew our men from the Prize and quitted her ... and made all sail to effect our own escape.' Astern, he watched the French frigate *Thémis* take possession of *Santa Ana*.[41]

Meanwhile, Don Cayetano Valdés, commander of *Neptuno*, claimed that as the French and Spanish ships approached, 'the English who were on board cut the [anchor] cable, but in a short while ... they surrendered themselves prisoners and my men took possession of their arms and of the hatches.' Valdés had been wounded in the head and neck during the action of the 21st, had remained unconscious below decks throughout the subsequent events, and his official report was compiled according to the testimony of others. A member of the seventy-five-man prize crew, William Thorpe, recalled that their surrender was not so passive as the Spanish account implied. On seeing the enemy's ships coming out of port, and expecting no assistance from their own, he and his mates had crafted an ungainly improvisation to allow themselves a chance of escape. '[We] riggd a spar to the stump of the main mast and an other to the [mizen], set a top Gallant [sail] upon each, and got an other to the Fore Mast, in lieu of a fore sail.' After casting off the anchor '[we] stood toward our own Fleet with all sail we could set, – but the enemy was gaining upon us fast from Cadiz.' They cleared for action, manned the stern chasers – 'cannon ... placed in the after part of a ship, pointing astern, to annoy any ship which is in pursuit of her' – and broke open the powder magazine. The Spanish prisoners, choosing this critical moment to make their move, 'rose upon our people and retook the ship, in doing which they met with little opposition'. Indeed, added Thorp, 'it would a been madness to resist,' although at the same time conceding that the surrender was not entirely docile. 'A slight resistance was made by some men who narrowly escaped with their Lives.' The French frigate *Hortense* towed her to the mouth of Cadiz harbour, where she rode at anchor until three o'clock the following morning. Her anchor cable then parted and she drifted north, grounding on rocks off the coast of Puerto de Santa María.[42]

With between twenty-five and twenty-eight British ships ranged against him, and about half 'seeming to be in good condition', Cosmao 'did not think it [his] duty to run the risk of a skirmish, seeing the bad state of the ships which composed [his own] division'. He accordingly signalled them to withdraw and they re-entered the bay, his own ship, *Pluton*, 'in a sinking condition'. *Rayo* was particularly decrepit, undermanned and 'practically crewed by soldiers'. A strong south-south-easterly wind against her, and with a fractured mainmast, she was unable to regain the harbour and anchored some eighteen miles to the north, off the town of Rota, close to the Sanlúcar shoals. Later that night her main topmast fell, followed by the rest of her main- and mizenmast, the wreckage smashing her tiller.[43]

*

Algésiras – recaptured earlier by her French officers and commanded by Lieutenant Valdémar de La Bretonnière – had spent the night of the 22nd insecurely anchored near the Diamante Rocks, in danger of wrecking should the anchor drag. As day broke on the 23rd they could see 'the *Bucentaur* ashore on the rocks of [Santa Catalina] and many boats ... going to take off the crew'. But repeated firing of distress signals throughout the morning and afternoon elicited no assistance from the passing ships of Cosmao's squadron as they set out from Cadiz and later returned. Lieutenant Pierre Philibert's journal account of the following day and night is a tale of 'touch-and-go' – a naval term used 'of anything within an ace of ruin; as in ... a ship very narrowly ... escap[ing] rocks'. *Algésiras* 'bumped'* first on the Diamante before a change of wind took them clear, only to be 'bumped heavily on the Galera'. They attempted to lighten the vessel's stern, 'throwing overboard four 18-pounder guns ... as well as all the shifting ballast, shot and other heavy objects that were in [that] part of the ship'. The aftermost tiers of casks were prised open with crowbars and the water pumped out one after another. The strategy worked and they floated clear, only to begin 'bumping heavily again on the rocks' the following day. Half an hour after midnight on the 25th, they 'bumped heavily' again, unshipped and lost their rudder, the chains securing it having been severed during the battle. Their guns fired with greater urgency. Several boats had already set out from the port to assist but foundered with all hands drowned. Eventually, at about ten o'clock on the morning of the 25th, a small two-masted brig was able to drop a best bower anchor well ahead of them and beyond the destructive power of the rocks. The anchor cable was with difficulty passed inboard to *Algésiras* and her crew was able to heave the ship to safety: 'until there remained 50 fathom scope' of water beneath her keel.[44]

*

Following Cosmao's raid, Collingwood's battle-torn fleet was reinforced by fresh ships – the 74-gun *Donegal*, frigates *Eurydice* and *Melpomene*, and the sloop *Scout* – to be employed with

---

* Constance Eastwick translated the verb as 'we bumped', the original French reading '*Nous talonnàmes*' – from *talonner*: (*en bateau*) to touch or scrape the bottom with the keel.

other seaworthy craft evacuating the prizes and preparing to destroy them.

HMS *Donegal* – formerly a French prize, *Le Hoche*, captured off the Irish coast in 1798 and renamed accordingly – had been ordered to Gibraltar on 17 October to fetch a consignment of water casks, missing the battle by three days.

III

THREE days of foul weather and the possibility of further troublesome incursions from Cadiz had made the retention and control of hard-won prizes impossible, and on the morning of the 24th, 'considering that keeping possession of the ships was a matter of little consequence, compared with the chance of their falling again into the hands of the enemy', Collingwood ordered signal 241 hoisted: 'QUIT AND WITHDRAW MEN FROM PRIZES AFTER HAVING DESTROYED OR DISABLED THEM.' *Euryalus*'s carpenter, Thomas Parrott, and his crew were sent on board *Santísima Trinidad* to cut holes in her sides below the waterline, while Lieutenant John Edwards of *Prince* had the task of overseeing the evacuation of Spanish wounded. 'We had to tie the poor mangled wretches round their waists, or where we could, and lower them down into a tumbling boat, some without arms, others no legs, and lacerated all over in the most dreadful manner.'[45]

HMS *Neptune* took off 450 of the Spanish prisoners, including 'a true Italian priest born at Malta', and Captain Fremantle acquired 'an excellent French cook', along with 'a true Spanish pug dog' that he proposed keeping to give to his daughter Emma, 'if she is a good Girl'. An officer of *Ajax* wrote that 'everything alive was taken out', the last creature saved being a cat which ran out onto the muzzle of one of the lower deck guns as the final boat was pulling away. There were reports, however, that the evacuation was not entirely comprehensive. William Robinson of *Revenge* wrote of Spaniards 'left on board' lining the gangway as the last British rescue boats were forced to depart fully laden. These unfortunates were 'displaying their bags of dollars and doubloons and eagerly offering them as a reward for saving them'. Lieutenant Edwards admitted to getting out all the wounded 'but about thirty-three or four, which ... it was impossible to remove'. Pérez Galdós's account of the gigantic vessel's final hours alleged that 'the wounded were forgotten, and several who had been brought on deck dragged themselves to the side in a sort of delirium, to ... throw themselves into the sea. Up through the hatchways came a hideous shriek ... from the poor wretches on the lowest deck who already felt the waters rising to drown them and vainly cried for help.' Rear Admiral Cisneros reported a similar story and suspected that, despite the best efforts of Lieutenant Edwards and the other British rescuers, 'more than eighty seriously wounded who were in the sick-bay must have been [drowned] in her on account of the scant time allowed by the sinking ship in which to take them off.' He arrived at this calculation because 'only 350 men' of the Spanish crew were later to be found on board *Prince*. He conceded that 'the rest [may have] got on board the English *Neptune*, who also gave assistance.' That ship's log mentions accommodating 'wounded Spanish prisoners' but neglects to say how many, while *Ajax*'s log records taking an additional 209 prisoners, condition unknown. Nevertheless, Cisneros insisted that, 'including [corpses] that were thrown overboard on the night of the battle and the succeeding days, I compute the total loss at 300 men, including those who, being wounded, were not ... saved.' The flagship's captain, Francisco Javier de Uriarte, made the same allegation, that regardless of three or four English vessels 'taking the people off between them ... they were not able to do so entirely in spite of much assistance and for all the activity they displayed they were obliged to abandon in this great extremity a large number of wounded and disabled, who went down in the *Trinidad* at dawn, at a distance of 7 or 8 leagues south of Cadiz.'[46]

Midshipman Badcock decried the Spaniard's sinking. 'She was

a magnificent ship and ought now to be in Portsmouth harbour.' Although totally dismasted, damage wrought by the British guns was largely superficial. 'Her top-sides, it is true, were perfectly riddled by our beautiful firing,' Badcock observed, 'but from the lower part of the sills of the lower-deck ports to the water's edge, few shot of consequence had hurt her between wind and water, and these were all plugged up. She was built of cedar, and would have lasted for ages, a glorious trophy of the battle; but "sink, burn, and destroy," was the order of the day.' Notwithstanding the breaches scuttled in her timbers by the axes of Parrott and his men, and the opening of the lower gun ports – 'that when she rolled a heavy sea might fill her decks' – it was with considerable difficulty that she was made to 'at last unwillingly go to the bottom'. Badcock made no mention of the Spanish wounded alleged to have gone down with her.[47]

The difficulty of evacuating and destroying the prizes was exacerbated, *Leviathan*'s Captain Bayntun remarked, by 'the vast rolling sea and the ships not being near each other' – and, as a consequence, 'many boats [were] lost' going between them.

Lieutenant Hargrave and his prize crew from *Defiance* had been sent on board *Argonauta* with orders to bring the prize to anchor, prior to taking out the prisoners and sinking her. The degree of cooperation in this task extended by about 600 Spaniards, the majority drunk, is unclear. 'It came on to blow a very heavy gale of wind [on the 25th] and continued to blow harder and harder during the night when it blew harder than [master's mate Colin Campbell] ever saw it.' It was not expected she would last until morning. 'The Spaniards were terribly frightened and all turned-to to pray.' With the sea crashing over them, they 'hove all the main deck guns overboard and let go the sheet anchor ... in case the best bow anchor should part'. Around midnight the rudder came loose, and 'knocked about so much [they] thought it would knock her stern post in'. Then at three o'clock 'it broke adrift altogether' and did no further damage, although making the ship impossible to manoeuvre. The two longboats in which Hargrave and his men had reached her had sunk astern during the night. Fortunately, on the 26th the gale abated sufficiently for *Donegal* and *Leviathan* to send boats to their assistance. When Campbell, Hargrave and the rest of the prize crew and prisoners had been taken off, *Argonauta* was scuttled at anchor.

Following *Intrépide*'s descent into anarchy, and Lieutenant Auguste Gicquel's timely prevention of fire in the liquor store, *Britannia* was ordered to take out her prisoners and prize crew, and to burn her regardless. The whole ship's company, including wounded, were safely brought off, but with the gale increasing 'almost to a hurricane', efforts to set the prize alight were 'effected with the greatest difficulty, the sea running very high'. Then, at about 8.30 in the evening, those watching from *Orion* 'perceived the fire to have taken' and as it strengthened the French officers on the quarterdeck of *Britannia*, 'while viewing the destruction of their fine Ship, instead of deploring the loss, stood admiring *le grand spectacle!*' There was a fitting climax to the show at 9.30 when the flames reached her powder magazine, and *Intrépide* blew up.[48]

More prisoners, a prize crew from *Leviathan*, and 'some warrant officers' stores' were taken from the *San Agustín*, but at the cost of a yawl, a longboat and ten members of the boat crew. The Spanish ship was then also set ablaze, an abattoir turned funeral pyre for the 184 corpses left on board. A Spanish lieutenant claimed that some of the most severely wounded, 'those without legs and arms who might as well have been dead,' still breathed. If so, their torment ceased abruptly when the ship exploded.[49]

*

Destruction of the prizes entailed finding accommodation for multitudes of French and Spanish captives. All told, Collingwood estimated, 'we took twenty thousand prisoners, including the troops.' On the day following the battle, *Prince* had 'victualled 154 prisoners', but by the 24th, following Collingwood's evacuation order, her log recorded: 'Employed ... all the afternoon fetching prisoners ... Got on board, supposed, 500 men, and a many wounded ... Expended, per captains order, shirts, trousers, frocks, beds, blankets, shoes and stockings to naked prisoners.' Having 'made a bonfire of *Intrépide*', *Orion* was crowded with 'a part of her people and also of [*San Agustín*]'. Captain Codrington estimated about another five hundred, 'besides my own men'.[50]

Britannia employed six boats to bring 'an enormous number of prisoners' from *Aigle* and *Berwick* and as a result was 'crowded to a dreadful degree', Lieutenant Halloran reported. 'A large proportion [were] wounded in addition to our own, numbers dying hourly, and the ship labouring in a heavy sea, in one of the most severe gales I ever witnessed, thunder, lightning, and torrents of rain.' She was also taking in a considerable quantity of water, 'leaking copiously through her sides'. This was not due to battle damage, according to Halloran – *Britannia*, arriving late to the action, had sustained minimal structural injury – but to her 'great age'. Launched near the end of the Seven Years War, in 1762, she was the oldest vessel in the fleet and suffered greatly from 'the concussion of her guns which shook the timbers to such a degree that they became quite loose'.[51]

By the end of October, *Orion* was 'getting to rights in her sails and rigging again and might perhaps be in some order,' Codrington told his wife, 'were it not for the number of prisoners, and the dirt, filth ... and confusion they occasion ... Besides our own people we [have] nearly 100 men of other ships, and 580 prisoners, French and Spanish.' He estimated having 'victualled nearly *twelve hundred people*'. An overcrowded man-of-war was a particularly unsavoury environment and the *Orion*'s must have been typical of conditions across the fleet as hundreds more prisoners were distributed between ships. The fastidious Codrington hoped soon to be relieved of the wounded prisoners at least: 'We have about thirty on board, and they not only take up much room and attention, but, poor creatures, the stench is most intolerable.' There was more to concern him than smell, however, and by the beginning of November, running short of fresh water, and with fever breaking out among the Spanish prisoners, he made sail in the hope of reaching Gibraltar before it spread to the rest.[52]

Leviathan was also 'much crowded with Spanish Prisoners' from *Monarca*, *San Agustín* and *Argonauta*. Among the ninety or so enemy wounded treated by William Shoveller there were some showing signs of mortal neglect. Several had tourniquets still applied to arms or legs after four to five days and – deprived of blood – 'most of the Limbs [were] in a state of Mortification or approaching it.' The surgeon was able to amputate in only four of these cases and with contrasting outcomes. Two undergoing upper limb procedures 'did well and were sent on shore at Algeciras', while the other two, operated on at the thigh, died on the third day 'the Stumps becoming mortified'.[53]

The days and nights of storm had exacerbated the suffering of the wounded, friend and foe alike. James Spratt, master's mate on *Defiance*, had his leg shattered by a musket ball. 'As [the ship] pitched to the heavy sea,' he recalled, 'I could hear as well as feel the broken ends of my marrow bones as they grated by derangement whilst I lay in my cot under the half deck.' Lieutenant John Clavell – advised by Collingwood prior to the battle to exchange his boots for silk stockings in case of injury – was lying, 'wounded and insensible' in his cabin when a wave stove in the larboard quarter gallery of *Royal Sovereign* and swept him into the wardroom. On board *Tonnant*, of sixteen amputations Mr Chevers performed during the action only two survived, the rest losing their lives 'in consequence of the motion of the ship during the gale, [when] their stumps broke out afresh, and it was impossible to stop the haemorrhage'. And in the cockpits of *Bellerophon* and *Colossus*, as they lurched, the wounded rolled upon one another, bursting their ligatures and bleeding to death. It was the same below decks on *Téméraire*. 'Ever since the battle,' Eliab Harvey wrote home to his wife, 'it has been very bad, almost a constant gale of wind with constant rain ... *Shocking* for our poor wounded.'[54]

*

Sea, rocks and storm destroyed what Collingwood's carpenters and incendiaries did not.

On board the grounded *Neptuno,* 'expecting the Ship every moment to go to Pieces, the Spaniards ... showed every simptom of Dispair,' wrote William Thorpe; 'they run about in wild Disorder nor made the last effort to extricate themselves from the Danger that threatened them.' Ropes were attached by the prize crew to the bowsprit, the foremast, and one of the catheads – among the sturdiest of a ship's timbers from which the heaviest anchors are suspended – 'by the assistance of wich, a number of men got safe on shore'. A raft was constructed 'to convey such as were unwilling to risk themselves by the ropes'. Twenty men reached the shore by this means but it was found impossible to retrieve it from among the rocks and another had to be built with the remaining lumber on board. A further twenty men hazarded the crossing with the loss of a single Spaniard to the surf. The raft was then dragged by rope back to the ship and twenty-eight more embarked. This time six Spaniards drowned in the crossing and the raft itself was found to be 'much damaged' when hauled again to the ship. Fully laden, it set out a third time but came apart before reaching the shore 'and every soul perished'. According to Thorpe, 'no further attempt could be made to save those unfortunate men who remained on board' and, like the occupants of the raft, 'All Perishd' when she broke up. Thorpe and the rest of the prize crew were escorted four miles overland to Puerto Santa María as prisoners of war, and may have been unaware of a more positive outcome reported by *Neptuno*'s Captain Don Cayetano Valdés, who claimed that 'only twenty men were drowned' from the rafts, and, with the assistance of local fishing boats, he himself abandoned the ship, accompanied by his wounded second-in-command, 'by the rest of the wounded among the crew, and by the officers'.[55]

Following her adventure with Cosmao's squadron, *San Francisco de Asis* shared *Neptuno*'s fate, and – driven by the same southwesterly gale and powerful swell – the same wreck site on the coast south of Rota. *Aigle* ran aground further south of the two Spaniards, below the Río Guadalete. In a final attempt to reach the safety of Cadiz, acting commander Asmus Classen had taken her from the danger of the Sancti Petri rocks to the edge of the Diamante, where she 'grounded hard and unshipped her rudder after several consecutive shocks'. At dawn on the 25th she drifted clear and was fortunate to ground again on a softer surface. Most of her crew were saved by Spanish boats arriving when the weather improved, although 'many of the French men were drowned who attempted to get ashore before the boats came.' Lieutenant Purchase and his men were well treated by their Spanish captors on shore, given 'plenty of mutton', and accommodation at Puerto Santa María, amounting to an open prison, 'rooms ... to live in and the key to go out and in when they chose'. Classen wrote his report on 1 November, still on board his ship, describing it as 'now stranded on a sandy mud bottom ... whence I am in hopes of getting her off'. Ever loyal to his adopted Emperor, the Dutchman concluded his account: 'My ambition will be rewarded if I am successful in ... restor[ing] to His Imperial Majesty a ship capable of making His name respected.' Classen's ambition went unrewarded and the ship was wrecked.[56]

Captured by the French from the Royal Navy in 1795, the 74-gun *Berwick* had been re-captured at Trafalgar by HMS *Achille* with the loss of more than fifty dead and 200 wounded. Prisoners were taken on board the British ship and sixty-seven casks hove overboard 'to make room in the fore-hold' to accommodate them. Anchored by her prize crew to weather the storm, it is believed that the prisoners remaining on board, 'in a fit of madness or desperation, cut the cables ... by which means she immediately drove towards the dangerous shoals of San Lúcar', some eighteen miles north-west of Cadiz. Loss of life in the ensuing wreck would have been greater had not *Donegal* pursued and intercepted her. Lieutenant Edward Barnard's prize crew was taken off along with 102 French wounded. Captain Malcolm had ordered his boats 'first to save all the wounded Frenchmen before they brought off any of the English, which order was most punctually complied with; the English were next removed, but before the boats could return [for the rest], the *Berwick* struck upon the shoals and every soul on board perished, to the number of three hundred.' According to Spanish records, however, sixty-one were saved.[57]

Meanwhile, wrapped in a Union Jack on the quarterdeck

of *Monarca*, and members of the prize crew lying around him sodden with looted drink, Midshipman Walker's instinct of self-preservation roused him from despairing lethargy. He and his still sober comrades, assisted by the Spanish officers, set about lightening the prize by heaving overboard several guns and shot, but still 'in such imminent danger of sinking, [they] determined to run the ship on shore'. Then, at dawn on the 24th, *Leviathan* reached them west of Sanlúcar, when Walker and the rest of the prize crew were taken off, along with most of the Spanish prisoners. Both ships anchored overnight in nineteen fathoms but the following morning *Leviathan*'s log recorded that '*Monarca* had parted [her anchor cable] and was driving on shore.' Walker mentioned that 150 Spaniards were left in the ship, 'who [had been] afraid of getting into the boats' sent to save them the day before. Captain Bayntun believed her to be lost 'with every one on board', but according to Spanish records, ninety-three survived the wreck. In the same vicinity as *Monarca* the dismasted Spanish *Rayo* – still flying Spanish colours – was forced to surrender, a belated prize. *Donegal* took off 626 prisoners and 'put above eighty of her own people on board to take care of her'. But three days later, *Rayo* also broke adrift from her cable and ran aground on the same part of the coast as *Monarca*. William Dunbar, her prize master, survived the wreck and told of witnessing 'about a hundred perish, including two boats loaded with men belonging to the *Donegal*'. Landed at Sanlúcar, with about fifty other English prisoners, Dunbar was amazed by his captors' generosity. 'A carriage was backed into the water for him to step into from the boat, all sorts of cordials and confectionary ... placed in the carriage for him ... women and priests presented him with delicacies of all sorts as the carriage passed through the streets ... and clean linen, bed, &c., prepared for him at a lodging on shore.' He questioned whether he would have received half the consideration, wrecked on an English coast, as he did from the Spanish, 'whose friends we had just destroyed in such numbers'.[58]

*

The *Indomptable* had suffered relatively few casualties during the battle of 21 October – twenty killed and thirty injured – having retired early from the action. She had subsequently taken on board as many as five hundred men from the foundering *Bucentaure*, including all her wounded. Participating in Cosmao's raid on the 23rd she was thought to have included extra hands among her crew, intended to man the prizes it was hoped to recapture. The result was that during the night of the 25th and 26th, when she crashed on the rocks of the Sanlúcar shoal and 'went to pieces at once', she was greatly overcrowded. Captain Pernot, whose 16ème Régiment de Ligne supplied the contingent of infantry manning the ship, claimed that as many as 1,400 sailors and troops were on board, of which no more than 150 survived the wreck, and although his gross total may be an exaggeration and was realistically closer to a thousand, no other estimate of survivors exceeds 180. Injured and temporarily blinded on the 21st, Pernot had remained on board the *Pluton* throughout the 'miserable days and nights' of storm that followed the battle, his hearing attuned to the distant gunfire in every direction signalling distress not belligerence, and the terrible fate of *Indomptable*'s crippled condemned, imagined rather than seen. 'The screams of the wounded were appalling. When the tide was low they tried to use the limbs they still possessed to drag themselves across the rocks away from a death that met them further on. It was indescribably ghastly and harrowing and mostly happening at night.' The wreck of *Indomptable* comprised the greatest collective loss of life attributed to the storm. The overall figure of French shipwrecked dead has been estimated at 2,300, far exceeding the 1,425 killed by shot and splinter during the battle.[59]

'We have lost more ships from the storm,' wrote Vice Admiral François Rosily, 'than the enemy have captured from us.' This meagre sop to national pride was, in essence, true. Of eight French ships captured only *Swiftsure* would remain in British hands, one being burnt on Collingwood's orders, one – *Algésiras* – recaptured, and the rest wrecked.

Nine Spanish prizes had been taken on 21 October, and a

tenth – *Rayo* – three days later. On the morning of 31 October Lieutenant Alexander Dixie and a barge's crew from HMS *Phoebe* were sent 'to set fire to and destroy two line-of-battle ships on shore to the westward of San Lúcar'. After ten and a half hours he returned having set alight the wrecks of *Monarca* and *Rayo*. He also reported seeing the wreck of *Berwick* nearby, 'totally lost having parted asunder amidships'. Since she was beyond any possibility of salvage by an enemy, Dixie did not trouble to burn her. At one o'clock the following morning *Monarca* was observed to blow up while *Rayo* was still 'in full blaze' three hours later. Only three Spanish prizes – *Bahama*, *San Juan Nepomeceno*, and *San Ildefonso* – reached Gibraltar, along with *Swiftsure*, as trophies of victory.[60]

*

When Midshipman Walker rejoined *Bellerophon* from his traumatic duties aboard *Monarca* he was dismayed to find that his hammock and bedding had been shot to shreds in the action – 'the more unfortunate as [he could] so ill afford to replace them'. In addition, his sea chest had been broken open, several articles of clothing stolen, 'and nearly all [his] linen either lost, or torn by the wounded for bandages'. He despaired of recompense for the loss, calculating that he would only receive about £20 in prize money, a fraction of the sum – upwards of £100 – that would have enriched him had not the prizes been destroyed. Another midshipman, William Hicks of *Conqueror*, wrote that 'the gale which came almost immediately after the fighting robbed us of our prizes and dashed the cup of fortune from our lips.' The full amount of prize money lost was estimated at 'near four millions, ... most of it gone to the bottom'. *Britannia*'s Lieutenant Halloran expressed the mood of exhausted disappointment better than any: 'After several days beating about at sea, the whole Fleet in distress, the greater part of the Prizes sunk or wrecked, and amidst a general scene of wretchedness and desolation, we made the best of our way to Gibraltar.'[61]

*

'We were cheered in to the mole by the ships laying in the bay,' recalled Lieutenant Nicholas. 'All the Garrison [were] under arms ... for the purpose of firing a salute. The sight was truly grand. The Artillery commenced by firing 121 guns, after which the infantry fired a *feu du joi* from right to left [and] this was repeated 3 times.' But the spectacle that hulks like *Belleisle* and the rest presented on arrival was difficult for some among the waterfront crowds to wholeheartedly exult in: victory looked too much like defeat. 'Grand beyond all idea,' wrote Dr Fellowes, '& yet ... enough to strike a terror into the bravest heart ... Wreck after Wreck came up ... the Hulls only of many ... towed in, horribly shattered, & without a Mast standing.'[62]

A ball was held at the Governor's residence in honour of the victory, and Captain Codrington attended, in company with Captains King and Hope, of *Achilles* and *Defence*. Coming directly from battling elements and enemy, all three went in dirty boots befitting men of action. It would have been their first opportunity to exchange views with comrades in arms on the conduct of the action and its aftermath. And if the contents of Codrington's letters home are an indication, he would have been particularly vocal in complaint, much of it directed at their commander-in-chief's failings in contrast to Nelson. '*He* made the signal to prepare to anchor; and had Admiral Collingwood *acted upon that hint* we might now have secured almost all our prizes.' *Orion*'s captain even believed that, had all fourteen been preserved, there might have been far-reaching consequences for the wider European war. 'The news would, ere this time, have been public at Vienna, and in the army of Buonaparte, where it would have made a sensation advantageous to the Austrian cause.' But that cause had already suffered a setback in the week before the battle – with the Austrian capitulation at Ulm – which no amount of maritime success a thousand miles away could reverse; nor would it have tipped the scales against a decisive French victory over combined Austrian and Russian forces at Austerlitz in early December.[63]

Collingwood's lack of leadership and aloofness was a contentious issue. 'Where our admiral is, God knows ... We are all here [at Gibraltar] without orders or instructions, and know not what he is about, or where he is pottering.' Codrington considered Collingwood 'a very good man in his way', and 'as brave a man as ever stepped on board a ship', but felt he lacked the judgement and flair of the man he had replaced. He was disgusted that the fleet would not be going home together, but instead 'by *driblets*' – in squadrons of four or five at a time – prejudicial both to the safety of disabled ships, and injurious to the manner in which their achievement would be represented. Collingwood was 'drivelling away' their hard-fought-for triumph, and had, in effect, 'frittered away ... the *éclat* of so grand a victory'. *Éclat*. It was a favourite word of Codrington's – expressive of brilliance, glamour, glory – all that a sniper's bullet through the smoke had lost them. 'Had our Nelson lived, what *éclat*, what dignity there would have been in all his proceedings!' But from that loss, and from Collingwood's neglect of compensating leadership to inspire unanimity across the fleet, morale suffered. 'The ships' companies are beginning to abuse each other,' Codrington declared. A recurring theme in some survivors' accounts – that some vessels had been less prominent in the action than others – reflected this. *Prince*'s dearth of injury was a distinction clearly regarded by able seaman John Brown of the *Victory* as a mark of shame, that she had 'nobody Killd or Wounded'. Even *Neptune* – with ten killed and forty wounded – was disparaged by Edward Harrison of *Téméraire*, for being 'of [so] little Service in the Action', that 'she might as well have been laying in Cawsand Bay' and never left Plymouth Sound. It was believed she would be 'sent [on blockade duty] up the Mediterranean for punishment'. The inequality of casualties from vessel to vessel gave rise to a rumour, recounted by Brown, that only fourteen of the fleet took part in any fighting at all, that 'most of our heavy Ships sculk't away', and that indefinite cancellation of shore leave had been imposed in retribution: 'some of our Ships ... to be Kept out of the Land for 7 Years for not coming into Action'.[64]

Insinuations of cowardice – or at best of shirking – became more serious when they appeared in the public prints. Captain

Fremantle was embarrassed to read an article in the *Star*, 'a long panegyric of the *Neptune*', and her meritorious conduct in the battle, clearly written by one of his own officers. 'Several of our ships', the anonymous author declared, 'were unable to get into action until it was nearly over; among which were the *Prince* and *Dreadnought*, of 98 guns each. This was the cause of many of our leading ships ... being so much cut up.' *Neptune*'s commander was particularly annoyed because 'of course this will make us enemies in those Ships, and it is very ill judged in those who were so impudent as to put it in print'.[65]

Codrington conceded that 'in a battle of such note there will always be some whose vanity leads them to paint their conduct in too warm a tint, and to sound their trumpets without regard to concord or harmony.' Such a man was Eliab Harvey.

On 29 October, the storm at an end, Midshipman Hercules Robinson, as 'youngster of the watch', was in charge of a jolly boat bringing Harvey – the commander of *Téméraire* – to visit Collingwood aboard *Euryalus*. The sixteen-year-old was bemused and flattered by the attention paid him during the crossing by one so senior in rank, 'the Captain of a three decker speaking freely to a green boy' being 'out of all rule'. Harvey regaled Robinson with 'his exploits and fought [his ship's] share of the battle over again'. And having rehearsed the account he was about to give at dinner, 'he did not hide his light under a bushel when he put it on Collingwood's table.' For this reason, the young man claimed, '*Téméraire* shines the brightest star of the Trafalgar constellation,' and the only vessel that would be singled out for especial praise in the commander-in-chief's official dispatch to the Admiralty as published in the *London Gazette Extraordinary*: 'A circumstance occurred during the Action which ... strongly marks the invincible Spirit of British Seamen, when engaging the Enemies of their Country ... The *Téméraire* was boarded by Accident, or Design, by a French Ship on one Side, and a Spaniard on the other; the Contest was vigorous, but in the End, the combined Ensigns were torn from the Poop, and the British hoisted in their Places.' Aside from the inaccuracy of this anecdote – only *Redoutable* and

Fougueux, both of them French, struck to *Téméraire* – Harvey's table talk aboard *Euryalus* could not have influenced the wording of Collingwood's dispatch which had been sent three days earlier and was already north of Lisbon on its way to England by the time the two men sat down to dinner on the 29th.

Even without a mention in the *Gazette*, Harvey would have been a man to avoid at the governor's ball. No longer content with bending the ears of midshipmen, he moved among his peers, telling any who would listen of his martial contribution. 'His head is turned,' Fremantle wrote, 'he thinks every Ship was subdued by him, and he wears us all to Death, with his incessant Jargon*.' Worse than mere bombast, he deprecated the conduct of another ship to the aggrandisement of his own, claiming that '*Victory* did nothing whatever towards effecting the capture of the *Redoutable*.' While Codrington even-handedly admitted that *Téméraire* had 'behaved certainly very well' in the fighting, that she had indeed been 'in a most conspicuous situation', and was fully deserving of praise, he nevertheless declared that her commander 'is become the greatest bore I ever met with'.[66]

*

During November many of *Leviathan*'s crew, uninjured in the battle and storm, were 'attacked with Bowel Complaints' and among others, it was noted, 'the slightest injury or scratch became a foul spreading Sore'. The conditions may have been physical manifestations of what is now called post-traumatic stress disorder, and, according to one authority, could 'illustrate the enormous demands on the body's reserves by a naval action like Trafalgar, which compromised the immune system and made the participants susceptible to opportunistic infections'. Mr Shoveller ascribed the plethora of 'Diarrhoeas', and the 'Catarrhs and Ulcers', to a change in the crew's accustomed diet of salted pork

---

* 'Unintelligible talk; gabble; gibberish.' Johnson's *Dictionary of the English Language*, 9th edn, 1805

and beef on 'long cruizes', and to their 'being ... abundantly supplied with Fresh Meat and Vegetables', following the ship's arrival at Gibraltar. How this accounted for the skin lesions – 'black, stringy and dry ... with inflamed Edges, the Ulcer spreading itself beneath the [skin]' – was unclear. These were, in the early stages, treated with 'Bark & Wine'. Sulphur balsam mixed with oil of terebinth was applied to the sores, as well as warm oatmeal and carrot poultices, 'the latter most beneficial'.[67]

William Burnett, the surgeon on *Defiance*, had believed James Spratt's right leg – broken by musket shot during the fight to capture *Aigle* – impossible to save. But Spratt had refused amputation, arguing that he would never otherwise find a better match for his left leg. Burnett dressed the limb as best he could and reluctantly consigned his patient to the torture of the damned with every lurch of the storm-tossed ship. By the time he reached the Gibraltar Hospital on 3 November, Spratt had developed a high fever. 'In my delirium I fancied I was playing at foot ball: so suiting the action to the thought I dislocated the broken bone as often as the surgeon put it to rights.' At Gibraltar the leg was encased in a long, narrow wooden box to immobilise it and 'facilitate the formation of Callus', the organic material generated in ossification by which fractured bones knit together. As his delirium receded Spratt became maddened by persistent itching, that he was only able to relieve by thrusting the blade of his knife down a crack in the wooden casing. After nine days the box was opened and the dressing removed to reveal 'hundreds of large red headed maggots nearly an inch long ... sticking into [his] precious limb'. They were produced by the flies 'which beset the Hospital, blackening the ceiling of the sick ward and depositing their eggs on and about the wounded'. When hatched the grubs began to feed. Only the tips of their tails could be seen but Spratt imagined 'their heads could not be far from the bone'. Attempts to remove them with forceps resulted in them breaking off short leaving their heads embedded, and only an astringent chemical poured 'into [the] honey combed calf' proved effective, although excruciatingly painful. The action of the maggots may well have saved Spratt's life, feeding as they did only on the diseased and suppurating parts of his wound and allowing the healthy tissue to heal. As a result, the formation of 'a surprising strong Callus' preserved Spratt's leg, although at nearly three inches shorter than his other.[68]

IV

THE two-masted schooner *Pickle*, second smallest vessel in the fleet, had departed for England with Collingwood's dispatches to the Admiralty five days after the battle, Lieutenant John Richards Lapenotière – native to Ilfracombe but from French Huguenot stock out of Holland – in command. Carrying official news of victory was an honour customarily conferred upon a 'man of rank in the service ... who bore a conspicuous part in the action'. The bearer might expect a substantial gratuity for his efforts and a guarantee of professional advancement. Speed being essential, the commander of a frigate was an obvious candidate, but none could be spared – Captain Blackwood and *Euryalus* being indispensable to the commander-in-chief – and so, 'having no means of speedier, or safer conveyance', the choice fell on Lapenotière and his schooner. 'As I trust you are fully aware of the great importance of those despatches being forwarded as soon as is possible,' Collingwood told him, 'I rely on your using every exertion, that a moments time may not be lost in their delivery.' Equipped with only fourteen 12-pounder carronades – four of them laid in the hold as ballast – but with her hull bottom re-coppered two years earlier guaranteeing speed, *Pickle* could at least hope to outrun, if not outgun, a pursuing enemy. Lapenotière's orders in the event of her failing to do so however, were clear: 'If necessary those despatches are to be thrown overboard and for which you are to be prepared.' And lest *Pickle* should founder or indeed be taken, two days later, on 28 October, Lieutenant Robert Benjamin Young, commanding the single-masted cutter *Entreprenante*, was sent with a duplicate of the dispatch to Faro, the nearest port on neutral Portuguese territory. From there the news would be taken 150 miles overland to the British ambassador at Lisbon.* Lieutenant Young would receive no reward for this service, apart from the so-called '100 guinea sword' presented by the Patriotic Fund to all commanders at Trafalgar.[69]

Collingwood also entrusted Lapenotière with 'a few lines' to his wife Sarah, reassuring her he was safe. Among the complaints voiced by Codrington was that others had not been given the same opportunity before *Pickle* set out, and that, without such reassurances, 'the publicity of Admiral C's dispatches' would create widespread anxiety at home. 'We are all in distress about our poor wives hearing of the action [without] knowing if we are dead or alive ... Can anything be so cruel as to send his dispatch away ... and *not* take the *very, very first* opportunity of relieving the minds of the [relatives] of those in the action?' He was later gratified to learn that Collingwood had 'sent word by the schooner ... that [he] was well', but rather ungraciously wondered whether this merely meant that he had not been reported otherwise.[70]

*

Pickle's homeward voyage began at half past noon on 26 October, her log recording 'fresh breezes and cloudy' but 'with a heavy swell from the westward'. The only mishap on the following day occurred some five leagues off Capo de Santa María on the Algarve, when the sailor taking soundings 'lost the deep sea lead & Ninety fathom of line'. By eleven o'clock in the morning of the 28th, she was rounding Cape St Vincent, when her lookout reported 'a strange sail in the NNW standing towards us'. Following the

---

* This dispatch would be forwarded from Lisbon on board the packet *Lord Walsingham* on 4 November and arrive at Falmouth on the 13th.

necessary exchange of coded signals to ascertain friend or foe, she proved to be the 18-gun sloop *Nautilus* commanded by Captain John Sykes, who came aboard the following day, and, being apprised of Lapenotière's news, departed for Lisbon to report to the British embassy. He did not, however, report directly, but sent the ambassador a brief note giving bare details of the victory, as recounted to him aboard the *Pickle*. He also wrote to Collingwood: 'The wind now being a fresh and favourable gale to proceed further Northward, and finding with care and economy, I could make the provisions and water last to reach England, I have ventured to proceed, solely activated by a zeal for the service, and in hopes to meet your wishes on the occasion, in becoming a security for the information of the *Pickle* should any accident befall her.' Given the honours and rewards that would be bestowed on the messenger arriving first with such information, it is perhaps not unreasonable to doubt that he was 'solely activated by a zeal for the service'. Whatever construction was to be laid upon it, it seems clear that Sykes was acting on no other authority – and to no advantage – but his own.[71]

Over the next two days, *Pickle* sailed nearly 300 miles north along the Portuguese coast with *Nautilus* astern but gaining. As night fell *Nautilus* overtook and was lost sight of. From then on, the *Pickle*'s crew had other concerns. By the 30th she was off Oporto and meeting heavy weather, a foretaste of conditions awaiting her the following evening as she rounded Cape Finisterre into the Bay of Biscay. Sails were reefed and hauled down one after another throughout the night, the log at midnight recording 'fresh Gales & Squally with a heavy head Swell'. It was this swell, as it crashed directly into her prow, that caused *Pickle*'s first difficulties, carrying away her spritsail and its yard, and inundating her bow section. Limber holes were designed to drain water aft but they had become 'stopt' with debris. As the flood level rose, the 'People [were] Emp^d Bailing the Water out of the fore Peak ... one pump continually Going,' but neither operation kept pace with the ingress. At five o'clock in the morning 'the Gale increased' and to lessen the weight in the forward part of the ship they 'hove four guns with their carriages over Board'. Jettisoning these larboard and starboard bow carronades – each about six hundredweight – steadied the *Pickle* and, as the wind eased, reefing was no longer necessary. By ten at night on 1 November, men were climbing the masts, lengthening sails and clambering along the bowsprit onto the lance-like boom to set the jib. Even studdingsails were set for extra speed. Early the next day they passed the westernmost point of France, the island of Ouessant – 'Ushant' to British navigators – and entered the English Channel, 150 miles from the Lizard. After forty-eight hours battling high seas and gales to make headway, Biscay's turbulent conditions were reversed and replaced by 'light airs & fogg'. As the wind dropped, headway ceased, and her 'People [were] Emp^d at the Sweeps to Keep the vessels Head the Right way'. A gruelling and unpopular occupation, only feasible aboard a ship of frigate class or smaller, sweeps were pairs of long heavy oars used galley-fashion to propel the vessel in a dead or near-dead calm. With three men to each, a maximum speed of one and a half knots – or nautical miles per hour – was possible.[72]

In the early hours of Sunday 3 November, an easterly breeze, freshening later, enabled the crew to stow the sweeps and make sail. At half past seven an approaching ship was sighted and identified – after an exchange of signals – as the 74-gun *Superb*, wearing a Vice Admiral's blue flag at her foremast. *Pickle* hoisted signal 351: I HAVE SOME INTELLIGENCE TO COMMUNICATE. Lapenotière was summoned aboard and reported to her commander, Nelson's friend and protégé, Captain Richard Goodwin Keats.[73]

A twelve-year-old naval volunteer, Edward John Trelawny, witnessed the exchange as the two men spoke in undertones, but neither he, nor the watching officers could make out more than a few unconnected words: 'Battle' ... 'Nelson' ... 'Ships'. The boy had never seen his captain 'much moved', being customarily 'cool, firm and collected on all occasions'. But now, his face flushed, Keats 'stamped the deck, walked hurriedly, and spoke with passion'. Going below he reported the news to Admiral John Thomas Duckworth: 'A great battle has been fought ... off Trafalgar. The combined fleets of France and Spain are annihilated, and Nelson is no more.' Then he added, in an undertone: 'Had we not been detained we should have been there.'

Trelawny's memoir, published a quarter-century later, claimed that Duckworth was blamed for their missing 'the most glorious battle in naval history', that subsequently 'a death-like stillness pervaded the ship ... sorrow and discontent ... painted on every face,' and the admiral was treated like a pariah on his own flagship. *Adventures of a Younger Son* has been dismissed as containing a 'proportion of truth to fiction [amounting to] not more than one tenth', as can only have been expected from this anecdotalist and myth-maker of the romantic poets.*,74

Captain Keats's disappointment, however, was understandable. A month earlier *Superb* had figured prominently – between *Victory* and *Téméraire* – in Nelson's 'order of battle', his preliminary plan for defeating the Combined Fleet when at last it emerged from Cadiz. In early September he had even outlined to Keats the tactics he proposed using: 'formed in two Lines ... [to] go at them at once [to] surprise and confound the Enemy [and] bring forward a pell-mell Battle.' But a lengthy refitting at Portsmouth had prevented *Superb* from sailing earlier than 27 October. A further five days' delay at Plymouth, awaiting the arrival of Admiral Duckworth, the delivery of his thirty-five cases of wine, and re-victualling the ship with Cornish mutton and potatoes at his insistence, though frustrating, would have made no difference to her chances of participating in the action.75

Absentee bitterness was common to many ambitious young naval officers as news of the battle became known. Like Pulteney Malcolm aboard *Donegal*, Francis Austen, commander of HMS *Canopus*, had been sent to Gibraltar on a useful but unillustrious errand for fresh water. The novelist's younger brother wrote home on 27 October: 'Alas! ... all my fears are but fully justified. The fleets have met ... Our situation is peculiarly unpleasant and distressing ... to find ourselves at last thrown out of any share

---

* See his *Records of Shelley, Byron and the Author* (1878).

of credit or emolument ... to be away at such a moment, and ... to lose all share in the glory of a day which surpasses all which ever went before, is what I cannot think of with any degree of patience.' Captain Malcolm's feelings at missing the battle are not recorded.[76]

As the disconsolate *Superb* resumed her voyage to the wreck-strewn waters of southern Spain, *Pickle*'s was nearing its end. She had travelled about 1,500 miles in ten days at an average speed of six and a half knots. Monday morning, 4 November, brought fresh breezes and cloud. With 'all Sail Set to advantage' she rounded the Lizard and after four leagues, at a quarter to ten, she 'shortend Sail' and anchored in sight of Pendennis Castle. Her log reads 'out Boat our Commander went on Shore at Falmouth with his dispatches for London'.

*

Meanwhile, at daybreak on 4 November, HMS *Caesar* – under the command of Sir Richard 'Mad Dick' Strachan* – was within long gunshot of four French men-of-war, off Finisterre, one of them wearing a rear admiral's flag at her mizen. He believed them to be part of a larger enemy force that had escaped from the Royal Navy's blockade of Rochefort on 18 July and had menaced English and neutral shipping ever since. Comprising five ships of the line, three frigates and two fast-sailing brigs, the Rochefort squadron had lost no time beginning its campaign of depredation and on the 22nd had captured the English merchantman, *Mary and Ellen*, out of Guernsey. Captain Radford and his crew had been taken prisoner and their ship burnt. During his captivity Radford claimed the squadron 'took and destroyed forty vessels sailing under neutral flags: five of them ... Americans, 25 Swedes, several Danes and Prussians.' According to another report, by the end of October they 'had ... in their possession an English frigate, ten English merchantmen, and thirty neutrals; had burnt an

---

* Pronounced 'Strawn'.

English sloop of war, and several merchantmen.' This energetic force had acquired near mythical status in the corridors of the Admiralty and the coffee houses of the City of London where it was known as the Invisible Squadron, 'from the adroitness with which it has steered clear of our squadrons sent in pursuit of it'. The threat it posed to shipping was, to Admiral Collingwood, all that marred the total victory so recently achieved. 'If I can get hold of the Rochefort squadron,' he remarked, 'the naval war of our enemy is over, till they build another fleet.'[77]

Strachan would not realise until after their capitulation that the ships he had been pursuing for two days were not in fact part of the marauding force that so worried the readers of *Lloyd's List*, but instead, the splintered and leaking rump of Villeneuve's Combined Fleet that had made its escape from the waters off Cape Trafalgar a fortnight earlier. Three 74-gun men-of-war – *Duguay-Trouin*, *Mont Blanc* and *Scipion* – were led by Dumanoir's flagship *Formidable*. Strachan held back, shortening sail to keep pace, but allowing time for the rest of his own squadron – *Hero*, *Courageux*, *Namur* and four frigates – to come up.

First to arrive and open fire was the frigate *Santa Margarita*, with orders 'to get under the enemy's stern and rake them [and] cut away some of their rigging to retard their sailing'. This rearguard action continued for a short time without eliciting a response – until *Scipion*'s helmsman 'luffed up', bringing her head to windward and 'her after guns to bear'. The first shot across the *Santa Margarita*'s forecastle took boatswain Thomas Edwards's head off, while another, low into her hull, left the hold flooded four feet deep, and the powder magazine 'over the [gunner's] shoe tops in water'.

At a quarter past eleven, with their enemies gaining and 'finding an action to be unavoidable', the signal was given to form a line of battle on the starboard tack – *Duguay-Trouin*, *Formidable*, *Mont Blanc*, and *Scipion* to the rear – bringing them broadside-on to their pursuers. *Formidable*'s eagle standard was placed in a prominent position on the quarterdeck forward of the main mast, and Dumanoir addressed his crew, exhorting them 'to defend it gallantly and to behave as befitted Frenchmen fighting valiantly for the honour of the flag'.[78]

Caesar, *Hero* and *Courageux* – the *Namur* still some distance behind – tacked in turn and formed their line on a course parallel with the French, those in range 'firing away with great vigour for nearly an hour', first into *Scipion* and *Mont Blanc*, and then at *Formidable*, 'and going at the rate of near five knots through the water, by which time the *Caesar* was nearly up with their van ship', *Duguay-Trouin*. Meanwhile, Strachan's nimble frigates, *Santa Margarita* and *Phoenix*, now joined by *Aeolus* and *Révolutionnaire*, harried them from astern.

At 11.45 Dumanoir signalled his ships to tack again, 'preserving the order', and sending them in the opposite direction to Strachan's line, reducing the distance from his antagonists to 'half a musket shot'. The French line now had three enemy men-of-war to larboard, and four frigates 'at a very short distance' starboard. Francis Romney, a nineteen-year-old midshipman on board *Aeolus*, writing to 'a young lady, his relation', recounted 'a running fight' to impress her, 'hot and warm, pelting away for three hours and twenty-five minutes'. Strachan's ships went about again and bore down on the French, who were by now manoeuvring with difficulty, *Scipion*'s main topmast tottering and *Formidable*'s damaged by two round shot. 'The action recommenced with renewed vigour.' Around three o'clock, *Scipion* had lost her topmast and Dumanoir himself was badly splinter-wounded in his side. Half an hour later, devastation to his ships increasing and 'their masts much damaged', the admiral received a shot in the left leg which pitched him from the poop to the quarterdeck and resulted in his being carried below. By this stage, 'almost all the men on the *Formidable*'s upper works were killed or wounded, [and] the [gun] batteries half disabled.' There was eight feet of water in the hold and her masts were no longer secured by rigging. While his wounds were being dressed, Dumanoir was approached by a midshipman with a message from Captain Letellier, urgently requesting his orders. His reply was 'to continue to fight to the last'. Shortly afterwards, a Lieutenant – Jean Baptiste Silhouette – appeared at his side. He reported that several round shot had struck their rudder and one – wedged between it and the stern-post – made it impossible to steer. 'It is my intention to fight on as long as the masts are standing,' Dumanoir replied. Then Letellier himself came to report that the ship – now unmanageable – was being fired into from three directions and could only reply with a few rounds; that besides this, the gun decks were abandoned, that there was now nine feet of water in the hold, that the masts were tottering and all the yards shot away. It was for these reasons, the captain declared, 'he found himself obliged to strike in order to save the ship from being sunk.' It was nearly four o'clock and, as though to emphasise the gravity of Letellier's report, 'at that very moment the mainmast fell . . . followed by the mizen-topmast and the crossjack yard.' *Scipion* struck her colours at about the same time, *Mont Blanc* and *Duguay-Trouin* some fifteen minutes later.

The disparity of casualties between the opposing sides in this postscript to the main action was wider than at Trafalgar. British losses were dismissed as 'not more than is to be expected on these occasions' and 'trifling considering the closeness of the action'. The French, by contrast, 'suffered much'. Dumanoir's official report estimated dead and wounded across his four ships at seven hundred and ten. *Duguay-Trouin* had lost 150 men disabled, including her captain, Claude Touffet, killed early in the action, and his second-in-command François Boisnard, severely wounded by a ball to the knee. Then Lieutenants Jean Baptiste Lavenu and Nicolas Cossé, and two midshipmen – Victor Guillet and Charles de Tocqueville – 'who had successively commanded the ship' – were also wounded, Guillet with 'his cheek pierced by a bullet'. Captain Gemähling of the 67ème Régiment de Ligne, found himself with three-quarters of his men lying dead around him. 'It was not war as one understands it,' he wrote, 'it was butchery, a fearful slaughter.' Two hundred more were killed and wounded aboard *Scipion* while *Mont Blanc* lost 140, with 37 known dead and 103 wounded, 'amongst whom [were] 55 dangerously hit'. The flagship *Formidable* had, 'besides the men wounded in the engagement on [21 October], ... fever cases and others who were in the hold ... something over 200 men disabled,' including Dumanoir himself. Commander Guillaume Donnadieu was injured too, as were all the officers and midshipmen attached to the admiral's staff. Midshipman Adrien Murat had his arm shot off and died after surgery. When *Formidable* had struck and firing ceased, a few shots, accidentally fired from on board, provoked several more enemy broadsides which 'killed or wounded a score of men'.[79]

British losses were just 24 killed and 111 wounded. 'I dare say their Lordships will be surprised that we have lost so few men,' Strachan wrote to the Admiralty. 'I can only account for it from the enemy firing high, and we closing suddenly.'[80]

For his part the flagship's captain, Jean-Marie Letellier, had no doubt where the blame lay: 'my guns were badly served ... from the beginning of the engagement I had remarked the bad aiming of my gunners ... and ... had neglected nothing that would obviate it.' And Dumanoir reported that while he had 'nothing but praise to bestow upon the captains, officers and crews' of his four ships he was pained 'to have to complain as greatly of the lack of skill among the gunners, since after 4 hours of running fight and the same length of time abeam at a range of a musket shot and even half that distance, the enemy were without any apparent injuries.' Admittedly, *Formidable* was at a serious disadvantage. She had guns dismounted and a carronade burst during the action of the 21st. She had also been obliged to throw overboard twelve of her guns to lighten the ship during Strachan's chase, reducing her armament from eighty to sixty-four, and her 'best gunners and seamen ... killed or wounded'.[81]

Strachan gave the French full and generous credit: 'the Enemy having fought to Admiration, ... did not surrender till their Ships were unmanageable.'

An article published on 30 November in the *Royal Cornwall Gazette* contrasted the squalor of defeat with the fastidious victors. 'When Sir Richard Strachan's officers and seamen took possession of the four men-of-war captured off Cape Ortegal, they found them in the most dirty and filthy condition, the mangled dead bodies not all thrown overboard, and the ... wounded in a terrible state: they immediately put the prisoners ... on board to work, to throw overboard all the dead bodies, get the poor wounded into a state of comparative comfort, and the ships (as far as the wreck of masts, yards, rigging, &c. would permit) into a state of tolerable cleanliness. The French officers, who were sent on board our ships from their own, appeared astonished at the neat, clean, and orderly state in which they found everything, decks all washed and fumigated, and every dead body thrown overboard, so recently after a severe and bloody battle.

The four ships of Strachan's squadron arrived in Plymouth Sound on 10 November, each with a battered French prize in tow, 'most confoundedly peppered from stem to stern on the sides they [had] engaged'. This compensation, in miniature, for the seventeen wrecked, scuttled and burnt vessels captured from the Combined Fleet three weeks earlier, drew thousands of spectators from Plymouth Dock and Stonehouse, who all assembled on the different points of land, and gave the victorious vessels, as they passed, 'three such cheers as made the welkin ring, ... on which each ship piped all hands on deck ... and returned three as hearty cheers – the men of war in the Sound and Hamoaze all cheering at the same time, and the bands of the different regiments ... playing and beating "God Save the King", "Rule Britannia", and "Britons Strike Home".' It was said that the occasion 'called out [on] the Hoe old people, who were lame, and had not been there for several years'.[82]

Here the last fatal shot of the Trafalgar campaign was fired. A young Royal Marine from the *Caesar* was employed on board *Formidable*, packing away captured musketry and pistols, and discharging any found to be still loaded. A comrade nearby was holding a musket under one arm when it went off accidentally into the young man's hip. The ball shattered the top of the femur and lodged in his pelvis. Before he eventually expired in agony from mortification of the wound, 'the poor fellow ... declared he would not have minded being killed in the action – but to die

AFTERSHOCKS

from so foolish an accident was dreadful!' The coroner's inquest returned a verdict of accidental death, and HMS *Caesar*'s toll of fatalities from the engagement of 4 November increased from four to five.[83]

*

On the morning of Monday 4 November, as Sir Richard Strachan prepared to engage Admiral Dumanoir's squadron, and exactly two weeks after the Combined Fleet was first sighted off Cape Trafalgar, Lieutenant John Lapenotière stepped ashore at Falmouth's Fish Strand Quay, bearing the news of its destruction. He had chosen this smaller port for his landfall, in preference to Plymouth, to avoid delaying his onward road journey by having to deal with overly conscientious quarantine officials.

A line in *Trewman's Exeter Flying Post* headed 'Falmouth, Monday, Nov 4th, 1805', reads only: 'The *Pickle* schooner arrived off the harbour this day from which an officer landed and went off express for London, with dispatches.' Nobody bothered to enquire as to his business and, perhaps learning a lesson from his encounter with Sykes, Lapenotière seems to have made no mention of it during the hour or so he spent ashore hiring a post-chaise for the first stage of his journey to London. Not so the crew of the *Pickle* when they dropped anchor at Plymouth the following morning. It was here, on 5 November, that the first English news of the victory appeared in print: a broadsheet, decorated with two men-of-war in woodcut, and bearing the headline: AN ACCOUNT OF THE VICTORY OVER THE COMBINED FLEETS OF FRANCE AND SPAIN; AND THE DEATH OF LORD NELSON. It contained the error, common to all early accounts, that Nelson had been struck in the breast by a musket ball fired from the tops of *Santísima Trinidad*. It included the incidental information that 'the *Nautilus* is also arrived [in Plymouth]' and that 'Captain Sykes . . . went off express for London.' On his arrival late the previous night, Sykes reported the news to Vice Admiral Sir William Young, the Commander-in-Chief, Plymouth, on board his flagship *Salvador del Mundo*. Young then ordered Sykes to the Admiralty, bearing a letter of congratulation to their lordships on the victory.

Meanwhile Lapenotière had left Falmouth shortly after noon on the 4th, changing horses at Truro, and again at the Blue Anchor Inn, south of Fraddon. His carriage was drawn by four horses, a necessary extravagance for the climb onto and across Bodmin Moor, and for maximum speed over the leveller stretches of road on the rest of his 270-mile journey. A driver was unnecessary, the vehicle being controlled by a postillion mounted on the near, that is left, side horse of each pair. After another change of horses at Launceston he crossed into Devon. Horses were changed again at Okehampton, skirting the northern edge of Dartmoor, and again at Crockernwell before entering Exeter. From here he would be travelling on the same roads as Sykes, but whether in front or behind is uncertain. Changing horses again at Axminster, he crossed into Dorset.

Lapenotière made a note of all the changes of horses – twenty-one of them in all – and what each stage had cost him so as to claim back from Mr Wright, the Admiralty's chief clerk, the large sum of £46 19s 1d that the journey cost. Sixteen miles from Exeter to Honiton cost £2 14s, while only nine miles from Honiton to Axminster had cost just £1 11s 7d. He did not trouble to make a note of how long each stage took, nor the times of arrival and departure. The testimony of one single eye-witness of the journey comes down to us, providing a specific location and time, and incidentally a fleeting but inconclusive impression of the rivalry between Sykes and Lapenotière. Captain Robert Tomlinson wrote from Dorchester on 6 November, to his brother Nicholas of the Sea Fencibles in Maldon, Essex: 'Yesterday about Noon, two officers of the Navy came through this Town, following each other, at about an hour's Space of Time, in two Post-Chaises and four Horses to each, from the Westward; the first reported that he brought good News of great Importance, and the second, that his Dispatches contained the best and most capital News that the Nation ever experienced.' Too much might be read into such a scrap of information, but it is tempting to see the tight-lipped commander of *Pickle* in the lead at this point, tersely divulging 'good News of great Importance', while the man with only hearsay to communicate could indulge in hyperbole.[84]

From Dorchester they passed through Blandford Forum, Woodyates and – crossing the border into Wiltshire – the city of Salisbury, relieving the exhausted horses at each stage, Lapenotière keeping scrupulous note of the mounting expenditure. The next twenty miles, entering Hampshire, to Andover cost him £2 15s, then ten and a half miles for £1 13s from Andover to Overton. Across the North Downs into Surrey brought him to Basingstoke, Hartfordbridge, Bagshot and Staines, then finally Hounslow. The shorter distances between these six stages, and correspondingly lower tariffs, might suggest the horses were urged harder on the improving roads and required more frequent changes, as they approached London. From Hounslow to Whitehall cost £2 1s, but for all the speed at which this final eleven miles was accomplished, the coach might as well have been pulled by the two postillions as by four powerful fresh horses.

*

On the morning of 5 November, Henrietta, Countess of Bessborough set out from her home in Chiswick to visit friends in Queen Street. 'The fog, which was bad when I set out, grew thicker and thicker, but when I got into the park was so compleat that it was impossible to find the way out. My footman got down to *feel* for the road, and the holloing of the drivers and screams of people on foot were dreadful. I was one hour driving thro' the park; Queen St. it was impossible to find, [even] with two men walking before the horses with flambeaux, of which we could with difficulty perceive the flame – the men not at all. Every ten or twenty yards they *felt* for the door of a house to ask where we were – it was frightful beyond measure.'

Henrietta's friend, Lady Villiers, a woman prone to mishaps, had ridden out to meet her, and 'was overtaken by [the fog] in her return, and nearly drown'd by riding into the Thames. How many accidents she has!'[85]

It was the densest London fog in twenty years; starting early in the morning, 'it increased with the progress of the day, until five o'clock when the Metropolis was involved in great darkness.' In the Strand, Bond Street, Piccadilly, Oxford Street, 'and other busy [thoroughfares] the thickness of the fog obscured entirely the light of the street lamps; and it was with difficulty that the glare of a shopwindow, full of patent lamps, could be discerned at the distance of a few yards.' Venturesome private carriages, like Lady Bessborough's, moved at foot pace, while 'hackney and stage-coachmen alighted from their boxes, and led the horses.' Near panic prevailed: 'At the corners of streets and in narrow passages particularly, carts, carriages, and pedestrians might be found huddled together, not knowing how to move or extricate themselves, without incurring the greatest possible danger.' Despite all precautions, accidents were inevitable. 'Lord Mulgrave's carriage drove against the *Cheveaux-de-frieze* inclosing the great gun in St. James's Park. A carriage, with four ladies in it, was upset in Oxford street, but they did not receive any material injury; and a servant of Mr Christie, of Pall Mall, was run over by a horse in Picadilly, and very much hurt.'[86]

Through this tenebrous chaos the two post-chaises trundled in search of Whitehall. Whichever had been in the lead leaving their final staging stop at Hounslow, it was the bearer of Collingwood's original Trafalgar dispatch who passed the Admiralty gates first, a little before one in the morning of 6 November, a matter of minutes before Sykes. It is said that they met at the entrance of the building, but it was Lapenotière alone who was shown to the Board Room where William Marsden was about to finish work for the day. Thirty-seven hours of solitary, jolting travel on pitted roads across the 270 miles between Falmouth and Westminster had allowed him ample time to formulate, refine and rehearse the words of his conflicted message to the First Secretary:

'Sir, we have gained a great victory, but we have lost Lord Nelson!'

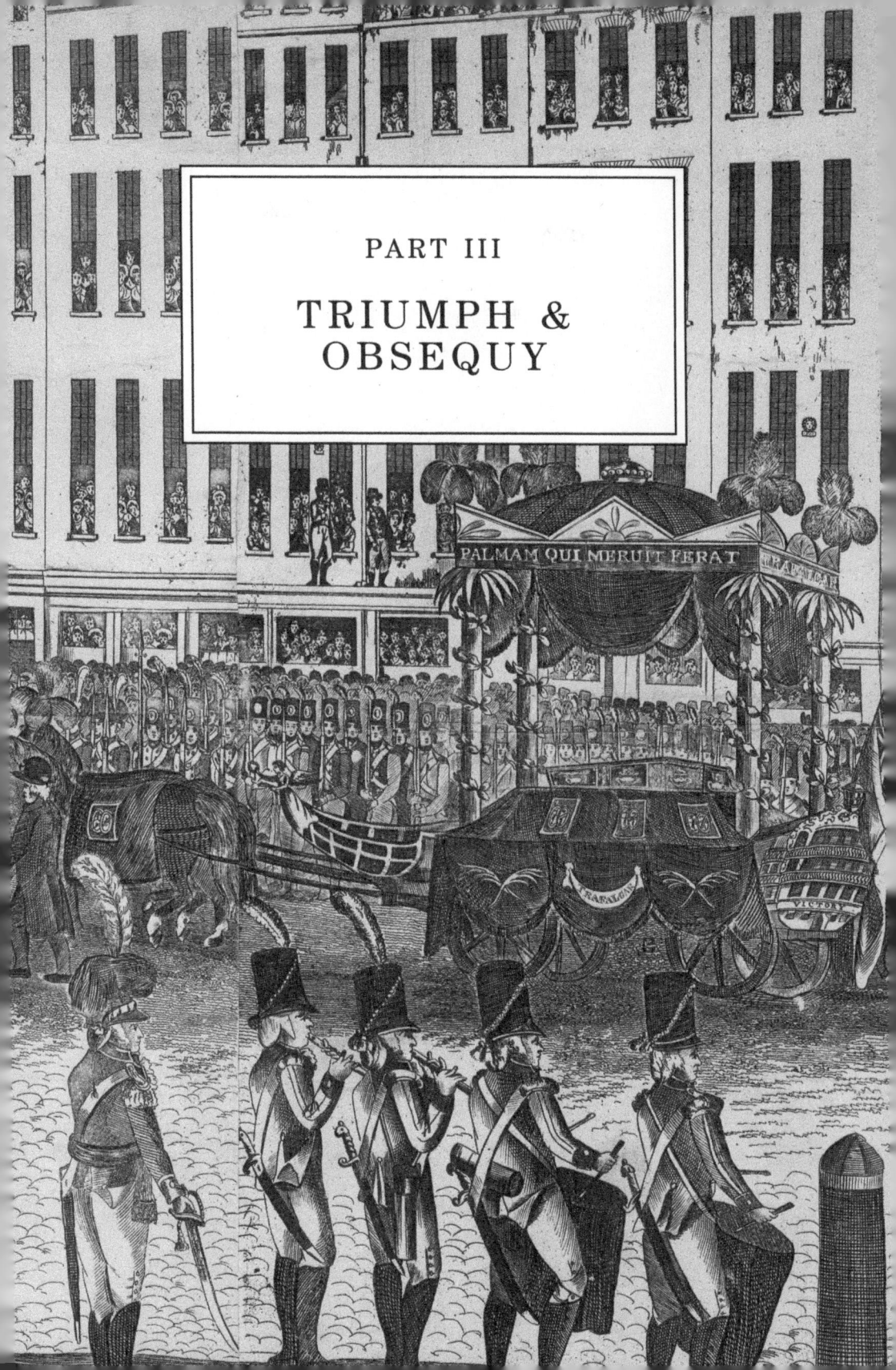

PART III

TRIUMPH & OBSEQUY

I

TOWARDS midnight on 21 June 1815, when the battle-soiled Major Henry Percy arrived in London – two captured French eagle standards protruding from the windows of his carriage – bringing word of Napoleon Bonaparte's final defeat at Waterloo, it was the memory of a ten-year-old national trauma that spread reassurance through the crowds thronging Piccadilly and St James's Street: 'The Duke is safe! Wellington is safe!' That significant corollary to the joyous intelligence of victory meant jubilation this time would be unalloyed. A decade earlier, reaction to news that the Combined French and Spanish Fleet had been destroyed off Cape Trafalgar, but the British commander-in-chief killed, was ambivalent, emotion confused, celebration muted.[1]

The Prime Minister, William Pitt had been awoken at various hours of the night during the course of an eventful political career by the arrival of momentous news, but whether good or bad he could always lay his head on his pillow and sink again into sound sleep. On this occasion, however, 'the great event announced brought with it so much to weep over, as well as to rejoice at, that he could not calm his thoughts, but at length got up, though it was three in the morning.'[2]

Mrs Fitzherbert, consort of the Prince of Wales, wrote to her friend Mrs Creevey that he had 'this moment rec'd an account from the Admiralty of the death of poor Lord Nelson, which has affected him most extremely... upon any other occasion [it] might be called a glorious victory... Excuse this hurried scrawl: I am so nervous I scarce can hold my pen.' The Prince's father, George III, was said to have 'remained silent for nearly 5 minutes', on being told the news, and by another account, had wept, exclaiming, 'We have lost more than we have gained.' More in keeping with the known coolness of the King's feelings towards Nelson, however, was the terse remark: 'He died the death he wished.'[3]

Walter Spencer-Stanhope, industrialist and Member of Parliament for Carlisle, echoed this sentiment, believing that such a glorious death was 'more to be envied than lamented and to die wept by the land he perished for [was] what he himself would have wished'. The father of thirteen also expressed the wish that his 'little William had been on board Collingwood's ship on that glorious day whatever might have been the risque!' William Spencer-Stanhope was twelve years old and would embark on his naval career as midshipman aboard HMS *Ocean* the following March, joining Collingwood's squadron off Cadiz. William's sister Marianne affected the impatience of a nineteen-year-old to the most momentous news of the day: 'Every letter Mamma has had has been full of nothing else,' she complained, '[and] if care is not taken, it will be like the invasion, a constant topick when you have nothing to say.' Writing to her other brother John she declared, 'I have made a vow not to name Lord Nelson or the Victory or Victories in any of my letters.' She wrote this in a postscript, 'but postscripts are exempt'. And she added, 'I think it is a great proof of genius to have written a letter without naming the event.'[4]

It seemed, indeed, all anyone else spoke or wrote of. 'Wasn't you sorry for Lord Nelson?' Charles Lamb enquired of William Hazlitt. 'I have followed him in fancy ever since I saw him walking in Pall Mall... looking just as a Hero should look, and I have been very much cut about it indeed. He was the only pretence of a Great man we had. Nobody is left of any Name at all.' Hazlitt's feelings on Nelson's death, the battle of Trafalgar and the temporary setback of Napoleon's endeavours are not recorded. A fervent republican, he is said to have taken the later news of Waterloo particularly badly: 'prostrated in mind and body, he walked about unwashed, unshaved, hardly sober day by day, and always intoxicated by night, literally without exaggeration, for weeks.'[5]

Lady Bessborough's elder sister, Georgiana, Duchess of Devonshire, had hastened from Chiswick to the Admiralty on first hearing the news, accompanied by her devoted friend – and incidentally the mistress of her husband, the Duke – Lady Elizabeth Foster. Each was anxious for the welfare of near relations: Elizabeth for her son Clifford, illegitimate product of their notorious *ménage à trois*; Georgiana for her fourteen-year-old nephew, Midshipman Robert Spencer.* The ladies' fears proved groundless. 'Your Grace, Mr Spencer was not in the action,' the Duchess was informed, while Clifford's ship, her companion learnt, had been 'sent ... on other service'.

Although she had no more than a dinner-table acquaintance with the fallen hero, Lady Elizabeth was particularly affected, writing to her eldest son, Augustus, secretary to the British legation in the United States: 'Really there is such a gloom over every thing. You cannot conceive how knocked up I feel.' This was an understatement. Indeed, if Georgiana's twenty-year-old daughter Harriet is to be believed, her response was histrionic and she still appeared to be in despair three weeks later. 'Her private affectation is enough to destroy the effect of a whole nation's public feelings, for she has so much grimace about her grief that one can hardly prevent one's own disgust of her operating upon one's pity for [Nelson]. She sobs and she sighs and grunts and she groans ... and whilst she is regretting that she could not "have died in his defence," her peevish hearers almost wish she had.' There was little warmth between Harriet and her father's handsome mistress.[6]

At Lady Elizabeth's urging the Duke of Devonshire contributed six 'noble lines' to a nationwide corpus of amateur commemorative verse that proliferated in variable quality over the following months:

---

* Her brother George's third son.

Oft had Britannia sought midst dire alarms
Divine protection for her sons in arms.
Generous and brave, though not from Vices free,
Britons from Heaven received a mixed decree,
To crown their merits but to check their pride
God gave them Victory but Nelson died.⁷

The third line – referring to Nelson's adultery – suggests his death in the sixth to be a kind of retribution. Georgiana's own ten-line tribute contained, in a single iambic pentameter, an admirably concise account of his demise: 'He conquer'd, knew it, "blessed his God", and died.'⁸

*

The Admiralty had provided Lloyds and the Lord Mayor with pertinent details of the battle in a bulletin at one o'clock in the morning of 6 November. The Park and Tower of London guns fired at eleven. Nine miles away, at Merton Place, Lady Hamilton, 'feeling rather unwell', was in bed, 'on account of a rash'. Hearing the distant explosions, she assumed they announced 'some victory perhaps in Germany, to retrieve the credit lost [at Ulm] by [General] Mack'.* Mrs Bolton, Nelson's elder sister, was with her.

'Perhaps it may be news from my brother.'

'Impossible, surely', said Emma. 'There is not time.' His ship had only left England on 26 September, and it seemed far too soon for the announcement of any decisive naval developments.

Five minutes later a carriage pulled up at the door and Captain Whitby from the Admiralty was announced.

'We have gained a great Victory . . .' he began.

'Never mind your victory. My letters – give me my letters.'

---

* The fortified city on the Danube had capitulated to the French on 15 October 1805 resulting in the capture of the entire Austrian force numbering twenty-five infantry battalions, ten squadrons of cavalry and fifty-nine field guns. News of this disaster had reached London on 28 October.

Whitby was pale, unable to speak and there were tears in his eyes. Lady Hamilton screamed and fell back on the pillows.[9]

*

The City of London 'soon became all bustle and enquiry'. Public Offices and coffee-houses overflowed, newspaper offices were besieged, those of the *British Press* and of the *Globe* were so crowded that it became impossible to transact business in them. The commercial world was greatly agitated as 'the Funds immediately began to move'. The value of Three Per Cent Consols – fixed-interest government bonds – rose significantly between half past ten and midday. 'It was expected that they would continue to rise still higher.'[10]

The Times had already gone to press on 6 November when the contents of Collingwood's dispatch became known. The *Globe* was printed later, announcing DESTRUCTION OF THE COMBINED FRENCH AND SPANISH FLEETS, AND DEATH OF LORD NELSON, followed by three exclamation marks. A hastily printed second edition of *The Times* set the tone and pattern for every other report that was to follow: 'We know not whether we should mourn or rejoice. The country has gained the most splendid and decisive victory that has ever graced the annals of England: but it has been dearly purchased. The great and gallant Nelson is no more.' The *Courier and Evening Gazette* matched that lead at some length: 'It is with mixed sensations of transport and anguish, of the deepest joy and the sincerest sorrow, that we communicate the most welcome and unwelcome news at once, that ever it fell to our lot to communicate. Providence has blessed His Majesty's Arms with a most signal Victory over the Combined Fleets; but it has thought fit to chasten our exultation by depriving us of a Man whose very name was a host and tower of strength – Lord NELSON was KILLED in the ACTION.' The *Sun*'s announcement followed a similar formula: 'We have this day to announce to our Readers the most GLORIOUS the most DECISIVE VICTORY ever obtained by the NAVY of GREAT BRITAIN; but we have at the same time to communicate an event, the knowledge of which will fill every British bosom with the deepest anguish – the GREAT, the GALLANT NELSON is NO MORE!'[11]

A week before the publication of these repetitive accounts, one London newspaper obtained and circulated a partial, and partially erroneous, version of the story, while at the same time wholly denying it credence. On Friday 1 November the *Star* had recounted that: 'Letters are said to have been received in Town from Lisbon, which state that a report prevailed there, that Lord NELSON had succeeded in destroying a great part of the combined fleet in the harbour of Cadiz.' Confused and incomplete though it was, this was the first news of the battle printed in England. 'We wish we could add,' the paragraph continued, 'that there were grounds for believing this intelligence; but as no such accounts have been received at the Admiralty, we can hardly give it credit.' When *The Times* reiterated the Lisbon rumour the following morning, it was again discredited: 'rather as an anticipation of what may be expected, than what has been really atchieved'. But in the sensational flood of reports published four days later, the *Star* was able to claim priority over all competitors in reporting the 'GREAT NAVAL VICTORY', and take 'great satisfaction in announcing that the intelligence given in this Paper on Friday last . . . is confirmed'. This time the desire expressed was not for verification of the news, but for denial. 'We wish we could add that it has been accompanied with no cause of regret to the Nation, but that, alas! we cannot do.'[12]

The *London Gazette* – 'Published by Authority of His Majesty's Britannic Government' – appeared twice weekly, on Tuesdays and Saturdays. It customarily contained royal proclamations, notices of parliamentary Acts, military and naval promotions and the names of gentlemen recently declared bankrupt, together with proceedings against them in the Court of Insolvency. 'Supplements' to the *Gazette*, containing important additional information, might occasionally be published on Mondays or Thursdays. But truly momentous events called for an issue that was not merely supplementary to the one preceding. And so, on Wednesday 6 November, a *London Gazette* EXTRAORDINARY was published, containing – without editorial rhetoric – copies of Collingwood's dispatches received by Admiralty Secretary William Marsden in the early hours of that morning. Countering the recent, less welcome, news of crushing Austrian defeats at Ulm and Verona, the next day 'two thousand copies of the *Gazette Extraordinary* were ... dispatched by Government, to be dispersed over various parts of Italy and Germany, to revive the drooping spirits of the people after the late unexpected successes of the French Usurper.'[13]

*

Over the days that followed, victory was marked in the capital by all the usual expressions of patriotism – illuminations, fireworks, and bells – but 'I never saw so little public joy,' Lord Malmesbury recorded in his diary. 'The illumination seemed dim and as it were half-clouded by the desire of expressing the mixture of contending feelings; every common person in the streets speaking first of their sorrow for [Nelson], and then of the victory.' The *Morning Chronicle* likened it to 'the funeral honour paid ... to departed worth ... the illumination of the tomb'. Everywhere Lord Nelson's name was to be seen 'blazing in letters of living fire', recalled Benjamin Silliman. The young American chemist, passing through London on his way to university in Edinburgh, remarked that 'the blaze of the illumination threw a noon-day splendour over the city, and rendered the countenances of the people distinctly visible; but their expression was sorrowful; the victory was won, but Nelson was dead, and every thing wore the aspect of a nocturnal funeral, lighted by death fires.' A telling metaphor appeared in several publications: 'the cypress entwined with the laurel'. Even bells sounded the ambivalence: they rang in alternating cadences of exultation and solemnity, and between each joyous peal for the victory they tolled sonorously for the death of the man that had achieved it.[14]

Contrary to Lord Malmesbury's impression of moderated illumination, London, according to numerous reports, was aglow, and the only reason a 'general illumination' was deferred until the following night, the *Globe* reported, was because 'time did not permit the necessary preparations'. Nevertheless, by nightfall on 6 November, the Navy Office, the Mansion House and the Navy Coffee House in Newcastle Street, off the Strand, were 'lighted up with great brilliancy'. The East India Company's directors – owing perhaps the largest commercial debt to Nelson and the Royal Navy's protection – ensured their vast frontage on Leadenhall Street surpassed every other building in splendour, its six pillars 'nearly covered with lamps, the windows ... completely so'. There was a huge star in a frame of lamps at either end of the building, the initials G.R. framed in the same manner in honour of the King, and an anchor supported by laurels emblazoned the central portico. 'It was hardly possible to move along the street, the grandeur of the illuminations had attracted such a crowd of people.' The Guildhall also 'made a very splendid appearance' featuring a bust of Nelson crowned with laurel, and 'the Crown, Anchor, &c., extending almost over the whole front of the building'. In Whitehall, the 'splendid design' adorning the Admiralty also featured 'an anchor, the flukes in blue lamps, surmounted by a crown, and supported by G.R.' Nearby, the Treasury building 'exhibited similar devices, although the *tout ensemble* was not so splendid'. In the glare that spilled along the pavement opposite, the forgotten battle-maimed of St Vincent, the Nile and Copenhagen importuned alms. 'A squadron of shattered tars were drawn up *in line of battle*, at anchor,' *The Times* commented wryly, 'with their lights* *aloft*, all *well stowed* with *grog*, flourishing their mutilated stumps, *chearing all hands*, and making the best of their position, in collecting *prize-money*.'[15]

London tradesmen attempted to outdo rivals with the splendour of their illuminations and were well rewarded with mentions by name in the press. Three firms of glass-cutters and sellers, in St Paul's Churchyard, the Strand and Ludgate Hill, 'had each very handsome illuminations', although the glittering showroom of Mr Blades at the last address 'attracted the attention ... most

---

* Slang for eyes, but here, more literally, links or torches.

particularly' with 'a transparency of a first-rate man of war in full sail'. Bland's music shop in Oxford Street exhibited 'Britannia leaning on the Royal Oak' while Mr Joshua Trewinnard, a watchmaker in the Strand, 'had a bust of Lord Nelson, the stern of the *Victory*, and Britannia with a lion couchant'. In Fleet Street, Mr Taylor, a baker, opted for a spirit of playful decoration and 'amused the crowd with a representation of . . . perpetual motion, by placing two spiral pieces of foil on the end of a piece of wire, so as to be drawn round almost constantly by the blaze of each candle to which they were affixed'. For the most part, however, spectacle and solemnity were the rule; while the display might be elaborate, some single reverent phrase was central to it: 'Peace to the Soul of the Hero', for example, or 'Clarum et Venerabile Nomen'.* Mr Salter, a sword-cutler, exhibited 'a transparency very neatly painted' which read:

The Vict'ry's great – but
The Loss irreparable.

The print dealer and publisher Rudolph Ackermann could always be relied upon for a spectacular graphic display, and did not disappoint, not least because it served to promote his Repository of Arts in the Strand: 'A very beautiful transparency, from a painting by Sir William Beechey, of a handsome female figure, kneeling before an altar, on which is placed an urn, enveloped with smoke, laurels, and oak branches', and underneath: 'Sacred to the Memory of the Immortal Nelson.'[16]

But although the illuminations continued the following night, it was reported that the 'honest and proper feelings of the public prevented them from being general . . . Several houses that illuminated for the victory, decorated their candles with crape, testifying at once their joy and their sorrow.' Abraham Goldsmid of Finsbury Square set up in variegated lamps the message, 'I REJOICE FOR MY COUNTRY, BUT I MOURN FOR MY FRIEND.'

---

* 'Illustrious and Venerable Name'.

Even the destructive impulses, 'usual upon occasion of an extraordinary Victory' – the furious rapping on doors, the imperative chanting of 'Lights! Lights! Lights!' and the stoning of households thought lacking in due respect by neglecting to illuminate their windows – were curbed. The correspondent of the *Morning Chronicle* 'did ... not see a single pane of glass broken from one end of the town to the other'. This moderation on the part of the mob, he remarked, 'did honour to their feelings as Englishmen'. There were, however, shouts from the street in front of some unlit dwellings in Cheapside, and a man who had retired with his family 'at the sober hour of ten o'clock', placed a disarming notice in his window:

> Good Gentlemen, why
>   So loud do you cry?
> Ah! Why would you wish me to light?
>   Poor Lord Nelson is dead,
>   And my wife ill a-bed;
> So I hope you'll excuse me to-night.[17]

The restraint exercised in the City did not prevail further west, however, and 'a gang of disorderly persons, of the lower order, paraded the streets of Mary-la-bonne on Wednesday night, and committed outrages ... by breaking the windows of the houses which were not lighted up. These depredations were carried to extremities in Charlotte street, Rathbone place, Oxford street, and Hanover square, at which place it was necessary to obtain the assistance of Police Officers to disperse the rabble.'[18]

On the following night too 'the populace were very clamorous for lights'. The composer and songwriter Thomas Dibdin's windows in Charlotte Street, Fitzroy Square were saved from destruction by the courageous defence mounted by a house guest. Ironically, Dibdin and his wife were at the Theatre Royal, Covent Garden that Thursday evening, attending the opening performance of his one-act sketch, *Nelson's Glory* – one of the first dramatic responses to recent events – when a mob 'paraded the streets, breaking every window which did not happen to be illuminated in celebration of the ... Victory'. Hearing the approach of 'the "Light Company" ... vociferating for illumination', the guest, 'forgetful of his own safety ... deliberately presented himself at the most conspicuous [window] with a tall candle in each hand, and remained there till the house was completely lighted up' by the servants. Even well-lit streets were not spared the unruly attentions of such patriots. 'Opposite the Admiralty [in Whitehall], they were very troublesome, and caused terror and confusion by firing muskets and blunderbusses and throwing squibs ... A man and two boys, who were thus employed, were brought to Bow-street Office, and thence committed to Bridewell.'[19]

*

Oak, laurel and ribbon bedecked mail coaches – chocolate-brown vehicles of lifelong fascination to Thomas De Quincey – spread 'the heart-shaking news of Trafalgar' in all directions out of London, their drivers acting as unofficial, full-throated broadcasters at every stop. And as they travelled, towns and cities across the country lit up in their turn. The Mayor of Canterbury announced a 'GENERAL ILLUMINATION' to begin at six o'clock on Tuesday 12 November. Anxious to discourage the worst excesses of the London crowd, local magistrates proscribed 'the illegal practice of letting off Squibs, Rockets, and other fire-works', which 'not only [is] extremely dangerous and tend[ing] to produce tumult and disorder, but also prevents many of the inhabitants, and particularly Ladies, from partaking the pleasure of viewing the illumination'. The law was to be enforced with the utmost rigour and 'Constables ... placed in various situations, in order to apprehend those ... detected in any of the aforesaid practices'. The Canterbury illumination was a great success, although it was admitted that 'the exhibition would have been more splendid had not the wind prevented some part from having the desired effect.' The mayor himself surpassed his neighbours with 'a large and well executed transparency, representing Britannia, ... a lion couchant at her feet, entwining an urn with laurel which contained the bust of the late gallant Lord Nelson; under which was ... the ... inscription, "The much lamented Hero of England"'. In another part of the composition, French and Spanish colours were covered by the shield of Britannia, and a distant view of the fleets in battle could be discerned with a cherub flying over them, holding the sentence 'Heaven Will Reward Him.' Above this there was a likeness of Lord Nelson, another cherub crowning him with a wreath of laurel:

Sons of Britain Shed a Tear,
The Victory's Great, but Paid for Dear.[20]

Alderman Simmons displayed a more modest transparency and variegated lamps but compensated for deficient spectacle by presenting 'a butt of beer' to the populace, 'and appeared to enjoy the hilarity of those who partook of it'. Because magistrates had prohibited squibs and rockets, 'the passing throng were uninterrupted [by] noise, confusion, or indecorous behaviour.'[21]

At Winchester Cathedral the bells rang out in jubilation, 'then changed to the doleful muffled and concluding knell for the departed'. Fifteen miles away, at Andover, the opposite pattern prevailed, 'a muffled peal to the memory of Lord Nelson' followed by 'round ringing for the discomfiture of the Combined Fleet'. The Mayor of Southampton was attending a performance at the Theatre Royal when he was handed a letter informing him of the victory. Interrupting the entertainment he had it read from the stage. 'The utmost exultation ensued, and *Rule Britannia* was sung.' Later, the Southampton Loyal Volunteers fired a *feu de joie* in the High Street, opposite the Audit House, where the mayor assembled the gentlemen of the town to drink a bumper to the glorious victory. In the evening the town blazed with a general illumination, Mr Baker's library attracting much notice and Mr Bell, proprietor of the George Inn, exhibiting an elegant transparency, executed by a local artist. The Crown Inn, the Star and the Dolphin were also very splendidly illuminated. Meanwhile, the band of the Loyal Volunteers paraded the streets, playing the Dead March from *Saul* – Handel's staple for mourning – accompanied by muffled drums.[22]

In Bath, while 'the burst of transport ... equalled, if not surpassed, every former exulting occurrence of the kind; the bells incessantly rang, flags were displayed from the churches, and universal congratulations filled the streets – but there was no firing of cannons, or other tumultuous demonstrations of joy – which was attributed to the ... recollection that the illustrious lady of the great Nelson, and his amiable sister* ... and her family, were residents.'[23]

When news reached Brecon, 'alternative joy and grief was visible in every countenance,' and the following morning bells of the town churches rang out in honour of the victory, 'but in the afternoon they were muffled, and their mourning peals produced a solemn and impressive effect'. At Carmarthen, the response was less complicated. The mayor and corporation assembled at the Old Ivy Bush Inn and paraded behind the Volunteer Band who played 'God Save the King', 'Rule Britannia' 'and occasionally a solemn dirge ... with drums muffled'. A bonfire and 'several large bowls of punch' awaited their arrival in Market Street, where 'loyal and patriotic toasts were drank in copious libations'. At ten o'clock the company returned to the Old Ivy Bush 'and devoted the remainder of the evening to agreeable conviviality'.[24]

Elsewhere too, the victory was celebrated with revelry: simple, unambiguous and indulgent. At Tewkesbury, the local Volunteers fired three volleys in honour of the occasion and 'were regaled with plentiful libations of ale, by their Officers, and the evening was spent with great harmony'. An ox was slaughtered and roasted whole in Norwich, cut up and distributed with an unsparing quantity of bread and ale. In Shrewsbury fifteen sheep were roasted, and twelve barrels of ale supplied to the thirsty. Sheep and oxen were roasted in Chesterfield and gangs of men yoked themselves

---

* It is unclear whether this refers to Catherine Matcham or Susannah Bolton.

together to drag wood and coals for bonfires. French officers – prisoners of war quartered in that town awaiting parole – found it too much to bear and shut themselves up in their enforced lodgings until the celebrations were over.[25]

And so the news travelled northwards. The College Youths of Ashton-under-Lyne rang their muffled bells in 'a peal of grandsire caters, consisting of 611 changes', this having been calculated as corresponding to the precise number of lunar months 'in the Noble Admiral's life'. In Yorkshire a 'splendid Illumination' took place at Thornville Royal, home of the celebrated sportsman Colonel Thomas Thornton. The *York Herald* reported: 'a large concourse of people assembled in the Park, and in the style of ancient BRITISH HOSPITALITY, the memory of the regretted Hero and the health of the gallant survivors, together with the Fleet were drank with enthusiasm, in copious libations of Ale.' On the lawn, a band played 'several national and popular airs' while a large Chinese gong provided 'dismal jarrings ... to express the sorrow of the Groupe for the lamented Hero'. Seven years earlier a grove of oak trees had been planted on the estate to commemorate the battle of the Nile, and it was then that the mid eighteenth-century octagonal domed folly that crowned a nearby hill became known as the 'Temple of Victory'. By 1805 the grove was described as being 'in a luxuriant flourishing state, [that] may ... some day add strength to the British Navy'. In the meantime it furnished branches to decorate the illuminated 'Temple', festooned 'by the fair hands of several ladies'.[26]

The citizens of Wigton in north Cumberland had, for many years, relied upon a bell on top of the old market cross to summon them each market day to trade. But when news of the victory arrived, 'the populace, transported with joy, surrounded the ancient wooden cross of the place with bonfires, and actually burnt it to ashes.'[27]

The Wordsworths were told the news at breakfast in Patterdale on 10 November during a week-long walking tour in the vicinity of Ullswater. A maidservant put her head around the door and 'with an uncouth stare and a grin of pleasure', told them that there had been a great victory and Lord Nelson 'was shot'. Dorothy burst into tears but William counselled restraint 'till he had made further inquiries'. When told that there was 'great rejoicings at Penrith – all the Bells ringing', his sister was reassured: 'Then he cannot be dead!' she reasoned. When she learned to the contrary she was 'shocked' at the celebrations. Ten years later she would view the jubilation greeting Bonaparte's defeat at Waterloo with equal distaste – 'the joy of victory [being] an awful thing' – and profess 'no patience for the tinkling of ... Ambleside bells on [that] occasion'. Of Trafalgar she wrote no more in her diary, preoccupied as she was by the possible purchase of a piece of land by her brother.[28]

For William, writing in February the following year, 'there was little [in Nelson's death] to regret'. The poor state of his health meant 'that he could not have lived long', even if he had not been struck down by a French musket ball. Indeed, believed the poet, there was a strong likelihood that had he survived the battle he might have succumbed to the celebration: 'the first burst of exultation upon landing in his native country, and his reception here, would have been dearly bought ... by pain and bodily weakness.' Accompanying these observations to his patron Sir George Beaumont, Wordsworth enclosed a couple of verses 'written several weeks ago'. The poem began with a question:

Who is the happy Warrior? Who is he
That every man in arms should wish to be?[29]

The eighty-three lines that follow are a meditation on the heroic human character, 'allusive to Lord Nelson' but making no mention of him by name. They can be read – as they probably were by Lord Beaumont – as a paean of praise for the man whose dazzling career and death were being celebrated and mourned alike with idolatrous fervour across the nation. But, speaking thirty-six years later, Wordsworth declared that Nelson's life, 'was stained with one great crime, so that though these ... lines were suggested by what was ... excellent in his conduct, I have not been able to connect his name with the poem as I would wish, or even to think of him with satisfaction in reference to ... what a warrior ought to be.' The eleventh line – extolling the warrior paragon as one who 'makes his moral being his prime care' – suggests Nelson's disqualifying 'crime' was his adultery.

By contrast, in conversation with Isobel Fenwick in 1843 the poet went on to say that 'many of the elements of the character ... pourtrayed [in the poem] were found in my brother John.' Nearly nine months before Trafalgar, on 5 February 1805, the East Indiaman *Earl of Abergavenny* sank within sight of land in Weymouth Bay, after ripping open her hull on the Shambles sandbank southeast of Portland Bill. Over 260 crew and passengers perished in the freezing water, among them her commander, John Wordsworth, aged thirty-two. Later that year, during the Patterdale excursion with his sister, William composed an elegy which included the lines:

> The meek, the brave, the good, was gone;
> He who had been our living John,
> Was nothing but a name.

At its end *The Character of the Happy Warrior* contrasts the glamorous hero whose spectacular funeral rites were being planned during its composition, with the lowly, the decent, and the forgotten:

> 'Tis, finally the Man, who, lifted high,
> Conspicuous object in a Nation's eye,
> Or left unthought-of in obscurity ...
> Who, whether praise of him must walk the earth
> For ever, and to noble deeds give birth,
> Or he must fall, to sleep without his fame,
> And leave a dead unprofitable name ...

And it is this obscure, uncelebrated figure, who is extolled in the closing lines, and who:

Finds comfort in himself and in his cause;
And, while the mortal mist is gathering, draws
His breath in confidence of Heaven's applause.

The poem's last couplet answers the question posed in the first:

This is the happy Warrior; this is he
That every man in arms should wish to be.[30]

*

Sarah Collingwood was in a shop when the mail coach, 'covered with ribbands', arrived at the centre of Newcastle. She emerged onto the street as the coachman, his hat bound with black crape, 'declared the great victory'. But through repeated halts and iterations of the news on the 300-mile journey from London, the tragic sequel had been embellished: 'that Lord Nelson and all the Admirals were killed'. Sarah – who had not yet received the 'few lines' her husband had sent on board the *Pickle*, reassuring her he was safe – 'immediately fainted'.[31]

In Edinburgh, 'a round of the great guns was fired from the Castle' at eleven o'clock in the morning of 9 November, and again on the 14th to honour Strachan's later victory over the enemy. The publishing house of Constable & Co. in the High Street contributed to the city-wide show of illuminations, with an 'elaborate transparency' featuring 'Britannia sitting at the base of a Pyramid, in deep distress, contemplating the portrait of her hero, NELSON ... the words, *Death*, *Victory*, and *Immortality*, [and] a fine figure of *Fame* crowning the whole with the wreath of victory'. Below this, in front of 'the *British Lion* in an angry attitude' and a distant view of 'ships in close action', was arranged 'a number of Naval Engines and Trophies'. Sailors to left and right carried pennants bearing the names of Collingwood and William Carnegie, 7th Earl of Northesk, third-in-command at Trafalgar. The composition provided an opportunity to advertise the publisher's own tenuous contribution to the victory. Prominently displayed in the foreground still life was a copy of *An Essay on Naval Tactics* by John Clerk of Eldin, first published in 1790, and said to have originated the tactic of breaking the enemy's line employed by Nelson at Trafalgar. It had been recently re-issued by Constable in a one-volume, quarto second edition. The transparency painting was the work of the now forgotten Alexander Smiton, 'and when it is considered that the whole was *designed and executed* in the short space of *a day and a half*,' the *Scots Magazine* declared, 'it cannot but be regarded as a happy presage of what may hereafter be expected from this promising young artist'.[32]

On the north side of Edinburgh's George Square, the widow of Admiral Duncan kept the curtains of her drawing room windows open, showing to the street 'the grand family picture' of her late husband's greatest victory, the 1797 battle of Camperdown. In honour of Trafalgar, Lady Duncan had the canvas 'illuminated with lamps displayed in a very ingenious manner, making arches over two full rigged ships, with festoons, forming a fine drapery to the picture'. Deference was observed towards a more recently bereaved Edinburgh household – as it had been in Bath to Lady Nelson and her sister-in-law – 'out of respect to the memory of the gallant Captain DUFF, who fell in the action, the inhabitants of South Castle Street, where his Lady resides, much to their honour, did not illuminate.'

The *Caledonian Mercury* reported that 'a general illumination took place at Glasgow, and similar demonstrations of joy were manifested over the whole country.' Major General the Marquess of Huntly, celebrating the victory in Aberdeen 'with his usual generosity, ordered 100 bolls* of coals to be distributed among the poor of [the city]', and gave an elegant ball and supper to local worthies. The entrance to his house was embellished with an ornamented portico, decorated with various coloured lamps on its

---

* 'A measure of capacity for grain, etc., used in Scotland and N England, in Scotland *usu* = 6 imperial bushels, in England varying from 2 to 6 bushels; also a measure of weight, containing, for flour, 140lb' (*Chambers Dictionary*).

pediment and pillars. Above was a very beautiful transparent picture which included the now customary bust of Nelson crowned with laurel, a rock inscribed 'Britannia Rules the Waves!' and a dismasted ship of war, with the Union standard flying above a French tricolour. 'The whole, strongly illuminated and decorated with a border of coloured lamps, had a beautiful and impressive effect on thousands, who crowded from all quarters of [the] town to see it.'[33]

The same spectacular use of lamps and candles was manifest across Ireland, from Dublin to Belfast, and Londonderry to Limerick. At Newtown Limavady in the north, the elegant mansion of Fruithill was brilliantly illuminated, 'and from its elevated situation, and profusion of lights in every window, both front and rear, had a most beautiful effect'. The Marquess and Marchioness of Donegall celebrated with a lavish banquet for local gentry at their Belfast home. Decoration followed an arboreal theme: three great arches formed of green branches – probably oak – extending the entire length of the table, 'a beautiful transparency' in each. The central design pictured the King having French and Spanish standards laid at his feet by a naval hero. The inscription read, 'Now We are Crowned with Honour and Glory.' Toward the table's head two warships were framed, 'lashed in close action' and inscribed 'We have Finished the Work which Nelson Began.'[34]

Widely reported in the Irish papers as well as elsewhere, was the unfortunate experience of a Dublin resident who failed to illuminate his house in Dame Street. Mr Shannon, a Quaker whose religious principles did not permit him to illuminate on any occasion, least of all in celebration of war and conquest, was particularly persecuted by the zealous mob. 'They demolished almost every pane of glass in front of [his] house and broke many of the sashes.' They also threw squibs and firecrackers into every coach passing along the same thoroughfare and College Green, as well as 'firing horse pistols close to the ears of women and children, and hustling groups of people into corners to the amusement and benefit of the pickpockets'.[35]

II

LONDON theatres had rapidly supplemented their programmes when news of the victory arrived, and Thomas Arne's stirring 'Rule Britannia' – played on deck by the bands of the Royal Navy three weeks previously as ships moved slowly into firing range of the French and Spanish guns – was to be heard everywhere, bawled out from stage, pit, boxes and 'two shilling gallery' by performers and patrons alike. The audience were already singing it on Wednesday night at the Theatre Royal, Drury Lane, before the curtain rose on Storace and Cobb's comic opera *The Siege of Belgrade*. Then the entire company assembled to sing 'this most patriotic and loyal air'. It was reprised at the end of the performance, and 'if possible, with more spirit and enthusiasm than before', concluding 'amidst universal acclamations'. Then, 'amidst the ecstatic plaudits of every part of the house', Richard Wroughton declaimed 'with great effect' lines especially penned for the occasion by 'a veteran favourite of the Muses', Richard Cumberland*:

---

* Richard Cumberland (1732–1811), prolific author of sentimental domestic comedies, such as *The Brothers* (1769), *The West Indian* (1771) and most recently *The Sailor's Daughter* (1804). He figured in Sheridan's satire of theatre, *The Critic* (1779) as Sir Fretful Plagiary.

Is there a man, who this great triumph hears,
And with his transports does not mingle tears?
For, whilst BRITANNIA'S Flag victorious flies,
Who can repress his grief when NELSON dies?
Stretch'd on his deck amidst surrounding fires,
There PHOENIX like the GALLANT CHIEF expires;
Cover'd with trophies, let his ashes rest –
His memory lives in every BRITISH BREAST –
His dirge our groans – his monument our praise –
And whilst each tongue this grateful tribute pays,
His soul ascends to Heaven in Glory's brightest blaze!³⁶

That same night, at Covent Garden, following Colley Cibber's vintage comedy *She Wou'd and She Wou'd Not*, the audience was presented with 'a charming little spectacle, strikingly in unison with that mingled sentiment of exultation and regret, that now pervades the bosom of every British subject'. Following the overture – a medley of nautical ballads including 'A sweet little cherub sits up aloft' from Thomas Dibdin's sentimental nautical poem 'Poor Jack' and 'Cease, rude Boreas' from George Alexander Stevens's 'The Storm' – the curtain rose on an heroic tableau: 'a group of naval officers and sailors ... supporting the flag of Great Britain, with the prostrate ensigns of France and Spain at their feet, ... returning thanks to Heaven for the victory with which our arms have been blessed'. The theatre's scene painters had been hard at work producing a backdrop representing 'a view of the sea, and the fleets engaged'. It was described variously as 'a tolerable good stage effect' and 'a most pleasing *coup d'oeil*'. To either side of the stage was 'a naval pillar, with the names of our most renowned Commanders inscribed'. The ubiquitous *Rule Britannia* was sung by Mr Taylor, featuring an extra verse, dashed off by a Mr Ashley of Bath:

Again the loud toned trump of Fame,
   Proclaims that Britain rules the main;
While Sorrow whispers NELSON'S name,
   And mourns the glorious victor slain;

> Rule, brave Britons, Britons rule the main,
> Avenge the Go-o-o-o-od-like hero slain.[37]

By the following night, in the wake of Thomas Otway's tragedy, *Venice Preserv'd*, Dibdin's *Nelson's Glory* had been expanded and billed as a 'Loyal Musical Impromptu'. It opened with the inhabitants of an English village reading newspaper accounts of the victory, and singing what the *Monthly Mirror* described as 'a very good comic song', mocking the imperial pretentions of that 'Great Nation' France as contrasted to their own little island:

> O! It's a very great Nation,
> > Inspiring such trepidation;
>
> Our Island they scorn, and all folks that were born,
> > Independent of such a Great Nation.
>
> Their King they destroy'd, and all Europe annoy'd,
> > About Freedom and Equalisation;
>
> Yet the farce was scarce done, when behold they all run,
> > To the shew of a new Coronation ...
> > Now as to invasion there's little occasion,
> > For us to indulge speculation,
>
> Unless we send over and fetch 'em to Dover
> We never shall meet the Great Nation.
> Then while here we've true civilisation,
> And laws which apply to each station,
> > We'll stand by our King,
> > Heart and hand, and still sing.
>
> Little England against the Great Nation.

The previous night's tableau of Collingwood and sailors posed in triumph on the French tricolour was repeated, but with the addition of a mechanical stage effect: 'They all point up to heaven, from whence descends a bright cloud, enveloping [a painting of] NELSON, in a reclining posture, supported by *Britannia*, [and] an angel bending over him.' While its 'poetical merit [was] not very great', it was well received, and 'allowance made for the promptitude with which it was brought forward'. Dibdin admitted he had 'written [it] in a day', and that 'the performers in consequence of the few hours allowed in which to produce the piece, were generally indulged, by permission to read their parts publicly.' 'Rule Britannia' was reprised by the full band, 'every person in the house standing [heads] uncovered'. This rendering included yet another additional verse:

> Rest, rest in peace, bright honour's Son,
>   Thy Sires above will smile on thee;
> Glorious thy race on earth was run,
>   Who dar'd to die to keep us free:
>   Then mourn Britannia,
>   Britannia's Son so brave
>   Your laurels strew o'er NELSON's grave.[38]

The theatre critic of the *Monthly Mirror* did not disguise his contempt for such productions, 'brought out on the spur of the occasion', regarding them as an unfortunate but necessary concession to popular taste. 'They afford us no pleasure. They are puerile and trifling. But the people have been led to expect them, and the managers, no doubt, did their best to meet the public expectation.' The following week it was announced that the Loyal Musical Impromptu, 'having been presented a 4th time and having again been received with reiterated shouts of approbation,' was to be repeated every evening until further notice. Dibdin himself conceded that topicality alone 'ensured this flimsy drama a good reception: it was acted nine nights'.[39]

Meanwhile at the rival house in Drury Lane, Mr Cumberland's lines, first heard the previous week, were now extended into a 'New Melodramatic Piece', entitled *The Victory and Death of Lord Nelson*. The jaded correspondent of the *Monthly Mirror* knew well what to anticipate from 'these little temporary pieces', and that they were 'seldom suitable to the glorious occasion which calls them forth'. He envisaged 'a few pasteboard ships, a squib or two let off by the [theatre's] carpenters, and some sorry daub, bearing the name of the victorious hero, [guaranteed to] throw a sort of ridicule upon events that, *out* of the theatre, we contemplate with mingled gratitude, delight, and admiration.' His expectations were lowered still further because 'the late victory, clouded as it was with the death of the conqueror, increased the difficulty of bringing the subject upon the stage.' And so he was relieved to find that the comparatively restrained presentation adopted by the Drury Lane management 'was very judicious'. The lines, 'partly elegiac, partly encomiastic', from Mr Cumberland's 'classical pen', were spoken 'alternately, by Mr Elliston and Mrs Powell', the intervals 'filled up with solemn and appropriate music', and 'a well-composed air [was] most affectingly sung' by the eminent operatic tenor John Braham:

> In death's dark house the Hero lies
> Cold his heart and clos'd his eyes,
> His flag that to the foe ne'er bow'd,
> His signal once but now his shroud.[40]

Further particulars were supplied by the *Morning Post*. Although the overture and music were credited to Mathew Peter King, the 'pathetic air [performed] with the most happy effect' was not only sung, but composed by Braham:

> The Partner of his former wars,
> Views his dead body trenched with scars,
> He gave the wreck he could no more,
> All but his life was lost before.

Scenery was 'appropriate and splendid', the battle 'managed with good effect', and there were calls for Mr Braham's song to be encored:

> Death the great Conqueror could not win the whole,
> Earth keeps his ashes, Heav'n receives his soul.

The entire piece lasted no more than fifteen minutes. 'The most striking incident', according to the *Sun*, 'very ingeniously introduced', was the final tableau, as 'FAME descend[ed] with a scroll, on which appeared the emphatic words of the lamented Chief ... *England expects every man will do his duty*.'⁴¹

At Covent Garden, in addition to *Nelson's Glory*, a new comedy provided further topical interest. On 14 November, the first performance of *The Delinquent, or Seeing Company*, 'from the prolific pen of Mr. REYNOLDS',* incorporated a supposedly spontaneous recitation lauding the fallen hero, and featured a surprising costume transformation. The young heroine of the piece, Olivia Tornado – played by a twenty-three-year-old actress and dancer, Nannette Johnston – had 'neatly delivered' an amusing epilogue and appeared to be leaving the stage, when instead, 'throwing off some of the front of her dress', she turned round and presented herself to the audience, with a purple ensign 'hanging from the waist like an apron, the English Jack in one of the corners', and NELSON embroidered on it in gold thread. 'The effect was electric,' and 'the house rang with the most enthusiastic plaudits.' She waited, allowing the applause to subside, then abandoned her comic role to deliver what pretended to be the performer's true heartbroken sentiments:

> Thus having finish'd all my flippant part
> I now must speak the dictates of my heart.
> Each smile I wore conceal'd a tear,
> Which long'd to flow on NELSON's honoured bier!

Her eulogy continued with 'extraordinary feeling and force' for a further four couplets and concluded:

> The tidings Fame with muffled trumpet brings,
> And Victory mourns his loss, in sable wings.
> Britons she cries – tho' now my bosom bleeds.

---

* Frederic Reynolds (1764–1841).

Your naval sons shall emulate his deeds.
Thus shall his spirit, rising from his grave,
Make future NELSONS triumph on the wave!⁴²

While her concluding tribute was warmly applauded, Mrs Johnston's performance earlier in the evening had been heckled by a raucous element in the second tier of boxes. Two young gentlemen, Mr Jukes and Mr Mingay, were accompanied by a pair of prostitutes, Mrs Ross and Mrs Martin. While their protectors 'ridicul[ed] the characters and the performers as they came on the stage, in ... a loud tone of voice,' to the annoyance of other patrons, the 'two Cyprians'* – as one report euphemistically called them – peered through their opera glasses, 'frequently ... ridiculing Mrs. Johnston's dress, and talking very loud'. Sitting in a neighbouring box, the Scottish actor Henry Erskine Johnston – celebrated as the 'Edinburgh Roscius'† – was watching his wife's performance and becoming increasingly irritated as the interjections persisted. He frequently 'called out for silence, but in vain'. In honour of the recent naval engagement, and anticipating her dramatic 'reveal' at the end of the play, Mrs Johnston had pinned a pearl ornament into her coiffure representing a ship, and one of the observations shouted by the rowdy crew was that 'her head carried too much *sail*'. But the comment that most provoked the actress's husband concerned the degree to which she was exposing her legs, and 'that she ought to have let out a reef or two‡ in her petticoats'. Blows were exchanged, Mr Jukes's eye blacked, and 'his clothes, as also Mr. Johnston's, were much torn' during the ensuing scuffle. The combatants would appear the following morning at the magistrates' court – a couple of doors down Bow Street from the theatre – and as the matter had become 'the subject

---

* The island of Cyprus was said to have been the birthplace of Venus.

† Quintus Roscius Gallus (c.126–62 BC), a Roman actor, 'supreme in comedy, he also played tragic parts. His name became typical for a consummate actor' (Simon Hornblower and Anthony Spawforth, eds, *The Oxford Classical Dictionary*, 3rd edn (1996)).

‡ A nautical term for lengthening sail.

of legal investigation', the *General Evening Post* refrained from further comment in its report, apart from concluding that the incident had been all too typical 'of a species of Nuisance, which has of late encreased greatly, and threatens to drive all decent company from a quarter of the Theatre, formerly select, but now the vortex of indecency and impertinence'. Nevertheless, the fracas having subsided by the play's end, the epilogue and its sequel were performed without further distraction. A more chivalrous and gentler wit remarked – on seeing Nelson's name glittering across the region of Mrs Johnston's thighs – 'that though the Hero died in the arms of VICTORY, he yet lived in the lap of BEAUTY'.[43]

*

Drury Lane and Covent Garden were not the only houses to celebrate the victory and profit from its dramatic and popular potential. Another 'new loyal impromptu', called *Nelson's Farewell, or Victory and Death*, was performed just off the Strand, at Mr Laurent's Loyal Theatre of Mirth, in the Lyceum.[44]

East of the Strand, Bow Street and Covent Garden, the Royalty Theatre in Goodman's Fields advertised a 'New Grand Naval Spectacle' entitled HE DIED FOR HIS COUNTRY, or NELSON VICTORIOUS. It was played out in front of a series of backdrops, beginning with Cadiz Bay and the engagement of Combined and British Fleets and climaxing on Tower Hill and the arrival of the 'Glorious News'. This was followed by a 'Grand Allegorical Sketch', BRITANNIA'S CONSOLATION and NELSON IMMORTAL, featuring the characters of Nelson himself, Captains Hardy, Duff and Cooke, Admirals Villeneuve and Gravina, the British tars Jack Junk, Tom Reef and Ben Tack, and the figures of Fame, Mars and Britannia.[45]

Towards the end of November, Mr Friedrich Schirmer's 'elegant little theatre' in Leicester Place – described in the *Globe* as a 'grand emporium of fashion and taste', and licensed for 'Musical and Dramatical Interludes in the German Language' – departed from its customary repertoire to offer 'a new Optical Piece' in commemoration of the 'VICTORY and DEATH of the Ever Lamented Lord Nelson.' The entertainment comprised a series of 'most interesting, new, and appropriate Optical Sceneries' projected onto a screen in the darkened auditorium, effects made possible by the 'magic lantern' technology of the Phantasmagoria, a popular novelty, recently introduced from France. The show began with a small figure of Fame bearing a laurel wreath and descending to a bust of Nelson. 'This figure increased in size and when nearly as large as life, placed the wreath on the head of Nelson, and vanished.' Next, a projection of the hero himself appeared from the darkness 'exalting the British flag in Egypt'. Then followed Britannia contemplating his bust and a monument to his memory, 'appropriate music accompanying every change'. The spectacle ended with a transparency of George III and the band playing 'God Save the King'. 'The audience greeted the image of their beloved Sovereign, with reiterated applause.' Mr Schirmer, the chief London exponent of Phantasmagoria, had advertised an 'Optical Masquerade' earlier in the month, and during the following year, an 'Optical Ballet', presumably offering similar wonders, although no indication was given of either attraction's content or relevance to current loyal sentiments. However, a 'beautiful transparency' of Britannia blazed on the outside of the building, bearing the words: '*Victorious Nelson, I will Revenge thy Death.*' Commemorative tributes continued at the German Theatre with 'a New Musical Drama, NELSON'S ARRIVAL IN ELYSIUM', and a Prologue performed by the proprietor's fifteen-year-old son, Master Albert Schirmer, 'in the character of a Sailor'.[46]

*

The establishment best equipped to do dramatic justice to the Navy's latest triumphs was the Aquatic Theatre at Sadler's Wells, under the inventive management of Charles Dibdin.* At its inaug-

---

* Charles Isaac Mungo Pitt-Dibdin, elder brother of Thomas John Dibdin, author of *Nelson's Glory*.

uration in 1804, the public had been promised 'superb naval spectacle[s] on real water, through the medium of which will occasionally be exhibited every naval exploit of consequence that may occur'. Eight thousand cubic feet of water, supplied from the New River which ran alongside the theatre, was collected in a tank on stage measuring ninety feet long, twenty-five feet wide and about five feet deep. 'The judicious advantage made of [this] by the Management, is a novelty no other Theatre can boast,' the *Daily Advertiser* enthused, 'and must unquestionably excite considerable interest.' The first production to make use of the new facilities was advertised with a title in Greek:

Ωχέανέια

It was, recalled Dibdin, 'intended to excite public notice from its singularity'. The word translated as 'Oceania' and was meant 'to convey, to those who understood it [an] intention of producing a series of representations, connected with every species of aquatic exhibition'. The full advertisement gave further particulars of the attraction:

> A Grand Naval Spectacle
> on
> Real Water;
> representing the
> *Siege of Gibraltar*
> with
> Real Ships
> built and rigged (on an inch scale)
> by Shipwrights and Riggers
> from his
> Majesty's Dockyard, at Woolwich.[47]

The blockade of the British garrison by French and Spanish sea and land forces was a distant, three-year-long sideshow of the American War of Independence. It culminated in mid September

1782, with the catastrophic failure of a combined assault, and the destruction of ten Spanish floating batteries by hot shot fired from gun emplacements on land, and a naval relief convoy led by Captain Roger Curtis. During the resultant carnage, Curtis gained celebrity, and a subsequent knighthood, by coordinating the rescue of several hundred burnt and drowning Spanish sailors.

Mr Dibdin later recalled the popular reception of his Aquatic Theatre's first success. 'The representation of the Rock and fortress of Gibraltar on one side, and the mimic ocean spreading itself on the other ... acted like electricity; a pause of breathless wonder was succeeded by stunning peals of acclamation; and when the Ships sailed down, in regular succession, "rolling on their way", their sails shifting to the wind; their colours and pennants flying; and their ordnance, as they passed the front of the Stage, firing a grand salute to the Audience, [they] seemed in an extacy ... Ships were dismantled, dismasted and sunk; the memorable "*red hot balls*" ... played upon and occasioned the blowing up of the Spanish Gun boats; and when these were in flames, burning down to the water's edge, the effect produced by the reflection of the fire ... in the water, was truly magnificent.' Compensating for the reduced size of the 1:12 model ships, children – known as 'water boys' – were employed both to manoeuvre the craft into position and, suitably costumed, 'affecting to struggle with the waves', as drowning Spanish sailors. 'The enthusiasm of the Audience exceeded all bounds.' It was, declared the *Monthly Mirror*, 'a contrivance so highly meritorious and clever, as to insure crowded houses for a considerable time.'[48]

But two years later, the Aquatic Theatre was unable to swiftly capitalise on Nelson's victory and death, because Dibdin had taken a lease on the Royal Amphitheatre in Dublin for the winter season to revive an entirely un-nautical pantomime: *Harlequin Aesop or Wisdom versus Wealth*. The Irish venture was not a success, losing the management between one and two thousand pounds, and on Dibdin's return to town, in the new year, he 'produced, as quickly as [he] could', a programme of entertainment for Sadler's Wells which included a new piece featuring 'the Battle of Trafalgar on real water'. It received its first performance on Easter Monday, 7 April 1806. The model ships made for the *Siege of Gibraltar* were once again pressed into service for the battle and 'when the Enemy struck, a most splendid representation of the "*Apotheosis of Nelson*" rose out of the water and ascended into the Cloud Borders of the Scene.' But apart from the following morning's *Advertiser* deeming it to be 'well managed, well conceived and executed as well as a subject can be on the boards of a Theatre', it met with near total indifference in the press. Even the applause on the night had been lacklustre, 'general, but not *heart and hand*'. Despite its potential for patriotic appeal and being a perfect aquatic subject to exploit this theatre's unique facilities, the spectacle failed to impress. Dibdin later admitted he had underestimated the insatiable demands of his audience, their craving for novelty, and their resentment at being short-changed. 'People had seen the Ships before, the surprize they had excited had subsided, and they were disappointed.' It dropped from the repertoire, and from further notice in the press, after only a fortnight.[49]

*

Men of the Navy were darlings of the British public. At once, the simple epitome of heroic service, and a subject of comical anecdote in the press, they were generally treated with indulgence. Even before Trafalgar, the character of 'honest Jack Tar' had been a popular favourite. In 1804, at Sadler's Wells, a sailor slid down one of the pillars from the gallery onto the edge of the stage, in order to settle a dispute as to the veracity of the 'Real Water' featured in the *Siege of Gibraltar*. It was only by plunging in and splashing about that he was able to test this to his satisfaction and shout up to his mates that it was indeed real. 'It became such a mania with our Naval Friends ... that scarcely a night passed for a week or ten days, without one or other performing a similar feat,' recalled Charles Dibdin, 'till at length, to prevent what at first was a joke, but now became an annoyance, I threatened to send one to the Watch House, after which we had no more divers.' But after Trafalgar they could do no wrong. On 27 December 1805, at Covent Garden, a performance of *Romeo and Juliet* was attended by 'a party of musical sailors in the two-shilling gallery, who sang favourite airs, *gratis*, almost without intermission, the entire night'. Despite this competition, Miss Smith as Juliet displayed 'much ability', although the fourteen-year-old Master William Betty in the male lead was judged 'unsuccessful'. Covent Garden, it seemed, particularly attracted seamen. The previous night, during a performance of Matthew Lewis's five-act tragedy *Alfonso, King of Castile*, the audience had been greatly entertained by a sailor described as being 'a little in liquor' – and such was the uproar he caused that 'few words of many scenes were distinctly heard'. He began by shouting up from the pit to his messmates in the gallery 'to stow their jabber', only to raise himself on one of the seats a little later and call for 'three hearty cheers for Nelson and the Nile', drawing a roaring response from the entire house. At this point he took from his pocket a medal that he announced had been struck and awarded to all those who had fought at the aforesaid battle. Strung on a length of black ribbon, it was in mourning, he declared, for his late commander. This was greeted again with much applause and he swung the treasured artefact around his head throughout the rest of the night. The band had, unaccountably, neglected thus far to include 'Rule Britannia' in the evening's programme and the sailor called repeatedly for it between each act of *Alfonso*. When the play came to an end, he clambered his way to the front row of the pit, where he leant on the rail separating orchestra from audience and appealed directly to the musicians, flourishing his medal, until it was played. Satisfied, he remained tranquil throughout *The Wild Islanders*, a new ballet set in China. It was during the interval between this and the ever-popular *Nelson's Glory* that the sailor pushed his way through the orchestra and succeeded in climbing onto the stage, where, intoxicated as much by celebrity as rum, he addressed the audience, offering them a dance or a song. 'A Song! A Song!' roared the gallery. But before he could comply with the request, he was lured offstage by one of the company beckoning from the wings and persuaded to remain there until *Nelson's Glory* was nearing its climax. Then Mr Charles Incledon, the resident tenor – himself a former seaman – came forward and made an announcement:

> LADIES and GENTLEMEN, One of the brave Crew of the VICTORY begs your permission to appear before you on this occasion, that he may join in the chorus of 'RULE BRITANNIA.'[50]

Welcomed back onto the stage among the assembled cast, the sailor seized a Union flag from one of the performers and waved it wildly until the chorus was finished, and even then, refused to give it back. From a drunken figure of fun, he was at that moment transfigured in the eyes of the audience into the living embodiment of national heroism. 'When the honest Tar indicated a resolution not to part with the flag ... the Theatre resounded with the highest acclamations of spontaneous approbation. It was a scene of such true sensibility, that the cheeks of numbers of the spectators, both male and female, were bedewed in tears of sorrow, gratitude, and joy, on the recollection of the GLORIOUS VICTORY.'

The sailor's name was Thomas Jackson. He was 'apparently about thirty years of age' and had served under Nelson at Santa Cruz de Tenerife in 1797. As his medal testified, he had also fought at the Nile – though not, it seems, at Trafalgar.

*

The theatre-going public was quick to applaud but just as quick to condemn. A glaring misjudgement of popular taste was committed at the King's Theatre, Haymarket on Saturday 7 December 1805, the opera season's opening night. 'Uncommonly crowded' and with well over a score of assorted aristocrats in attendance, it promised to be a glittering occasion. The refurbished house had 'undergone a complete repair, the painting look[ed] extremely fresh, and the drop-scenes [had] been retouched in many places'. The singers – Elizabeth Billington and Josephina Grassini – were 'in fine voice and divided the applause which was enthusiastic' for

Peter von Winter's 'Grand Serious Opera with Chorusses', *Il Ratto di Proserpina* that began the evening's programme. Then came, at great expense, a 'new Melo-Dramatic Ballet, entitled *Naval Victory and Triumph of Lord Nelson*'. It was the 'invention' of the ballet master, Signor Rossi, and was set to music by the Austrian pianist and composer, Joseph Woelfl, 'whose genius [was] universally acknowledged'. In addition to 'all the first DANCERS', the tenor John Braham, contralto Grassini and soprano Billington, were to 'contribute their wonderful powers for the success of the piece'. It comprised four scenes: the quarterdeck of *Victory* and the wounding of Nelson, his death below decks, celebrations in front of the Admiralty and, finally, an allegorical pageant featuring the entry of Britannia and attendant Roman deities in a chariot drawn by lions, together with the Temple of Immortality, containing a painted likeness of the Hero, descending from the clouds.[51]

Audience displeasure was apparent from the start, at 'the incongruity of *British* Seamen singing *Italian* duets and trios', but it was when the performer playing Nelson made his appearance that 'the House, as with one voice, expressed its dissatisfaction.' The objection was not to the actor's performance in the role as such, but to the role's being performed at all. 'To personify Lord Nelson,' the *Morning Chronicle* argued, 'to delineate his attitudes, expressions, and action – to see him receive the fatal shot – and, finally, to represent the workings of nature in the moment of his dissolution, was a thing beyond the reach of the dramatic Muse, much less of Ballet.' The *Sun* suggested that 'if only a graphic representation [of Nelson] had been introduced, the Audience would doubtless have testified the highest respect and sympathy.' It was, however, 'injudicious in the extreme to exhibit a mimic appearance of his death while the People [were] deeply bewailing the reality'. And it was during the second scene, 'at the exhibition of the dying agonies of their beloved hero, in his last and solemn moments', that the offence became most audible and hissing could be heard from every part of the theatre. The *Monthly Mirror* pronounced that 'the circumstances were too ... sorrowful [to] bear sporting with.' The critic of the *Morning Herald* – who had objected to the

Royal Navy singing Italian – placed the blame on Signor Rossi, in that 'the structure of the Piece was committed to the hands of a Foreigner, who ... could certainly be no judge of the feelings of a British Audience.' The *Sun* conceded that 'at a future period such [a production] might be well received, but the impression of the loss is at present too recent,' and the *Morning Chronicle* agreed, declaring that 'it must be to griefs of other times, to passages of our history, which, however grand, awful, and impressive, at the time, have been softened down to a lenient recollection, that it is the province of the dramatic art to apply its powers.' It was, in short, too soon for theatrical presentation. Between the second and third scenes, the management sent Mr Braham on stage to placate the audience. He announced that 'any offensive part should [in future performances] be suppressed,' but begged their indulgence to allow the less contentious second half of the spectacle – being 'altogether allegorical' – to continue. The performance went on 'amidst a general murmur', despite Signor Rossi's talents as both choreographer and dancer in the third scene being 'displayed with a most auspicious felicity', and Billington, Grassini and Braham singing 'with exquisite effect' in the roles of Britannia, Minerva and Mars. Nevertheless, 'the Spectators having taken an impression against the piece in the first instance, were not to be reconciled to it.' The management bowed to public pressure and Mr Braham was again sent out after the final curtain fell to announce that the ill-conceived piece would be entirely withdrawn. The Haymarket debacle must have seemed especially crass just forty-eight hours after the National Day of Thanksgiving and its attendant gravity.[52]

*

Twenty-four hours after the battle Admiral Collingwood had issued a General Order from on board *Euryalus*, that 'a Day should be appointed of general Humiliation before God, and Thanksgiving for his merciful Goodness, imploring Forgiveness of Sins, a Continuation of his Divine Mercy, and his constant Aid to us in Defence of our Country's Liberties and Laws, without which the utmost Efforts of Man are nought.' The date planned for this holy purpose was left blank and a note appended: 'The Fleet having been dispersed by a gale of wind, no day has yet been able to be appointed for the above purpose.' Originally intended by Collingwood as applying only to the fleet, the scope of thanksgiving was extended by Royal Proclamation to the nation.[53]

'Perhaps at no period has the extinction of our national glory been so contemptuously menaced, and our utter extirpation so formidably pursued,' the Revd Andrew Hatt reminded worshippers from the pulpit of St Paul's on Thursday 5 December. 'And on no occasion has our national character been raised to a more glorious pre-eminence; or the anticipated triumph of an implacable enemy been succeeded by a more humiliating reverse.' The order of service included Handel's setting of Exodus, chapter 15, verses 3 and 4, from *Israel in Egypt*:

> The Lord is a man of war; the Lord is his name; Pharoah's Chariots, and his Host, hath he cast into the Sea; his chosen Captains also are drowned in the Red sea.[54]

Elsewhere that day, sermons were composed and declaimed and money collected. 'Think on the Widow, and the Orphan,' the Reverend Robert Wood urged his parishioners in Sneinton, Nottinghamshire, 'think on a Husband lost – a Brother maimed, and Children helpless left as doves unfledged.' Nicholas Bull at Saffron Walden gave thanks that Britain – an island nation – did not have the experience of war fought over its native soil and accordingly, he did not spare his listeners a harrowing account of those who had, '[their] fields devastated, ... rivers swelled with carnage, ... cities burnt with fire'. Warming to his theme, he reminded his wide-eyed flock of the horrors they had escaped: 'We know not what it is to see the fruits of our land swept down untimely as forage for the war-horse, our stores of provision consumed by the rapacious plunderer, our wives and our daughters defiled by violence and brutality, and the mangled bodies of our countrymen and friends scattered unburied on the field of battle, with garments rolled in blood! We have not been startled, at the solemn hour of midnight, by the approach of an insidious and unrelenting enemy, nor been compelled to fly, half naked, by the light of our blazing habitations; whilst the shrieks of our companions and the shouts of their murderers, have swelled after us upon the wind.' And despite Bonaparte's latest invasion plans being averted, there were no grounds for complacency. James Rouquet, in West Harptree, Somerset, warned his congregation that a continued threat of imperial aggression remained, of foreign armies bearing before them the same warlike emblems of earlier conquerors: 'succeeding Scipios, yet, to spread the terror of the Roman eagle'.

A more abstruse discourse was delivered by Samuel Horsley, Lord Bishop of St Asaph. The published text of his sermon ran to nearly twenty-five pages, largely devoted to expounding on the status and function of angels and archangels – 'Watchers and Holy Ones' – in delivering the will of God. Only in the final pages did he begin to address the nation's principal reason for giving thanks that December, and even then, only on the very last page was reference made to the 'Great Commander, whose grave is strewed with laurels, and bedewed with his country's tears'. The bishop's lesson was that 'the fortunes of kings and empires are in the hand of God' and mortal intervention largely incidental to that design. 'In the case of Antichrist', he declared, prophesy is explicit. So clearly is it foretold, that he shall rise; so clearly is it foretold that he shall fall. So clearly is it foretold, that he shall raise himself to power by successful War; so clearly is it foretold, that War, fierce and furious War, waged upon him by the faithful, shall be, in part, the means of his downfall.' This martial tool of the Almighty, he argued, refuted 'the despicable cant of puritans about the unlawfulness of War'. Regarding the present crisis, His Grace concluded: 'if, as we hope and trust, it is the will of God, that the vile Corsican shall never set foot upon our shores; the loyalty and valour of the country are, we trust, the appointed means of his exclusion.'[55]

Since its formation at Lloyd's Coffee House in 1803, on the renewal of hostilities with France, the committee of the Patriotic Fund had served the purpose 'of assuaging the anguish of wounds, or palliating in some degree the more weighty misfortune of loss of limbs – of alleviating the distresses of the widow and orphan – of smoothing the brow of sorrow for the fall of dearest relatives, the props of unhappy indigence or helpless age – and of granting pecuniary rewards or honourable badges of distinction for successful exertions of valour or merit'. The battle of Trafalgar and Sir Richard Strachan's action of 4 November were expected to present 'about 1,300 cases more to the notice of the Committee, and ... require a provision from the Fund to the extent of about £80,000.' The Committee's coffers were greatly swelled by the Day of Humiliation and Thanksgiving, although not to the requisite provision mentioned. £18,000 had already been donated to the Fund, and collections on 5 December yielded a further £14,600. At St Paul's the collection was made in four golden bowls 'of large dimension' presented by the Lord Mayor. His Worship also donated £50, as did the Duke of Cambridge, bringing that total to £300 11½d. At the Surrey Chapel in Southwark about £360 was collected, a considerable portion of it donated by a single individual. One of the sidesmen noticed a sealed paper which proved to contain a £100 banknote wrapped around a new halfpenny piece. The paper was inscribed, 'A Widow's Mite'.[56]

III

'HOW is the Body to be landed?' John Tyson asked. 'In a Cask of Spirits and rolled into the Painted Chamber? Or decently carried there in his Coffin?' As Nelson's former purser, secretary, and now custodian of his late master's dignity in death, it was only right that Tyson should address the arrangements for transferring his corpse from HMS *Victory* to the most opulent ceremonial space the Naval Hospital at Greenwich had to offer. Trundling it ashore in a barrel was clearly unthinkable when a respectable alternative had been bespoke six years earlier.[57]

In May 1799 – two years prior to his ship's capture by the French – Captain Benjamin Hallowell, of *Swiftsure*, sent Nelson a coffin constructed of pine and iron taken from the main mast of *L'Orient*, the 118-gun French flagship that blew up during the battle of the Nile. The captain's macabre gift 'was made of deal planks not more than an inch thick; being six feet in length, but rather narrow'. A covering letter explained that 'when you are tired of this life you may be buried in one of your own Trophies'. Nelson kept the *memento mori*, standing it upright behind his chair in the Great Cabin of his own flagship *Foudroyant*, but later left it in the care of a cabinetmaker in Brewer Street. Mr Peddison claimed that, before he left England for the last time in September 1805, his lordship left instructions that an attestation of its warlike origins was to be engraved on the lid because, he said, 'I think it highly probable that I may want it on my return.' The remark has fed speculation regarding a supposed death wish.[58]

Taken from its cask at Spithead on 11 December, the corpse was found to be in 'a state of perfect preservation, without being in the smallest degree offensive'. Internal examination, however, showed 'the condition of the bowels ... to be much decayed, and likely in a short time to communicate the process of putrefaction to the rest of the Body'. Surgeon William Beatty therefore took the precaution 'to remove from the body the greatest part of the contents of the Chest and Abdomen ... excepting the Heart'. That exception – traditionally the seat of reason, emotion and spirit – was largely symbolic, subject as it was to putrefaction like the rest. Then, 'surrounded with Cotton and Linnen Wrappers ... and rolled throughout with bandages of the same in the antient mode of Embalming,' the corpse was placed in a leaden coffin full of camphor- and myrrh-laced brandy, the ship's stock of pure wine spirit being exhausted.[59]

It remained immersed in the pungent liquor until 21 December when, in the presence of the *Victory*'s officers, the body was examined again. Two months dead to the day, it was 'found still in most excellent condition, and completely plastic ... its undecayed state ... excit[ing] the surprise of all who beheld it'. Admittedly, when the face was exposed, its features 'were somewhat tumid, from absorption of the spirit', but after judicious rubbing with a napkin 'they resumed in a great degree their natural character'. It was, however, a deceptive and transient condition. Beatty was concerned that removal of the linen bandages 'may be attended with the unpleasant circumstance of the skin coming off the body' as well. And even were the delicate operation to be successfully accomplished, he confessed that the Admiral's facial features could not 'at this distant period of his demise be easily traced', and, therefore, 'the features being lost, the Face cannot with propriety be exposed during the time which the body may lay in state.'[60]

The deceased's eldest sibling William – rector of Hilborough, prebendary of Canterbury Cathedral, newly ennobled, and soon to be greatly enriched by Act of Parliament to support his status as 1st Earl Nelson of Trafalgar – was kept informed by the Revd Alexander Scott concerning 'the remains of his exceeding lamented, and late brother'. His lordship expressed himself 'perfectly satisfied' with the measures Beatty had taken, but 'cou'd have wished to have known what was done with the bowels, whether they were thrown overboard or whether they were preserved to be put into the Coffin with the Body'. Scott neglected to enlighten him as to the integrity of the corpse, but Jacob Richards of *Euryalus*, writing home from Spithead, claimed that the body 'was Opened & his Entrails taken out & hove Overboard in a Ledden Case'.[61]

On 22 December Gaetano Spedillo, Nelson's Sicilian valet, dressed the corpse in 'a shirt, a pair of silk stockings, and uniform breeches... a white cambric handkerchief... tied round the neck, and another bound round the forehead to the back part of the head', before it was laid in the pine sarcophagus upholstered for it by Mr Peddison in 'white silk, stuffed with cotton'. This was enclosed in 'a leaden coffin lined with thick planks of oak', which was in turn placed in yet another, of elm. As *Victory*'s carpenter William Bunce performed his admiral a final service and soldered the lead coffin shut for ever, Beatty observed that this was 'the last time the mortal part of the lamented Hero was seen by human eyes'. The long-retarded corruption of that part resumed unobserved, the rest granted immortality and elevation to national icon.[62]

The three-fold weight of coffins enclosing the frail corpse now amounted to nearly a quarter of a ton, and, with a handle at head and foot and three to either side, was 'Slung so that six or eight men [could] carry it'. Wrapped in one of *Victory*'s colours and secured by a length of stout rope, it was lowered from *Victory* to the *Chatham*, a yacht commandeered by Tyson from the Sheerness Dockyard. Arriving at Greenwich in the early afternoon of Tuesday 24 December, the body was carried from the water's edge to the Hospital.[63]

*

By the year's end, *Victory* was docked at Chatham, a convenient carriage drive for the London curious. 'We scarce have room to move,' Able Seaman John Brown complained, 'the Ship is so full of Nobility ... looking at shot holes.' She had received, it was said, 'upwards of eighty shot between wind and water'. A rumour had spread among the crew that 'there is three hundred of us Pickt out to go to Lord Nelson['s] Funeral we are to wear blue Jackets white Trowsers and a black scarf round our arms and hats.' That number was reduced to forty-eight, in the final funeral arrangements – thirty-six seamen and twelve marines – the total coinciding with the forty-seven years of Nelson's lifespan, rounded up for ceremonial symmetry. The reduction was not the only shortfall in expectation. Brown had been told that all would receive a 'gold medal for the battle of Trafalgar Valued £7 1s. round our necks'. True, Matthew Boulton – proprietor of the Soho Mint in Handsworth, outside Birmingham* – had recently announced the intention of striking, at his own expense, a medal to commemorate the battle, 'and to present one to every seaman who served that day on board the British Fleet'. But Boulton's patriotic generosity did not extend to gold. Officers would receive one in copper, the rest in pewter. Many presented with the base 'white metal' products are said to have thrown them overboard in disgust on discovering they were not even silver, and therefore worthless in a pawnshop.[64]

*

At eight o'clock in the morning of Friday 3 January 1806, Nelson's fourth, final and most splendid coffin was carried from a shop in Pall Mall, the premises of Mr France, 'Upholder† to the King'. Carefully wrapped in cotton sheeting, it was loaded into the hearse, a quantity of straw laid on the bed of the vehicle to protect the precious artefact from damage. 'Considered as the most elegant and superb ever seen in Europe,' it was constructed of mahogany,

---

* Boulton's Soho steam presses were responsible for producing most of the government's coinage and he had earlier designed and manufactured the Nile medal at cost price.

† Upholsterer, and by extension one dealing in furnishing. In this case, undertaker.

although no one seeing it during the following week would be able to identify the wood, tautly covered as it was in black Genoa velvet, secured by 'treble rows of double gilt nails', numbering 'upwards of 10,000'. It was further decorated with 'gold matt, enclosed and chased' emblems. In addition to the orders and crests awarded the deceased in life, the designs included a British lion, 'one of his paws laid on the Gallic Cock', a sphinx and a crocodile, Britannia and Neptune drawn in triumph by sea horses and, also denoting maritime supremacy, a dolphin, 'noblest fish of the sea'. This last motif was intended as a subtle affront to Britain's traditional enemy, being formerly the exclusive entitlement of an heir to the French throne: the 'Dauphin'.

As soon as the doors of the hearse were secured, Mr Chittenden,* 'fearful lest the velvet or his workmanship should suffer any injury through the carelessness of the common driver', mounted the box, took up the reins and elected to drive the vehicle himself the six-and-a-half miles to Greenwich. 'He proceeded at a very slow pace, picked his road, and did not arrive till one o'clock,' five hours after leaving Pall Mall.[65]

*

The following day, Saturday 4 January, the Princess of Wales and her retinue entered the sombrely transformed Painted Hall in Greenwich Hospital and 'remained for a considerable time contemplating with silent sorrow the last solemn obsequies paid to the remains of the gallant Hero'. Afterwards a few 'persons of respectability were also admitted'. Among these was Georgiana, Duchess of Devonshire, who had previously made private application, presenting her compliments to Mr Marsden, First Secretary to the Admiralty, and expressing herself 'most extremely obliged ... if he would obtain for her tickets of admission for the lying in state ... She would wish to have enough for her whole party, which is eight

---

* The report in the *Sun* and *British Press* on 4 January gives the craftsman's name as Mr CHIPPENDALE. This is probably a mistake.

persons.' Among them was the emotional Lady Elizabeth Foster, who remained calm up to the moment of passing the coffin, when she was 'quite overcome'.[66]

On the Sunday morning – the first day on which the public was to be granted access – newspapers reported that the 'rage of curiosity' outside the Painted Hall created dangerous chaos. 'Before eight ... every avenue from the metropolis to Greenwich was crowded with carriages of every description till past eleven, exhibiting a scene of confusion beyond description; but the approach to Greenwich Hospital Gates, a little before that hour, must baffle the conception of those who did not witness it.' A guard of the Greenwich and Deptford Volunteer Association, reinforced with groups of midshipmen and River Fencibles, was stationed on the approach, armed with pikes, 'to prevent too great an influx at one time'. Even so, 'when the clock struck eleven, the doors were thrown open, and the scene now became very alarming. The most frightful female shrieks assailed the ear on every side. Several persons were trodden under foot and greatly hurt. One man had his right eye literally torn out, by coming in contact with one of the gate posts – Vast numbers of Ladies and Gentlemen lost their shoes, hats, shawls, and the ladies fainted in every direction.'[67]

After the riotous behaviour outside the Hall, silence descended on the crowd inside, and 'all appeared impressed with a reverential awe befitting the grandeur and solemnity of the scene then opening to their view.' The walls were hung from floor to lofty cornice in black baize, entirely obliterating light from the eight tall window alcoves to north and south, but at intervals, in compensation, 'lamps were distributed sufficiently to throw a still religious glimmer over every part of the place'. Entering the main body of the hall from its lower vestibule, the eye would naturally be drawn upwards to the sinuous, tangled complexity of Sir James Thornhill's ceiling, though in the absence of natural light the expansive allegorical fantasy celebrating the foundation of the Hanoverian state was barely visible in that vast shadowy space, and only the distant glow issuing from the central archway at the far end focused the crowd's attention. Channelled between a four-foot-high central wooden partition running the entire length of the chamber, and another, somewhat higher to the right and five feet in from the wall, the packed mass of devotees shuffled slowly forward. The partitions, like the walls, were shrouded with black baize, as was the floor, and the flight of six steps that brought the awestruck, hushed crowd to the upper chamber. Here a curved, waist-high partition preventing further progress afforded those in front their first close view of the dread funerary trappings of the fallen hero. At the centre of a dais running the whole breadth of the saloon and covered like walls and floor in ubiquitous black, the coffin was mounted on a draped catafalque, its foot towards the visitors. A heavy black velvet pall was drawn back from it, revealing a white silk lining and parts only of Mr Chittenden's gold handiwork: the crocodile, the dolphin, a weeping woman and a cluster of captured enemy flags surmounted by a hapless Phrygian cap, symbol of Revolutionary France. At the coffin's head was a richly fringed black velvet cushion supporting a viscount's coronet. To either side tall tapers blazed in branched candle sticks, mounted on cylindrical plinths, the surrounding matte black surfaces only intensifying their 'very brilliant effect'. A low pedestal covered alike with black velvet, and fringed with black and gold, displayed the symbols of nobility to the slowly passing throng: shield, gauntlets, sword, helmet, crown, and the jewelled *chelenk* or 'Plume of Triumph', presented by the Turkish Sultan to the victor of the Nile.

Uniformed naval officers stood erect around the body, and six gentlemen were seated 'in full dress, bag[wig]s and swords', two at the head of the coffin and four at the foot. The faithful Revd Scott sat in an elbow chair, dressed in his cassock. His hair – indicating woe or personal neglect – was 'without powder'.[68]

*

The disorderly scenes outside were repeated the following day, despite the gates being opened an hour earlier, at ten o'clock, to accommodate the crowds. Even so, 'there were some who waited until between one and two o'clock before they could even get a sight of the gates.' The extreme congestion proved fatal in one case. 'A woman with one child in her hand, and an infant at the breast, imprudently got into the midst of the croud, from which she was with great difficulty extricated, and on examining the infant immediately found it quite lifeless.'[69]

Further measures were taken on the third and final day to impose order. The crowd on Tuesday, undeterred by appalling weather, was as immense as on the Sunday and Monday. A troop of the First Dragoon Guards brought from London were stationed close to the gates, facing the waiting multitude. Then a trumpet, sounding from the steps of the Great Hall, gave a signal for the gates to be unbarred. The dragoons parted and the crowd surged into the courtyard until it was nearly full, when with another trumpet blast the gates were closed and barred against the rest. 'As soon as the curiosity of those who were admitted [to the Hall] was gratified, the signal, by trumpet, was given again, and a similar scene followed. By this arrangement, the constant pressure at the gates was prevented.' But, despite these precautionary measures, 'great numbers were ... thrown down and trampled underfoot ... A gentleman had his leg shockingly fractured and was otherwise much bruised. He was carried away senseless on a bier. A woman had her arm broken, and several others were trampled upon, and carried away apparently lifeless.'[70]

*

Directives had been sent to St Paul's Cathedral 'to all the principal artificers there employed, desiring them to expedite the finishing of their different orders on or before the 7th of January'. It had been decided that '[the] corpse shall not be taken down the steps ... to the vault, as all others have been, but that it shall be let down under the dome, where the brass grate is.' The existing opening being insufficient for its passage, 'a number of workmen [were] daily employed, using every possible exertion to make the hole large enough to let the coffin down [there being] an immense body of stone to cut through.'

The four cathedral vergers were said to be charging sixpence a time just 'for letting people see the scaffolding inside, & the hole'. They were then sharing the profits with the dean and precentors. It was reported that 'the door money is taken as at a puppet-shew, and has amounted ... to more than £40 each day.' Lady Elizabeth Foster visited and was much impressed and, needless to say, moved by a pyramid or obelisk covered with the flags which had struck to Nelson at Trafalgar. This structure would be removed prior to the funeral as it was found to obscure the choir's view of the nave, causing them to miss their cue to begin the dirge as the procession entered the Western Gate. Preparations in the cathedral resulted in only one death – the day before the funeral – when a workman fell from scaffolding 'and was killed on the spot'.[71]

*

Meanwhile Londoners prepared for the spectacle that was to come. 'You know lord Nelson is dead,' Charles Lamb wrote to William Hazlitt. 'He is also to be buried. And the whole town is in a fever. Seats erecting, seats to be let, sold, lent, &c.' As soon as the date of the ceremony and the processional route were announced, advertisements began appearing in the press. One of the first, in *The Times* of 28 December, informed prospective spectators that seats offering 'the best SITUATION in London for viewing the PROCESSION' were to be had at St Paul's Coffee House for 'One Guinea each' and that 'select parties may be accommodated with separate rooms, making early application'. During the following week, residential properties and business premises alike touted accommodation. The Dublin Hotel, Tavern and Coffee House – offering front rooms overlooking Charing Cross and affording a view of the entire length of Whitehall – advertised 'Tickets at One Guinea each, refreshments included'. A gentleman had hired a 'large ROOM on the First Floor in the most eligible part of Ludgate-hill', and finding it too large for him and his friends, offered part to a family group. 'As profit [was] not the Advertiser's object, the most respectable references [would] be required.' In the same vicinity, a south-facing house, 'commanding a view from St Paul's to the top of Fleet street', was offered to 'two or three respectable families'. Here profit was the sole object: offers had already been made 'but as it is one of the best houses in the neighbourhood, none need apply who will not offer a handsome sum'. Two first-floor-windows giving a view onto 'the heart of Fleet street', were offered for ten guineas each, or a guinea per person for single individuals. A first floor 'commodious bow window' at 184 Fleet Street 'command[ed] an extensive view from St Dunstan's Church nearly to the Old Bailey'. No mention being made of the cost, applicants were invited 'Please to ring the bell'. Mr Bundock, an upholsterer, advertised rooms on the first and second floor of a property 'in a grand part of Fleet street which commands a very extensive view', suitable for families 'that would wish to be by themselves', at a 'reasonable' but otherwise unspecified price. 'Good fires will be kept, and everything ... done for their accommodation.' Seats in Mr Bundock's ground floor shop were available at a guinea each. The *Morning Advertiser* reported one resident of Ludgate Street successfully letting the use of his house to a family for 'the astonishing price of 500 guineas'. The paper predictably commented: 'Fools and their money are soon parted.'[72]

Mrs Salmon's Wax-Works – boasting '200 Wax Figures in various groups' and recently enhanced by 'A Presentation of the Death of Lord Nelson' – benefited from a prime situation on the south side of Fleet Street by offering 'Whole Rooms to be Lett for the day of the Funeral, for separate Parties and single places'. Patrons were informed that 'the interesting dying Figure of Lord Nelson supported by his Sailors [would] continue to be exhibited, as usual ... the day after [the] Funeral.' But, to make room for the lucrative press of custom expected on the day itself, 'the Naval Groupe must necessarily be removed'.[73]

Elsewhere, regular customers took advantage of their previous patronage of shops along the processional route. Charles Lamb gleefully conjured imaginary negotiations as the normally obsequious tradesman and his discriminating customer exchanged roles – the fashionable lady becoming a wheedling supplicant:

'A favour to beg of you Mr Tape. To let my young Ladies come and see the funeral procession on Thursday. My girls are coming home from school, and young folks love sights.'

'How many, Ma'am?' enquires the cautious haberdasher.

'O! there'll be only *me* . . . And my three daughters . . . And perhaps their cousin Betty . . . And the two young men to escort them . . . Unless my *Cousin* . . . happens to come to Town . . .'

And, chancing one extra for good measure:

'Then there'll be nine of us.'

'I am afraid it will be impossible to accommodate so many,' says Mr Tape gravely. 'But . . . we perhaps shall be able to put [one of the young ladies] in the second floor.'

And the customer goes on her way with fulsome thanks, only to return on the morning of the funeral, 'with fourteen more than the number first begg'd for'.[74]

*

The coffin's progress by river from Greenwich to Westminster Stairs was not neglected by entrepreneurs and the spectacle was to be enjoyed from numerous waterfront vantage points. A first-floor room with a double sash window, 'centrally situate between London and Blackfriars Bridges close alongside the Thames', was suitable for a single family of between ten and twelve, with terms described as 'easy'. The boat-building firm of Martin's offered 'A Good VIEW of the Grand Procession . . . by Water' from their 'spacious Lofts, fitted up with Seats for the occasion'. At five shillings each, hardier souls could hire seats in 'two large Barges . . . with awnings to keep off the weather . . . opposite . . . Bull Stairs, just above Blackfriars Bridge'. Complicated negotiations must have ensued when a householder offered his riverside property – 'the most centrical, and commanding a view of the three Bridges on the Thames' – in exchange for four places in St Paul's or, failing that, in a house providing a view of the cathedral entrance. The landlord of the Dundee Arms tavern in Wapping had prepared his 'LONG and COMMODIOUS ROOM with SEATS ... it being the best View on the River', tickets priced at five shillings. This seemed to be the standard rate for a river view, although cheaper still could be found. The Turk's Head tavern, at Union Stairs near the London Docks, for example, offered 'an extensive View as any other on the Water-side', with prices ranging from two shillings on the first floor, to three shillings on the third. One-and-sixpence secured more exposed accommodation on the leads of the roof. 'Tickets to be had at the Bar.'[75]

*

On the stroke of eleven, Wednesday morning, 8 January, gunboats of the River Fencibles began firing at one-minute intervals, an hour and a half before the coffin left the Painted Hall, and they continued firing during embarkation and throughout the slow passage upriver to Whitehall. As the procession came opposite the Tower, at a quarter to three, the great guns began firing from Tower Wharf, also at sixty-second intervals and synchronised with the Fencibles' minute guns.

The leading barge contained trumpeters and drummers to play the requisite anthems and dirges, six naval officers and a small retinue of Nelson's closest servants, together with two junior officials of the College of Arms, the Pursuivants Rouge Croix and Blue Mantle. At the barge's head, borne by Captain Laforey of HMS *Spartiate*, and supported by two lieutenants, an elaborate quartered standard comprised a Union Jack, a naval crown adorned with trident and palm-branch, the *chelenk*, and the stern of the *San Josef*, Nelson's Spanish prize from the battle of Cape St Vincent in 1797. More College of Arms heraldry followed, the eccentricities of that arcane institution much in evidence throughout this and the following day. The second barge carried four more trumpeters and heralds bearing the medieval emblems of nobility painted on silk – surcoat, shield and sword, helm and crest, gauntlet and spurs.

A 'Great Banner' was supported by Captain Moorson of *Revenge* and two lieutenants. The hulls of both the first and second barges were covered in black cloth.

The third was draped more expensively in black velvet, befitting the gravity of its burden, referred to unequivocally throughout the printed Order of Procession as 'the BODY'. Shrouded thus, the painted and gilded royal barge built for Charles II in 1670, and lent by the present King, was unrecognisable. Rowed by men of *Victory*'s crew, it contained six more trumpeters, six naval lieutenants – five from *Victory*, one from *Defiance* – and the third most senior officer of the College, Sir Ralph Bigland, as Norroy King of Arms, whose sole ceremonial function was holding the viscount's coronet on its black velvet cushion. Also crouched in this vessel the Revd Alexander Scott, his long faithful vigil from the waters off Cape Trafalgar to the Thames nearing its end. A canopy decked with black ostrich plumes flapped above in the wind.

Cladding of the fourth and last of these 'mourning barges' reverted to the undifferentiated 'black cloth' of the first two. It contained sixteen admirals – rear admirals and vice admirals – and also the Admiral of the Fleet, Sir Peter Parker. As holder of the highest rank in the Royal Navy, Sir Peter was officially designated 'Chief Mourner'. Henry Blackwood, captain of *Euryalus*, was his train bearer, while Captain Hardy carried the 'Banner of Emblems'. Conspicuously absent from this company was Vice Admiral Cuthbert Collingwood, unable to be spared by the Navy, and continuing blockade duty off Cadiz.

The King's barge was fifth in line. Because protocol precluded His Majesty's attending a commoner's funeral, it also demanded his vessel be rowed empty, but, due to the late arrival of the Admiralty's barge, it carried those unable to find accommodation elsewhere. The Lords Commissioners of the Admiralty occupied the sixth barge, the Lord Mayor of London the seventh, and the Corporation of London's special committee appointed for the funeral occupied the eighth. 'The only ornaments of this Barge were the actual colours of the *Victory*, borne by seven select Seamen.' These quasi-sacred relics would figure prominently in the land procession of the following day, and during the final obsequies in St Paul's.

Last of all came the ceremonial barges of the Worshipful Companies of London. The Drapers' Company, of which Nelson had been granted honorary membership following the battle of the Nile, deservedly took the lead, followed by the Fishmongers'. Next came the Goldsmiths' Company, then the Skinners', and the Merchant Taylors'. The most ornate of the Company barges was that of the Ironmongers', decorated with gilded mermaids, sea lions, a brace of salamanders and an ostrich. The Stationers' barge followed and, bringing up the rear, the Apothecaries' Company, proud beneath their rhinoceros banner, emblematic of the supposed medicinal efficacy of that creature's powdered horn.

The ten gunboats and eighteen rowboats of the River Fencibles that flanked the procession were to keep three boats' length distance apart, and the barges twice their lengths. The rowboats ensured no other vessels intersected the line of official vessels, that the proper distances were maintained between the great barges, and that sufficient room was preserved either side for the passage of their oars. Rowers had been ordered that 'the Rest on the Oars must be long' and to pull 'half-minute strokes', the riverine equivalent of a slow march. But although the incoming tide flowed upstream in their favour, a strong south-westerly wind blowing against them made any faster progress impossible. As they strained towards Westminster, the firing of the Fencibles' minute guns seemed to slow the pace even further.

*

Both banks of the Thames were lined with spectators: every opening to the river from Greenwich to Westminster filled, every eminence commanding a view 'completely covered', church steeples and house roofs 'numerously inhabited'. William Watson, watching from a house at St Katharine's Dock 'cram full of people', thought it 'the finest sight [he] ever saw'. He noted 'thousands of boats covering the water' and people 'clinging like Bees upon the rigging' of moored vessels. A boy fell from the mast of a ship at Rotherhithe 'and was drowned before he could be got out of the water'. Elsewhere, 'a Lady, of the name of Bayne, was so affected by the [procession], that she fell into hysterics, and died a few minutes after.' More than two hundred watched from the tower of St Bride's church between Fleet Street and the river, and a similar throng from the roof of Somerset House in the Strand. The Inner Temple also commanded a fine view and 'was greatly crowded' in consequence, jammed with carts and carriages, each filled to capacity. This area became particularly congested when 'the multitude who had watched the procession from Blackfriars Bridge, as soon as it passed through the arches, rushed in that direction along Fleet Street and the Strand, in expectation of catching another view of it, further towards Whitehall.' The Admiralty's navigation barge, *Crosby*, moored off Temple Gardens, hosted members of the London Livery Companies clad in 'deep mourning and violet gowns'. They were sustained by a lavish meal served on board while they viewed the procession. Temple lawyers watched from the Gardens' terrace.[76]

Accidents were inevitable as inexperienced citizens ventured onto the crowded river. 'A boat, having four persons, sank above Westminster bridge, and three of them perished, notwithstanding the exertions of other boats. The person who was saved was in a senseless state.' Another boat capsized opposite Somerset House but all seven of the party were picked up and safely landed. One journalist was particularly entranced by the spectacle of young female excursionists, 'strangers to all fear ... in the most dangerous situations, perfectly free from all apprehension, and intent only upon the passing show'. He watched fascinated as they disembarked from boats and cross[ed] ranks of closely tethered barges, lighters and wherries extending a hundred yards from the shore. While the accumulated mass of vessels were tossing about ... the most delicate females ... stepped from boat to boat with as much ease and agility as if they felt themselves upon a grass plot in Kensington Gardens.' The correspondent reported an incongruous, erotic frisson as 'many a beautiful leg was displayed in this extraordinary march, across a bridge of boats, and many a youth felt happy in assisting the fair in this perilous journey.' But one woman was not so nimble: Mrs Miffin, the young wife of a carpenter in Shoe Lane, was drowned with her infant, near the Temple. She had been walking on a plank between two lighters, one end of which gave way, and precipitated mother and child into the water. Neither body was recovered.[77]

*

The cosmopolitan writer, biographer and diarist, Miss Mary Berry was watching from Lord Fife's garden which bordered the Whitehall steps and had a view eastward across the river's bend as far as Blackfriars Bridge. She was unimpressed by what she saw of the aquatic spectacle. 'On the water it was a crowd of boats, in which the immense city barges only were conspicuous.' Clarity was not enhanced, she observed, by 'the foggy atmosphere of the Thames'. She also complained that 'the distance of time between the minute guns ... was too long to command continued attention, and therefore ... failed in their effect. The music, too, was not sufficiently loud to have any effect at all; and the barge which contained [the] honoured remains was neither sufficiently large nor sufficiently distinguished to command the eye and the attention of every spectator, which by some means or other it ought to have done.' From her vantage point, Miss Berry was able to see the coffin being landed. And this, she thought, was 'the only really impressive moment' in its progress. It was also the least capable of being controlled. At that instant 'the sky, which but a few minutes before had been clear, poured down at once a torrent of rain and hail, and a sudden gust of wind arose, the violence of which was not less remarkable than the moment at which it took place.' In a more superstitious age, she mused, it might have been recorded as the moment the hero's spirit took flight.

The same sudden gust of wind-blown hail and rain passed on to the east along the Strand, where it led to a dash for shelter and the injury of an elderly woman, knocked down by a hackney coach, 'her skull ... dreadfully fractured'. A three-year-old child suffered a similar accident at the other end of the street and 'both its legs were broken'. Meanwhile, people watching the arrival of the coffin from the tops of buildings 'were in great danger [and] a lady who was on top of the Horse Guards, was in the most imminent peril, and must have been blown down, had not a gentleman, at the risk of his life, run to her assistance'.

From the Stairs – with the canopy and black ostrich feathers dishevelled by the wind – the body was carried on a bier the short distance into Whitehall, emerging opposite Horse Guards, then turning right towards the Admiralty. The dense crowd, even in that small locality, was a portent of the hordes that would turn out for the following day's procession. 'The very beggars left their stands,' observed Alexander Scott that evening, 'and seemed to pay tribute . . . tattered and on crutches, shaking their heads with plain signs of sorrow.'[78]

Meanwhile, William Marsden, 'without any effort . . . or intention of going the least out of [his] way', had a fine view of the water procession and the arrival of the body from his office window in the Admiralty. Professing indifference to the funeral, he remarked sourly that it was 'a matter of the utmost importance [to everyone else], which people think more about than of the disasters on the Continent, or the safety of our troops'. News of Bonaparte's catastrophic victory at Austerlitz was only nine days old.[79]

Elizabeth Foster and Georgiana were in Whitehall. 'Soon we heard distant music and distinguished the Dead March in *Saul* – all besides was profound silence – the music sounded louder and louder . . . the procession entered the great gates – the trumpets drew up and continued playing – and the attendants, the Admirals and officers bearing . . . flags, in solemn slow pace, scarcely heard on the sand which had been everywhere spread, advanced to the Admiralty doors through the great columns'. A more rugged covering than sand would be demanded for the following day's traffic to St Paul's.[80]

The funeral procession was to go through several parishes and their paving committees were requested to spread gravel for its passage. To encourage the efficiency of this operation councillors from each parish were promised seats inside the cathedral. A total of 3,767 yards of roadway required covering from kerb to kerb. Between Wednesday and Thursday 'London could not be said to have slept'. Paviers shovelled gravel 'by candle and flambeau ... during the whole night,' while carpenters erected scaffolding along the route to accommodate the anticipated crowds. On the north and west sides of St Clement Danes, banks of seating were 'capable of holding several thousands of persons'. These structures were of variable quality and stability, however, and a newspaper correspondent deplored the 'sordid and avaricious people [responsible for] the erection of ... miserable, ill-constructed wooden balconies in the front of houses in the Strand and Charing cross'. Money was to be made from such structures, however ramshackle, but, surprisingly, there were no reports of any *ad hoc* perches collapsing under the weight of spectators.[81]

The streets began to fill 'while it was still dark, hundreds more than what are usually seen at mid-day'. Gentlefolk were abroad at an uncommonly early hour and 'beautiful females, elegantly dressed, were seen ... braving the chill air of the morning, all anxious to take possession of seats as early as possible.' By daybreak every window along the route was filled, as were the roof leads. The lawyer William Watson had secured seats for himself, his brother Chatto and a friend, in the premises of Mr Clarke, near Temple Bar, and by eight o'clock the house and shop accommodated more than 250 people, distributed in the different rooms and on the roof where benches had been placed. An hour later tea and coffee were served and handed round by the gentlemen. At midday, as far as could be seen 'every window housetop & chimney [was] swarming with Ladies and Gentlemen.' Lady Bessborough, attended by her nineteen-year-old son, the Hon. William Francis Spencer Ponsonby, had set out early from Chiswick, anxious to occupy her seat in the cathedral before the stipulated time of eight o'clock. But her journey was to prove as frustrating as her fog-bound ordeal the previous November. Forced by traffic restrictions to alight from her carriage in Holborn, she attempted to continue the remaining distance on foot. However, 'the crowd in Fleet market became so oppressive, that her Ladyship could neither proceed to St Paul's, nor return to her carriage.' Instead, she decided to forego her seat and, 'with the greatest difficulty' William succeeded in escorting her to Charing Cross where she was able to join her sister Georgiana, Lady Elizabeth Foster and several illustrious foreigners, taking advantage of the Dublin Hotel's offer of viewing places for a guinea inclusive of refreshments.[82]

Those unable to gain an elevated view from scaffolds, upper floors and roofs, packed the pavements behind files of yeomanry and volunteers – 20,000 of them according to one estimate – that, by half past eight, had lined the route 'two deep, and in close Order ... officers and men [with] crape round their arms, fifes and drums muffled'. In Fleet Street and Ludgate Hill considerable damage would be caused to tradesmen's shop windows by the concerted pressure of the crowd. 'Not one from Temple Bar [and beyond] but experienced a fracture, and glaziers were wholly employed [the following day] in mending the demolished panes.' Such dense crowds were expected to attract the light-fingered and the *Morning Chronicle* recommended readers 'to leave at home their pocket books, watches, and purses, as well as to secure their handkerchiefs, it being likely that pickpockets [would] be unusually numerous'.[83]

The lines of militia were supplemented by special, petty and other constables of every description, belonging to London, Westminster and Middlesex, whose duty was to ensure that nothing disrupted the proceedings. 'Carts, coaches, and waggons were placed at the openings of several streets into the line of the procession, so that none but pedestrians could possibly intrude upon the cavalcade.' In the Strand coal waggons were parked as barriers across each side street to the north and south. Even these were 'filled on the instant by the eager multitude', scrambling for the best view. It was said that 'large sums of money were given even for standing in a cart'. At the bottom of Southampton Street, Newcastle Street and Catherine Street, hackney coaches drew up above the coal waggons, providing further vantage places. These streets to the north sloped down to the Strand and people who had congratulated themselves on gaining elevated positions further up found their view of the procession ruined by the improvised grandstands at the bottom. 'On the roofs of these vehicles ... many groups of young ladies and well dressed women, [were seen] *standing* ... in most eminent hazard.' Only the day before in Whitehall a man had fallen from a carriage roof while trying to get a glimpse of the coffin and 'was killed on the spot, his head being beat to pieces', and nearby a cart overladen with spectators collapsed 'by which several had their limbs broken, and others dreadfully bruised'. On the day of the funeral itself a woman and child who attempted to cross Fleet Street during the procession were knocked down by a troop of cavalry. 'She had her arm broken and was taken to the Hospital. The child was not hurt.' It was also claimed that a man, a woman and a child, 'through their own imprudence ... were crushed to death by the crowd', although what they had done to bring about their fate was not entirely clear.[84]

During the long wait for the parade to begin, conversations were struck up between strangers. On the scaffolding opposite St Clement's a gentleman was gratified to learn that the man sitting beside him 'had taken care to provide himself with a pack of cards and a cribbage board'. To pass the time they played a few hands, then a few more, and within an hour the gentleman had lost the considerable sum of £20. Nearby an exhausted West-countryman, who had travelled from Exeter the day before and occupied his seat in the early hours of Thursday, might have benefited from some distraction as he waited. 'Overcome with fatigue, and the [increasing] heat of the sun, he fell asleep.' Even the long-awaited approach of the funeral procession did not wake him, and the incessant dirge from *Saul*, accompanied by the muffled drums of the regimental bands, apparently served only to deepen his slumber.[85]

*

The military force that had assembled in St James's Park and which then snaked across Horse Guards Parade and along Whitehall towards Charing Cross was said to be 'far beyond what any one would think requisite ... and amount[ed] in number and character, as well as in appearance to a formidable army.' Reports vary as to how many. The *Morning Post* put it at nearly ten thousand, although eight thousand was probably nearer the mark. Given the importance of the Nile in Nelson's battle honours it was no coincidence that the regular troops taking part were drawn from 'regiments that had fought and conquered in Egypt ... delivering that part of the world from the tyrannic ambition of the French' – albeit during the land campaign of 1801, three years after Nelson's celebrated naval engagement. They included men of the Queen's Royal Regiment of Foot, second oldest in the British army, and the Gordon and Cameron Highlanders. The 28th North Gloucestershire Regiment – who fought back-to-back at the battle of Alexandria, earning the distinction of badges at the front and rear of their hats – and the 10th Lincolnshire Foot, their emblem a sphinx, were also represented. 'They were fine looking fellows ... truly picturesque ... the finest soldiers the universe ever beheld.' Two troops of cavalry, the 14th and 10th Light Dragoons, and the whole regiment of Scots Greys followed. Eleven pieces of light, or 'flying' artillery brought up the rear, with four companies of Grenadiers. The primary purpose of such a display was the same as any exhibition of military might through the heart of a civilian community: to demonstrate that 'with such defenders, ready to repair, at a moment's warning, to any threatened point of attack, no enemy, or combination of enemies, could make any impression in the attempt to invade.' This was especially needful, of course, in time of war, regardless of the French invasion threat being so recently neutralised by the efforts of the man this parade honoured. On their arrival in front of St Paul's the troops not assigned for duty in the cathedral proceeded north to the artillery ground at Moorfields, there to await a signal to perform their final ceremonial duty of the day.[86]

Following this formidable show of military strength, came the main procession, led by six Marshal's Men walking abreast, notionally 'to clear the Way'. A Messenger of the College of Arms came next in a mourning coach carrying a 'Staff tipped with Silver and furled with Sarsnet'. He was followed by six 'Conductors' in black mourning cloaks, bearing 'Black Staves headed with Viscounts Coronets'. Next came forty-eight Greenwich Hospital Pensioners, 'Two and Two', also in black cloaks and carrying black staves. After the brash splendour of the terrestrial forces, the crewmen of HMS *Victory*, 'in their ordinary Dress, with Black Neck Handkerchiefs and Stockings, and Crape in their Hats,' were the crowd's favourites. 'We had rather see them than all the show,' Lady Elizabeth Foster claimed to have overheard among the 'common people'. Next came officers enshrining the College of Arms' esoteric mysteries: the pursuivants Rouge Croix, Blue Mantle and Rouge Dragon, each 'in close Mourning, with his Tabard over his Cloak, Black Silk Scarf, Hat-band and Gloves'.

A dour parade of about 150 unadorned, black private carriages succeeded the pageantry. They contained Privy Councillors, Knights of the Bath, law officers, physicians and divines, esquires and gentlemen, together with the different degrees of nobility – dukes, marquesses and earls, viscounts, barons and baronets, as well as their eldest and younger sons. With their windows raised against the cold, they might as well have been empty, but although indistinguishable from the outside, they processed in reverse order of precedence, younger sons of barons to the fore, dukes at the rear. The final carriage contained representatives of the blood royal: the Prince of Wales and his brothers, the Dukes of Clarence and of Kent.

To avoid undue congestion in front of St Paul's, as this long line of carriages disgorged their occupants, the departure of the next part of the procession was delayed. The result was that following the longueur of drab coach traffic, spectators were left staring at empty road, 'an elapse of 35 minutes between ... the passing of the Prince of Wales's carriage & that of the Funeral Car supporting Lord Nelson's Coffin'. The *Morning Chronicle* called it 'a chasm in the process'.[87]

It was shortly after one o'clock that the centrepiece of the mournful pageant was brought from behind the Admiralty to its appointed place in Whitehall. Sprung and mounted on four sturdy wagon wheels, it was drawn by six 'Belgium Black' horses, each led by a liveried coachman. The bed of the car followed a nautical theme: its rear fashioned to resemble the stern quarters of Nelson's flagship, a Union Jack at half-staff and draped over the taffrail, while at the bow, a winged figure of Nike, bare-breasted, flourished a wreath of laurel in her right hand, and clasped a palm frond in her left. The angle of the right arm suggested it was designed to accommodate a trumpet should a change of symbolism be demanded, transforming her from 'Victory' to 'Fame'. The platform supporting the coffin was decorated, fore and aft, with Nelson's escutcheons of nobility, laurels, and the names of four French and Spanish men-of-war, 'taken or destroyed' by him: *San Josef*, *L'Orient*, and the most recent, *Santísima Trinidad* and *Bucentaure*. On each side of the car – TRAFALGAR embroidered in gold across the centre – three heavy swags of black velvet hung down to axle level. The car was roofed by a domed canopy fashioned from the same material and supported by four tall wooden posts, carved to resemble the trunks of palm trees, 'silvered and shaded, and glazed with green', entwined with real cypress and yet more laurel. The *Morning Post* reported that 'the carved work has been executed by artificers employed in his Majesty's dock-yards [and] it is scarcely necessary to add, . . . the carving is exquisitely finished.' Across the front of the canopy was embroidered NILE, and across the rear TRAFALGAR. Latin mottos ran along either side: PALMAM QUI MERUIT FERAT and HOSTE DEVICTO REQUIEVIT.* Corners and sides of the canopy were topped off by six black ostrich plumes. Mr Townsend, proprietor of a feather repository on Ludgate Hill, calculating each 'plume' as comprising eighteen individual feathers, or 'falls', at five shillings apiece – and 'nothing less . . . wo'd look worthy the present melancholy occasion' – had presented a bill for £27 in plumage alone, together with an additional twelve guineas for labour, or 'making up'.[88]

The whole structure towered about eighteen feet from the

---

* *'Let Him Bear Away the Palm who has Deserved it'* and *'He Conquered and went to Rest.'*

ground. It was to have been twenty until someone thought to take the clearance of the Temple Bar arch – marking the boundary between the Cities of London and Westminster – into account and made adjustment accordingly. A further modification proved impossible, when it was found to be too wide to pass through the Admiralty gates, and it was necessary instead for the vehicle to receive the coffin outside in Whitehall on the morning of the funeral. Two features of the original conception were abandoned completely: four naval lieutenants were to have sat on the platform 'one at each angle of the Coffin', and projecting 'on either side ... four Poles, to be held by Seamen of the *Victory*'. The conceit of sailors appearing to 'row' the car forward was doubtless thought 'rather an overstretch of fancy, which was too light for the solemnity of the occasion'. Another omission was by popular demand. 'At the earnest request' of the watching crowd, the undertakers stripped [the coffin] of the black velvet pall, exposing the whole of Mr Chittenden's gilded craftsmanship to public gaze for the first time.[89]

The historical painter Benjamin Robert Haydon quoted an unidentified 'clever foreigner' as saying that Nelson's funeral 'showed the nation's generosity and its utter want of taste'. Ever eager to draw attention to the British establishment's failures in patronage, and neglect of the fine arts, Haydon declared that 'instead of employing the first artist of the day, [Rudolph] Ackerman[n] in the Strand designed the whole thing'. He was partially correct. The printseller was indeed responsible for designing the gold embellishments on the coffin and the 'Banner of Emblems', depicting the doleful figure of Britannia, seated with her lion, and gazing at the armorial ensigns of her fallen hero, amongst the captured flags of France, Spain and Denmark. But the funeral car – arguably the most outlandish and vulgar feature of the occasion – was the exclusive conception of Denis Macquin of the Herald's Office.[90]

Haydon claimed to have witnessed the procession but curiously made no further remark upon it. Not so the censorious Miss Berry, for whom it fell both short of anticipation and at the same time was entirely equal to her limited expectations. 'I had certainly hopes that it would have been more considerable than it was, although I had little hope of its being conducted with any real taste or solemn effect, knowing that its conduct had not been entrusted to any persons of approved taste themselves, ... who would have summoned artists to their assistance.' Resigned though she was to 'the disproportions and perfect bad taste' of Mr Macquin's funeral car – 'good taste in forms', she declared, 'I never expect here' – she was disappointed in the want of 'good taste in moral feeling' to have entrusted 'the conduct of such a ceremony, the tribute of such a nation to such a chief, as a job to the Heralds' office and their hireling undertakers!'[91]

Shortly after departing from the Admiralty, the car stopped for some moments, immediately opposite the statue of King Charles I at Charing Cross, on the edge of what would, in thirty years' time, become Trafalgar Square. A crowd that assembled on the roof of the King's Theatre at the bottom of Haymarket was rewarded with an uninterrupted but distant view along Cockspur Street, while Lady Bessborough – consoled after forfeiting her seat in St Paul's – witnessed the moment in congenial company from the upper window of the Dublin Hotel 'which look'd over a mass of heads'. As the car approached, her ladyship recalled, 'You might have heard a pin fall, [then] without any order to do so, they all took off their hats. I cannot tell you the effect this simple action produc'd; it seemed one general impulse of respect beyond any thing that could have been said or contrived. Mean while the dead march was play'd in soft tones, and the pauses fill'd with cannon and the roll of the muffled drums.' Elizabeth Foster, having not missed a single opportunity to indulge her emotions – during the 'funeral pomp' in Greenwich, and the body's arrival in Whitehall – found it all 'affecting beyond measure'. Like Lady Bessborough, she remarked on the stillness of the vast crowd 'which nothing broke through but a sort of murmur of "Hats off!" as the Car passed'. And, so scathing about every other aspect of the procession by water and land, Miss Berry was also impressed by this, 'the only moment in which the mind the most disposed to enthusiasm could for a moment indulge it . . . Here nothing could be seen on every side but myriads of heads, and every head uncovered, from respect of the object, on which every eye was entirely bent. One general feeling pervading a great multitude must ever tend to the sublime.'[92]

As the car moved off and turned right into the Strand, at street level the soft crunch might have been heard of freshly laid gravel under wheel, foot and hoof.

In contrast to her mother's bosom companion, young Lady Harriet Cavendish 'rejoice[d] at escaping' the entire occasion. 'It would', she said, 'have been the greatest fatigue and exertion and most likely to be able to see very little after all.' But a more impressionable youth, the thirteen-year-old Frederick Marryat, future pioneer of nautical fiction – and shortly to begin his naval career as midshipman – watched the procession in the company of his father. 'As the triumphal car upon which [Nelson's] earthly remains were borne disappeared from my aching eye, I felt that death could have no terrors if followed by such a funeral.'[93]

Following the funeral car came another fifty or sixty 'Mourning Coaches', marking the end of the procession. The first contained Garter Principal King of Arms attended by two 'Gentlemen Ushers'. Next Sir Peter Parker, the Chief Mourner, followed by six Assistant Mourners. Norroy King of Arms came next, and 'highly gratified the spectators' by displaying the deceased viscount's coronet on its black cushion, 'alternately at each window'. The *Star*'s correspondent remarked, however, that there was a depletion of the crowd the moment the funeral car had passed. 'It was enough, they said, to have seen that . . . they wished to see no more.' The long line of undifferentiated black mourning coaches ground on across the thinning gravel, bearing the 'Relations of the Deceased, [and] Officers of the Navy and Army, according to their respective ranks, the Seniors nearest the body'. The *Morning Chronicle* correspondent thought the procession as a whole would have been 'much more gratifying to the feelings of the people had the greater part . . . not been buried as it was in coaches'.[94]

Last of all, and unnoticed by many in the dispersing crowd,

was a carriage with its window blinds drawn up, the driver and two footmen in deep mourning, the latter carrying bouquets of laurel. Otherwise empty, it bore Nelson's coat of arms and was accordingly referred to in newspaper accounts of the procession as 'the private chariot of the deceased Lord'. It belonged, however, to Lady Nelson who, in keeping with contemporary custom, was not expected to attend her husband's funeral in person.[95]

*

From his hired window above Mr Clarke's shop William Watson could see, waiting below in the roadway near Temple Bar, a small group of 'seamen of the *Victory* with the Nelson Colours'. The committee appointed by the City of London's Court of Common Council to oversee arrangements between the Bar and St Paul's, 'conceiving it would add much to the spectacle if a number of those brave men ... could be procured' had applied to Captain Hardy who 'not only instantly ordered seven of the men to attend but directed that the colours under which they so gloriously fought ... should be borne in the procession mutilated and imbued as they were by the blood of [their comrades] in the ever-memorable Battle of Trafalgar'. These were the seven who had brought the battle-torn relics from Greenwich the previous day. As the funeral car rumbled slowly along the Strand towards them – woodwork creaking and black ostrich feathers swaying from side to side – the men awaited their moment to join the solemn choreography. The scale of Mr Macquin's fantastical invention was about to undergo its final crucial test. A young Welshman, John Williams, was standing nearby and noted that 'in passing under Temple Bar the plumes of the Car had not 6 inches to spare', adding in a letter to his father, 'Judge of the height of it!' As it cleared the arch and emerged into Fleet Street the sailors fell in behind the body of their late commander for the last mile and a half of its journey to St Paul's. They played to the spectators on either side, exposing the two Union flags, and the twenty- by forty-foot, shot-riddled White Ensign – St George's cross, with the Union Jack in the upper hoist quarter – ensuring that the significance of no rent or bloodstain was lost on the crowd. And the crowd responded rapturously, no longer watching in awed, respectful silence, but clapping wildly and even reaching out to snatch at the sacred relics, as one newspaper reported, 'so many wishing to partake of a part'.[96]

*

So long was the procession 'that it was upwards of four hours from the time of its first motion [in Whitehall] until the last coach stopped at the gate of St. Paul's'. Its head had reached the cathedral at half past one, the final part at about three o'clock. The Prince of Wales and his brothers – Clarence and Kent now joined by the Royal Dukes of York, Cumberland, Sussex and Cambridge – had been waiting outside for at least half an hour when the last of the procession arrived. As they ascended the steps to the cathedral entrance, the Duke of Clarence stopped and approached the group of sailors who had followed the funeral car. He exchanged a few words with them, took hold of one of the colours they carried and began to weep. One of the crew is said to have offered somewhat unlikely words of comfort to His Royal Highness: 'Cheer up my Noble Commander, let the enemy give us another opportunity, and our Royal Master [King George], who is the father of a British seaman, will not be disappointed.' Clarence was dressed for the occasion in his naval uniform. By 1811 he would be Admiral of the Fleet, the future 'Sailor King', William IV.[97]

*

On either side of the nave, tiers of scaffolding accommodated seats and benches 'to a great height', while in the circular space beneath the dome and surrounding the grave opening down to the crypt, the seating formed a steeply banked amphitheatre. Provision had been planned for nine thousand, although the

Morning Post suggested that '10,000 ... in all probability were present.'

A tradesman's quotation of £84 has survived: the cost of erecting two temporary scaffolds equipped with rails. One was to bear five rows of seating on the outside of the building – under the pediment porch above the west door – which afforded a view down Ludgate Hill and Fleet Street. Allowing eighteen inches per person this accommodated 170 spectators, thirty-four to a row. The other scaffold – to be erected inside the cathedral – spanned the gallery below the west window and faced down the nave to the crossing and on to the choir. This was to be furnished with four rows of seats and estimated to bear another 108 persons. The two banks of seating were to be furnished with 'A Water closet to Each' for relieving the urgent needs of gentlemen and ladies enjoined to occupy their places no later than eight o'clock that morning, and unable to leave until six in the evening. Calculating on an average of 140 persons for the use of each facility, it can be assumed there would have been about seventy such necessary receptacles strategically placed around the cathedral.[98]

*

The grave was concealed until the moment of interment by a 'canopy ... 11 feet long, 7 feet 9 inches wide, and about 12 feet in height ... covered with rich black velvet, with festoons in gold ornaments ... finished with a row of deep fringe, and ... supported by four light pillars, covered with black velvet.'[99]

At one o'clock the great west door was thrown open, but it was not until half past that General Sir David Dundas entered at the head of Grenadiers of the 21st and 31st foot, followed by the 79th and 92nd Highlanders, moving in slow time by single files, they formed lines either side of the nave, around the crossing and on to the gates of the choir, then, turning to the front, they rested on their arms reversed – muzzle to the ground, palms crossed over the stock – and so remained until the whole of the ceremony was concluded.

At two o'clock the main procession entered, led by naval officers carrying standard and guidon, and followed by Gentlemen of the Herald's Office, the City of London aldermen, the Prince of Wales and the Royal Dukes. They were followed by the Lord Mayor and his suite. Then the coffin was brought in, carried by eight undertaker's men. The *Victory*'s men followed with their flags, commanding most attention inside the building, as they had the length of Fleet Street and Ludgate Hill. The forty-eight Greenwich Pensioners terminated the procession. As they entered and the west door closed behind, the organ thundered and the combined choirs – boy choristers from St Paul's, Westminster Abbey, and the Chapel Royal, St James's, accompanied by a contingent of nearly forty gentlemen, sang 'I am the resurrection, and the life: he that believeth in me, though he were dead, yet shall he live, and whosoever liveth and believeth in me shall never die.'

The *Star* correspondent claimed that it took fully two hours for the whole procession – accompanied by choral settings of texts from Job and Timothy – to move from the west door to the choir. The funeral service was conducted there, the Bishop of Lincoln officiating 'in a most impressive and affecting manner' and supported by the Bishop of Chester.

As the service proceeded, light faded and 'by a most excellent previous arrangement, a great number of torches were lighted up in the choir, both below and in the galleries'. The space under the dome, focus of the sombre theatre still to come, was brilliantly lit, for the first time in the building's history. A temporary 'lanthorn' had been contrived, comprising 'an octagonal framing of wood, boarded on the outside, and finished at top by eight angles and at the bottom by a smaller octagon'. It was painted black and contained about 130 'patent lamps'. When hoisted by a rope from the centre of the dome it 'had a most impressive and grand effect and contributed greatly to the splendour of [the] spectacle,' rendering other lamps in the aisles 'of no great consequence'.

The funeral service finished at ten minutes to five and the *Morning Post* timed the subsequent interment to the second: 'at thirty-three minutes and a half past five precisely, the coffin was lowered into the grave, whither it was followed by the regrets of all that witnessed the affecting scene.' An 'excellent contrivance' had been devised by James Wyatt, the cathedral's surveyor general, allowing for 'the great weight of the different coffins in which [the body] was inclosed' to descend smoothly and slowly into the crypt. 'Made upon the same principle as [a] stage trap-door', it consisted of a platform, suspended within a square wooden frame, and supported by pillars some four feet in height. The body, placed on the platform, was lowered on four ropes controlled from the crypt floor by means of a windlass. Its principal virtue was that the mechanism and supporting structure lay below the level of the cathedral's pavement and entirely hidden from the congregation. The discretion of this arrangement was supposed to avoid 'all those disagreeable and disgusting circumstances which too often occur at the funerals of the Great, arising from the weight of the coffins and the comparative weakness or want of energy of the persons who are called upon to carry their superiors to interment'. The descent, when the time came, took ten minutes. As it disappeared from sight a prearranged signal was transmitted from the cathedral's Stone Gallery to a dome on the 'Temple of the Muses', James Lackington's palatial bookshop in Finsbury Square, three-quarters of a mile away. Then, on the adjacent artillery ground at Moorfields the assembled troops fired to mark the hero's burial: 'the infantry by regiments, three volleys each, and the artillery three salutes of eleven guns each'.[100]

*

At the graveside, Sir Isaac Heard, Garter King of Arms – reading from a single manuscript sheet of foolscap – pronounced, according to custom, the 'Styles and Titles' of the deceased:

> The Most Noble Lord Horatio Nelson, Viscount and Baron Nelson of the Nile, and of Burnham Thorpe in the County of Norfolk, Baron Nelson of the Nile, and of Hilborough in the same County; Knight of the Most Honourable Order of the Bath; Vice Admiral of the White Squadron of the Fleet, and Commander in Chief of His Majesty's Ships and Vessels in the Mediterranean; also Duke of Bronté in Sicily; Knight Grand Cross of the Sicilian Order of St Ferdinand and of Merit; Member of the Ottoman Order of the Crescent, Knight Grand Commander of the Order of St Joachim.

Sir Isaac's concluding words, a departure from the age-old rubric, were underlined as though to emphasise the breach of custom: '*and the Hero who, in the moment of Victory, fell covered with mortal Glory! let us humbly trust, that he is now raised to bliss ineffable, and to a glorious immortality!*' Then, his duty done, he broke his wand of office and threw the pieces into the gulf. The colours of HMS *Victory* were to have followed, but before depositing them in the grave, the seven custodians who had carried them from Greenwich insisted on retaining mementoes of their commander. They 'tore off a considerable part of the largest flag, of which most, if not all of them, obtained a small portion, though few other persons were able to get any of it'. Officially unsanctioned, but as officially winked at, this spontaneous breakdown of naval discipline by the 'honest tars' was silently applauded by those who witnessed it, as a rare moment of humanity amidst the ritual. 'That was *Nelson*,' remarked Mrs Codrington, 'the rest was so much the Herald's Office.'[102]

The lady had other reservations regarding the ceremony: 'It was certainly as fine a national spectacle ... as can possibly be seen,' she admitted, 'It was magnificent; it was solemn and impressive to the utmost degree.' But at the same time, she was conscious of 'its having not had the *great* and powerful effect on [her] feelings which [she] expected'. She had anticipated 'the most affecting scene', that she would 'see faintings and swoonings', and that she herself, although not customarily subject to such transports, 'should not be far from it'. Instead, she was disappointed at being 'not moved beyond *self-control*' and 'not having wept bitterly and severely the whole time'. She conceded, also, that 'expectation and *heart* were ... worn out in so many long hours of waiting.'[103]

William Windham had been sitting next to fellow Whig Charles James Fox and, like Mrs Codrington, felt a sense of anti-climax, being 'not impressed throughout so much as [he] ought. Attention disturbed with the cold.' Close and warm proximity to the corpulent Fox and the massed body heat of that vast assembly had not taken the chill off Wren's cavernous masterpiece. Notwithstanding the contribution of gentlemen choristers and boy trebles 'amounting altogether to upwards of one hundred', the *Morning Chronicle* blamed 'the want of an orchestra in the Cathedral' for a lack of engagement and pointed out that 'with the heart so predisposed to emotion, the effect would have been inexpressibly pathetic'. Mrs Billington – 'the St. Cecilia of Song' – unabashed by her association with the disastrous 'Melo-Dramatic Ballet' at the King's Theatre the previous month, had 'made a respectful tender of her fine talents to assist in the solemnity ... but it was not thought proper to accept the offer'.[104]

Of the vast congregation assembled in St Paul's that day, there was only one reported instance of illness when a gentleman suffered an apoplectic fit and had to be carried outside. Despite receiving immediate medical assistance there, and later at his home in Great Queen Street, he died about twelve o'clock the same night. Captain Richard Whitford was a man 'of amiable manners and highly esteemed in an extensive circle of respectable friends and acquaintance'. He was 'many years in the Jamaica Trade', often a euphemism for the traffic in slaves. Another indisposition was suffered by Sir Edmund Nagle, 'occasioned by a carriage passing over his foot as he was coming out [of the cathedral]'. A week later it was reported that 'the gallant Admiral has been confined to his room in consequence'.[105]

The gentleman from Exeter awoke in his seat opposite the church of St Clement Danes to find 'the procession had not only passed, but the soldiers [and crowds] had actually dispersed'.[106]

Many who had neglected to heed the *Morning Chronicle*'s warning to leave their valuables at home returned thither poorer than they came. It was reported that 'the greatest gang of thieves and pick-pockets ... ever heard of' had preyed on the dense press of humanity, enjoying 'a feast they had been looking to for some time; and ... made great spoils, repaying them their trouble and expense in coming to town'.[107]

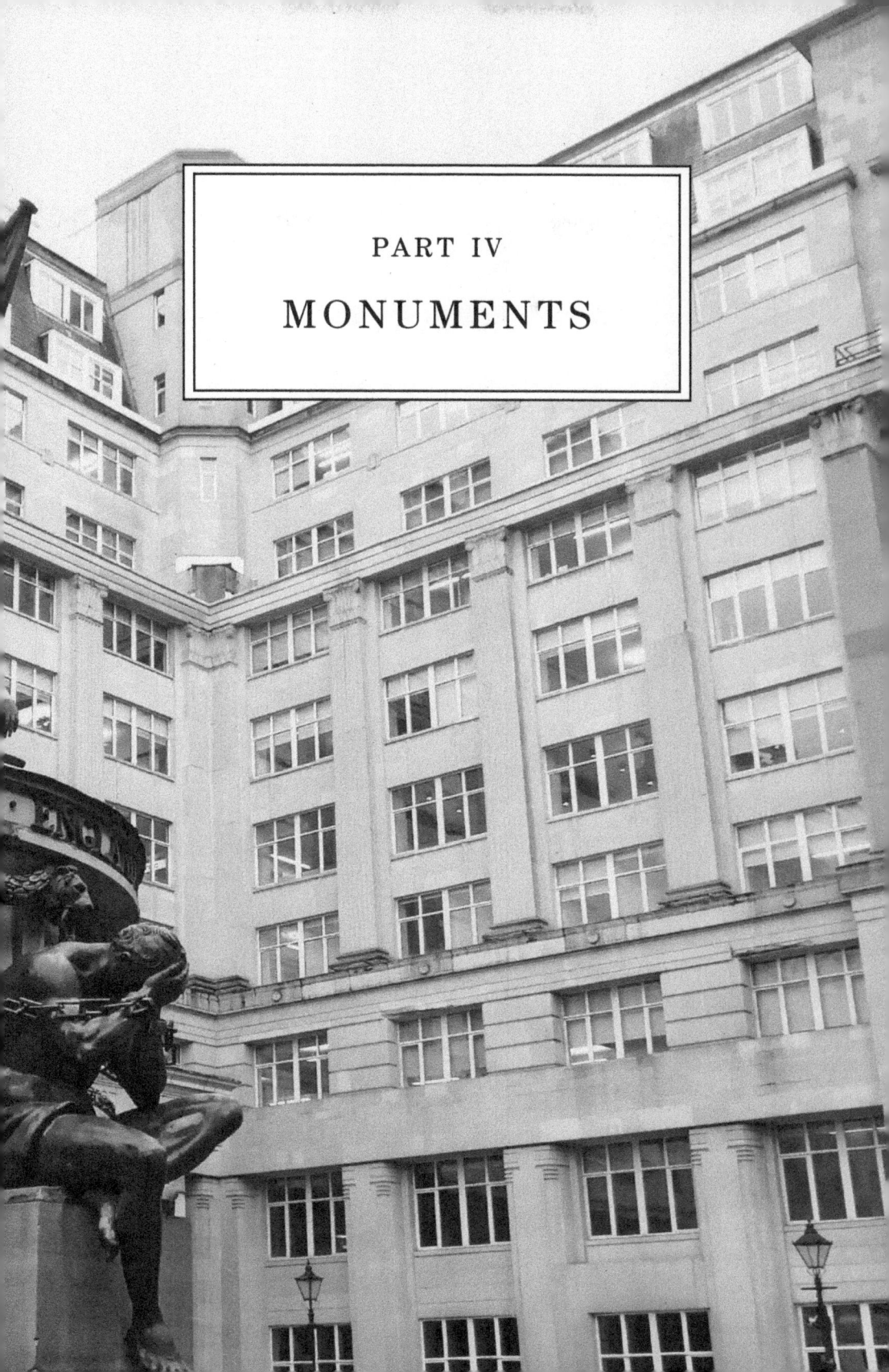

PART IV
MONUMENTS

I

FOLLOWING the coffin's disappearance into the cathedral crypt, Robert Mylne, Surveyor of the Fabric at St Paul's, wrote a terse entry in his diary for 9 January 1806: 'Lord Nelson's funeral but no interment.' Then, on the following day: 'Coffin – 7ft. from floor.' It had been left suspended above the tomb which Mr Mylne had had constructed 'in the most massy ... and durable manner, and of stone and brass materials, which time can never injure'. That it was not lowered further – into the two-and-a-half-feet-deep cavity left in the granite to receive it – was due to uncertainty regarding Earl Nelson's wishes as to his late brother's 'final disposition'. However, before that uncertainty was resolved – and the coffin definitively enclosed under a nine-by-three-foot slab of stone – the cathedral's vergers continued to supplement their income, already greatly enhanced before the funeral. Throughout the following Saturday crowds flocked to the cathedral and, after paying at the door, were permitted to enter the enclosed area below the dome and stare down into the excavated opening – 'a distance of about ten feet' – to where the splendid coffin hung above the sable-draped open tomb. 'They were suffered, however, to remain but a few moments, and as fast as they were dismissed a fresh company was admitted.' The *Morning Herald* was indignant: 'The whole world cries out shame on the exposure of the Coffin with its sacred remains ... as a *common shew* ... like *Mother Salmon's*

Waxwork, at one shilling per head. The four *Vergers* had made £500 a-piece in shewing the preparations for the funeral. This might have satisfied them. Surely the DEAN will put a stop to this indecent proceeding!' The *Sun* compared it to other contemporary London tourist attractions, declaring that 'the remains should lie in awful silence, not be exhibited to the gaping crowd, like the Lions at the Tower or Exeter 'Change* . . . for the aggrandisement of a few mercenary individuals,' while the *Public Ledger & Daily Advertiser* concluded its report with the pious sentiment that 'The House of God ought not to be made a Theatre of Extortion!'[1]

*

An early concept for a monument to Nelson in St Paul's, mooted by Robert Mylne – and 'much objected to on the ground that it would disfigure the appearance of the Church' – was for 'a large stone pillar', presumably to be built on top of the granite tomb, 'to rise from the grave a considerable distance above the brass grate, and a very elegant colossal figure of the gallant Lord to be on top of it'. Objections prevailed and the monument eventually approved by a government-appointed 'Committee of Taste' would be sculpted in white marble by John Flaxman and installed in the south transept, a short distance from the brass grating. Larger than life, but considerably smaller than that envisaged by Mr Mylne, the figure stands on a circular pedestal, decorated with sea gods in relief, at the base of which crouches the watchful British lion, while Britannia directs the attention of two adoring young midshipmen to the heroic exemplar above. Sir William Hamilton – elderly connoisseur and husband of the vivacious Lady Emma – is said to have secured Nelson's tacit approval some years earlier when he

---

* Lions and other wild beasts had been kept at the western entrance to the Tower of London since the thirteenth century. The other menagerie, run by Edward Cross, was in a building erected on the site of Exeter House, at the eastern end of the Strand. Its most famous resident was 'Chunee' the elephant, who ran amok and was destroyed by a keeper with a harpoon after a contingent of troops from Somerset House had failed to dispatch it.

introduced him to the country's foremost exponent of neoclassical sculpture:

'Pray, stop a little, my Lord. I desire you to shake hands with Mr Flaxman, for he is a man as extraordinary in his way as you are in yours. Believe me, he is the sculptor who ought to make your monument.'[2]

'Is he?', Nelson replied, gripping Flaxman's hand; 'then I heartily wish he may.'[3]

Sir William was also present at Nelson's meeting with another memorialist — albeit in a different medium. On 23 December 1800, two years after his victory at the Nile, Nelson sat at table among company that included Benjamin West, President of the Royal Academy of Arts. West was at this time most famous for his portrayal of an incident during the American War of Independence — *The Death of General Wolfe*, painted thirty years earlier in 1771. Nelson remarked to Sir William that he regretted never having acquired a taste for art. Then he turned to West. 'But there is one picture,' he said, 'whose power I *do* feel. I never pass a print-shop with your "Death of Wolfe" in the window, without being stopped by it.' He asked the painter why he had done no more pictures like it.

'Because, my Lord, there are no more subjects,' the painter replied, meaning no more subjects of comparable nobility or heroism in the modern world.

'Damn it,' said Nelson, 'I didn't think of that.'

Then, referring to the extraordinary bravery in battle, bordering on recklessness, that had already lost Nelson his right arm, the sight of an eye, and mutilated his forehead, West went on: 'But, my Lord, I fear your intrepidity will yet furnish me with such another scene; and if it should, I shall certainly avail myself of it.'

'Will you?' said Nelson excitedly, '*Will* you Mr West? Then I hope I shall die in the next battle.'

Although failing to get himself killed during the battle of Copenhagen the following April, Nelson fulfilled his pledge off Cape Trafalgar, and within a month of the news arriving in London, West had begun work on a canvas six feet high and eight wide, a foot wider and taller than *The Death of General Wolfe*, and which accommodated fifty-eight individual portraits to the other's fourteen. The composition mirrored that of his earlier picture: Wolfe reclining diagonally from left to right, Nelson from right to left, the native American Indian contemplating the general balanced on the right by the kneeling figure of Able Seaman Saunders laying a Spanish flag at the admiral's feet. Like others of the *Victory*'s crew who came to London from Chatham to sit for their portraits, Saunders was given a guinea by West to defray his expenses. He told the diarist Joseph Farington that he had not in fact seen Nelson after he was shot as he was carried below decks immediately. This was far from the only liberty West took with the accuracy of the scene. Although master's mate and secretary to Captain Hardy, Thomas Goble – depicted standing between Lieutenants Andrew King and Edward Williams – had made himself available for three months offering technical advice, West felt under no constraints to execute a piece of slavish documentary realism. It was, Farington believed, a picture 'of what might have been, not of the circumstances as they happened'. Instead of showing Nelson stripped of his uniform in the cramped, windowless cockpit, lit only by oil lamps, West depicted him fully dressed, dying on the quarterdeck, surrounded by a reverent crowd of onlookers for whom the battle – still raging in the background – seems to have come to a halt out of respect. By May 1806 the painting was finished. In the space of just over a month, thirty thousand members of the public came to West's studio to see it, instinctively doffing their hats as they approached. It was the reaction he had strived for. 'There was no other way of representing the death of a Hero but by an Epic representation of it. It must exhibit the event in a way to excite awe & veneration,' he declared. 'Wolfe must not die like a common soldier under a Bush, neither should Nelson be represented dying in a gloomy hold of a ship, like a sick man in a Prison Hole.'[4]

Another painter, however, did just that and yet produced a scene no less inspiring: a semi-recumbent, white-shrouded central figure picked out by light from its brown, crepuscular surroundings, like the Christ child in a Rembrandt Nativity. Arthur William Devis's canvas was the most meticulously researched contemporary depiction of Nelson's death. Striving for authenticity the artist had attended the shipboard autopsy conducted by Beatty in Portsmouth and made a forensic drawing of the musket ball with its attached fragments of epaulette and woollen cloth, just as it was extracted from the corpse. He would also make preparatory sketches on *Victory*'s orlop deck, with the aid of which he was able to construct in a corner of his painting room a full-size model of the place where Nelson died: an empty stage set for the solemn drama he was planning to depict. Even so he had to enlarge the dimensions of the cramped space and raise the overhead beams in his composition to comfortably accommodate the more than six-foot-tall figure of Captain Hardy and sixteen other attendants.

Two years after finishing his epically conceived 'Death of Nelson', West would produce another, following Devis's example – *The Death of Lord Nelson in the Cockpit of the 'Victory'*. Commissioned as a book illustration for a factual biography* of Nelson, former liberties taken with the subject were necessarily curtailed, but the portrait format, most suitable for reproduction on the page, made of it a stilted and uncomfortable performance.

When a monumental wall painting – twelve feet high and nearly forty-six long – was commissioned for the Royal Gallery of the newly built Palace of Westminster in 1858, West's preference for imagined heroism over historical accuracy was favoured by the Irish painter Daniel Maclise. Again, Nelson expires on deck, Dr Beatty bending over him, a kneeling sailor presenting a captured enemy flag – in this case a French tricolour. Again, he is attended by officers, common seamen and marines, apparently pausing for the moment from fighting while a black sailor at the back points upward towards the source of the fatal shot. Maclise's incidental research is apparent in the 'still lifes' occupying the foreground: Nelson's hat with its attached eyeshade; Mr Scott's secretarial

---

* *The Life of Admiral Lord Nelson K.B.* (1809) by James Stanier Clarke and John McArthur.

papers lying next to the meagre trickle of blood from his evisceration; a signal slate, 'ENGLAND EXPECTS' and the rest chalked upon it with the numbers of Popham's code. Elsewhere there is a bar shot, a canvas-bound bundle of grape and assorted gunnery paraphernalia: a wad, a wadhook or worm, and a rammer.

Like its companion picture – *The Meeting of Wellington and Blücher after the Battle of Waterloo* – on the opposite wall, *The Death of Nelson* was painted by Maclise using the water-glass technique, a variety of fresco in which the painted plaster is coated with potassium or sodium silicate which dries to a protective film. This method was thought necessary to preserve the murals against damp from the Thames and filth of the London air. Nonetheless, after only a decade both paintings had deteriorated so rapidly that the *Art Journal* declared, 'we look forward eagerly to the removal of these unfortunate frescoes which year by year blacken on the wall.' They remain in place today but, fortunately, a finished oil study by Maclise – scaled down to just under twelve feet in length – preserves the original colours.*

*

Commissioned in 1808, Flaxman's marble statue would not be finished and installed in St Paul's for another ten years, while at Westminster Abbey the professional singers employed as choirmen, or lay vicars, were quicker off the mark in raising their own, somewhat vulgar monument.

The decision to stage Nelson's funeral and interment in the newer cathedral on Ludgate Hill had marked a considerable change in government policy regarding future ceremonials of its kind. Seeking royal approval, the Secretary of State for Home Affairs, Lord Hawkesbury, had explained: 'As Westminster Abbey is at this time so very crowded with monuments, and as it was thought proper to lodge Standards taken from your Majesty's enemies in

---

* It is exhibited in the same room of the Walker Art Gallery, Liverpool, as Benjamin West's 1806 version.

the different naval victories in the last war, at St Paul's, your Majesty will perhaps consider that cathedral as the fittest place for this melancholy ceremony, as well as for the erection in future of such monuments ... to the memory of those who ... have rendered considerable naval and military services to the country.' In brief, St Paul's was to be a pantheon of sorts, dedicated to Mars and Neptune. And so, when Westminster's overcrowded mausoleum was denied the accommodation of both Nelson's remains and monument, and the choirmen thereby lost a significant source of revenue, they were quick to invest in a rival attraction.[5]

The Abbey already housed a collection of life-sized royal and aristocratic effigies, originally carried in funeral processions, fully and sumptuously clothed, then later shown to visitors by choirmen to supplement their salaries. The earliest were carved and painted wooden mannequins of Henry V's queen Catherine de Valois, of Henry VII and Elizabeth I. Among the most recent, their heads and hands realistically modelled in wax, were the 2nd Duke of Buckingham and his wife Catherine Sheffield, illegitimate daughter of James II. The Duchess's effigy was the last to have been displayed at its subject's funeral in 1743, long after the tradition and practice of processing such likenesses had passed. When William Pitt the Elder, 1st Earl of Chatham, died in 1778, the abbey choirmen commissioned the American modeller, Mrs Patience Wright to supply a wax head and hands to a figure of the statesman, in the hope of attracting paying visitors. Dressed in a specially made parliamentary robe, it proved a great success with the public – despite the customary threepence admission fee being doubled – and soon defrayed the twenty guineas paid to Mrs Wright.

Press criticism levelled at the mercenary exposure of Nelson's coffin, like one of Mrs Salmon's exhibits, found an ironic echo in the Abbey choirmen's presentation of a waxwork created by Catherine Andras, modeller to the Crown. Miss Andras had made a profile drawing in 1800 of the then rear admiral, and at about the same time created a wax portrait which received a prize at the Society of Arts and Sciences in March of the following year.

A week before Nelson's funeral she placed an advertisement in the *Morning Herald*, informing the public that the model 'for which his Lordship did her the honour to sit, having met with the decided APPROBATION OF HIS Lordship's most intimate Friends', copies were offered for sale, either by direct application to her, 'or at Mr Shrapnel's Jeweller, Charing Cross'. Later that year she exhibited a full sized effigy, at Bowyer's Historic Gallery in Pall Mall, 'made so exactly to resemble nature that it is with truth described as a perfect facsimile'. Emma Hamilton declared that 'the general carriage of the body was exactly his, and altogether the likeness was so great it was impossible for anyone who had known him to doubt about or mistake it.' Having made a final adjustment to a lock of hair, she is said to have only refrained from kissing the lips when told that the paint was still wet. The *Morning Post* reported that Miss Andras had 'with great liberality [been] presented . . . with the whole of the cloaths in which the model appears, and which was often worn by the gallant NELSON.' In fact only the shirt, embroidered 'HN24' as a laundry mark, was authentically his own, the coat having been made for the exhibition and the cocked hat supplied by James Lock, hatter, of St James's Street. Although particular attention was paid to attaching a green eyeshade to the hat, the glass 'blind' eye was secured in the left socket instead of the right. When the choirmen of the Abbey bought it from Miss Andras following the Pall Mall exhibition, it was placed in St Andrew's Chapel against a painted background of ships at sea. The words of Nelson's apocryphal battle cry, 'Victory or Westminster Abbey', were inscribed on the display case as if to validate the effigy of one not actually buried there.[6]

*

It would take four years to complete the tomb in St Paul's Cathedral crypt. By 1810, a heavy black marble plinth, deeply incised in gilt, HORATIO VISC. NELSON, with white marble moulding top and bottom, was placed onto Mylne's original austere granite structure, and surmounted by a massive, highly polished ornamental chest of black Lydian stone* measuring seven feet by four, and two and a half feet high, to which was affixed a large decorative cushion supporting an oversized viscount's coronet. Both plinth and chest had been designed and sculpted nearly three centuries earlier for the burial and glorification of someone else: at the height of his prosperity, power and influence in the court of King Henry VIII, Cardinal Wolsey commissioned the Florentine sculptor Benedetto da Rovezzano to create an ostentatious resting place for his own mortal remains. Following his fall from royal favour in 1529, his subsequent death, and less grandiose burial at York, the unfinished Benedetto monument was appropriated by the King for his own eventual use. However, following his death it remained, unused, throughout the reign of Elizabeth I at Windsor Castle. King Charles I later planned to be buried beneath it. But following the Civil War and Commonwealth, when the metalwork trappings intended to decorate the tomb – the bronze pillars topped with candlestick-bearing angels, kneeling angels in gilded bronze, small figures of saints, and 'four naked children' – were sold off to finance the army, the forgotten stone monument remained in twenty-nine pieces, with other 'lumber', in a chamber adjacent to St George's Chapel. It is not known precisely when George III gave his permission for the Wolsey tomb to be repurposed for the national hero, nor was it mentioned in the London newspapers,† but the lumber cluttering the chamber was removed towards the end of 1810 by labourers preparing it as a vault 'his Majesty intended ... for the interment of the remains of his family'. That work was assuming particular urgency by the long decline and imminent death on 2 November of his youngest

---

* Basanite, a variety of flinty slate, also known as 'touchstone' from its property as a test for gold or silver according to the colour of the mark each makes on it.

† Although an item appearing in early 1810 only served to confuse the issue, by mistakenly assigning it to the recently deceased second-in-command at Trafalgar: 'It is a curious fact, that the remains of Lord Collingwood are deposited in the very stone coffin which Cardinal Wolsey had prepared for himself ... and for its last purpose was given as a present by his Majesty' (*General Evening Post*, 24 May 1810).

and favourite child, the twenty-seven-year-old consumptive Princess Amelia.[7]

The impressive article of monumental masonry that Nelson inherited from Wolsey is usually referred to as a sarcophagus, its implied purpose the containment of the body. This is a misleading term. 'The body of Wolsey would [have] rest[ed] in a vault under the tomb, as, in point of fact, Nelson's does, and not in the sarcophagus itself.'[8]

II

WHEN the officers and ship's company of HMS *Orion* had assembled on 14 November, their captain read to them a proposal from Admiral Collingwood that two thousand pounds should be deducted from the prize money for the action – money that everyone knew to be a fraction of the sum lost to them by the destruction of ships captured on 21 October – for the purpose of erecting a monument on Portsdown Hill, above Portsmouth, to the memory of Lord Nelson. The officers and ship's company all agreed to this, 'and as much more if required'. Captain Codrington added a note to the ship's log in his own hand: 'The people thought it too little.' *Conqueror*'s log recorded the same decision, 'unanimously agreed to'. This ship's figurehead had been decapitated during the battle and her crew requested it be replaced by a bust of Nelson, made and fitted at their own expense. Three months later, it was reported to be 'carving at Plymouth ... more than ordinary care devoted to its execution'.[9]

Over the following decades, across the United Kingdom and the Empire, iconography would be crafted in wood, iron, bronze, marble, Portland and artificial stone, concrete, wax, oil paint and embroidery. Monuments and memorials varied in form, but all were generated by a single death in action.

Ephemeral tributes to Nelson and the battle were devised to meet the demands of fashion. 'The Trafalgar turban is much worn,' the *Ipswich Journal* reported, 'and is extremely elegant; the crown of royal purple, with a Turkish roll of muslin, caught up in front, with the word Trafalgar beautifully embroidered on purple velvet; it encircles an ostrich feather, or a sprig of laurel.' Lady Elizabeth Foster was said to have dressed for a time in 'black cockades, with [Nelson's] name embroidered on every drapery she wears'. Elsewhere the name of the battle was a mark of virility for equine bloodstock when a three-year-old bay horse – '15½ hands high, full of bone, with good action; promis[ing] to be a remarkable fast trotter' – was called 'TRAFALGAR', and advertised to 'COVER THIS SEASON', at Ditton Hall, near Cambridge, for a fee of 'One GUINEA a Mare and one shilling the Groom.' During the naval action off San Domingo in February 1806, a portrait of Nelson hung from the mizen stay of HMS *Superb*. Her captain, Richard Goodwin Keats – doubtless still remorseful at missing his own chance of immortality – had placed it there to encourage the men, as the ship's band played 'God Save the King', 'Off she goes', and 'Nelson of the Nile' before hostilities began. By the end of the engagement the portrait 'was completely covered with the blood and brains' of Mr Brookbank, the coxswain's mate, as was Keats himself.[10]

Ireland provided the first permanent monument, on a hill outside Castletownshend in County Cork: a crude granite arch, '20 feet in clear height above its base; the walls ... every where 12 feet in thickness'. It was erected on 11 November, the first Sunday following the arrival of the news, by a party of local Sea Fencibles under the command of Captain Joshua Rowley Watson. In a 'most animated and animating speech' he announced that 'he had brought them there that they might dedicate [the] day, he hoped not unworthily, to the erecting on the spot, visible from all the surrounding land and sea, a Memorial of the Fall of the greatest of Heroes, in the acquisition of the most splendid of Victories.' Within just six hours the work was complete. It would be partly demolished by Irish nationalists in 1920 but restored within two years before being definitively blown up in 1966, some days after a better-known memorial suffered the same fate in Dublin.[11]

A ready-made monument was raised above Loch Etive in

Argyllshire. On 25 December 1805, workers of the Lorne Iron Furnace dug up a monolith from the 'Druidical circle near Aird's Bay' and dragged it to the summit of Cnoc Aingeal, or 'Hill of Angels'. The foundry was said to have once made cannonballs for the Royal Navy and this explained the iron workers' Christmas Day labour. A local schoolmaster penned a dedicatory ode that would not have disgraced the later career of William McGonagall:

> 'Twas for Nelson's great victorie
> This monument was erect you see;
> When the combined he did defeat,
> And captured twenty of their fleet.
>
> But, alas! Dear was the prize,
> For therein our Nelson dies:
> For a rifle from their tops
> Strikes our hero, and – he drops!
>
> But altho' he is no more,
> Still his memory we adore;
> And ever to the end of time,
> Keep his great exploits in mind.[12]

Three gigantic, outcropped rocks at the highest point of Birchen Edge in the Peak District of Derbyshire became natural memorials, their weathered sides carved with the ships' names, 'VICTORY', 'DEFIANCE', and 'ROYAL SOVERIN'. Nearby, a simple twelve-foot-high, square gritstone pillar surmounted by a ball of the same material was erected at the expense of John Brightman, a local worthy.

*

Among the nine models and designs for naval monuments shown at the Royal Academy's Exhibition in March 1807 – the majority destined for oblivion – one was under construction: a 'Cenotaph, erecting on Portsdown Hill, to the memory of Lord Nelson by the officers, seamen, and marines of the fleet under his command at the Battle of Trafalgar'. The £2,000 of prize money – unanimously voted following the action – had been supplemented by donations of two day's pay by all who served, amounting to a further £1,000. The foundation stone had been laid on 4 July 1806, 'the farmer holding the lease of the ground on which it [was] to be erected, as well as Mr Thistlewaite, the Lord of the Manor, having offered the grant of it without purchase'. It was unveiled towards the end of 1808: a granite obelisk, 150 feet tall, with a niche at the top containing a bust of Nelson sculped by John Groves that watched over Portsmouth and the Channel.[13]

Close by – a more substantial memorial – the angular ramparts and gun emplacements of Fort Nelson face inland, protecting the heights of Portsdown Hill from capture by a potential foreign invader intent on attacking the Royal Navy's dockyards below. The threat of invasion fifty years after Trafalgar was posed by another French emperor – Napoleon III, Bonaparte's nephew. This time it would be supported by a growing French 'ironclad' navy and launched from a newly strengthened port and garrison at Cherbourg, 'a dagger pointed at the heart of this country', according to Lord Palmerston. Despite Britain's military alliance with France against Russia during the Crimean War of 1853–6, she was still the most likely future enemy to be reckoned with. Second in a line of fortifications along the chalk ridge – between Wallington in the west and Purbrook in the east – construction of Fort Nelson began in 1861 and was completed a decade later. By that time – and the arrival of the first troops to defend it – the threat of an invasion mounted from Cherbourg had, in fact, been permanently removed by France's defeat in the Franco-Prussian war of 1870–71, followed by Napoleon III's surrender and capture at Sedan and his subsequent abdication. The redundant fortifications, built at the behest of the Prime Minister and on the recommendation of a Royal Commission on the Defence of the United Kingdom, became known as Palmerston's Follies.

Another design displayed at the Academy's 1807 Exhibition

was an elaborate allegory by Benjamin West. Conceived and completed between his epic first *Death of Nelson* and mundane second, it marked a decisive departure from both. Most of the *Sketch for a Monument to Lord Nelson* – the base, pillars, entablature and flanking figures of sailors and marines that frame its central painted composition – was rendered in *grisaille*, or monochrome, suggesting architectural or sculptural form. The allegory itself, as West explained in the Exhibition catalogue, 'represents Victory presenting the dead body of the hero to Britannia ... from the arms of Neptune ... Britannia sits in shaded gloom, as expressive of that deep regret which overwhelmed the United Kingdom at the loss of so distinguished a character.' Although the monument was never realised as depicted in West's *Sketch*, he subsequently adapted his composition of the principal figures – Neptune, Nelson, Victory, Britannia and an accompanying lion – into the gigantic sculptural group he created with Joseph Panzetta to occupy the ten-foot-high, forty-foot-wide pediment on the Royal Naval College, Greenwich.[14]

*

The first civic monument raised by public subscription was in Glasgow: a 144-foot sandstone obelisk, its foundation stone laid on 1 August 1806 and finished, at a cost of £2,075, a year and a week afterwards, on 7 August 1807. Three years later, on the fifth day of a month that was proving to be momentous, August 1810, it suffered a lightning strike, 'the column torn open for more than 20 feet from the top, and several of the stones ... thrown down ... A number of the stones [were left] hanging in such a threatening posture that a military guard [was] very properly ... placed around the monument to keep at a distance too thoughtless or too daring spectators.'[15]

Hearing that the monument was to be repaired, and a poetic inscription placed on it, the following 'effusion' was submitted by the Revd James Grahame, who believed that the result of a providential act of God should not be tampered with:

Withold, withhold, the sacrilegious hand!
That lofty ruin still a ruin stand!
Nor let those lines, which Heaven's own fire hath traced,
By mortal numbers ever be effaced.
What record so sublime, of him who fell
Where thousand thunders peal'd his parting knell,
As Nature's sculpture, trench'd by forky leven!
As characters engraved by bolts from Heaven!
Inscribed by Fate. Leave then th'unrivalled plan:
The monument an emblem of the man.[16]

Equipped belatedly with a lightning conductor – or 'thunder rod' – the obelisk still stands on Glasgow Green, all evidence of heavenly intervention effaced by mortal restoration. There is no accompanying verse.

In 1807 the Lord Provost of Edinburgh laid the foundation stone on top of Calton Hill for a 105-foot castellated circular tower designed by Robert Burn. Construction stopped the following year when money ran out and was not resumed until 1814, to be completed two years later. An inscription above the entrance reads:

TO THE MEMORY OF
VICE-ADMIRAL
HORATIO LORD VISCOUNT NELSON,
AND THE GREAT VICTORY OF TRAFALGAR,
TOO DEARLY PURCHASED WITH HIS BLOOD,
THE GRATEFUL CITIZENS OF EDINBURGH
HAVE ERECTED THIS MONUMENT:
NOT TO EXPRESS THEIR UNAVAILING SORROW FOR HIS DEATH:
NOR YET TO CELEBRATE THE MATCHLESS GLORIES OF HIS LIFE:
BUT BY HIS NOBLE EXAMPLE TO TEACH THEIR SONS
TO EMULATE WHAT THEY ADMIRE, AND LIKE HIM,
WHEN DUTY REQUIRES IT,
TO DIE FOR THEIR COUNTRY.

Burn's creation was 'differently and yet, in both cases aptly compared to a telescope and a butterchurn' according to Robert Louis Stevenson, who added that 'comparisons apart, it ranks among the vilest of men's handiworks.' Rooms on the ground floor were originally intended 'as accommodation to a few disabled seamen' but subsequently 'leased to a vendor of soups and sweetmeats... and the visitors to the monument [given] the opportunity of eating... and drinking, under certain restrictions, to the memory of the great hero'. In 1853 a mechanism was devised on crosstrees at the top that caused a five-foot-diameter black ball to drop down a mast every day on the stroke of one o'clock, allowing ships' masters in the Firth of Forth to set and adjust their chronometers. Eight years later this facility was supplemented by firing a one o'clock gun each day from the Castle ramparts – an audible signal should the falling of the time-ball be obscured by fog.[17]

A subscription had been opened in Dublin and submission of designs invited in early 1806. On 15 February 1808 a foundation stone was laid in Sackville – now O'Connell – Street, close to the General Post Office. The winning design, by the Norfolk architect William Wilkins, was for a fluted Greek Doric column on a plinth resembling a 'chaste Grecian mausoleum', raised on fourteen steps. He proposed an eight-oared Roman galley for the top, but the selection committee recorded that – with only £3,827 collected, and an estimated cost of £5,000 for the plinth and column alone – 'means were not placed in their hands to enable them to gratify [Mr Wilkins], as well as themselves, by executing his design precisely as he had given it.' Francis Johnston, an Irish architect, subsequently modified the design, bringing it in for £4,503, and – because the funds raised by public subscription had since increased to £6,299 – the column could be surmounted by a thirteen-foot-high Portland stone statue of Nelson, carved by a young Dublin sculptor, Thomas Kirk. Completed in 1809, an internal spiral of 168 steps allowed visitors to reach a viewing platform below the figure. James Joyce would describe the experience:

They give two threepenny bits to the gentleman at the turnstile and begin to waddle slowly up the winding staircase, grunting, encouraging each other, afraid of the dark, panting ... praising God and the Blessed Virgin, threatening to come down, peeping at the airslits, Glory be to God. They had no idea it was that high ... they go nearer to the railings ... Two old Dublin women on the top of Nelson's pillar ... But they are afraid the pillar will fall ... They see the roofs and argue about where the different churches are ... But it makes them giddy to look so they pull up their skirts ... And settle down on their striped petticoats, peering up at the statue of the onehandled adulterer ... It gives them a crick in their necks ... and they are too tired to look up or down or to speak.[18]

Completed in Birmingham in the year following Kirk's lofty Dublin statue, and for a subscribed sum of £2,500, Richard Westmacott's bronze presented Nelson at less than life size, his left arm resting on the stock of a ship's anchor, with the bow of HMS *Victory* behind him. The round pedestal bore on its face a low relief carving of a female figure representing 'the town of Birmingham ... in a dejected attitude ... mourning her loss; ... accompanied by Groups of Genii, or children, in allusion to the rising race, who offer her consolation by bringing her [a] Trident and Rudder'. The statue was unveiled on 25 September 1810, a month before the end of George III's Golden Jubilee year. The original pedestal would be replaced by a plain one in 1961, when the monument was moved during the redevelopment of the Bull Ring Centre and its allegorical relief lost. Westmacott created a similar figure of Nelson in 1813, for Bridgetown, Barbados, but without the accessories of ship and anchor.[19]

The earliest memorial to Nelson outside the British Isles was Robert Mitchell's sixty-two-foot-high column and statue in Montreal, completed in 1809. The figure was moulded in an artificial material perfected about 1770 and manufactured by the London firm of Coade and Sealy. Originally called 'Lithodipyra' – ancient Greek for 'stone fired twice' – but more commonly known as Coade stone, it was highly valued for its resistance to weathering.

Nevertheless, after nearly 190 years Mitchell's statue was relocated to the city's museum for preservation, and a copy replaced it on the column.

Another column, completed in September 1819, was surprisingly slow in the raising considering it was intended to honour the county of Norfolk's most celebrated son. It had been first mooted following the battle of the Nile, but only after Trafalgar did it again become a subject for consideration. Even so, the proposal for a monument, either at Burnham Thorpe, the hero's birthplace, or the county town of Norwich, 'foundered from lack of support'. It would be ten years before a committee had been established to raise funds, and a decision made that the monument serve the additional purpose of a 'seamark' for mariners – disqualifying both the landbound sites previously considered – and designating Great Yarmouth instead. It was designed by the Norfolk-born William Wilkins, using the plan he had submitted to the Dublin commissioners, but without the Roman galley. In its place, above the Doric capital, a podium supported six Coade stone caryatids – described as 'Victorys' – supporting in their turn a stone canopy bearing a globe on which stands the figure of Britannia, also in Coade stone, carrying an olive branch and trident. Given the monument's intended use as a navigational aid it had been hoped to receive funding from Trinity House – the body responsible for lighthouses – but that would only have been forthcoming for a considerably taller column, and Wilkins's had already required reducing by 20 feet because the ground at the site would not have sustained the height and weight originally proposed.

A monument to Nelson stands on a rocky shore in North Wales and was also intended to serve a nautical function. Lord Clarence Paget had been four years old when his father lost a leg at the battle of Waterloo. The younger son of the 1st Marquess of Anglesey, he entered the Royal Navy aged sixteen as a midshipman and rose, in the course of a fifty-year career, to the rank of vice admiral, and eventually to Nelson's former position as Commander-in-Chief of the Mediterranean Fleet. Following his retirement, at Plas Llanfair on the island of Anglesey, and under the bronze gaze of his illustrious father on top of a nearby column, he indulged an amateur passion for sculpture. He was originally planning a statue of Neptune, until persuaded otherwise. 'What has Neptune done for us?' he is said to have been asked. 'Nelson is the proper subject.' Paget's particular enthusiasm was for the unprepossessing sculptural medium of concrete, 'his primary object ... to show that statues can be constructed of a material little inferior to marble in appearance, and probably more durable, at one tenth the cost.' Made from a combination of limestone and Portland cement, strengthened by the insertion of a central iron core, the figure stands nineteen feet in height including plinth, on a pedestal and basement tower twenty-two feet high, forty-one feet in total. Its precise location on the Menai Strait was requested by maritime surveyors, its object, his lordship explained, 'to form a good leading mark through the Swilly channel* on the north side, and to clear a rock to the southward, pointing out to the mariner an unerring path from which it is dangerous to digress'. Lady Paget unveiled the monument on 9 September 1873, dedicating it 'to all mariners'. As salutes boomed from the Admiralty steamer and from the land, as the Naval Reserve and Coastguard fired a *feu de joie* and the band played 'Rule Britannia', it was already marked on all the latest official charts of the area.[20]

---

* The Swillies (or Swellies) is a particularly turbulent stretch of water beset with rocks at the confluence of two tides. Safely negotiable only at slack – either side of high – water, its passage requires careful timing. There is a local tradition that Nelson once claimed a sailor who could successfully navigate the Menai Strait could navigate anywhere on earth. There is no evidence, however, that he ever sailed in that area, or held any such opinion either way.

III

TRAFALGAR Square was not so named until the reign of William IV. On his accession to the throne in 1830, the square – then still in development – was to have been given the monarch's name, until 'the opportunity of recording the victory at which Nelson fell a sacrifice' was suggested to him by the architect George Ledwell Taylor. 'I like the idea,' said the King and scrawled a note to Lord Duncannon, Chief Commissioner of the Office of Woods, Forests, Land Revenues, Works and Public Buildings: 'TRAFALGAR SQUARE, WILLIAM REX'. And so it was decided.

In 1798, while still Duke of Clarence, William had presided over a committee 'for raising a Naval Pillar or monument' to commemorate the battle of the Nile. A public subscription was launched and a competition proposed but, despite the euphoria following the victory at Aboukir Bay, it came to nothing and the funds collected were returned to subscribers.

In the welter of conflicting emotions following news from Trafalgar, the Court of Common Council of the City of London lost no time in inviting submissions for a monument to Nelson in the Guildhall. A little-known sculptor, James Smith, won the commission and his white marble extravaganza, twenty-four feet high, was installed by April 1811 at a cost of £4,211 10s 10d. It incorporated a nude figure of Neptune, reclining with his trident against a dolphin and cornucopia on a rocky base strewn with shells and seaweed. A doleful Britannia, seated on the back of an equally doleful lion, contemplates a roundel portrait of the hero, while a female figure representing the City inscribes on an upright stele the names of Nelson's last three victories. At either side of the main group are the draperies of five captured flags, from which a cable and anchor stock and the breech of a cannon protrude. At the centre of the fourteen-feet-wide pedestal, below a lengthy encomium from Richard Brinsley Sheridan, is a bas-relief of the final battle, and inscribed underneath, the fervent hope of the Lord Mayor, Aldermen and Common Council, that the monument 'WILL REMAIN AS LONG AS THEIR OWN RENOWNED CITY SHALL EXIST'.

Standing in niches to right and left of the pedestal are miniature figures of sailors, stripped to the waist, one carrying a ramrod, the other a fathom line and lead weight – implements of warfare and navigation. Originally intended to represent prisoners of war, the alteration was intended to emphasise the contribution to victory of the common seaman.[21]

For more than thirty years, Smith's Guildhall confection remained London's only public monument to Nelson. In 1816 a National Monument to the armed services was proposed – its naval component commemorating the battle of Trafalgar – but the project was postponed in the climate of austerity following nearly a quarter-century of war. Then a committee was established in 1838 to oversee the raising of a monument to Nelson, specifying at first only that it should be 'in a conspicuous part of [the] metropolis', and later, inevitably, that 'every possible endeavour [be made] to obtain a space of ground in Trafalgar Square as the site of the proposed monument'. A contribution of £5,545 19s from the Patriotic Fund – amassing interest since 1805 – was made to the subscription, which by February 1839 amounted to £15,255 18s.

In all, 168 models and drawings by more than fifty-five architects and sculptors were submitted for the committee's consideration. They included a 'very sweetly moulded' maquette by Benedetto Pistrucci for a colossal trident, and three recumbent female figures draped on a segment of a sphere. It was uncertain how the 'prongs and handle' of this novelty would translate when 'magnified to the gigantic scale' required, to 'say nothing of [its] sufficiency ... to fulfil the idea of a national monument to an individual hero'. Walter Granville offered a 218-feet-high pedestal, column and statue in cast iron and brass. It was to be surmounted by Britannia 'standing on a globe, hurling ... thunder-bolts as emblems of naval power with her right hand, and holding in her left hand the sceptre of the sea'. This, explained the sculptor, was 'a more appropriate termination to a lofty column ... than the statue of the hero himself'. The design and material might also have been regarded as tempting fate, when the wrecking of Glasgow's obelisk by lightning strike nearly thirty years earlier was recalled. And, considering the English climate and the effects over time of rust, one critic asked how long the iron pillar would last. Thomas Moule suggested a statuary group: Nelson with a captain and boatswain in attendance. 'Without diminishing the importance of the principal figure, this,' he argued, 'would show the different grades of the navy, and form a just tribute to their successful co-operation.' He also denigrated, by implication, a number of his competitors' plans. 'To place a lofty column in such a situation is objectionable in point of taste, as its height would overpower the facade of the building erected as a National Gallery, in front of which [it] is intended to be placed.'[22]

William Railton won the first prize with just such a column, Edward Hodges Baily the second with an obelisk, and the third prize went to a joint submission by the sculptor Robert Sievier and architect Charles Fowler, presenting a 128-foot tiered tower, surmounted by a statue of Nelson and incorporating at its various levels, antique ships' prows or *rostra*, and colossal figures of Caledonia, Hibernia and Britannia accompanied by couchant lions. For good measure, it would also feature Neptune 'reclining on a sea-horse, 23 feet in length'. Both Railton and Baily had included statues of Nelson in their designs, Railton's on top of his column, Baily's at the base of his obelisk, and it was eventually decided that the various elements of the monument were to be assigned to different individuals. Railton's column would constitute the main component, at an estimated cost of £16,500 – including scaffolding – and another £1,000 for the Corinthian capital and mouldings, while Baily was asked to estimate the cost of a statue in bronze. An unsuccessful competitor, John Graham Lough, was considered for the Egyptian – later African – reclining lions, radiating from the column's base, that had formed part of Railton's original design. However, Lough's estimate of 3,000 guineas for the four twenty-feet-long beasts to be carved in red granite was deemed prohibitively expensive and deferred, as were the bronze reliefs of St Vincent, Nile, Copenhagen and Trafalgar also conceived by Railton to be set into each face of the pedestal.

*

Baily had originally estimated that casting the statue of Nelson in bronze, not more than seventeen feet high, would cost £5,000, but should the metal be supplied by the Committee its market value could be deducted from that sum. Competitive tenders by rival sculptors were submitted for carving the figure in artificial stone, Portland, or Roach Abbey limestone. One proposal for using such materials in preference to bronze was supported by the argument that it 'would not be resorted to as plunder in revolutions'. Asked to estimate the cost of a figure in Portland stone, Baily agreed to undertake it for £1,000. The Committee's chairman, the Duke of Buccleuch, owned the Granton quarry near Edinburgh – source of a particularly fine type of Craigleith sandstone, denser than Portland stone, and when this was finally chosen, Baily was awarded an additional £112 for the increased labour involved in its carving. Even so, it proved impossible to ship a single block large enough to accommodate a sixteen-feet-high figure and the roughed-out stone was instead landed at Westminster in two parts on 25 June 1842. It was also decided that Railton's column would be surmounted by a Corinthian capital in bronze, and cannon from Woolwich Arsenal were donated for its casting.[23]

Just over a year later the statue was nearly finished, and on 3 and 4 November 1843 the two main sections were hoisted into position on top of the pillar. The separately sculpted left arm, fitted with its bronze sword, was the last piece to be attached. Only when the scaffolding was taken down was it noticed that, seen from the ground, the large coil of rope serving as a buttress at the rear of the statue created an alarming 'appearance as if the figure was not in a perfectly erect position'. Scaffolding was re-erected for adjustments to be made and canvas placed around the statue to shelter the masons from the inclement January weather. When it was finally exposed again to view, judicious 'clippings' had cured the impression of imbalance, 'the coil of rope ... much diminished, and the left-hand tail of the coat being likewise lessened'. This 'undoubtedly much improved' the effect.[24]

It would be twelve years before the bronze reliefs of Nelson's triumphs – modelled by different hands* – were installed on the faces of the pedestal, and more than twenty before the lions, designed by the painter Edwin Landseer and cast in bronze by the sculptor Carlo Marochetti, were in place. Because Landseer – albeit the most celebrated animal painter of the day – was not primarily a sculptor his commission had been felt by one critic to be 'an unwise and unjust arrangement', while *The Times* roundly declared him to be 'the wrong man in the wrong place'. He had begun work making studies of a sick, elderly lion on loan from the London Zoological Society's collection until the creature died and he had to content himself with drawing its corpse. Later, he would spend time with more vigorous specimens, 'studying the habits of lions' and 'making himself thoroughly acquainted with their attitudes'. When all four were in place by the end of January 1867, they were highly praised and *The Times*, retreating from its former position, judged that 'never before has the king of beasts been so nobly and so truthfully treated in sculpture'. The *Illustrated London News* declared them to be a credit to the nation and would 'do honour to the English school of sculpture'.

---

* *Battle of Cape St Vincent* (west face) by M.L. Watson and W.F. Woodington; *Battle of the Nile* (north face) by W.F. Woodington; *Battle of Copenhagen* (east face) by J. Ternouth; *The Death of Nelson* (south face) by J.E. Carew.

However, their very excellence, and particularly their proportions, rendered them, it was felt by one commentator, to be at odds with the monument as a whole. 'The column is shrunk into a walking-stick, and the statue of the hero on its summit is reduced, in its almost forgotten aerial limbo, to a mere puppet by the magnitude of the animals and the masses they form.'[25]

*

At 1.30 in the morning of Tuesday 8 March 1966 – the half-centenary year of the Easter Rising – the Doric column and statue of Nelson in O'Connell Street, Dublin, blew up. Access had been gained to the interior by forcing the door at its base and the charges laid at the top of the spiral staircase – 'a necklace of explosives' – underneath the observation platform. The effect, on detonation, was to direct the force of the explosion upwards to the statue itself, smashing it to pieces and leaving just two-thirds of the monument standing as a broken reminder of British dominion. The authorities described it as 'the work of experts' and it was long assumed to have been perpetrated by the IRA, although their responsibility was denied in an official statement: 'We have refused to settle for the destruction of the symbols of domination; we are interested in the destruction of the domination itself.' In fact, the monument was destroyed by former members of the organisation and the operation was codenamed 'Humpty Dumpty'. The battered head of Nelson was recovered from the rubble, later stolen by art students and is today preserved in the Gilbert Library on Pearse Street. The bronze sword was said to have been picked up by an opportunist souvenir hunter, and its present whereabouts are unknown. The remaining stump was demolished by the Irish Army's Corps of Engineers at half past three on the following Monday morning. The charges were less expertly laid than previously and instead of tilting northwards as intended, the truncated column disintegrated on the plinth, shattering windows in the vicinity. A piece of masonry crashed through a jeweller's display, setting off the alarm, and glass in the Royal Bank, Burtons and the

General Post Office was smashed. 'Thousands of Dubliners and groups of Welshmen, still in the city after Saturday's rugby international, cheered the blast.'[26]

The destruction of a landmark known to generations of Dublin residents simply as 'The Pillar' – a convenient meeting place and a point marking the town centre for trams and, later, buses from the suburbs – was neither greatly regretted nor particularly celebrated, but viewed with amused tolerance – although one journalist did go so far as to say that 'the whole of Dublin' was 'secretly delighted'. A folk group calling themselves the Go Lucky Four wrote and recorded a jaunty accordion-backed song to the tune of 'John Brown's Body'. Embodying a mid-sixties perception of Irish republicanism as romantic, dashing and mischievously subversive, it reached number one in the Irish charts and stayed there for ten consecutive weeks:

> One early morning in the year of sixty-six
> A band of Irish laddies were knocking up some tricks
> They thought Horatio Nelson had overstayed a mite
> So they helped him on his way with some sticks of gelignite.
>
> Up went Nelson in old Dublin
> Up went Nelson in old Dublin
> All along O'Connell Street the stones and rubble flew
> As up went Nelson and the Pillar too.

More lethal operations during the following decade and beyond would alter British public perception and teach it the epithet 'terrorism'.

IV

IN June 2020 – at the height of the 'Black Lives Matter' campaign – a petition was submitted to Parliament to 'Remove the statue of racist and white supremacist Horatio Nelson from Nelson's Column in Trafalgar Square, instead displaying it in context elsewhere. The statue should be replaced by a plaque that explains its removal on the grounds of its glorification of a racist.' The statement continued: 'In our current political and social climate it is clear that it is inappropriate to continue to ignore the abhorrent views of an individual who is celebrated by one of London's most famous landmarks ... Nelson was a racist and white supremacist who fought against the abolition of the slave trade in the 19th century, instead encouraging slavery and its atrocities to benefit himself and his associates. We should discuss this history in a more appropriate setting, not celebrate it.'

In the same year a similar petition to take down the Richard Westmacott statue from National Heroes – formerly 'Trafalgar' – Square in Bridgetown, Barbados, was supported by over 10,000 signatures and it was accordingly removed to the city museum.

The London petition was rejected on the grounds that it called for action on an issue that only the local authority, and not the UK government or House of Commons, was responsible for. But had it been considered or even been successful, the proposed contextual display would undoubtedly have made much of a letter written by Nelson to his friend Simon Taylor – a plantation owner and the largest proprietor of slaves in Jamaica. It was written and dated 10 June 1805, aboard HMS *Victory*, as Nelson was pursuing Admiral Villeneuve's fleet from Antigua back across the Atlantic. His intention seems to have been to reassure Taylor and the other colonists of his and the Royal Navy's continued protection against the French. It constitutes the only known documentary evidence of Nelson's opinion on slavery, either positive or negative: 'Kind Providence may some happy day bless my endeavours to serve the Public of which the West India Colonies form so prominent and interesting a part. I ever have been and shall die a firm friend of our colonial system. I was bred as you know in the Good old school and taught to appreciate the value of our West India possessions, and neither in the field or the Senate shall their just rights be infringed whilst I have an arm to fight in their defence or a tongue to launch my voice against the damnable cruel doctrine of Wilberforce and his Hipocritical allies ... who would certainly cause the murder of all our friends and fellow subjects in the colonies.' The abolitionist Member of Parliament for Yorkshire, in attacking the practice of slavery – so Nelson reasoned – was destabilising and endangering the colonies and colonists themselves, in a time of war. Protecting Britain's colonial system against her enemies – as his naval officer's duty demanded – regardless of the slavery underpinning that system – proved him to be neither a racist nor a white supremacist. Following the abolition of the slave trade two years after Trafalgar the Royal Navy, tasked with applying the new legislation, captured over 1,600 slave ships and freed some 150,000 slaves. Had he lived, it must be assumed, Nelson would have seen it as no more than his duty to enforce the law of prohibition with the same vigour as he had previously preserved and protected the then legal slaving routes to and from the West Indies.[27]

Perhaps nowhere in Britain was the issue of the preservation or abolition of that trade more relevant than in Liverpool. The port's prosperity throughout the second half of the eighteenth century had been entirely based on the traffic in slaves. Admittedly, the triangular transatlantic trading route generally kept the noxious aspects of the business well away from Liverpool itself. Slave ships sailed from West Africa to the Caribbean and North American plantations and only the more wholesome merchandise of tobacco, sugar and cotton returned in them to the Mersey waterfront, departing thence with trading goods to exchange on the Gold Coast for their shackled westward-bound human cargoes. But the wealth enriching the port and people of Liverpool accrued from the entire interdependent cycle. 'Throughout this large-built Town', the Revd William Bagshaw Stevens declared in 1797, 'every Brick is cemented to its fellow Brick by the blood and sweat of Negroes.' And it should not be forgotten how broadly the profits and dividends were spread, implicating far more than those families who made vast fortunes from slavery and gave their eminent names to so many of the town's streets. A contemporary account made clear that 'almost every man in Liverpool is a merchant ... Almost every order of people is interested in a [slave] cargo ... It is well known that many of the small vessels that import about an hundred slaves are fitted out by attornies, drapers, ropers, grocers, tallow-chandlers, barbers, taylors, &c. some have a one-eighth share, some a fifteenth, and some a thirty-second.' By the beginning of the nineteenth century the heyday of the trade was past and the traffic – although not the overseas ownership – of slaves would be abolished under British law on 1 May 1807. But until then local newspaper advertisements provided ample reminders of the logistics, while at the same time suggesting that some far-sighted owners, anticipating the end, were selling off their assets:

> ON SALE, The Schooner WHIM, Burthen 110 ton ... copper fastened complete, and sheathed in copper, has only made two voyages ... this vessel from having great depth of hold, will answer for the African or general purposes of trade, and is capable of carrying 160 negroes. Also, the Ship BETSEY, likewise Coppered, 200 tons, three years old, a handsome swift sailing vessel, well found, and competent to any trade her size may suit, well adapted to the African trade, to carry about 230 slaves.[28]

Both vessels could be inspected by prospective buyers in the Nova Scotia graving dock,* a short distance from Liverpool's business quarter.

The sinister basis of the port's prosperity was well known, and on occasion the butt of dark humour, so that when the celebrated Irish actress Harriet Mellon appeared at the town's Theatre Royal in September 1805 attracting packed houses, a London paper made it the excuse for a gratuitous pleasantry: 'The west India merchants of Liverpool prove their respect for Miss MELLON, by making the Theatre, every night of her performance, as hot and as full as *a slave ship*.'[29]

*

News of the victory at Trafalgar and death of Nelson arrived in Liverpool by the mail coach from Plymouth on 7 November and within a week the mayor, Mr Henry Clay, had convened a meeting at the Town Hall 'to take into consideration the means of raising a Fund for defraying the expense and to adopt measures for erecting a PUBLIC MONUMENT ... to commemorate the VICTORIES and the ever to be lamented DEATH of Lord NELSON.'[30]

The location of the proposed monument was to be behind the Town Hall, at the very heart of the commercial centre, 'the square of the new Exchange Buildings now in so forward a state – Buildings which, but for our lamented Chief, might perhaps have mouldered to decay and served as the melancholy proofs of the triumphs of our enemies in the West Indies'. The monument, in short, was not so much to celebrate a national hero but, rather, the champion and protector of Liverpool's commercial interests and trading routes with the Caribbean.[31]

Liverpool's perceived indebtedness to Nelson was reflected in remarkably expeditious fundraising for his monument, its anticipated cost of £8,000 being met and exceeded in two months.

---

* A dry dock where 'graving', or cleaning a ship's hull below the water line, can take place.

£4,500 was collected by public subscription within a week of the Town Hall meeting and the fund had nearly doubled to £8,930 three months later. There were further contributions of £1,000 from the Liverpool Corporation, £500 from Lloyd's underwriters, and, significantly, £500 from the West India Association of traders and planters. The Memorial Committee made clear who had reason to be grateful and for what. 'The people of Liverpool, and their descendants to remote ages should, in the midst of their mercantile transactions, and daily concerns, be perpetually reminded of the man to whom they are so greatly indebted, for the vindication of their rights, and the protection of their commerce, at a period when they were threatened with destruction by a vindictive and powerful enemy.'[32]

Of the twenty-one-man committee formed to deliberate on the choice of design, fourteen were merchants actively engaged in the African trade. William Harper invested in fifty-two slaving voyages out of Liverpool between 1784 and 1799, leaving an estate in Cheshire and a fortune of £7,000 at his death in 1815. Arthur Heywood, scion of a family that for three generations invested in more than 140 voyages, ploughed the profits into the bank he established with his brother Richard. Thomas Rodie and John Staunton not only traded in slaves but co-owned the Alliance and Bel Air sugar plantations in Demerara, Guyana. John Gladstone, chairman of the West India Association, and father of the future Prime Minister, owned several Demerara plantations, the largest being Vreedenhoop* worked by over 400 slaves. He would receive more than £109,000 compensation from the British government following emancipation in 1833. John Bolton – self-styled lieutenant colonel of the 800-strong corps of volunteers he raised and financed to defend Liverpool against French invasion – invested in seventy-three transatlantic expeditions during the last twenty years before abolition, trafficking, according to an official statistic, 22,124 slaves in the final decade alone. He would be compensated £35,240 13s 7d for emancipating the 783 slaves he

---

* Dutch, translating as 'Peace and Hope'.

owned in Demerara, St Vincent and St Croix. George Case and John Gregson were part of a syndicate that owned the notorious *Zorg*, a vessel that in 1783 had become a legal test case when underwriters were successfully sued by the owners over insurance for loss of 'cargo' – 132 sick and chained slaves thrown overboard to preserve the rest – when the ship ran short of drinking water. The owners' claim was rejected on appeal, but only because the crew were judged at fault for inadequate stowage of water, not for drowning the cargo. Another member of the *Zorg* syndicate was James Aspinall, who died in 1787, but his son John Bridge Aspinall – Henry Clay's predecessor as mayor – flourished in the family trade and sat on the 'Committee for Superintending the Erection of the Monument' with fellow slavers.

> Shame to Mankind! But shame to Britons most,
> Who all the sweets of Liberty can boast;
> Yet deaf to every human claim, deny
> That bliss to others which themselves enjoy:
> Life's bitter draught with harsher bitter fill;
> Blast every joy, and add to every ill;
> The trembling limbs with galling iron bind,
> Nor loose the heavier bondage of the mind ...
> Blest were the days ere Foreign Climes were known,
> Our wants contracted, and our wealth our own ...
> Ere the wide spreading ills of Trade began,
> Or Luxury trampled on the rights of Man.[33]

William Roscoe, poet, art historian, and avowed abolitionist, was sitting in uneasy company as chairman of the Committee, having previously chaired the original public meeting summoned by the mayor in November 1805. Roscoe was generally regarded as the prime mover of the memorial project and had personally contributed fifty guineas to the fund, alongside John Gladstone's twenty. Another of the minority of committee members having no involvement in the slave trade, was the architect John Foster who would take over as chairman following Roscoe's election in

October 1806 to a seat in parliament as Member for Liverpool, a seat he would lose the following year having voted in favour of abolition. Foster's close working relationship with James Wyatt in the recent re-building of the Town Hall after fire, and the latter's role as external adviser to the Committee, has led to the suspicion of nepotism in the selection of a design for the Nelson monument by Wyatt's relatively unknown and unestablished son. Matthew Cotes Wyatt won the commission, although the complexity of the cenotaph he envisaged, and his inexperience, led to Richard Westmacott being engaged to execute it. The London sculptor's greater skill – particularly in bronze casting – was reflected in the unequal division of the fee, Wyatt himself receiving just eight per cent of the agreed £8,000.

The monument stands at the centre of a large, paved area known as Exchange Flags, where Liverpool business had traditionally been conducted in the open air. A bronze composition representing the hero's Apotheosis comprised five principal figures: Nelson himself, nude, his right foot resting on the muzzle of a cannon, his left upon the back of an enemy corpse, raises a sword slung with three crowns – his previous battle honours – while, above, Victory, bearing in her right hand a furled enemy flag lowered in token of submission, with her left bestows a fourth and final crown to the upraised sword. At the same moment the skeletal figure of Death emerges from the drapery of another captured flag to lay a bony hand across Nelson's heart and, to one side, a sailor armed with a pike embodies 'the zeal of the navy to wreak vengeance'.* The viewer must walk around to the back of the group to find the fifth figure, kneeling and easily unnoticed against the bronze cluster of flags: Britannia, 'with laurels in her hand . . . leaning regardless of them on her shield and spear' in token of 'the feelings of the country, fluctuating between the pride and the anguish of a triumph so dearly purchased'.

On the upper rim of the drum-shaped Westmorland marble pedestal supporting the Apotheosis – in letters of brass and repeated

---

* The pike has long been missing from the monument.

on the rest of the circumference – are the words: ENGLAND EXPECTS EVERY MAN TO DO HIS DUTY. Below are four rectangular bronze bas-reliefs depicting the battles of Cape St Vincent, the Nile, Copenhagen and Trafalgar. In between, seated on blocks of marble at each point of the compass, and emblematic of those victories, are four bronze 'captives or vanquished enemies', loins loosely draped, each in a different posture, ranging from resignation to agonised despair. They are manacled and chained to a series of laurel-linked lions' heads mounted under the lettering. Because the signal is repeated, the words EVERY MAN appear directly above the north- and south-facing figures.[34]

Prisoners of war as motifs of Nelson's achievements and service to his country were briefly considered in James Smith's plan for his Guildhall monument, only to be replaced by British sailors carrying instruments of conquest and seamanship. Prisoners also figured in another design submitted for the Liverpool commission, by the principal local contender, the cabinetmaker and sculptor, George Bullock. He proposed a statue of Nelson on top of a cylindrical plinth, encircled by four figures of Victory, their arms outstretched at shoulder height to either side. Below, protruding from each face of a rectangular pedestal was to be a ship's prow, or *rostrum*, and underneath – anticipating by sixty years the London monument – recumbent lions, radiating from the base on four more pedestals, inscribed St Vincent, Nile, Copenhagen and Trafalgar. And sitting on each corner of the upper pedestal, between the *rostra*, Bullock envisaged four male figures, barefoot, stripped to the waist and bound at the wrists. Dressed in seamen's trousers, they are clearly intended to represent French or Spanish captives, unlike the more ambiguous figures designed by Wyatt and moulded by Westmacott: naked, chained, and – despite their Caucasian features – reminiscent of the black, human merchandise of the African trade. Of the myriad monuments, statues, columns and obelisks that sprouted across the country and the world in the decades following the battle of Trafalgar, Wyatt's is surely the most striking, complex and disturbing, viewed in the context of Liverpool and its then still recent slaving past. A constant reminder to the community of the man to whom they were indebted 'for the vindication of their rights and protection of their commerce', it could not, at the same time, fail to remind them of the source of their prosperity, and of the violation of other's rights that had so long contributed to their commerce. And lest such an interpretation of the 'prisoners' be dismissed as twenty-first-century overthinking, Herman Melville was struck by the same disquieting connection when he first encountered it in 1839. 'I never could look at their swarthy limbs and manacles, without being involuntarily reminded of four African slaves in the market-place. And my thoughts would revert to ... the historical fact, that the African slave-trade once constituted the principal commerce of Liverpool; and that the prosperity of the town was ... indissolubly linked to its prosecution.'[35]

As a scholar of the Renaissance and biographer of Lorenzo de' Medici, William Roscoe would have recognised Wyatt's debt to Pietro Tacca, and his four bronze, specifically Moorish, slaves chained on the 1626 monument to Ferdinand I at Livorno. But as an abolitionist – who had written thirty years earlier of 'the trembling limbs' bound 'with galling iron' and the 'trampled ... rights of Man' – Roscoe must also have applauded and championed Wyatt's less overt competition entry as an incidental, veiled message of the cause he espoused. That the rest of the Committee for Superintending the Erection of the Monument agreed, and awarded the commission to Wyatt's design, is a tribute more perhaps to Roscoe's influence and persuasion than to the others' lack of imagination and inability to recognise an implied criticism of their business interests. Certainly, men like John Bolton and, particularly Gladstone, as committed to preserving slavery as Roscoe was to abolishing it, would have baulked at anything more explicitly critical.

The alacrity with which so elaborate and expensive a monument was erected – within eight years of Nelson's death – was in marked contrast to the comparative apathy greeting the memorialisation of figures with less direct commercial significance for Liverpool. A foundation stone was laid on 25 October 1809, at the official start of a nationwide celebration of the fiftieth anniversary of George III's accession to the throne, and a subscription was opened to finance an equestrian statue of the monarch – in Portland stone for £2,000 or £5,000 for one in bronze. But the flow of money proved sluggish.

The end of this Golden Jubilee year coincided, almost to the day, with the renewed symptoms of stress and agitation on 24 October that would pitch the king into permanent insanity, and withdraw him from the public eye for the remaining nine years of his life. Despite the cost of the preferred bronze option for an equestrian statue – by the ubiquitous and industrious Richard Westmacott – having been pared down from £5,000 to £3,000, even that more modest target had not been reached by 1820, the accrual of ten years' interest notwithstanding. The following year the sculptor's fee was only covered by the donation of a further two hundred guineas from the £850 surplus originally raised for the Nelson monument. Westmacott's statue of the king – based on that of Marcus Aurelius in Rome – was belatedly unveiled in 1822, two years after its subject's death.

There was a comparable lack of enthusiasm when the Duke of Wellington died in 1852 and the Corporation proposed a commemorative statue and column reminiscent of Nelson's in Trafalgar Square, erected eight years earlier. Had the Duke been killed at Waterloo on 19 June 1815, the warmth of local, patriotic sentiment might have erected column and statue in the centre of Liverpool as swiftly as Nelson's monument in Exchange Flags. But instead, Wellington outlived his glorious victory by nearly forty years, long enough for his heroic reputation to sully in the less glamorous world of politics – and briefly as a deeply unpopular Prime Minister. After four years the fund raised by public subscription amounted to £5,893 16s 6d, far short of the estimated ten to twelve thousand pounds required. It was then calculated that, for a column sixty feet shorter than Nelson's in London, the Liverpool monument could be completed for £7,000. The proceeds of the subscription having languished unspent for so long, the shortfall in funding was confidently expected to be made up by interest. The foundation stone was laid on 1 May 1861, and the work, beset by difficulties of subsidence, completed in 1863.

Forty-seven years after Nelson's coffin disappeared below the pavement of St Paul's Cathedral, the circular brass grating under the dome would be removed to enable the Duke of Wellington's corpse to be lowered into the crypt. The mechanism employed at his lavish state funeral on 18 November 1852 was identical to that used in January 1806, but its descent would this time be interrupted – 'lowered from the midst of the great and noble of the land to the flat top of the sarcophagus which covers Nelson'. The viscount's coronet and supporting cushion had been removed to allow the wooden platform bearing the Duke's ornate coffin to hang suspended by chains, inches above the funerary monument of his predecessor. For the next two years – until an adjacent tomb had been prepared for him in the crypt, forty feet away to the east – the victor of Waterloo dangled in limbo above the victor of Trafalgar.[36]

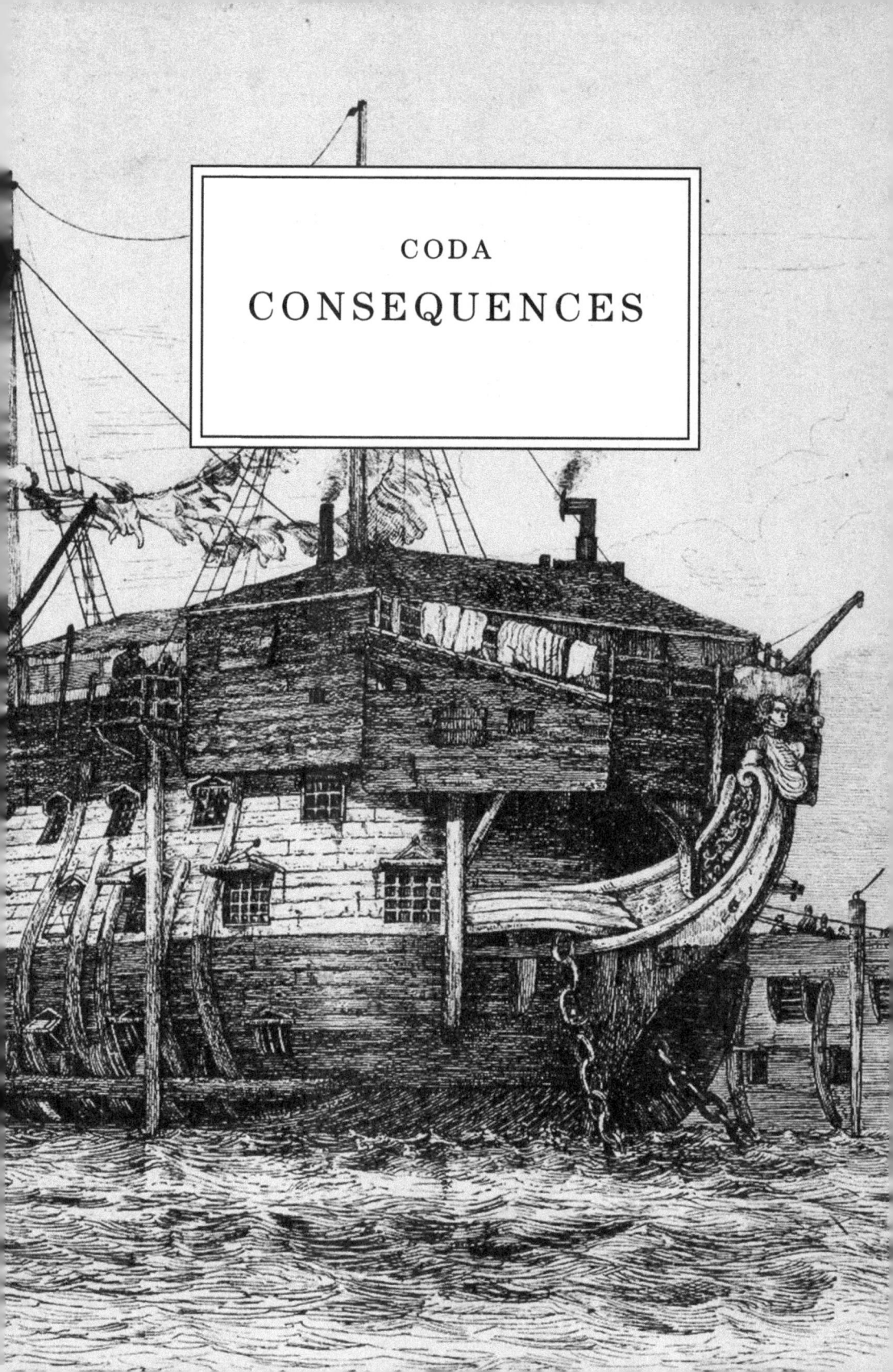

CODA
CONSEQUENCES

DEPLETED by scuttling, fire and storm, prize money for the battle of Trafalgar was distributed in 1807. Each captain was awarded £973, lieutenants £65 11s, warrant officers £44 4s 6d, petty officers £10 14s, and 'Trumpeters, Quarter Gunners, Carpenters' Crew, Stewards' Mates, Cooks' Mates, Gunsmiths, Coopers, Swabbers, Ordinary Trumpeters, Barbers, Able Seamen, Ordinary Seamen, and Marines ... and all other persons doing duty and assisting on board', each received £1 17s 6d. Although these shares ranged – in today's equivalents – from about £76,000 for captains to £146 15s for the lowliest member of the ship's company, they were so far below those expected from such a tremendous victory as to seem deeply disappointing. To compensate officers and men for these comparatively paltry sums, £300,000 was voted by Parliament giving every captain an extra £2,389 7s 6d, a further £161 to lieutenants, £108 12s to warrant officers, petty officers £26 6s and £4 12s 6d apiece to the rest. Nelson's combined share enriched his brother by £7,303 8s 2d. Prize money accrued from the four French ships captured by Sir Richard Strachan's squadron off Cape Ortegal – distributed as it was among far fewer beneficiaries – gave them more than five times the amount received by the men of Trafalgar.[1]

The French prize *Duguay Trouin* would become one of the two longest-surviving Trafalgar veterans. She entered the Royal

Navy re-named HMS *Implacable*, and over the following 150 years saw active service in the Baltic, off the Iberian Penninsula, in the West Indies and Mediterranean, and latterly as a training vessel for sea scouts and cadets. By 1949, requiring half a million pounds' worth of restoration, the decision was taken to dispose of her. The figurehead and stern gallery carvings were removed to the Maritime Museum at Greenwich then, on 2 December, explosive charges were attached to her hull, and she was towed into the Channel, a tricolour flying at her taffrail alongside the British White Ensign, and scuttled off Selsey Bill. The weight of ballast carried her hull to the bottom but large portions of her superstructure remained afloat – a hazard to shipping – before being washed up on the French coast close to Rochefort. The World Ship Trust, established in 1979 for the protection and preservation of historic vessels, deplored the loss in its motto: '*Implacable, Never Again*'.

A more cherished relic endures, buttressed in Dry Dock number two at Portsmouth harbour since 1922. From the time of her launch in the mid eighteenth century, HMS *Victory* has undergone more than 260 years of repair, restoration and the gradual replacement of most of her damaged and decayed timbers with new. At present undergoing a ten-year-long conservation process costing between forty and forty-five million pounds, she is the embodiment of a philosophical paradox known as the 'Ship of Theseus' which playfully questions to what extent, if at all, the vessel still exists after such fundamental renewal.*

*

---

* 'The thirty-oared galley in which Theseus sailed [from Athens to Crete] and returned safely was preserved by the Athenians down to the time of Demetrius of Phaleron. At intervals they removed the old timbers and replaced them with sound ones, so that the ship became an example used by philosophers when they disputed the "argument about change", some of them arguing that it remained the same, and others that it was not the same' (Plutarch's *Life of Theseus*, trans. Ian Scott-Kilvert). A modern equivalent of the paradox featured in an episode of *Only Fools and Horses*, aired on 25 December 1996, in which Trigger, the road sweeper, describes his twenty-year-old broom as having had seventeen new heads and fourteen new handles.

A court martial held aboard HMS *Circe* at Carlisle Bay, Barbados on 24 June 1805 deliberated on the loss, three weeks earlier, of HMS *Diamond Rock*. It was a formality that would have been followed after the capture or destruction of any of His Majesty's vessels, of whatever description. When the court had heard Captain James Wilkes Maurice's defence read to them, they ruled that he and the officers and men under his command 'did everything in their power to the very last ... and against a most superior force ... and ... did not surrender the Diamond until ... unable to make further defence for want of water and ammunition'. The defendants were 'unanimously and honourably acquitted accordingly'. There was an addendum to the judgement: the court could not 'dismiss Captain James W. Maurice without expressing their admiration of his conduct in the whole of the occasion', and also expressed 'the highest approbation of the support given by the officers and men under his command; a circumstance that does high honour to them [and] does no less credit and honour to the discipline by Captain J.W. Maurice.' It appears to have been unnecessary to consider the exonerating letter sent to Maurice by Lord Nelson: 'While I regret the loss of the Diamond, I have no doubt that every exertion [was] used ... for its defence, and that its surrender [was] occasioned from the circumstances you represent.' It was particularly gratifying, he added, 'that so few lives were lost in the contest'.[2]

The following December, another court martial, this time at Portsmouth, concerned the failure to bring Villeneuve's squadron to a decisive action off Finisterre in July. Vice Admiral Sir Robert Calder was tried aboard his flagship, *Prince of Wales*, 'for not having done his utmost to renew the ... engagement, and to take or destroy every ship of the enemy, which it was his duty to engage accordingly'. The defendant had demanded a court martial as a means of clearing his name of the dishonourable imputations published against his conduct in the London press. One strand of his defence was that this conduct had enabled the combined fleet to be pursued into Cadiz, which 'laid the foundation of that splendid victory which engages the attention of the country'. Furthermore, 'by being placed under the necessity of demanding this inquiry,' he declared, 'I have been prevented from sharing in the glories of that day.' And, he assured the court, 'that has been no small part of my suffering'. At this moment, it was reported, he turned aside 'and wiped a tear from his eye'.

The transcript of Calder's statement in his own defence ran to five and a half pages of small print in the *Naval Chronicle*. The judgement arrived at on 26 December – after three days' witness testimony, examination and cross-examination, followed by one of deliberation – consisted of eighty-five words: 'The Court is of the opinion, that the charge of not having done his utmost to renew the said engagement, and to take or destroy every ship of the enemy, has been proved against the said Vice-Admiral Calder; that it appears that his conduct has not been actuated either by cowardice or disaffection, but has arisen solely from error in judgement, and is highly censurable, and doth adjudge him to be severely reprimanded, and the said Vice-Admiral Sir Robert Calder is hereby severely reprimanded according.'[3]

Although the decision went against him, he at least avoided the terrible fate of Vice Admiral John Byng who – despite being likewise cleared of cowardice in 1757 – was executed for 'failing to do his utmost to take or destroy the enemy's ships'. In the London streets the mob chanted 'Swing, swing, Admiral Byng' but he was slain instead by firing squad on the quarterdeck of his own flagship, the bayonets of the first rank nearly touching his chest. Voltaire famously remarked of the case that the English like to 'kill an admiral from time to time to encourage the others'.[4]

*

Three weeks after the battle of Trafalgar, the *Gibraltar Chronicle* reported that 'French ships, under a Rear Admiral, who had no share in the action, in their flight, fired for some time upon the *Santísima Trinidad*, and others of the Spanish prizes after they had struck their colours to the English ... by which several hundreds of the Spaniards were killed and wounded.' The paper was able to confirm, 'from the concurring testimony of several Spanish Officers of rank, who were on board the ships ... that Rear Admiral Dumanoir was the person who led on his division to the perpetration of this bloody deed'. Such ruthlessness, the correspondent declared indignantly, recalled horrors of all too recent French domestic history, and he denounced it as 'worthy the days of ROBESPIERRE'.[5]

Reprinted in the London *Star* on 3 December, it was later brought to the attention of Dumanoir himself – then a prisoner of war at Tiverton, in Devon – who lost no time in defending his conduct and honour in a letter to *The Times*. He rejected the charge of deliberately firing on captured Spanish ships and accused the *Gibraltar Chronicle*'s editor of making that assertion with the 'express design of raising the animosity of the Spaniards against the French'. He did however concede that 'in the heat of the action some guns which were ill aimed might ... possibly have borne on the vessels of our friends.' This, to do him justice, might have been the case when a smoke-obscured English prize was identified only by the glimpse of a union flag at the masthead. As for the charge that ships under his command had taken 'no share in the action' and that 'he prudently chose to be a distant spectator' of the battle, Dumanoir stressed his initial difficulty in changing course, 'the wind being very weak', but that, having done so he 'bore towards the centre ... where the fire was hottest', only to find *Bucentaure* and *Santísima Trinidad* already in enemy hands, as well as other vessels and part of the rearguard.[6]

Having already defended himself in the pages of *The Times*, he was made to do so again – following his parole and return to France – in two courts of enquiry. The first was convened on 30 September 1809 to investigate four questions relating to his conduct four years earlier: did he 'manoeuvre conformably' with the signals telegraphed by his commander-in-chief 'and with the dictates of duty and of honour?'; did he do all that he was able to do 'to relieve the centre of the Fleet and the flagship [*Bucentaure*] in particular?'; did he 'engage the enemy ship to ship and did he approach the action sufficiently to take part in the engagement at as close a range as he should have done?'; and, lastly, 'Did Rear-Admiral Dumanoir quit the action when it was in his power to have engaged?' The court ruled on the first question, that he had so manoeuvred; on the second, that he had done 'all that the wind and circumstances would allow'; third, that he had engaged 'all the ships that he fell in with ... at as close a range as he was able', and, finally that he 'did not quit the action until obliged by the injuries ... sustained by his ship, and especially from the impossibility of manoeuvring owing to the condition of his masts'.[7]

But the findings of a second court of enquiry investigating the encounter with Sir Richard Strachan in November 1805 were not so favourable. Although 'the 4 ships which had the misfortune to yield in this engagement were fought gallantly', Dumanoir himself was blamed for 'committ[ing] tactical errors and display[ing] too much irresolution in all the manoeuvres that he carried out'. Although he was completely exonerated by the court martial that followed, a verdict of honourable acquittal by the nine naval officers sitting in judgement on him may not have been unanimous. As the tribunal's president handed Dumanoir back his sword, Rear Admiral Cosmao-Kerjulien is said to have broken his own in protest.[8]

*

Vice Admiral Charles Villeneuve, after four months' confinement, at first in Bishop's Waltham, but for the most part in Reading – during which time he is said to have been given permission to attend Lord Nelson's funeral – was paroled for four British post captains, 'according to the regulation rate of exchange'. On Saturday morning, 5 April 1806 he and an entourage including Captains Lucas and Infernet – of *Redoutable* and *Intrepide* – took their departure from the comfortable captivity afforded high-ranking prisoners of war. 'Their reception in the town of Reading [had] been highly flattering and hospitable, and their expressions of gratitude, on leaving ... were warm and sincere.' At Plymouth 'many hundreds of people assembled at the Pier to see Villeneuve embark, [and] he was treated with great respect by the populace.' The former commander-in-chief of the Combined Fleet was described as 'a thin mean-looking man'. His party sailed on 9 April aboard a local fishing smack – the *Betsey* – commissioned to ferry paroled prisoners between the still-warring countries. Landing under a flag of truce at the Breton port of Morlaix two days later, Villeneuve's 'dejection appeared very great on leaving the cartel, as to what reception he might meet with in France'. From Morlaix he travelled east a hundred miles or so as far as Rennes where, on 17 April, he took a room in the Hôtel de la Patrie, to await instructions from the Minister of Marine. Lucas and Infernet continued to Paris, where they would be warmly received by the Emperor at Saint-Cloud, 'compliment[ing] them on their gallant behaviour in the battle', but declaring ominously 'that certain other commanders should be brought to their merited punishment by a Court Martial'.[9]

What occurred in Villeneuve's bed chamber on the night of 21 April remains a mystery. He was found the following morning naked, with five stab wounds to the chest and a table knife sunk to the hilt in a sixth. The door was locked with the key on the inside and a letter of remorseful farewell addressed to Madame Villeneuve lay on the table, suggesting a suicide, albeit of extreme tenacity. This was the verdict of the local coroner. Press reports sought to explain how such a desperate act could have been accomplished, surmising that 'after stabbing himself, he threw himself on his bed, leaning on the handle of the knife, to thrust it in deeper, and thereby accelerate his death.' Other evidence suggested the wounds could not have been self-inflicted because 'the weapon ... was found literally in his heart [and] his heart was wounded in two other places, in such a manner as must, in either case, have occasioned instant dissolution, and prevented him repeating the blow, should he ... have struck the first.' Suspicion of foul play pointed to Napoleon, whose animosity towards Villeneuve for failing to support his invasion plans on England, and for the defeat at Trafalgar, was considered sufficient motivation for ordering his murder.[10]

Along with the farewell to his wife, a second document was allegedly found in the chamber, although its authority has ever since been in question. Copies were 'expedited to several Officers in French naval stations' and the text was published as a pamphlet in France a fortnight after the admiral's death, then promptly translated for circulation in the British press. Villeneuve's supposed letter to the Emperor – impertinently addressed as 'MONSIEUR!' – began by asserting that he had wished to resign his command of the Toulon fleet in late 1804 or early 1805, 'convinced [as he was], that whoever headed or directed the adventurous and badly planned expedition [against Great Britain], would be disgraced as well as defeated'. He also claimed to have tendered his resignation while at Martinique, El Ferrol and at Cadiz, each time being refused. Whether authentic or not, the letter certainly reflected his understandable fears of what he might suffer for failure at the hands of a vengeful and capricious leader. He had heard about the Emperor's reception of news from Trafalgar: 'When in the midst of your prosperous and ambitious career in Germany, my report reached you, did you not, with your usual petulance and cruelty, say – "*I see that the example of a FRENCH BYNG* is absolutely necessary to make victory the order of the day in my navy?*"' It was, he continued, a 'sentence of death pronounced against a patriotic French Admiral, by a foreign Usurper, while my dispatch was left unnoticed, unheard of, and perhaps unread'. Ironically, the damning indictment of Bonaparte contained in the document, acquits him of complicity in Villeneuve's death and only confirms the intention – and the coroner's verdict – of suicide, by declaring that the 'writer is out of reach of your ferocious vengeance, and fears no longer either your racks or dungeons, your poisoners or your tormentors'.

Villeneuve had remained in Rennes after receiving instructions 'not to approach the capital without permission from [the emperor]',

---

* 'Un brigand Français' in the French text of a copy of the original letter found among the papers of Sir Arthur Paget, British Envoy Extraordinary and Minister Plenipotentiary to the Court of Vienna 1801–6 (see Paget, *The Paget Papers*, vol. 2, pp. 278–82). The reference to Admiral Byng was presumably an embellishment to the translation in the British press.

and – if the letter be genuine – an assassination plan of his own, long brooded in England, had thereby been foiled. 'Resolved not to survive the ruin of the French navy, I meditated on dispatching you before I punished myself for having been your tool, to the disgrace of my honour, of my duty, of my birth and my profession.' And, he envisaged, had his plan succeeded and 'had your murder preceded my suicide, not only the present generation, but ages to come, would have hailed me as a deliverer, and revered me as a saviour. Altars, as well as statues, would then have been erected to my memory.' While regretting the 'blind and unjust fortune, that from inscrutable motives, still permits the continuance of . . . barbarous tyranny', the letter concluded with an assurance that Bonaparte's 'end must be untimely and terrible [and that] an assassin or an executioner shall finish a career of atrocities, which to the shame of humanity and our age, has already been too long endured . . . Tremble, tyrant. You live abhorred, and will expire with the curses of the universe, following you even on the other side of the grave.'[11]

The signature that followed, 'de Villeneuve', has been thought an indication of forgery because, like many post-revolutionary French aristocrats, he had long renounced use of the *particule nobiliaire* in his correspondence. It might, however – like the salutation 'Monsieur' – have been intended as a final snub to the foreigner whose family, in the words of Andrew Roberts, 'occupied that social penumbra encompassing the *haute bourgeoisie* and the very minor nobility'.[12]

The last, and least credible, testimony relating to this strange death in the Hôtel de la Patrie merits mention only because it came from the lips of Bonaparte himself. The erstwhile Emperor, when in exile on the South Atlantic island of St Helena, told his physician and confidante, Barry O'Meara, that Villeneuve, a prisoner of the English and 'so much grieved at his defeat', had 'studied anatomy on purpose to destroy himself'. Having purchased some anatomical plates of the heart he had 'compared them with his own body, in order to ascertain the exact situation of that organ'. Receiving orders on his return to France 'that he should remain at Rennes, and not proceed to Paris', and fearing that this icy reception boded ill for a sympathetic treatment of his case at the inevitable court martial, he studied again his plate of the heart. 'Exactly in the centre ... he made a mark with a large pin, then fixed the pin as near as he could judge in the same spot in his own breast, shoved it in to the head, penetrated his heart, and expired.' O'Meara noted down everything his patient told him, including his final words on the subject: 'He need not have done it. He was a brave man, though possessed of no talent.'[13]

The *Naval Chronicle* observed that 'history will remark that the three Admirals, French, Spanish, and English, engaged in the battle of Trafalgar, have all lost their lives. The English Admiral was killed outright; Admiral Gravina died of the wounds he received; and the French Admiral Villeneuve finished his mortal career by his own hand.'[14]

Don Frederico Gravina had been wounded in the left arm by grapeshot, and later in the left leg, but remained on the quarter-deck of his flagship, *Príncipe de Asturias*, fainting intermittently from loss of blood. Having evaded capture during the battle, he lingered at Cadiz for four and a half months, where he died, it was said, 'a victim of his doctors'. They had disagreed 'as to the necessity of amputating his arm, and he preferred to accept the views of the minority, who had expressed hopes of saving the limb'. By the end of February 1806 it had mortified and within ten days he was dead.[15]

*

'How this letter is to go to you I know not.' Collingwood was writing home to his wife in the summer of 1809 from HMS *Ville de Paris*, off Toulon. Lonely and depressed as he was, the distance from Mediterranean to Morpeth seemed more than a mere matter of land or sea miles. 'I never hear from your world, and cannot tell whether any thing from ours ever reaches you.' In sixteen years he had 'been only one year at home' and, since that domestic idyll during the Peace of Amiens, 1802–3, he had been continuously at sea. 'To my own children' – Sarah, aged seventeen, and sixteen-year-old Mary Patience – he declared, 'I am scarcely known.' He had been promoted from Vice Admiral of the Blue to the Red and raised to the peerage for his 'valour, judgment, and skill' at Trafalgar. He had also succeeded to Nelson's former command of the Mediterranean Fleet, condemning him to seemingly interminable blockade duty – his closest companion Bounce, an elderly dog. Ship after ship commanded by his subordinates had been relieved 'two or three times', he reported ruefully, while 'Bounce and I seem to be the only personages who stand our ground.' The Admiralty, it seemed, was unable to spare him, and the most that could be promised 'from England [was] being relieved at the end of the war'. He had shifted his flag from the storm-damaged *Ocean* to the *Ville de Paris* in April – 'the best ship in the Navy', he told Lady Collingwood; 'but what I most want is a new pair of legs and a new pair of eyes. My eyes are very feeble; my legs and feet swell so much every day, that it is pretty clear they will not last long.' Nor was Bounce in the best of health and when he fell overboard and drowned in August, it may have been the work of a crew member wishing to end the animal's suffering from rheumatic pain. Collingwood's own condition declined during the remainder of that year. He complained of 'headache by day, and cramps by night' and observed that 'this mortal body of ours is but a crazy sort of machine at the best of times; and when old, it is always wanting repair.' In October he wrote 'I am an unhappy creature, old and worn out.' He was fifty-nine. 'I wish to come to England, but some objection is ever made to it ... My health and strength are wearing fast away, and I am become an infirm old man.' Towards the end of November he reported having 'been ill and confined ... yet I cannot tell what to say on the subject of my coming on shore. My declining health will make it necessary soon; my weakness unfits me for the arduous situation which I hold.' New Year's Day 1810 brought more of the same: 'Old age and infirmities are coming on me very fast, and I am weak, and tottering on my legs.' In the following month there was no improvement: 'Lately I have had a very severe complaint in my stomach, which has almost prevented my eating. It is high time I should return to England, and I hope that I shall be allowed to do so before long. It will, otherwise, be soon too late.' He was, he said, 'almost past walking across my cabin.' He wrote to John Wilson Croker, First Secretary to the Admiralty, with a final appeal to be relieved, and permitted to return to England. He was 'past service, being at present totally incapable of applying to the duties of [his] office'.[16]

He died on 7 March, not twenty-four hours into his homeward voyage. An autopsy revealed that, 'with the exception of the stomach, all the other organs of life were peculiarly vigorous and unimpaired.' Death was ascribed to 'a contraction of the pylorus' – the valve connecting the stomach to the duodenum and small intestine. This pyloric stenosis was probably caused by a narrowing of the valve due to scar tissue from a duodenal ulcer, not, as was believed at the time to 'his continually bending over a desk while engaged in his Correspondence'. The exceptional condition of his stomach would have been thin-walled and distended by the failure of its contents to find egress towards the bowel, his gradual debility and miserable death due to lack of nourishment.

Aside from a Newcastle street – laid out in 1810 from Cloth Market to Westgate Road – bearing his name, and a carved bust in the cathedral paid for by his family, for nearly thirty years Collingwood was all but forgotten in his place of birth. Then, in 1838, the news that a committee had been formed in London to consider the possibility of raising a monument to Nelson appears to have whetted an appetite for something comparable to honour the northern city's own naval hero, and a public subscription was established for a 'Memorial in some eligible Situation'.

One of the variety of designs fielded by the London competition was that of John Graham Lough, a native of Northumberland, who had proposed for Nelson a monument that was 'national and intelligible to all classes' and – with North-country bluntness – one that 'studiously avoided allegory'. For £2,600 he had offered London a structure forty feet in height, comprising a twenty-four-foot pedestal and a statue of the hero, sixteen feet high, wearing a boat cloak, and holding a telescope, 'as emblematic of his constant vigilance'. At the base, raised six and a half feet from the ground were to have been four figures of sailors, twelve feet high, bearing flags 'supposed to have been taken in battle'. The figures were to be so adapted to the form of the pedestal 'that the eye is carried to Nelson at once'. The local sculptor's second-hand design was decided to be just as suitable for Collingwood by the Newcastle committee, an additional attraction being that the estimated cost of £2,600 would be 'very much reduced' if the 'four subordinate figures' were dispensed with. A site in St Nicholas's Square was initially favoured. Then, in September another location was proposed, at Tynemouth, overlooking the North Sea. Someone styling himself 'Blue Jacket' – having a naval background or sympathies – had argued against placing the monument in an urban setting, on 'some vile confluence of brick and mortar avenues', and suggested one – like that at Great Yarmouth – with maritime associations that might encourage naval enlistment and be 'worth a dozen press gangs'.[17]

Statue, pedestal, base and surrounding terrace were completed by 1845. Three years later, four 32-pounder cannon from *Royal Sovereign* – verified as such and selected by the inspector of artillery at Woolwich Arsenal – were installed, flanking a broad frontal flight of steps, 'where they will be both ornamental and useful', according to the *Durham Chronicle*, though the nature of their usefulness was unclear. Except for the telescope, Lough's design for the statue was retained, the boat cloak 'giv[ing it] a classical appearance ... the folds ... boldly modelled and made to hang with grace and dignity'. Forfeiture of the supernumerary 'sailors' seemed compensated for by the enlargement of Collingwood's figure from its proposed sixteen to twenty-three feet in height, seven feet taller than Nelson's in Trafalgar Square. The height of base and pedestal, designed to enable 'the features [to] be clearly recognised', makes the figure appear even more colossal, bringing it so much closer to the eye.[18]

*

Between 1793 and 1815 approximately 122,440 enemy soldiers and sailors were incarcerated in Britain, some on land, most on water. A decade after Trafalgar, on 14 June 1815 – the anniversary of his victories at Marengo and Friedland* – and four days before his final battle against an allied army commanded by the Duke of Wellington, Napoleon issued a proclamation to inspire his troops with animosity against the enemy and remind them of what they might expect in the event of defeat: 'Soldiers ... Let those who have been prisoners of the English tell you about the hulks and the terrible sufferings they endured there.'† Ironically, his army's defeat on 18 June, his subsequent abdication and exile would expedite the release of all remaining French prisoners of war.

During the three years prior to Trafalgar, in a climate of insecurity and threatened invasion from across the Channel, the Admiralty's Transport Office – 'for the Care and Custody of Prisoners of War' – had come to regard the continued accommodation of hostile foreigners aboard hulks in close proximity to naval arsenals at Plymouth, Portsmouth and Chatham as a danger to national security. In October 1805, tenders were invited 'from such Persons as may be willing to CONTRACT FOR THE BUILDING OF A PRISON, for the Confinement of Five Thousand Prisoners of War, on Dartmoor, in Devonshire', the proposed site being a safe fifteen miles from Plymouth. Applications were to be received not later than one o'clock on 16 December. 'Buildings and boundary walls [were] to cover about fifteen acres ... to be constructed of Moor Stone ... broken from the scattered rocks on the spot, where there is also fine gravel, sand and water.' The prison was to be 'floored with timber and roofed with timber and slate'. A foundation stone was laid in March 1806 and the establishment was expected to be ready for occupation by Christmas of the following year. It would not, however receive its 5,000 inmates until June 1809.[19]

---

* 1800 and 1807.

† *Ordre du Jour*, Avesnes, 14 June 1815: 'Soldats ... Que ceux d'entre vous qui ont été prisonniers des Anglais, vous fassent le récit de leurs pontons et des maux affreux qu'ils yont soufferts!'

In the meantime, 4,800 French prisoners, captured from the actions at Trafalgar and Cape Ortegal, had been brought to England. The 210 officers held in comparatively salubrious accommodation at Crediton and Wincanton might expect an early release, as soon as an exchange of prisoners could be arranged. But over 4,500 rank and file would be confined in varying degrees of wretchedness, the majority in floating prisons, for the duration of the war.[20]

'The prison ship as a British institution for the storage and maintenance of men whose sole crime was that of fighting against us,' wrote Francis Abell in 1914, 'must for ever be a reproach to us ... It lay, rather than floated, like a gigantic black, shapeless coffin.' The same analogy had been used in earlier, eyewitness accounts. Approaching *Prothée* in Portsmouth harbour on 15 May 1806, Louis Garneray beheld a 'shapeless black bulk [that] resembled an immense sarcophagus ... I looked despairingly at this sombre tomb in which I was to be buried alive.' Another prisoner, René-Martin Pillet, called them 'living tombs'. He was confined on *Brunswick* – one of nine hulks at Chatham, 'moored in the midst of fetid and stagnant mud, which at every tide is left bare. The air which is breathed being putrid, damp and salt, would be sufficient without ill treatment, or unwholesome food, to impair and destroy in a very short time the health of the most robust.' The same suffocating stench can be imagined arising from the sump of human waste and other concentrated pollution surrounding the stationary floating prisons of Plymouth and Portsmouth. The *Prothée* hulk, as described by Garneray, contained around eight hundred prisoners, conspicuously dressed to facilitate re-capture in ill-fitting yellow trousers and jackets stamped in black with the broad arrowhead symbol of three converging strokes denoting Government Property, and the large initials of the Transport Office. They lived and slept on the former gun deck and the orlop, each space around 130 feet long and forty wide, bare of furniture apart from a long bench running along each side. At either extremity 'a stout bulkhead made of particularly solid thick planks' separated the prisoners from their captors' quarters, officers astern, soldiers for'ard. 'For further security [each] partition was studded with a great quantity of large-headed nails, so tightly crammed together as to form practically a wall of iron.' In the event of riot or mutiny 'loopholes at regular intervals allowed the English to fire on [their charges] point blank without running the least danger.' *Prothée*'s gun deck ports, and the 'narrow scuttles' cut into the orlop timbers for supplying minimal ventilation, were fitted with 'cast iron grilles, two square inches in thickness'. These were tested for interference with the blow of an iron bar each morning, 'even though they would have been proof against any file'.[21]

On board *Brunswick*, hammocks for some 450 or so men on each deck were slung two deep, and three from one side to the other: 'The space allowed to a prisoner to suspend his hammock, is six ... feet long, and fourteen inches wide; but these six feet are reduced to four and a half, because it is so contrived that the cords of the hammocks run into each other, and consequently the head of every man in the second [or middle] rank when lying down, is placed between the legs of the two men who are in the first rank ... and his feet are placed between the two heads of those of the third rank, and so on from one extremity of the deck to the other.'[22]

Above these cramped, airless and unwholesome spaces, the quarterdeck, poop and forecastle served to muster prisoners every morning for head count, and for exercise. Poop and quarterdeck were known sardonically, for their latter function, as 'the Park', while the forecastle's recreational benefits were nullified by thick clouds of coal smoke belching from the galley's chimney, 'a horrible annoyance'.[23]

*

An HMS *Formidable* already figuring in the Navy List, Dumanoir's flagship was re-named HMS *Brave* on arrival at Plymouth. In 1808 she was fitted 'for a Prison Ship' at a cost of £4,444 and would hold French prisoners of war for the following six years. Likewise avoiding confusion with her English namesake, *Swiftsure* – the only French prize captured at Trafalgar to survive the subsequent storm and Collingwood's campaign of destruction – entered British service as HMS *Irresistible*. She docked at Chatham for repairs on 11 July 1806 in company with the Spanish prize *Bahama* and both were fitted out as prison hulks.

Bahama retained her exotic name, made more incongruous still by the unsavoury stories attached to her penitentiary career under the command of Lieutenant Milne, 'a drunken brute who held orgies on board at which all sorts of loose and debased characters from the shore attended. Upon one occasion a fire was caused by these revels, and [Milne] gave orders that the prisoners should be shot ... should the fire approach them, rather than that they escape.' During a break-out from one of the neighbouring hulks, three men did escape, but a fourth became stuck in mud and was drowned by the incoming tide. Milne ensured that the body remained there, in view, until it rotted away, a gruesome warning to would-be absconders from his own vessel.

It might have seemed apposite to house prisoners of war aboard captured enemy ships but by far the majority hulked and put to this degrading employment were British. The Georgian Navy was remarkably unsentimental about its veterans. 'Man took one of the most beautiful objects of his handiwork,' wrote Francis Abell, 'and [turned] it into a hideous monstrosity.' In 1813, eight years after fighting the most glorious sea battle in British history, *Britannia*, *Neptune*, *Defiance* and *Téméraire* were monstered in the way Abell described: 'masts and rigging and sails ... shorn away ... the symmetrical sweep of [their] lines ... deformed by all sorts of excrescences and superstructure'. But with the coming of a temporary – and then more enduring – peace in 1814 and 1815, their penal careers were short-lived. Not so Collingwood's one-time flagship, *Euryalus*. In 1825 she was 'Fitted for Criminals' at Chatham and served twenty years in that capacity on the Medway. Then in 1845 she was unmoored and towed to Sheerness where she underwent an £11,000 refit that included masts, yards, rigging and stores, and sailed for Gibraltar where she resumed her role as a prison hulk for a further thirteen years. She was sold in 1860 for £337 6s 8d. *Téméraire* remained a convict ship until 1819 when she found a kind of redemption as a Royal Navy receiving vessel at Sheerness, accommodating new recruits to the service. Ten years later she became a victualling depot to the fleet. Then, in 1838, she was sold. The ghostly spectacle of her last journey to John Beatson's breaker's yard in Rotherhithe, towed by the smoking tugboats *Sampson* and *Newcastle*, inspired J. M. W. Turner's painted elegy to the age of sail, and the advent of steam: *The Fighting Téméraire*.[24]

On 15 July 1815 *Bellerophon* received Napoleon's surrender at Rochefort and delivered him to Plymouth and the custody of HMS *Northumberland* for transportation into exile. *Bellerophon* was then ordered to Sheerness to be decommissioned, hulked, and – the war over – her lower decks fitted with iron cages for felons. As a convict ship, she was renamed *Captivity*. For the next ten years receding tides grounded her twice daily on the insanitary mudflats of the Medway. Also hulked for convicts in 1816, *Leviathan* served in that capacity at Portsmouth for the following thirty years, succumbing, in 1846, to an even more ignominious end. Partly scuttled, she was used as a target for gunnery practice, then sold and broken up for her timber. Mercifully spared such degradation, HMS *Conqueror*, having reached the end of her active service, was broken up at Chatham in 1821. But between 1816 and 1820, she served as a daily reminder to the former French Emperor of his greatest naval defeat. Adorned with a bust of Nelson, replacing the figurehead mutilated at Trafalgar, she was stationed off St Helena, guarding the captive Bonaparte.

NOTES

PRELUDE

1. *Correspondance de Napoléon Ier*, vol. 9, 7273, 12 Nov. 1803.
2. Ibid., vol. 10, 7832, 2 Jul. 1804.
3. Ibid., 8802, 27 May 1805.
4. Stuart and Eggleston, p. 9.
5. Norie, p. 72.
6. Stuart and Eggleston, p. 47.
7. *Naval Chronicle*, vol. 15 (Jan.–Jun. 1806), pp. 123–4.
8. CARTEL, see Moore.
9. *Naval Chronicle*, vol. 15 (Jan.–Jun. 1806), pp. 135–7.
10. *Correspondance de Napoléon Ier*, vol. 10, 8700, 8 May 1805; 9022, 26 July 1805.
11. *Naval Chronicle*, vol. 14 (Jul.–Dec. 1805), p. 170; *London Courier and Evening Gazette*, 1 Aug. 1805; *Morning Post*, 6 Aug. 1805.
12. *St. James's Chronicle*, 6 Aug. 1805.
13. *Star*, 18 Jul. 1803; *Morning Post*, 21 Jul. 1803.
14. *Sun*, 5 Aug. 1803; *Morning Post*, 6 Aug. 1803; *Star*, 8 Aug. 1803.
15. Hare, pp. 130–31; London Metropolitan Archive, ACC/1037/764.
16. *Calcutta Gazette*, 16 Feb. 1804; *Caledonian Mercury*, 15 Oct. 1804.
17. *Letters Intercepted*, No. XI; Ibid., No. XV; Ibid., Nos. XVIII and XIX.
18. *Evening Mail*, 2 Oct. 1804; Ibid., 1 Oct. 1804; *Letters Intercepted*; *Morning Post*, 1 Oct. 1804.
19. *Naval Chronicle*, vol. 13 (Jan.–Jun. 1804), p. 484; Schom, p. 266; *Correspondance de Napoléon Ier*, vol. 11, 9115, 22 Aug. 1805.

20 *Johnson's Sunday Monitor*, 1 Sep. 1805; *London Chronicle*, 7 Sep. 1805; *Morning Post*, 7 Sep. 1805.
21 Collingwood, vol. I, pp. 153–4.

PART I

1 Adkin, p. 12.
2 See White, *Encyclopaedia*, p. 262.
3 Beatty, p. 72.
4 Norie, p. 187.
5 Sturges Jackson, vol. 2, p. 272; Robinson, *Sea Drift*, p. 206.
6 [Robinson,] *Nautical Economy*, pp. 13–14; Lovell, p. 44; Martin, ff. 14–18.
7 [Nicholas,] p.66, quoted Allen, pp. 278–9; Thursfield, p. 364; BL, Add MS 30170 M; Martin, f. 14.
8 'Royal Proclamation for granting the Distribution of Prizes during the present Hostilities', 1803, reprinted Tracy, vol. 2, pp. 346–51.
9 Hill, *Prizes*, p. 65.
10 Tracy, vol. 3, p. 229; NNM WKR/2/1–9; Thursfield, p. 364; See Fraser, *Enemy*, p. 234 fn 1, and also Nicolas, vol. 7, p. 336.
11 *The Times*, 7 Nov. 1805.
12 Beatty, p. 14.
13 Sturges Jackson, vol. 2, pp. 238, 258. See also Kemp, p. 375 and Fraser, *Sailors*, p. 308.
14 *Notes and Queries*, 6th ser., vol. 4 (1881), p. 504.
15 'The Trafalgar General Order Book of HMS *Mars*', *Mariner's Mirror*, Jan. 1936, p. 104; Benito Pérez Galdós, *Trafalgar*, chapter X.
16 Fraser, *Sailors*, pp. 215–16; [Robinson,] *Nautical Economy*, p. 49; RNM 1981/435/46; Traill, p. 28.
17 James, vol. 4, p. 116; Ives, p. 451.
18 Northcote, vol. 2, p. 448; *Notes and Queries*, 6th ser., vol. 4, 24 Dec. 1881, pp. 503–5.
19 Northcote, vol. 2, p. 449; [Robinson,] *Nautical Economy*, p. 22; Blane, p. 580.
20 Atkins, p. 131.
21 Northcote, vol. 2, p. 447.
22 Ibid., vol. 2, p. 448; Ibid., vol. 1, p. 183; Guthrie, p. 76; Northcote, vol. 1, p. 184.
23 Nicolas, vol. 7, p. 444.
24 Collingwood, *Correspondence*, vol. 1, p. 174; Hibbert p. 386.
25 Beatty, p.12 fn 4; Ibid., p. 21; Fraser, *Sailors*, p. 247.
26 Ibid., p. 248.

27 *Naval Chronicle*, vol. 14 (Jul.–Dec. 1805), pp. 469–70.
28 See John Ashton, *English Caricature and Satire on Napoleon I*, 1888 (reissued NYC: 1968) p.165.
29 *Notes and Queries*, 4th ser., vol. 2, 10 Oct. 1868.
30 *Naval Chronicle*, vol. 15 (Jan.–Jun. 1806), p. 293.
31 See Bevan and Wolryche-Whitmore, p. 159.
32 Fraser, *Sailors*, p. 217; Smith and Campbell, p. 118; *Trafalgar Chronicle*, new ser., vol. 2 (2017), p. 99.
33 NMM WKR/2/1–9; Fraser, *Sailors*, p. 226; Huskisson, p. 71.
34 Beatty, pp. 23–4.
35 *Naval Chronicle*, vol. 3 (Jan.–Jun. 1800), pp. 363–4.
36 Ibid., vol. 4 (Jul.–Dec. 1801), p. 142.
37 Gravière, vol. 2 pp. 180–81.
38 Desbrière, vol. 2, p. 194.
39 Gicquel des Touches, p. 424.
40 Allen, p. 146.
41 *Naval Chronicle*, vol. 17 (Jan.–Jun. 1807), p. 361; Cumby, pp. 722–3.
42 Fraser, *Enemy*, p. 114.
43 Dwyer, *Citizen Emperor*, p. 175; Desbrière, vol. 2, p. 308; Dwyer, *Citizen Emperor*, p. 175; Quoted Roberts, *Napoleon*, p. 357; Saint-Chamans, vol. 1, p. 32.
44 Sturges Jackson, vol. 2, pp. 297, 235, 238, 199, 202.
45 Burney, p. 380; Haydon, vol. 1, p. 6 fn.
46 Fraser, *Enemy*, p. 214; Sturges Jackson, vol. 2, p. 225.
47 *The Times*, 21 Oct. 1912; Desbrière, vol. 2, p. 194.
48 Fraser, *Enemy*, p. 214; Collingwood, *Correspondence*, vol. 1, p. 290.
49 Allen, p. 282.
50 Desbrière, vol. 2, p. 282.
51 BL, RP 8864; Allen, p. 285.
52 *Naval Chronicle*, vol. 15 (Jan.–Jul. 1806), p. 272; RNM, MSS 1992/133.
53 *Naval Chronicle*, vol. 15 (Jan.–Jul. 1806), p. 272; RNM, MSS 1992/133; *Naval Chronicle*, vol. 15 (Jan.–Jul. 1806), p. 275.
54 TNA, PRO, ADM 51/1493; Goodwin, *Ships of Trafalgar*, p. 92.
55 Sturges Jackson, vol. 2, p. 241; Smith and Campbell, p. 118; [Robinson,] *Naval Economy*, p. 24.
56 *Leeds Intelligencer*, 18 Nov. 1805; [Robinson,] *Naval Economy*, pp. 55–6.
57 Warner, pp.109–10.
58 Bevan and Wolryche-Whitmore, pp. 59–61; Ibid.
59 Collingwood, *Correspondence*, vol.1, p. 186; *The Times*, 21 Oct. 1912.
60 Sturges Jackson, vol. 2, p. 203.

61 Allen, p. 123.
62 Desbrière, vol. 2, p. 215; Beatty, p. 29; 7 Nov. 1805. See also *St. James's Chronicle* and *The Globe* of the same date.
63 Turnbull, p. 259; James, vol. 4, p. 56 fn.
64 RNM 1981/435/46; RNM 1981/435/55; NMM JOD/48; RNM 1981/435/46; Lovell, p. 50.
65 Clowes, vol. 5, p. 139; James, vol. IV, p. 54.
66 Nicolas, vol. 7, p.241fn; Nicolas, vol. 7, p. 91; Clowes, vol. 5, p. 136 fn 5.
67 Fraser, *Enemy*, p. 116.
68 NMM WEL/30.
69 Sturges Jackson, vol. 2, p. 225; Beatty, pp. 30–31; RNM 1981/435/46.
70 Adkin, p. 509; Senhouse, p. 418.
71 RNM 1981/435/46.
72 Desbrière, vol. 2, p. 215 fn 1; *Dictionary of the English Language*, 9th edn, 1805.
73 Revd Scott, p. 186.
74 Revd Scott, p. 186.
75 RNM 1981/435/46; Southey, p. 356; *Kentish and Surrey Mercury* 30 May 1863.
76 NMM, WEL/30.
77 Northcote, vol. 1, pp. 189–90; NMM, AGC/4/15.
78 *Illustrated London News* 13 Apr. 1844.
79 RNM, 1998/41/1.
80 *Public Ledger and Daily Advertiser*, 6 Dec 1805.
81 NMM, MSS 73; Scott, p. 185.
82 [Nicholas,] p.75–6, quoted Allen, pp. 285–6.
83 Northcote, vol. 2, p. 449; TNA, Surgeons' Journals, Adm. 101/85, quoted Lloyd and Coulter, vol. 3, p. 59; Northcote, vol. 2, p. 449.
84 Royal Navy Articles of War (1757); Northcote, vol. 2, p. 449.
85 Collingwood, *Correspondence*, vol. 1, p. 289; Bevan and Wolryche-Whitmore, p. 164; Polwhele, vol. 2, p. 578; *Naval Chronicle*, vol. 14 (Jul.–Dec. 1805), pp. 494–5.
86 Ives, pp. 451–2; Watt *Letters*, p.233; NMM, MSS 73; See Jean Pierre Hamon, 'Les chirurgiens navigants français de la bataille de Trafalgar', thesis, University of Nantes (1982), pp. 194, 197; Fraser, *Enemy*, p. 155.
87 Desbrière, vol. 2, p. 238; Dillon, vol. 2, p. 58.
88 Cumby, pp. 725–6.
89 Norie, p. 29; Cumby, p. 724; NMM, MSS 73; TNA ADM 102/232; NMM, MSS 73; Sturges Jackson, vol. 2, p. 325.
90 Desbrière, vol. 2, p. 269.

NOTES (pages 80–100) 305

91 Halloran, p. 21.
92 Desbrière, vol. 2, p. 140; Sturges Jackson, vol. 2, p. 258; *The Times*, 19 Oct. 1905.
93 Desbrière, vol. 2 p. 156; Ibid., p. 195.
94 Ibid., p. 151; Ibid., p. 131.
95 Ibid., p. 326; Sturges Jackson, vol. 2, p. 251; Desbrière, vol. 2, p. 399; Ibid., pp. 135, 136.
96 Ibid., p. 329.
97 Beatty, p. 42.
98 Sturges Jackson, vol. 2, p. 235; Desbrière, vol. 2, p. 429.
99 Ibid., p. 232.
100 RNM, MSS 1992/133; *Naval Chronicle*, vol. 15 (Jan.–Jul. 1806), p. 272.
101 Desbrière, vol. 2, p. 247, 255; Fraser, *Enemy*, pp. 184–5.
102 Galiano, pp. 102–3.
103 Desbrière, vol. 2, p. 402; Fraser, *Enemy*, p. 270; Desbrière, vol. 2, p. 402.
104 *The Times*, 19 Oct. 1905.
105 Huskisson, p. 73.
106 Sturges Jackson, vol. 2, pp. 308, 254; Desbrière, vol. 2, pp. 219, 52; Sturges Jackson, vol. 2, p. 226.
107 Desbrière, vol. 2, p. 169; Ibid., p. 176; Sturges Jackson, vol. 2, p. 226; Desbrière, vol. 2, p. 219.
108 Desbrière, pp. 163–4.
109 Watt, *Letters*, p. 241; Collingwood, vol. 1, pp. 155–6; Gicquel, p. 419.
110 Watt, *Letters*, p. 231; Fraser, *Enemy*, p. 142; Senhouse, p. 419.
111 Plunkett, pp. 99–100.
112 Codrington, vol. 1, p. 62.
113 Fraser, *Enemy*, p. 220; Desbrière, vol. 2, p. 290; *Hull Advertiser*, 7 Dec. 1805.
114 RNM, 1992/436.
115 Desbrière, vol. 2, p. 290; Ibid., p. 288.
116 Bevan and Wolryche-Whitmore, p. 162; Fraser, *Enemy*, pp. 220–21.

PART II

1 [Halloran,] pp. 22–3.
2 *Naval Chronicle*, vol. 36 (Jul.–Dec. 1816), p. 372; Galiano, vol. 1, p. 98.

3 Sturges Jackson, vol. 2, p. 153; McCrea, RNM, 1992/436; Smith and Campbell, p. 119; Senhouse, p. 419; [Halloran,] p. 22; Robinson, *Sea Drift*, p. 207.
4 *Naval Chronicle*, vol. 36 (Jul.–Dec. 1816), p. 372; Ibid., vol. 18 (Jul.–Dec. 1807), p. 467; Galiano, vol. 1, p. 101; RNM, 1998/41/1.
5 Collingwood, *Correspondence*, vol. 1, pp. 189–95.
6 *Naval Chronicle*, vol. 18 (Jul.–Dec. 1807), pp. 466–7.
7 RNM MSS 1998/41/1
8 [Robinson,] *Nautical Economy*, pp. 55–6; Ibid., pp. 53–4; Allen, p. 285.
9 [Halloran,] p. 21; Sturges Jackson, vol. 2, p. 247; Cumby, p. 727.
10 Hall, vol. 3, p. 208.
11 Blane, pp. 88–9; Desbrière, vol. 2, p. 201; Smith and Campbell, p. 119.
12 Beatty, p. 48.
13 Ibid., pp. 76–7.
14 NMM, AGC/F/15.
15 Watt, *Letters*, p. 249; NMM, AGC/B/18; Steele, vol. 2, p. 9.
16 Robinson, *Sea Drift*, p. 207; *Trewman's Exeter Flying Post*, 2 Jan. 1806; NMM, AGC/M/5; https://bidefordbuzz.org.uk/history/trafalgar-women/.
17 Smith and Campbell, p. 119.
18 Fraser, *Enemy*, p. 308; also Ekins, p. 278.
19 Senhouse, p. 420.
20 Collingwood, *Correspondence*, vol. 1, p. 197 fn; Ibid., p.172.
21 James, vol. 4, p. 118; BL, Add MS 18048.
22 Sturges Jackson, vol. 2, p. 308.
23 Ibid., p. 155.
24 Fraser, *Enemy*, pp. 298–9; Desbrière, vol. 2, p. 236; Codrington, vol. 1, p. 73.
25 Fraser, *Enemy*, pp. 153–5; RNM, 1992/436; Sturges Jackson, vol. 2, p. 198; Desbrière, vol. 2, p. 220; Warwick, p. 284; Sturges Jackson, vol. 2, p. 283.
26 RNM 1992/436.
27 Codrington, vol. 1, pp. 72–3.
28 Adkins, *Trafalgar*, p. 231.
29 Colby, p. 265.
30 Desbrière, vol. 2, p. 257; Fraser, *Enemy*, p. 303.
31 Sturges Jackson, vol. 2, p. 255.
32 Desbrière, vol. 2, p. 244.
33 Dillon, vol. 2, p. 52.
34 Gicquel des Touches, p. 421.

35 Sturges Jackson, vol. 2, p. 326; *Naval Chronicle*, vol. 15 (Jan.–Jun. 1806), pp. 203–8.
36 Sturges Jackson, vol. 2, p. 260.
37 Desbrière, vol. 2, pp. 202–3.
38 *Gibraltar Chronicle*, 9 Nov. 1805.
39 Desbrière, vol. 2, p. 238.
40 Blackwood, pp. 12–13.
41 Colby, p. 265.
42 Desbrière, vol. 2, p. 400; See Moore; Adkins, *Trafalgar*, p. 236; Clayton and Craig, p. 302.
43 Clayton and Craig, p. 108.
44 See Smyth, p. 690.
45 Collingwood, vol. 1, p. 186; Sturges Jackson, vol. 2, p. 174.
46 Fremantle, vol. III, pp. 221, 236; [Robinson,] *Nautical Economy*, p. 34; Desbrière, vol. 2, p. 403; Ibid., p. 406.
47 Prothero and Badcock, pp. 767–9.
48 [Halloran,] p. 22.
49 'Documento: El navío *San Agustín*', p. 90.
50 Collingwood, *Correspondence*, vol. 1, p. 188; Sturges Jackson, vol. 2, p. 231; Codrington, vol. 2, p. 62.
51 [Halloran,] p. 22.
52 Codrington, vol. 1, p. 63; Ibid., p. 70.
53 TNA, Adm 101/106/1.
54 Bevan and Wolryche-Whitmore, p. 164.
55 NMM, JOD/41, quoted Adkins *Trafalgar* p. 239; Desbrière, vol. 2, p. 400.
56 Ibid., pp. 186, 209; Smith and Campbell, p. 120; Desbrière, vol. 2, p. 244; see also ibid., p. 127.
57 Sturges Jackson, vol. 2, p. 270; NMM, MSS LBK/38; Desbrière, vol. 2, p. 430.
58 Codrington, vol. 1, p. 73.
59 Dillon, p. 59.
60 Sturges Jackson, vol. 2, p. 312.
61 Ibid., pp. 325–7; *The Times*, 9 Oct. 1905; Collingwood, *Correspondence*, vol. 1, p. 191; [Halloran,] p. 23.
62 NMM, AGC/N/11; NMM, AGC/4/15.
63 Codrington, vol. 1, p. 69.
64 Ibid., pp. 68–78; Thursfield, p. 365.
65 *Star*, 5 Dec. 1805; Fremantle, vol. III, p. 240.
66 Codrington, vol. 1, pp. 71–2.
67 Watt, 'Surgery', p. 273.
68 NMM, JOD/281; MSS/77/163.

69 BL, Add MS 23207, f. 269. Quoted in Hore, p. 101; ibid., p. 102.
70 Codrington, vol. 1, pp. 70, 78, 80.
71 Hore, p. 104.
72 Quoted in Goodwin (2005) p.157.
73 Ibid.
74 Trelawny, pp. 18–19; Hill, Anne, p. 26.
75 Nicolas, vol. 7, p. 241.
76 Hubback, pp. 155–6.
77 *Naval Chronicle*, vol. 15 (Jan.–Jul. 1806), pp. 186–8; *Belfast News-Letter*, 26 Nov. 1805; Collingwood, *Correspondence*, vol. 1, p. 231.
78 Desbrière, vol. 2, p. 341.
79 *Naval Chronicle*, vol. 14 (Jul.–Dec. 1805), p. 379; Fraser, *Enemy*, p. 234; Desbrière, vol. 2, p. 338; Ibid., pp. 348–51.
80 *Naval Chronicle*, vol. 14 (Jul.–Dec. 1805), pp. 428, 373–80.
81 Desbrière, vol. 2, pp. 344–9.
82 *Morning Chronicle*, 13 Nov 1805.
83 *Naval Chronicle* vol. 14 (Jul.–Dec. 1805), p. 478.
84 Bullocke, J.G. (ed.) vol.2, p. 321.
85 Granville, vol. 2, p. 131.
86 *London Chronicle*, 7 Nov. 1805 (see also *The Globe*, 6 Nov. 1805).

PART III

1 Shelley, p. 87.
2 Malmesbury, p. 341 fn.
3 Creevey, p. 69, 6 Nov. 1805; Hibbert, pp. 381, 391.
4 Stirling, vol. 1, pp. 68–9.
5 Marrs (ed.), vol. 2, pp. 188–9; Benjamin Robert Haydon, quoted in O'Keeffe, *Haydon*, p. 147.
6 Leveson Gower and Palmer, p. 133.
7 Stuart, pp. 126–7.
8 Foster, p. 252.
9 Stuart, pp. 127–8.
10 *Globe*, 6 Nov. 1805.
11 *Globe*; *The Times*, 2nd edn; *Courier and Evening Gazette*; *Sun*, 6 Nov. 1805.
12 *The Times*, 2 Nov. 1805.
13 *Morning Post*, 8 Nov. 1805.
14 Malmesbury, p. 342; [Silliman,] vol. 3, pp. 74–5; *Morning Chronicle*, 8 Nov., and *Kentish Weekly Post or Canterbury Journal*, 12 Nov. 1805.

15 *Globe*, 7 Nov. 1805; *The Times*, 7 Nov. 1805.
16 *Star*, and *British Press*, 8 Nov. 1805.
17 *Morning Chronicle*, 8 Nov. 1805; *Star*, 9 Nov. 1805.
18 *Star*, 8 Nov. 1805.
19 Dibdin, Thomas, vol. 1, p. 393; *British Press*, 8 Nov. 1805.
20 De Quincey, p. 192; *Kentish Weekly Post or Canterbury Journal*, 12 Nov. 1805.
21 Ibid., 12 and 15 Nov. 1805.
22 *Salisbury and Wiltshire Journal*, 11 Nov. 1805; *Hampshire Chronicle*, 11 Nov. 1805; Ibid.
23 *St. James's Chronicle*, 12 Nov. 1805.
24 *Globe*, 21 Nov. 1805; Ibid.
25 *Chester Courant*, 26 Nov. 1805; Abell, p. 417.
26 *Sun*, 19 Nov. 1805; *York Herald*, 16 Nov. 1805.
27 *Carlisle Journal*, 16 Nov. 1805.
28 de Sélincourt, pp. 546–7; Journal MA 1581.233 pp. 11–12 (Morgan Library and Museum, New York); Knight, W. (ed.) vol. 1, p. 61, to Mrs Clarkson.
29 Ibid., pp. 215–16, to Lord Beaumont.
30 Curtis, Jared (ed.), p. 40.
31 Stirling, vol. 1, pp. 69.
32 *Caledonian Mercury*, 14 Nov. 1805; Ibid., 14 and 28 Nov. 1805; *Scots Magazine*, Nov. 1805.
33 *Caledonian Mercury*, 14 Nov. 1805; Ibid., 23 Nov. 1805.
34 *Belfast Commercial Chronicle*, 27 Nov. 1805; *British Press*, 28 Nov. 1805.
35 *Belfast Commercial Chronicle*, 11 Nov. 1805; *Dublin Evening Post*, 12 Nov. 1805.
36 *Globe*, 7 Nov. 1805.
37 *London Courier and Evening Gazette*, 7 Nov. 1805.
38 Wyndham, vol. 1, p. 311; *London Courier and Evening Gazette*, 11 Nov. 1805.
39 *Monthly Mirror*, Nov. 1805, p. 340; *Oracle and Daily Advertiser*, 11 Nov. 1805; Dibdin, Thomas, vol. 1, p. 393.
40 *Monthly Mirror*, Nov. 1805, p. 339.
41 *Morning Post* and *Sun*, 12 Nov. 1805.
42 *Westminster Journal, and Old British Spy*, 16 Nov. 1805, and *British Press*, 18 Nov. 1805.
43 *General Evening Post*, 16 Nov. 1805; *Morning Post*, 19 Nov. 1805.
44 *Globe*, 14 Nov. 1805.
45 *Sun*, 13 Nov. 1805.

46 *British Press*, 28 Nov. 1805; *British Press*, 9 and 11 Nov. 1805; *Morning Herald*, 7 Jan. 1806; *British Press*, 9 and 11 Nov. 1805; 22 and 29 Jan. 1806.
47 *Morning Advertiser*, 8 Apr 1806; Dibdin, *Memoirs*, p. 61.
48 *Morning Advertiser*, 8 Apr. 1806; *True Briton*, 31 Mar. 1804; *Oracle and Daily Advertiser*, 27 Mar. 1804; *Monthly Mirror*, Apr. 1804, p. 273.
49 *Morning Herald*, 7 Jan. 1806; *Morning Advertiser*, 8 Apr. 1806; Dibdin, Charles, p. 87.
50 Ibid., pp. 64–5; *Globe*, 28 Dec. 1805; *Sun*, 27 Dec. 1805.
51 *Morning Chronicle*, 4 Dec.; *British Press*, 9 Dec. 1805; *Oracle and Daily Advertiser*, 6 Dec. 1805.
52 *Morning Herald*, 9 Dec. 1805; *Morning Herald, Morning Chronicle, Sun*, 9 Dec. 1805; *Monthly Mirror*, Dec. 1805.
53 *Sun*, 7 Nov. 1805; Collingwood, vol. 1 p. 184.
54 *Morning Post*, 6 Dec. 1805.
55 Wood, p. 17; Bull, pp. 12–13; Rouquet, p. 11; Horsley, pp. 25–6.
56 *Naval Chronicle*, vol. 14 (Jul.–Dec. 1805), p. 463; *Star*, 12 Dec. 1805; *St. James's Chronicle*, 7 Dec. 1805.
57 Monmouth, Nelson Museum, E 214.
58 White, *Supplement*, p. 12; Hibbert, pp. 207–8 fn.
59 Beatty, p. 67; NMM, AGC/30/6.
60 Beatty, pp. 73–4; NMM, AGC/30/6.
61 NMM, LOA1715, f. 159; Watt, *Letters*, p. 249.
62 White, Joshua, p. 12; *Naval Chronicle*, vol. 14 (Jul.–Dec. 1805), p. 373; Beatty, pp. 73–4.
63 Monmouth, Nelson Museum, E 221; Monmouth, Nelson Museum, E 222.
64 White, Joshua, p. 13; *St. James's Chronicle*, 21 Dec. 1815.
65 *Sun*, 4 Jan. 1806.
66 Marsden, p. 124 fn.
67 *Hampshire Chronicle*, 13 Jan. 1806; *Gloucester Journal*, 13 Jan. 1806.
68 BL, Add MSS 34992, f. 58.
69 *Morning Advertiser*, 9 Jan. 1806.
70 *Hampshire Chronicle*, 13 Jan. 1806.
71 Marrs (ed.), vol. 2, p. 197; *Oracle and the Daily Advertiser*, 4 Jan. 1806; Stuart, p.130.
72 *The Times*, 30 Dec. 1805; *Morning Advertiser*, 8 Jan. 1806.
73 *Morning Herald*, 12 Nov. 1805; *The Times*, 2 Jan. 1806.
74 Marrs (ed.), vol. 2, p. 197.
75 *Morning Advertiser*, 1 Jan. 1806; *The Times*, 3 Jan. 1806; Ibid., 4 Jan. 1806.

76 White, Colin, 'Notes', p. 7; *Morning Advertiser*, 9 Jan. 1806; *Public Ledger*, 13 Jan. 1806; *Morning Chronicle*, 8 Jan. 1806.
77 *British Press*, 9 Jan. 1806.
78 Brockliss, Cardwell and Moss, p.172.
79 Marsden, p. 124.
80 Stuart, D.M. p. 131.
81 White, Joshua, p. 39; *British Press*, 9 Jan. 1806.
82 *Saunders' News Letter*, 14 Jan. 1806; White, Colin, 'Final Thoughts', p. 28.
83 *Morning Chronicle*, 8 Jan. 1806.
84 White, Joshua, p. 40; *Public Ledger and Daily Advertiser*, 10 Jan. 1806; Ibid.; *Morning Advertiser*, 9 Jan. 1806; *Morning Advertiser*, 11 Jan. 1806; *Morning Post*, 10 Jan. 1806.
85 *Morning Advertiser*, 11 Jan. 1806; *General Evening Post*, 14 Jan. 1806.
86 Collingwood, Adam, p. 112; Ibid., p. 113.
87 Farington, vol. 7, p. 2670; *Morning Chronicle*, 11 Jan. 1806.
88 *Morning Post*, 8 Jan. 1806; College of Arms Archive, RRG LXII A.
89 Ibid., RRG LXII A f121; *Star*, 10 Jan. 1806.
90 Haydon, *Autobiography* vol. 1, p31.
91 Lewis, vol. 2, pp. 309–1X.
92 Granville, Castalia, Countess, ed., vol. 2, p. 155; Lewis, vol. 2, p. 311.
93 Leveson-Gower and Palmer, p. 146; Marryat, p. 155.
94 *Star*, 11 Jan. 1806; *Morning Chronicle*, 10 Jan. 1806.
95 *General Evening Post*, 11 Jan. 1806.
96 Cited in Ward-Jackson, *City of London*, pp. 172–3; RNM, 9/56; *Oracle and Daily Advertiser*, 11 Jan. 1806.
97 *Morning Chronicle*, 10 Jan. 1806; Ibid., 11 Jan. 1806.
98 The London Archives (formerly Metropolitan Archives), CLC/314/MS29427-8.
99 *Morning Post*, 8 Jan. 1806.
100 Duncan, pp. 415–6; *Morning Post*, 10 Jan. 1806; *British Press*, 10 Jan. 1806; *Kentish Weekly Post or Canterbury Journal*, 14 Jan. 1806; *British Press*, 11 Jan. 1806.
101 College of Arms Archive, RRG LXII A f122.
102 Codrington, vol. 1, pp. 97–8.
103 Baring, p. 455; *Star*, 10 Jan.; *Morning Chronicle*, 11 Jan. 1806.
104 *Sun*, 15 Jan. 1806; *Evening Mail*, 15 Jan. 1806.
105 *General Evening Post*, 14 Jan. 1806.
106 Mann, p. 40.

PART IV

1. TNA, HO/42/86; *Public Ledger*, 13 Jan. 1806; *Morning Herald*, 15 Jan. 1806; *Sun*, 15 Jan. 1806; *Public Ledger*, 13 Jan. 1806.
2. *British Press*, 30 Nov. 1805.
3. Hibbert, p. 384.
4. Farington, vol. 8, p. 2806; Erffa and Staley, p. 222.
5. TNA, HO/42/86.
6. *Morning Herald*, 1 Jan. 1806; *Morning Post*, 24 May 1806.
7. *General Evening Post*, 1 Nov. 1810.
8. Higgins. p. 161.
9. Codrington, vol. 1, p. 69; *Public Ledger and Daily Advertiser*, 13 Jan. 1806.
10. 7 Dec. 1805; Leveson Gower and Palmer, p. 133; *Cambridge Chronicle and Journal*, 12 Apr. 1806; *Naval Chronicle*, vol. 15 (Jan.–Jul. 1806), p. 400.
11. *Belfast Commercial Chronicle*, 30 Dec. 1805; See Kennedy.
12. *Aberdeen People's Journal*, 7 Aug. 1880.
13. *Cambridge Chronicle and Journal*, 11 Jul. 1807.
14. Erffa, p. 233.
15. *Perthshire Courier*, 9 Aug. 1810.
16. Ibid., 23 Aug. 1810.
17. Stevenson, p. 28; Gifford, McWilliam and Walker, pp. 437–8.
18. Hill, *Irish Public Sculpture*, pp. 63–4; Joyce, James, *Ulysses – The Corrected Text*, edited by Han Walter Gabler with Wolfhard Steppe and Claus Melchior (London: 1986) pp. 119, 121.
19. Noszlopy, pp. 116–17.
20. *Liverpool Weekly Courier*, 13 Sep. 1873.
21. Ward-Jackson, *City of London*, p. 172.
22. Mace, pp. 252–3; *Bell's New Weekly Messenger*, 16 Jun. 1839.
23. Ward-Jackson, *Westminster* vol. 1, pp. 278.
24. *Morning Herald*, 26 Jan. 1844; *Sun*, 31 Jan. 1844.
25. *The Builder*, vol. 16, no. 811 (21 Aug. 1858); *The Times*, 14 Aug. 1858; *London Illustrated News*, vol. 50, no. 1412 (9 Feb. 1867).
26. Donal Fallon, *Irish Times*, 8 Mar 2016; *Belfast Telegraph*, 14 Mar. 1966.
27. 'Nelson and the Slave Trade: A Position Statement' (2020), https://nelson-society.com/nelson-and-the-slave-trade-a-position-statement-by-the-nelson-society/; 'Nelson Letter a Forgery' (2020): https://nelson-society.com/nelson-letter-a-forgery/.
28. Cited by Sharples, p. 10; [Wallace,] p. 230; *Gore's Liverpool General Advertiser*, 24 Oct. 1805.

29 *Morning Post*, 7 Sep. 1805.
30 Ibid.
31 *Gore's Liverpool General Advertiser*, 14 Nov. 1805.
32 *Report of the Committee for . . . the Monument to Lord Nelson*, p. 10.
33 Roscoe, William, *Mount Pleasant: A Descriptive Poem* (Liverpool: 1777), pp. 14–15.
34 Report of the Committee for . . . the Monument to Lord Nelson, pp. 17–21.
35 Herman Melville, *Redburn, His First Voyage*, ed. Harold Beaver (Harmondsworth, 1986), p. 222.
36 *Illustrated London News*, 4 November 1854.

CODA: CONSEQUENCES

1 Tracy, vol. 2, pp. 346–51.
2 *Naval Chronicle*, vol. 15 (Jan.–Jun. 1806), pp. 124, 128.
3 Ibid., pp. 79–86, 162–75.
4 Voltaire, *Candide, or Optimism*, trans. and ed. Theo Cuffe, (London: 2005), p. 69.
5 9 Nov. 1805, reprinted *Star*, 3 Dec. 1805.
6 *The Times*, 2 Jan. 1806.
7 Desbrière, vol. 2, pp. 330–33.
8 Ibid., p. 371; Fraser, *Enemy*, p. 240.
9 *Star*, 9 Apr. 1806; *Bristol Times and Mirror*, 12 Apr. 1806; *Morning Herald*, 22 Apr. 1806; *Scots Magazine*, May 1806.
10 *Oracle and Daily Advertiser*, 12 May 1806; Ibid., 26 May 1806.
11 *Les Nouvelles à la main*, no. 1 (5 May 1806); *Morning Post*, 26 May 1806.
12 Roberts, *Napoleon*, p. 3.
13 O'Meara, pp. 56–7.
14 *Naval Chronicle*, vol. 15 (Jan.–Jun. 1806), p. 456.
15 Fraser, *Enemy*, p. 247.
16 Collingwood, *Correspondence*, vol. 1, p. 125; Ibid., vol. 2, p. 380, 17 Jul. 1809; Ibid., p. 333; Ibid., p. 380; Ibid., pp. 387–8; Ibid., p. 395; Ibid., p. 400; Ibid., p. 402; Ibid., pp. 402–3.
17 Usherwood, Beach and Morris, p. 208.
18 *Durham Chronicle*, 4 Aug. 1848.
19 *British Press*, 19 Oct. 1805.
20 Abell, p. 445.
21 Ibid., p. 37; Garneray, p. 5; Pillet, pp. 221, 228; Garneray, pp. 6–7.
22 Pillet, p. 231.
23 Garneray, p. 6.
24 Abell, pp. 37–56.

BIBLIOGRAPHY

Archives

London, British Library (BL)
London, College of Arms
London Archives (formerly London Metropolitan Archives)
London, The National Archives (TNA)
London, National Maritime Museum, Caird Library (NMM)
Monmouth, Nelson Museum
Portsmouth, Royal Naval Museum (RNM)

Books, Articles, Etc.

Abell, Francis, *Prisoners of War in Britain, 1756–1815* (Oxford: 1914)
Adkin, Mark, *The Trafalgar Companion* (London: 2005)
Adkins, Roy, *Trafalgar: The Biography of a Battle* (London: 2004)
Adkins, Roy and Leslie, *The War for All the Oceans* (London: 2006)
Adkins, Roy and Leslie, *Jack Tar* (London: 2008)
Allen, Joseph, ed., *Memoir of the Life and Services of Admiral Sir William Hargood* (Greenwich: 1841)
Amos, Susan, and Louis Roeder, *Nelson's State Funeral 1806: How to Bury a National Hero* (Cranbrook: 2020)
Atkins, John, *The navy surgeon; or, practical system of surgery. With a dissertation on cold and hot mineral springs; and physical observations on the Coast of Guiney* (London: 1742)

Baring, Mrs Henry, ed., *Diary of the Right Hon. William Windham 1784 to 1810* (London: 1866)
Beatty, William, *Authentic Narrative of the Death of Lord Nelson* (London: 1807)
Berry, [Mary,] *Extracts from the Journals and Correspondence of Miss Berry from the Year 1783 to 1852*, ed. Lady Theresa Lewis, 2nd edn, vol. 2 (London: 1866)
Best, Nicholas, *Trafalgar: The Untold Story of the Greatest Sea Battle in History* (London: 2005)
Bevan, A.B., and H.B. Wolryche-Whitmore, eds, *A Sailor of King George: The Journals of Captain Frederick Hoffman* (London: 1901)
Blackwood, H., 'Memoir of Vice-Admiral the Honourable Sir Henry Blackwood, Bart. KCB KGH', *Blackwood's Edinburgh Magazine*, vol. 34, no. 210 (1833), pp. 1–24
Blane, Gilbert, *Observations on the Diseases of Seamen* (London: 1799)
Brockliss, Laurence, John Cardwell and Michael Moss, 'Nelson's Grand National Obsequies', *English Historical Review*, vol. 121, no. 490 (2006), pp. 162–82
Brownlow, Emma Sophia, Countess, *Slight Reminiscences of a Septuagenarian from 1802 to 1815* (London: 1867)
Bull, Nicholas, *A Thanksgiving Sermon* (London: 1805)
Bullocke, J.G. (ed.) *The Tomlinson Papers: Selected from the Correspondence and Pamphlets of Captain Robert Tomlinson, R.N., and Vice-Admiral Nicholas Tomlinson*, 2 vols. (London: 1935)
Cavanagh, Terry, *Public Sculpture in Liverpool* (Liverpool: 1997)
Clarke, Revd J.S., and John McArthur, *The Life and Services of Horatio Viscount Nelson*, 3 vols (London: 1806)
Clayton, Tim, and Phil Craig, *Trafalgar: The Men, the Battle, the Storm* (London: 2004)
Clement, Benjamin, 'The Battle of Trafalgar', *Cornhill Magazine*, vol. 24 (n.s.), no. 143, (1895), pp. 478–82
Clerk, John, *An Essay on Naval Tactics, Systematical and Historical*, 2nd edn (Edinburgh: 1804)
Clowes, W.L., *The Royal Navy: A History from the Earliest Times to the Present*, 6 vols (London: 1900)
Codrington, E., *Memoir of the Life of Admiral Sir Edward Codrington*, ed. Lady Bourchier, 2 vols (London: 1873)

Colby, Thomas, 'Journal of Commander Thomas Colby, RN 1797–1815', ed. Edward Fraser, *Mariner's Mirror*, vol. 13 (1927)
Coleman, Terry, *Nelson: The Man and the Legend* (London: 2001)
Collingwood, Adam, *Anecdotes of the Late Lord Viscount Nelson ... to which is Added the Ceremonial of his Funeral* (London: 1806)
Collingwood, G.L. Newnham, ed., *A Selection from the Public and Private Correspondence of Vice-Admiral Lord Collingwood*, 5th ed., 2 vols (London: 1837)
Correspondance de Napoléon Ier, 28 vols (Paris: 1857–69)
Creevey, Thomas, *The Creevey Papers: A Selection from the Correspondence and Diaries of the Late Thomas Creevey, M.P., Born 1768–Died 1838*, ed. Herbert Maxwell (London: 1923)
Cumby, William Pryce, 'Battle of Trafalgar: An Unpublished Narrative', *The Nineteenth Century*, vol. 46 (1899), pp. 718–28
Curtis, Jared (ed.) *The Fenwick Notes of William Wordsworth*, (London: 1993).
De Quincey, *Confessions of an English Opium-Eater and Other Writings*, ed. Barry Milligan (London: 2003)
de Sélincourt, Ernest, ed., *The Early Letters of William and Dorothy Wordsworth*, vol. 1: *The Early Years: 1787–1805* (London: 1935)
Desbrière, E., *The Trafalgar Campaign*, trans. Constance Eastwick, 2 vols (Oxford: 1933)
Dibdin, Charles, *Professional and Literary Memoirs of Charles Dibdin the Younger, Dramatist and Upward of Thirty Years Manager of Minor Theatres*, ed. George Speaight (London: 1956)
Dibdin, Thomas, *Reminiscences of Thomas Dibdin*, 2 vols (London: 1827)
Dillon, Sir William Henry, *A Narrative of my Professional Adventures*, ed. Michael A. Lewis, vol. 2 (London: 1956)
'Documento: El navío San Agustín en el combate de Trafalgar', *Revista de Historia Naval*, no. 52 (Madrid: 1996), pp. 83–90.
Douglas, General Sir Howard, *A Treatise on Naval Gunnery*, 5th edn (London: 1860)
Duncan, Archibald, *Correct Narrative of the Funeral of Horatio Lord Viscount Nelson* (London: 1806)
Dwyer, Philip, *Napoleon: The Path to Power 1769–1799* (London: 2007)
Dwyer, Philip, *Citizen Emperor: Napoleon in Power* (London: 2013)

Ekins, C., *Naval Battles from 1744 to the Peace in 1814* (London: 1824)
Erffa, Helmut von, and Alan Staley, *Paintings of Benjamin West* (New Haven and London: 1986)
Fairburn, J., *Fairburn's Edition of the Funeral of Admiral Lord Nelson* (London: 1806)
Farmer, George Henry, 'Our Bands in the Napoleonic Wars', *Journal of the Society for Army Historical Research*, vol. 40 (1962), pp. 33 ff.
Farington, Joseph, *The Diary of Joseph Farington*, ed. Kenneth Garlick, Angus Macintyre, Kathryn Cave and Evelyn Newby, 17 vols (New Haven and London: 1978–1998)
Foster, Vere, ed., *The Two Duchesses, Georgiana, Duchess of Devonshire; Elizabeth, Duchess of Devonshire* (London: 1898)
Fraser, Edward, *The Enemy at Trafalgar* (London: 1906)
Fraser, Edward, *Sailors Whom Nelson Led* (London: 1913)
Fremantle, Anne, *The Wynne Diaries* vol. III 1798–1820 (Oxford: 1935)
Galiano, D. Antonio Alcalá, *Memorias*, vol. 1 (Madrid: 1886)
Gardiner, Robert, ed., *The Campaign of Trafalgar* (London: 1997)
Garneray, Louis, *The Floating Prison*, trans. Richard Rose (London: 2003), first published as *Mes Pontons* (London: 1851)
Gicquel des Touches, Auguste, 'Souvenirs d'un marin de la république', *Revue des deux mondes*, 5th period, vol. 28 (1905), pp. 177–201, 407–36
Gifford, John, Colin McWilliam and David Walker, *Edinburgh* (Pevsner Architectural Guides: The Buildings of Scotland) (London: 1984)
Goodwin, Peter, *Nelson's Ships: A History of the Vessels in which he Served 1771–1805* (London: 2002)
Goodwin, Peter, *The Ships of Trafalgar: The British, French and Spanish Fleets, October 1805* (London: 2005)
Granville, Castalia, Countess, ed., *Lord Granville Leveson Gower ... Private Correspondence 1781–1821*, 2 vols (London: 1916)
Gravière, E. Jurien de La, *Guerres Maritimes Sous La République et L'Empire*, 16th edn, 2 vols (Paris: 1879)
[Guillemard, Robert,] *Adventures of a French Sergeant during his Campaigns in Italy, Spain, Germany, Russia, &c. from 1805 to 1823* (London: 1898)

Hall, Basil, *Fragments of Voyages and Travels by Captn. Basil Hall RN*, vol. 3 (Edinburgh: 1831)
[Halloran, L.B.,] 'In the Days of Trafalgar', *English Illustrated Magazine*, vol. 34 (1905–6), pp. 18–23
Hamon, Jean Pierre, 'Les chirurgiens navigants français de la bataille de Trafalgar', thesis, University of Nantes (1982)
Hare, Augustus J.C., *The Gurneys of Earlham*, 2 vols (London: 1895)
Harland, John, *Seamanship in the Age of Sail* (London: 1984)
Hatt, Revd Andrew, *Sermon, Preached in the Cathedral Church of St Paul* (London: 1805)
Haydon, B.R., *Autobiography and Memoirs* (London: 1926)
Haydon, B.R., *Correspondence and Table Talk*, 2 vols (London: 1876)
Heathcote, T.E., *Nelson's Trafalgar Captains and their Battles* (Barnsley: 2005)
Hibbert, Christopher, *Nelson: A Personal History* (London: 1994)
Higgins, Alfred, 'On the Work of Florentine Sculptors in England in the Early Part of the Sixteenth Century; with Special Reference to the Tombs of Cardinal Wolsey and King Henry VIII', *Archaeological Journal*, vol. 51 (1894), pp. 129–220
Hill, Anne, 'Trelawny's Family Background and Naval Career', *Keats-Shelley Journal*, vol. 5 (1956), pp. 11–32.
Hill, J.R., *The Prizes of War: The Naval Prize System in the Napoleonic Wars, 1793–1815* (Stroud: 1998)
Hill, Judith, *Irish Public Sculpture: A History* (Dublin: 1998)
Hore, Peter, *HMS Pickle: The Swiftest Ship in Nelson's Trafalgar Fleet* (Stroud: 2015)
Horsley, Samuel, Lord Bishop of St Asaph, *The Watchers and the Holy Ones: A Sermon* (London: 1805)
Howarth, David, *Trafalgar: The Nelson Touch* (Glasgow: 1969)
Howarth, David and Stephen, *Nelson: The Immortal Memory* (London: 1988)
Hubback, J.H. and Edith C., *Jane Austin's Sailor Brothers* (London: 1906)
Huskisson, Thomas, *Eyewitness to Trafalgar* (Orwell: 1985)
Ives, Edward, *A Voyage from England to India* (London: 1773)
James, William, *The Naval History of Great Britain*, 6 vols (London: 1826)
Jenks, T., 'Contesting the Hero: The Funeral of Lord Nelson, *Journal of British Studies*, vol. 39, no. 4 (2000), pp. 422–53

Kemp, Peter, *Oxford Companion to Ships and the Sea* (Oxford: 1976)
Kennedy, Dennis, 'Captain Watson and the Nelson Arch', *History Ireland*, vol. 24, no. 1 (Jan. 2016), pp. 18–20
Knight, Roger, *The Pursuit of Victory: The Life and Achievement of Horatio Nelson* (London: 2005)
Knight, Roger, *Britain Against Napoleon: The Organisation of Victory 1793–1815* (London: 2013)
Knight, W., ed., *Letters of the Wordsworth Family from 1787 to 1855*, 3 vols (London: 1907)
Lambert, Andrew, *Nelson, Britannia's God of War* (London: 2004)
Lavery, Brian, *Nelson's Navy: The Ships, Men and Organisation, 1793–1815* (London: 1989)
Letters Intercepted on board the Admiral Aplin . . . (London: 1804)
Leveson Gower, George, and Iris Palmer, (eds, *Hary-O: The Letters of Lady Harriet Cavendish 1796–1809* (London: 1940)
Lewis, Lady Theresa, *Extracts from the Journals and Correspondence of Miss Berry from the Year 1783 to 1852*, 2nd ed., 3 vols (London: 1866)
Lincoln, Margarette, ed., *Nelson and Napoleon* (London: 2005)
Lloyd, Christopher, and Jack L.S. Coulter, *Medicine and the Navy 1200–1900*, vol. 3: *1714–1815* (Edinburgh: 1961)
Lovell, William Stanhope, *Personal Narrative of Events from 1799 to 1815* (London: 1879)
Mace, Rodney, *Trafalgar Square: Emblem of Empire* (London: 1976)
Mackenzie, R.H., *The Trafalgar Roll of Honour* (London: 1913)
Malmesbury, James Harris, First Earl of, *Diaries and Correspondence of James Harris, First Earl of Malmesbury*, , ed. [James Harris,] Third Earl of Malmesbury, vol. 4 (London: 1844)
Mann, A.Y., *Last Moments and Principal Events Relative to the . . . Death of Lord Viscount Nelson* (London: 1806)
Marrs, Edwin W. Jr. (ed.) *The Letters of Charles and Mary Anne Lamb* vol. II 1801–1809, (Ithaca and London: 1976)
Marryat, Frederick, *The King's Own* (London: 1830)
Marsden, William, *A Brief Memoir of the Life and Writings of the Late William Marsden, Written by Himself*, ed. Elizabeth W. Marsden (London: 1838)
Martin, James, 'Book Concerning the Battle of Trafalgar', n.d., microfilm in NMM

McCrea, Robert Coutard, 'An Account of the Proceedings of His Majesty's Ship Swiftsure on the Glorious 21st of October 1805', RNM 1992/436, typescript
[Nicholas, Lt Paul Harris] 'The Battle of Trafalgar', *The Bijou: An Annual of Literature and the Arts* (London: 1829)
Nicolas, N.H., ed., *Dispatches and Letters of Vice Admiral Lord Viscount Nelson*, vol. 7 (London: 1846)
Nicolson, Adam, *Men of Honour: Trafalgar and the Making of the English Hero* (London: 2005)
Northcote, William, *The Marine Practice of Physic and Surgery*, 2 volumes, (London: 1770)
Noszlopy, George T., *Public Sculpture of Birmingham, Including Sutton Coldfield* (Liverpool: 1998)
O'Keeffe, Paul, *A Genius for Failure: The Life of Benjamin Robert Haydon* (London: 2009)
O'Keeffe, Paul, *Waterloo: The Aftermath* (London: 2014)
O'Meara, Barry, *Napoleon in Exile: A Voice from St Helena* (London: 1822)
Paget, Sir Arthur, *The Paget Papers*, ed. Augustus B. Paget, 2 vols (London: 1896)
Pérez Galdós, Benito, *Trafalgar* (Madrid: 1873)
Pillet, René-Martin, *Views of England, During a Residence of Ten Years; Six of them as a Prisoner of War* (Boston: 1818)
Plunkett, E., *The Past and Future of the British Navy* (London: 1846)
Pocock, Tom, *Horatio Nelson* (London: 1988)
Polwhele, Revd R., *Traditions and Recollections*, 2 vols (London: 1826)
Pope, Dudley, *England Expects: Nelson and the Trafalgar Campaign* (London: 1959)
Prothero, G.W., and William Stanhope Badcock, 'Battle of Trafalgar', *English Historical Review*, vol. 5, no. 20 (1890), pp. 767-9
Report of the Committee for Superintending the Erection of the Monument, to ... Lord Viscount Nelson, in the Area of the Liverpool Exchange (Liverpool: 1813)
Roberts, Andrew, *Napoleon the Great* (London: 2014)
Roberts, Andrew, *George III* (London: 2021)
Robinson, Hercules, *Sea Drift* (Portsea: 1858)
[Robinson, William,] *Nautical Economy; or Forecastle Recollections* (London: 1836)

Rodger, N.A.M., *The Wooden World: An Anatomy of the Georgian Navy* (London: 1986)
Rodger, N.A.M., *Safeguard of the Sea* (London: 1997)
Rodger, N.A.M., *Command of the Ocean* (London: 2004)
Rodger, N.A.M., *The Price of Victory* (London: 2024)
Roscoe, William, *Mount Pleasant: A Descriptive Poem* (Warrington: 1777)
Rouquet, James, *Thanksgiving Sermon* (Bristol: 1805)
Saint-Chamans, Alfred Armand Robert, Comte de, *Mémoires du general Cte de Saint-Chamans, ancient aide de camp du maréchal Soult* (Paris: 1896)
[Scales, J.,] *Correct Account of the Funeral Process of Lord Nelson by Water and Land* (London: 1806)
Schom, Alan, *Trafalgar: Countdown to Battle 1803–5* (London: 1990)
Scott, Revd A.J., *Recollections of the Life of the Rev. A.J. Scott DD, Lord Nelson's Chaplain* (London: 1842)
Senhouse, Humphrey, 'The Battle of Trafalgar', *Macmillan's Magazine*, vol. 81 (1899–1900), pp. 415–25
Sharples, Joseph, *Liverpool* (Pevsner Architectural Guides) (New Haven and London: 2004)
Shelley, Frances, Lady, *Diary of Frances Lady Shelley*, ed. Richard Edgcumbe (London: 1913)
Southey, Robert, *The Life of Nelson*, (London: 1916)
[Silliman, Benjamin,] *Journal of Travels in England, Holland and Scotland*, 3rd edn, vol. 3 (Boston: 1820)
Smith, David Baird, and Colin Campbell, '"The Defiance" at Trafalgar', *Scottish Historical Review*, vol. 20, no. 78 (1923), p. 116–21
Steele, R., *The Marine Officer, or Sketches of Service*, 2 vols (London: 1840)
Stevenson, Robert Louis, *Edinburgh: Picturesque Notes* (London: 1879)
Stirling, A.M.W., ed., *The Letter Bag of Lady Elizabeth Spencer-Stanhope*, vol. 1 (London: 1913)
Stuart, Dorothy Margaret, *Dearest Bess: The Life and Times of Lady Elizabeth Foster, afterwards Duchess of Devonshire* (London: 2012)

Stuart, Vivian, and George T. Eggleston, *His Majesty's Sloop-of-War Diamond Rock* (London: 1978)
Sturges Jackson, T., ed., *Logs of the Great Sea Fights 1794–1805*, vol. 2 (London: 1900)
Sugden, John, *Nelson: A Dream of Glory* (London: 2004)
Sugden, John, *Nelson: The Sword of Albion* (London: 2012)
Taylor, Stephen, *Sons of the Waves: The Common Seaman in the Heroic Age of Sail* (New Haven and London: 2020)
Terraine, John, *Trafalgar* (London: 1976)
Thursfield, H.G., ed., *Five Naval Journals 1789–1817* ([London]: 1951)
The Tomlinson Papers: Selected from the Correspondence and Pamphlets of Captain Robert Tomlinson, R.N., and Vice-Admiral Nicholas Tomlinson, ed. J.G. Bullocke (London: 1935)
Tracy, Nicholas, ed., *The Navy Chronicle*, consolidated edition, 5 vols (London: 1998–9)
Traill, H.D., *Life of Sir John Franklin RN* (London: 1896)
Trelawny, Edward John, *Adventures of a Younger Son* (London: 1835)
Turnbull, William, *The Naval Surgeon comprising the Entire Duties of Professional Men at Sea ... A System of Naval Surgery and a Compendious Pharmacopoeia* (London: 1806)
Uglow, Jenny, *In These Times: Living in Britain through Napoleon's Wars* (London: 2015)
Usherwood, Paul, Jeremy Beach and Catherine Morris, *Public Sculpture of North-East England* (Liverpool: 2000)
[Wallace, J.,] *A General and Descriptive History of the Ancient and Present State of the Town of Liverpool* (Liverpool: n.d. [c.1796])
Ward-Jackson, Philip, *Public Sculpture in the City of London* (Liverpool: 2003)
Ward-Jackson, Philip, *Public Sculpture of Historic Westminster*, vol. 1 (Liverpool: 2011)
Warner, Oliver, *Trafalgar* (London: 1959)
Warwick, Peter, *Tales from the Front Line: Trafalgar* (Newton Abbot: 2011)
Watt, Helen, with Anne Hawkins, ed., *Letters of Seamen in the Wars with France 1793–1815* (Woodbridge: 2016)
Watt, Sir James, 'Surgery at Trafalgar', *Mariner's Mirror*, vol. 91, no. 2 (2005), pp. 266–83
White, Colin, *The Nelson Companion* (Stroud: 1997)

White, Colin, *The Nelson Encyclopaedia* (Rochester: 2002)
White, Colin, ed., *Nelson: The New Letters* (2005)
White, Colin, 'Notes on Nelson's Funeral: The River Procession', *Trafalgar Chronicle, Journal of The 1805 Club*, No. 22 (2012), pp. 1–11
White, Colin, 'Final Thoughts on Nelson's Funeral', *Trafalgar Chronicle Journal of The 1805 Club*, No. 24 (2014), pp. 26–48
White, Joshua, *Supplement to the Life of the Late Horatio Lord Viscount Nelson ... and an Accurate Description ... of all the Ceremonies Attending The Funeral* (London: 1806)
Wood, Robert, *Sermon Preached in the Parish Church of Sneinton, Nottinghamshire* (Nottingham: 1805)
Wordsworth, William, *The Fenwick Notes of William Wordsworth*, ed. Jared. R. Curtis (London: 1993)
Wyndham, Henry Saxe, *Annals of Covent Garden Theatre, from 1732 to 1897* (London: 1906)

Dictionaries

Burney, William, *New Universal Dictionary of the Marine* (London: 1815)
Falconer, W., *Universal Dictionary of the Marine* (London: 1776)
Grose, Francis, *A Classical Dictionary of the Vulgar Tongue*, 2nd edition, corrected and enlarged (London: 1788)
Johnson, Samuel, *A Dictionary of the English Language*, 6th edition (London: 1785)
Moore, J.J., *The British Mariner's Vocabulary; or Universal Dictionary of Technical Terms and Sea Phrases* (London: 1801)
Norie, J.W., *The Mariner's New and Complete Naval Dictionary*, 3rd ed. (London: 1804)
Smyth, W.H., *Sailor's Word-Book: An Alphabetical Digest of Nautical Terms* (London: 1867)

Newspapers, Journals, Etc.

Aberdeen People's Journal
Belfast Commercial Chronicle Belfast News-Letter

BIBLIOGRAPHY

Bell's New Weekly Messenger
Blackwood's Edinburgh Magazine
Bristol Times and Mirror
British Press
The Builder
Calcutta Gazette
Caledonian Mercury
Cambridge Chronicle and Journal
Carlisle Journal
Chester Courant
Cornhill Magazine
Durham Chronicle
English Historical Review
English Illustrated Magazine
Evening Mail
General Evening Post
Gibraltar Chronicle
Globe
Gloucester Journal
Gore's Liverpool General Advertiser
Hampshire Chronicle
Hull Advertiser
Illustrated London News
Irish Times
Johnson's Sunday Monitor
Journal of British Studies
Kentish and Surrey Mercury
Kentish Weekly Post or Canterbury Journal
Leeds Intelligencer
Liverpool Weekly Courier
London Chronicle
London Courier and Evening Gazette
London Gazette
Macmillan's Magazine
Mariner's Mirror
Monthly Mirror
Morning Advertiser
Morning Chronicle
Morning Herald

Morning Post
Naval Chronicle
Nineteenth Century
Notes and Queries
Les Nouvelles à la main
Oracle and Daily Advertiser
Perthshire Courier
Public Ledger and Daily Advertiser
Revue des deux mondes
St. James's Chronicle
Salisbury and Wiltshire Journal
Saunders's News-Letter, and Daily Advertiser
Scots Magazine
Scottish Historical Review
Star
Sun
The Times
Trafalgar Chronicle
Trewman's Exeter Flying Post
True Briton
Westminster Journal, and Old British Spy
York Herald

ACKNOWLEDGEMENTS

My thanks, as ever, to the staff of the London Library. Also, to the London Archive, the National Archives, the British Library, Liverpool University's Sydney Jones Library, Liverpool Central Library and the Caird Library of the National Maritime Museum, Greenwich. Particular thanks to Victoria Ingles and Heather Johnson at the Royal Naval Museum, Portsmouth, Dr James Lloyd, Archivist of the College of Arms, Elesha-Joy Davis of the Nelson Museum, Monmouth, Rebecca Clarence at the Nelson Monument on Calton Hill, Edinburgh, and Margaret Hirst and Rob Williams at the Whitby Museum.

Thanks to Carys and Julian McCarthy for their unstinting New Malden hospitality. Thanks, also, to members of Llanfairfechan Sailing Club for responding to my lubberly queries with the benefit of their expert nautical knowledge and experience, particularly Mike Carter for explaining the perils of the Menai Straits 'Swellies'. And thanks to John Clark Ch.M., F.R.C.S. for providing a plausible explanation for what may have constituted the 'exceptional condition' of Admiral Collingwood's stomach at the time of his death.

Thanks to my agent Bill Hamilton, to Stuart Williams my publisher at The Bodley Head and to Henry Howard, copy-editor, for his meticulous scholarship that has spared the book lapses in my own. Thanks also to editorial director Jörg Hensgen and managing editor Graeme Hall for bringing the book to production with serene patience. Thanks also to proofreader Fiona Brown and indexer Alex Bell. Special thanks to Laura Reeves for her dogged pursuit of illustrations and Peter Pawsey for turning my mobile phone snap into a striking and useable image.

It was my partner, Sian Hughes, who first suggested that *Trafalgar* might round off the trilogy of books begun with *Waterloo*. We had both been fired up by a lecture in 2005 by the late Colin White, which inspired us to visit Portsmouth and HMS *Victory* for the first time later that bicentennial year. In 2022 I repeated the pilgrimage with Will Sulkin, my editor, mentor and friend of now thirty-five years. We paced the quarterdeck together, banged our heads on the oak beams of the orlop and ate fish and chips at the Ship Anson pub on the Hard. His wisdom, companionship and support have made the research and writing of this book a true joy.

And finally, for their warm and loving welcome to Portsmouth for a memorable long weekend in September 2024: my two nieces – Siobhan and Amy – and their families, to whom this book is dedicated.

LIST OF ILLUSTRATIONS

Prise du Rocher de Diamont, June 1805, Historical Galleries of Versailles. © National Maritime Museum, Greenwich, London.

Battle of Trafalgar © National Maritime Museum, Greenwich, London.

To Lord Collingwood... This representation of the destruction of the French and Spanish prizes after the glorious victory off Trafalgar. © National Maritime Museum, Greenwich, London.

The funeral procession of Lord Nelson, 1806. © The London Archives.

Nelson Memorial, Liverpool. © Paul O'Keeffe.

Prison-ship *York* in Portsmouth Harbour, c. 1828. © National Maritime Museum, Greenwich, London.

INDEX

Abell, Francis, 297, 299
Aboukir Bay, Egypt, 25, 30, 38, 172, 197, 203, 209, 223, 259, 261
Achille (French 74), 11, 53, 54, 93–5, 100, 110–11
Achille, HMS (74), 41, 120, 136, 140
Ackermann, Rudolph, 173, 226
Adair, Charles, 60, 64–5, 67
Admiralty, 160, 167, 168, 170, 171, 172, 175, 217, 219, 224, 226
Adolphus, Duke of Cambridge, 202, 230
Adventures of a Younger Son (Trelawny), 150
Aeolus, HMS (frigate 32), 153
Africa, HMS (64), 49, 83
Agamemnon, HMS (64), 113
Aigle (French 74), 11, 47, 53, 56, 78, 106, 118, 119, 123, 133, 135–6
Airy Hill, Whitby, 55
Ajax, HMS (74), 32, 40, 42, 129–30
de Álava, Ignacio María, 48, 117, 125
alcohol, 107–9, 119–20, 132
Alexander I, Emperor of Russia, 19, 20
Alfonso, King of Castile (Lewis), 196
Alfred, HMS, 34
Algarve, Portugal, 147
Algésiras (French 74), 53, 56, 76, 86, 117–18, 126–7, 139
Alliance plantation, Demerara, 272
Ambleside, Cumberland, 179

Ambleteuse, France, 20
Amelia, Princess, 249–50
American War of Independence (1775–83), 60, 193, 243
amputations, 25, 33–7, 68–79, 104–5, 144
Andover, Hampshire, 159
Andras, Catherine, 247–8
Anglesey, Wales, 259–60
Antigua, 10, 269
Aplin, Peter, 15
Apothecaries' Company, 216
Aquatic Theatre, Sadler's Wells, 192–5
Ardent, HMS (64), 75
Argonauta (Spanish 80), 120, 131–2, 134
Argonaute (French 74), 56
Argus, 7
Armide, 2
Arne, Thomas, 39, 184
Art Journal, 246
Articles of War (1749), 75
Ashton-under-Lyne, Lancashire, 177
Aspinall, James, 273
Aspinall, John Bridge, 273
Atcherley, James, 90
Atkins, John, 35, 36
Augustus Frederick, Duke of Sussex, 230
Austen, Francis, 150
Austria, 20, 140–41, 171
Authentic Narrative (Beatty), 74

Axminster, Devon, 158
Azores, 73

Badcock, William Stanhope, 28, 60, 90, 131
Bagshot, Surrey, 159
Bahama (Spanish 74), 47, 86, 100, 139, 299
Baily, Edward Hodges, 263
Ball, Arthur, 117
bands, 30, 39, 41
Barbados, 9, 10, 258, 268, 285
Barbara (English merchantman), 102
Barbary coast, 101
Barham, HMS (74), 111
Barker, Alexander, 28
Barnard, Edward, 136
Barof, Jean, 77
Basingstoke, Hampshire, 159
Batavian Republic (Netherlands), 13, 14
Bath, Somerset, 177, 182
Battle of Alexandria (1801), 223
Battle of Austerlitz (1805), 20, 48, 141, 219
Battle of Camperdown (1797), 75, 182
Battle of Cape Finisterre (1805), 11–13, 19, 285
Battle of Cape Ortegal (1805), 151–7, 181, 202, 283, 288, 297
Battle of Cape St Vincent (1797), 106, 172, 214, 264, 275
Battle of Copenhagen (1801), 172, 243, 264, 275
Battle of Crécy (1346), 1
Battle of Diamond Rock (1805), 1, 7–10, 124, 285
Battle of Fort Royal (1781), 44
Battle of Friedland (1807), 296
Battle of Marengo (1800), 296
Battle of the Nile (1798), 25, 30, 38, 172, 197, 203, 209, 216, 223
  memorials, 259, 261 264, 275
Battle of San Domingo (1806), 252
Battle of Santa Cruz (1797), 25, 37, 197
Battle of Sedan (1870), 254
Battle of Ulm (1805), 20, 141, 168, 171
Battle of Verona (1805), 171
Battle of Waterloo (1815), 165, 167, 179, 259, 277, 278, 296
Bavaria, 19

Bayne, William, 34
Bayntun, Henry William, 131, 137
Bazin, François Marie, 85, 114
Beatson, John, 300
Beatty, William, 26, 37, 38, 63, 66, 68–74, 75–6, 107, 204–5, 245
Beaumont, George, 179
Beechey, William, 173
Bel Air plantation, Demerara, 272
Belgium Black horses, 225
Belleisle, HMS (74), 10, 28, 32, 46, 49, 52–4, 56, 58, 63, 140
  anchoring, 113
  band, 39, 41, 46
  casualties, 74, 92
  clearing of decks, 31
  lie down order, 46–7
  Royal Sovereign, firing on, 51
  towing, 113
Bellerophon, HMS (74), 30, 32, 42, 47, 54, 56, 78, 86, 92, 105, 139
  Monarca prize taking, 120, 139
  Napoleon's surrender (1815), 300
  prison hulk conversion (1815–16), 300
  wounded on, 134
Benedetto da Rovezzano, 249
Bennett, Charles, 117–18
Berry, Mary, 218, 226–8
Berwick (French 74), 7, 133, 136, 137, 139
Bessborough, Henrietta Ponsonby, Countess, 159–60, 220, 227
Betsey (slave ship), 270, 289
Betty, William, 196
Bigland, Ralph, 215
Billington, Elizabeth, 197–9, 235
Birchen Edge, Derbyshire, 253
Birmingham, Warwickshire, 258
Bishop's Waltham, Hampshire, 288
Black Lives Matter, 268
Blackfriars Bridge, 213, 217, 218
Blackwood, Henry, 114, 123, 124–5, 146, 215
Blandford Forum, Dorset, 159
Blane, Gilbert, 34, 105
Blue Anchor Inn, Fraddon, 158
Bodmin Moor, Cornwall, 158
Boisnard, François, 154
Bolton, John, 272
Bond Street, Westminster, 160

INDEX

Bond, Will, 76
Bonduca, or the British Heroine (Fletcher), 39
Boulogne, France, 11, 13, 14, 19–20
Boulton, Matthew, 206
Bow Street Police Court, 175, 190
Bowyer's Historic Gallery, Pall Mall, 248
Boyer, Eugène-Edmond, 7–10
Braham, John, 188, 198, 199
Brave, HMS (formerly French *Formidable* 80), 298
Brecon, Wales, 177
Brest, France, 19
Bridewell Prison, London, 175
Bridgetown, Barbados, 258, 268
Bridgwater, Somerset, 27
Brightman, John, 253
Britannia, 173, 175–6, 181, 207, 226
  in theatre, 191–2, 198, 199
  on monuments, 242, 255, 259, 262
Britannia, HMS (100), 28, 40, 79, 83, 86, 91, 99, 100, 132, 133, 139–40, 299
British Press, 169
'Britons Strike Home', 39, 156
Britton, Simon Gage, 68
Brooke, Edward Freeman, 55, 104
Brown, John, 28, 41, 141, 206
Browne, George, 115
Brunswick (English prison hulk), 297, 298
Buccleuch, Walter Scott, 5th Duke, 264
Bucentaure (French 80), 5, 48, 58–9, 61, 62–4, 79–81, 82–4, 85, 111
  casualties, 90–91, 106
  prize, taking as, 114, 121–4, 225, 287
  recapture, 121–4
  sinking, 122–3, 127, 138
  wounded on, 120, 138
Buckingham, Catherine Sheffield, Duchess, 247
Buckingham, John Sheffield, 1st Duke, 247
Bull Ring Centre, Birmingham, 258
Bull, Nicholas, 200
Bullock, George, 275
Bunce, William, 205
Burgess, James, 70
Burgin, Joseph, 70
Burke, Walter, 73, 74
Burn, Robert, 255–6

Burnett, William, 144
Burnham Thorpe, Norfolk, 106, 259
Burstal, Richard, 85, 88
Bush, James, 73
Bush, John, 71
butcher's bill, 92
Butrón, Alonso, 86
Byng, John, 286, 290

Cadiz, Spain, 1, 5–6, 20–21, 40, 99–103, 114, 119, 122–7, 136, 292
Caesar, HMS, 151, 152–3, 156–7
Calais, France, 13, 14, 18
Calder, Robert, 11–13, 19, 285–6
Caledonian Mercury, 182
Calton Hill, Edinburgh, 255
Calvi, Corsica, 25
Cameron Highlanders, 223
Campbell, Colin, 41, 54, 100, 106, 131
Canada, 258
canister shot, 44
Canopus, HMS (80), 150
Canterbury, Kent, 175–6, 204
Cape Finisterre, Spain, 11–13, 148, 151, 285
Cape Ortegal, Spain, 151–7, 181, 202, 283, 288, 297
Cape St Vincent, Portugal, 106, 147, 172, 214, 264, 275
capital knives, 35
Capo de Santa María, Portugal, 147
Captain, HMS, 106
Captivity (prison hulk, formerly HMS *Bellerophon*), 300
carbines, 65
Caribbean, 1–11, 73, 269–70, 272–3
Carlisle, Cumberland, 166
Carlisle Bay, Barbados, 285
Carmarthen, Wales, 177
Caroline, Princess of Wales, 207
Carron Iron Company, 5
Case, George, 273
Cash, John, 41
Castle, George, 50, 51, 52, 57
Castle, William, 72
Castletownshend, County Cork, 252
casualties, 46, 47, 54, 60–61, 63, 71, 77, 84, 87, 90–92, 103–6
  disposal of bodies, 103–6
  shipwrecks, 138

Catherine de Valois, Queen consort, 247
Catherine Street, Westminster, 221
Catholicism, 40
catlin knives, 35, 36
Caunant, Jeanette, 110
Cavendish, Harriet, 167, 228
Centaur, HMS (74), 3, 4–5, 43–4
Chalmers, William, 76
Chapel Royal, St James's Palace, 232
Character of the Happy Warrior, The (Wordsworth), 180
Charing Cross, Westminster, 211, 220, 221, 222, 227, 248
Charles I, King, 227, 249
Charles II, King, 215
Charlotte Street, Westminster, 174
Chatham (English yacht), 205
Chatham, Kent, 205–6, 244, 295, 297, 299, 300
Chatham, William Pitt, 1st Earl, 247
Cheapside, London, 174
chelenk, 209, 214
Chelsea Pensioners, 70
Cherbourg, France, 13, 254
Chester, William Cleaver, Bishop of, 232
Chesterfield, Derbyshire, 177
Chevers, Forbes McBean, 33, 76, 134
Chiswick, Middlesex, 167, 220
Chittenden, Mr, 207, 209, 226
Cibber, Colley, 185
Circe, HMS (frigate 32), 285
de Cisneros, Baltasar, 86, 130
Classen, Asmus, 118–19, 136
Clavell, John, 134
Clay, Henry, 271, 273
clearing of decks, 31–2
Clerk, John, 182
Cnoc Aingeal, Argyllshire, 253
Coade and Sealy, 258
Coade stone, 258, 259
Cobb, James, 184
Cochinas Rocks, 122
cockpits, 33, 34, 76
Cockspur Street, Westminster, 227
Codrington, Edward, 115, 116, 133, 140–41, 142, 143, 147, 251
Codrington, Jane, 133, 234, 235
coehorn mortars, 65
Colby, Thomas, 117, 125

College of Arms, 214, 223
Collingwood, Cuthbert, 20–21, 38, 46, 49, 56, 58, 90, 100, 112, 140–41, 181, 292–5
  anchoring, 112, 113
  Belleisle firing incident, 51
  death (1809), 290
  dispatch, 146–8, 160, 169, 171, 181
  Euryalus, flag shift to, 114, 124
  Harvey, meeting with, 142–3
  humanitarian gestures, 102
  memorials to, 294–5
  Nelson's death, 57
  Nelson's funeral, 215
  Nelson's signal, 42
  Portsdown Hill monument, 251
  prizes, abandonment of, 92, 129, 132–3, 139
  Rochefort squadron, views on, 152
  stockings, 37, 52, 134
  Swiftsure prize, 117
  thanksgiving order, 199–200
  theatrical representation, 186
  Toulon blockade (1809), 292–3
Collingwood, Edward, 67
Collingwood, Sarah, 147, 181
Colossus, HMS (74), 56, 77, 86, 88, 92, 113, 134
Columbus, or a World Discovered (Morton), 40
Compiegne, France, 13
Concordat (1801), 40
Conqueror, HMS (74), 10, 27, 31, 60, 79–81, 86–7, 92, 100, 111, 121, 123, 139, 251
Constable & Co., 181, 182
Cooke, James, 105
Cooke, John, 47–8, 54, 78, 191
Copenhagen, Denmark, 172, 243, 264, 275
Cornwall, England, 149, 150, 151, 157–8
Corsica, 25
Coruña, Spain, 11
Cosgrove, James, 68
Cosmao-Kerjulien, Julien Marie, 7–8, 77, 124–7, 135, 138, 288
Cossé, Nicolas, 154
Courageux, HMS (74), 152–3
Courier and Evening Gazette, 169
Court of Common Council, 229, 261

INDEX

Covent Garden, London, 174, 185, 189–91, 196
Craigleith sandstone, 264
Cramwell, Henry, 72
Crediton, Devon, 293
Crimean War (1853–6), 254
Crocan, Aaron, 27, 31, 93
Crockernwell, Devon, 158
Croker, John Wilson, 294
Crosby (admiralty navigation barge), 217
Cross, Edward, 242*n*
Cumberland, England, 178–81
Cumberland, Richard, 184, 187–9
Cumby, William, 47, 78, 105
Curtis, Roger, 194

Daily Advertiser, 193
Danube River, 20
Dartmoor, 158, 296
De Quincey, Thomas, 175
Deal, Kent, 20
Death of General Wolfe, The (West), 243–4
Death of Lord Nelson, The (West), 243–4, 245, 255
Death of Lord Nelson in the Cockpit of the Victory, The (West), 245, 255
Death of Nelson, The (Devis), 244–5
Death of Nelson, The (Maclise), 245–6
Decrès, Denis, 2
Defence, HMS (74), 42, 87, 94, 106, 140
Defiance, HMS (74), 27, 41, 54, 100, 118, 120, 131, 134, 144, 215, 299
Delinquent, or Seeing Company, The (Reynolds), 189
Delivet, Jean-Baptiste, 79
Demerara, Guyana, 272–3
Deniéport, Louis Gabriel, 93
Denmark, 172, 243, 264, 275
Devis, Arthur William, 244–5
Devon, England, 158
Devonshire, Georgiana Cavendish, Duchess, 167–8, 207, 219, 221
Devonshire, William Cavendish, 5th Duke, 167–8
Diamante Rocks, 122, 126–7, 136
Diamond Rock, HMS, 1–10, 124, 285
Dibdin, Charles, 192–5
Dibdin, Thomas, 174, 185, 186–7, 196–7
Ditton Hall, Cambridgeshire, 252

Dixie, Alexander, 139
Dominica, 2
Donadieu, Antoine, 81
Donegal, HMS (74), 127–8, 132, 136, 137, 150
Donegall, Anna Chichester, Marchioness, 183
Donegall, George Chichester, 2nd Marquess, 183
Donnadieu, Guillaume, 155
Dorchester, Dorset, 158
Dorset, England, 158
Downfall of Paris (quickstep), 39
Dragoon Guards, 210, 223
Drapers' Company, 216
Dreadnought, HMS (74), 20, 49, 85, 88, 90, 92, 114, 117, 120, 142
Drury Lane, Westminster, 184, 187–9, 191
Dublin, Ireland, 183, 252, 257–8, 259, 266–7
Dublin Hotel, Westminster, 211, 221, 227
Duckworth, John Thomas, 149–50
Duff, George, 40–41, 53–4, 85, 104–5, 191
Duff, Norwich, 41
Duguay-Trouin (French 74), 59, 83, 89, 152–4, 283–4
Dumanoir le Pelley, Pierre, 82–4, 88, 89, 91, 152–5, 157, 287–8, 298
Dunbar, William, 137
Duncan, Adam, 1st Viscount, 182
Dundas, David, 231
Dundee Arms, Wapping, 214
Dunkirk, France, 13, 14, 18
Durham Chronicle, 295
Durham, Philip, 118

Earl of Abergavenny (English East Indiaman), 180
East India Company, 15, 172, 180
Eastwick, Constance, 127*n*
Edinburgh, Scotland, 181–2, 256–7
Edward, Duke of Kent, 224, 230
Edwards, John, 129–30
Edwards, Thomas, 152
Egypt, 25, 30, 38, 172, 197, 203, 209, 216, 223, 259, 261
Elizabeth I, Queen, 247, 249
Ellis, Samuel Burdon, 32, 42

INDEX

English Channel, 149
Entreprenante, HMS, 39, 111, 147
Ernest Augustus, Duke of Cumberland, 230
Essay on Naval Tactics, An (Clerk), 182
Étaples, France, 18, 20
Euryalus, HMS (frigate 36), 27, 38, 100, 101, 109, 205, 299
    Collingwood on, 114, 124, 142–3, 146, 199
    pig rescue, 110
    Royal Sovereign towing, 113
    Santísima Trinidad sinking, 129
Eurydice, HMS (frigate 24), 127
Evening Mail, 17
Exchange Flags, Liverpool, 274–8
Exeter Hall, Westminster, 242
Exeter, Devon, 158, 222, 235

Falkirk, Scotland, 5
Falmouth, Cornwall, 147n, 151, 157
Farington, Joseph, 244
Faro, Portugal, 147
Fellowes, James, 69, 108
Fencibles, 158, 208, 214, 216, 252
Fenwick, Isobel, 180
fer-de-lance vipers, 4
Ferrol, Spain, 11, 12, 19, 290
Fettes, William, 256
Feuillet, Pierre François, 118
Fife, James Duff, 4th Earl, 218
Fighting Téméraire, The (Turner), 300
figureheads, 40, 68, 70, 300
Fine (French schooner 14), 7, 9
Finsbury Square, London, 233
Firme (French 74), 11
Fischer, John, 120, 122, 123
Fishmongers' Company, 216
Fitzherbert, Maria, 165
Flaxman, John, 242–3, 246–7
Fleet Street, London, 173, 212, 217, 221, 222, 231
Fletcher, John, 39
fog, 159–60
food, 31, 41, 144
Forbes, George, 116
Formidable (French 80), 83, 89, 152–6, 298
Fort Nelson, Hampshire, 254
Fort Royal, Martinique, 1, 2, 3, 43–4

Foster, Augustus, 167
Foster, Clifford, 167
Foster, Elizabeth, 167, 208, 211, 219, 221, 224, 227, 252
Foster, John, 273–4
Foudroyant, HMS (80), 203
Fougueux (French 74), 44, 50, 51, 52–4, 56, 58, 63, 85, 88, 114, 115, 119, 143
Fournier, Fulcran, 81, 106, 121
Fournier, René-Marie, 77
Fowler, Charles, 263
Fox, James, 235
Fraddon, Cornwall, 158
France
    Concordat with Rome (1801), 40
    Prussian War (1870–71), 254
    Revolution (1789–99), 40
Francis II, Emperor of Austria, 19
Franklin, John, 32
Frederick, Duke of York, 230
Fremantle, Thomas, 129, 142, 143
Fruithill, Newtown Limavady, 183
Fry, Elizabeth, 14

Galdós, Pérez, 32
Galera Rocks, 122, 127
Galiano, Antonio Alcalá, 100
Galiano, Dionisio Alcalá, 86, 100
gangrene, 35
Ganteaume, Honoré Joseph Antoine, 11, 19
de Gardoqui, José, 57
Garneray, Louis, 297
Garrick, David, 40
General Evening Post, 17
George III, King, 38, 166, 192, 249, 258, 277
George IV, King, 165–6, 224, 232
Gibraltar Chronicle, 123, 286, 287
Gibraltar, 5, 69, 71, 74, 104, 108, 109, 128, 134, 139, 140, 144, 150
Gicquel, Auguste, 45–6, 90, 120, 132
Gilbert Library, Dublin, 266
Ginger, John, 16–17
Gladstone, John, 272, 273, 276
Glasgow, Scotland, 255–6, 263
Globe, 169, 191
Gloire (French frigate 40), 2
Go Lucky Four (folk group), 267

Goble, Thomas, 244
'God Save the King', 156, 177, 192, 252
Gold Coast, 270
Goldsmid, Abraham, 173
Goldsmiths' Company, 216
de Gomendio, Anselmo, 87
Goodman's Fields Theatre, London, 191
Gordon Highlanders, 223
Gordon, Joseph, 69
Grahame, James, 255
Granton quarry, Edinburgh, 264
Granville, Walter, 263
grapeshot, 44
Grassini, Josephina, 197–9
Gravina, Federico, 6, 54, 191, 292
Great Queen Street, Westminster, 235
Great Yarmouth, Norfolk, 259, 295
Greenly, John, 77, 90
Greenock, Scotland, 102
Greenwich, Kent, 203, 205, 207–10, 213, 214, 216, 227, 284
Greenwich Pensioners, 224, 232
Gregson, John, 273
grenades, 65–6, 78
Grier, Thomas, 104
Guernsey, 151
Guildhall, London, 172, 261–2, 275
Guillet, Victor, 154
guns; gun decks, 32, 33, 43–8, 49–50
Gurney, Priscilla, 14
Guruceta, Roque, 86
Guthrie, George, 37
Guyana, 272–3

Hall, Stuart, 17
Halloran, Lawrence, 28, 40, 80, 100, 101, 104, 133, 139–40
Hallowell, Benjamin, 203
Hamilton, Emma, 31, 74, 107, 168–9, 248
Hamilton, William, 242–3
Hampton, Sam, 76
Handel, George Frideric, 177, 200, 219, 222
Handsworth, Staffordshire, 206
Hanover, 17, 18
Hanover Square, Westminster, 174
Hardy, Thomas, 42, 57, 58, 59, 61, 62, 66, 72, 84, 108
  anchoring order, 112, 113
  Nelson's death, 106, 107, 109

Nelson's funeral, 215, 229
  theatrical representation, 191
Hargood, William, 46, 47
Hargrave, William, 131–2
Harlequin Aesop or Wisdom versus Wealth (pantomime), 194
Harlequin, 99
Harper, William, 272
Harris, Isaac, 70
Harrison, Edward, 141
Hartfordbridge, Hampshire, 159
Harvey, Eliab, 51, 85, 88, 89, 94, 134, 142
Hatt, Andrew, 200
Hawkesbury, Robert Jenkinson, Lord, 246–7
Haydon, Benjamin Robert, 49, 226
Haymarket, Westminster, 197–9, 227
Hazlitt, William, 166, 211
Heard, Isaac, 233–4
Hearts of Oak, 30
Hennah, William, 54, 85
Henry V, King, 247
Henry VII, King, 247
Henry VIII, King, 249
Herald's Office, 226, 232
Hero, HMS (74), 152–3
Héros (French 74), 59, 82, 84, 124
Heywood, Arthur, 272
Heywood, Richard, 272
Hicks, William, 80, 87, 139
Highlanders, 223, 231
Hilton, Robert, 116
Hoffman, Frederick, 56, 94
Honiton, Devon, 158
Hood, Samuel, 3–5, 7–8
Hope, George Johnstone, 42, 140
Horse Guards Parade, Westminster, 222
Horsley, Samuel, 201
Hortense (French frigate 40), 126
Horwood, Joshua, 93
Hôtel de la Patrie, Rennes, 289–92
Hounslow, Middlesex, 159, 160
Howard, Robert, 15
Hudson, William, 47, 52
Huguenots, 146
Huntly, George Gordon, 9th Marquess, 182
Huskisson, Thomas, 42
Huskisson, William, 87

INDEX

Ilfracombe, Devon, 146
illuminations, 171–83
Illustrated London News, 70, 265
imperial eagles, 48, 62, 80–81, 165
Implacable, HMS (formerly French *Swiftsure*), 284
Incledon, Charles, 197
India, 15, 18, 108n
Indomptable (French 74), 11, 51, 52, 122–3, 124, 138
Infernet, Louis-Antoine-Cyprien, 284–5
Inner Temple, London, 217
Intrépide (French 74), 11, 45, 82, 83, 91, 120, 132, 133, 288
Ipswich Journal, 252
Ireland, 17, 128, 183, 252, 257, 266–7
Ironmongers' Company, 216
Irresistible, HMS (formerly French *Swiftsure*), 295
Israel in Egypt (Handel), 200
Italy, 171
Ives, Edward, 33, 76

Jack Tar, 195
Jamaica, 108n, 235
James II, King, 247
James, William, 112
Jemappes (French 74), 2
Jewell, Richard, 70
'John Brown's Body' (Go Lucky Four), 267
Johnson, Samuel, 65–6
Johnson's Sunday Monitor, 19
Johnston, Francis, 257
Johnston, Henry Erskine, 190–91
Johnston, Nannette, 189–91
Jolley, John, 80
Jones, William, 70
Josephine, Empress consort, 3
Joyce, James, 257–8

Keats, Richard Goodwin, 149, 252
Kensington, Middlesex, 16, 217
King, Andrew, 244
King, John, 67
King, Mathew Peter, 188
King, Richard, 140
King's Somborne, Hampshire, 15
King's Theatre, Haymarket, 197–9, 227
Kirk, Thomas, 257

Knight, William, 71
Knights of the Bath, 224, 234

L'Hôpitalier-Villemadrin, Charles-Eusebe, 79
L'Orient (French 118), 203, 225
de La Bretonnière, Valdémar, 126
Lackington, James, 233
Laforey, Francis, 214
Lamb, Charles, 166, 211, 212–13
Landseer, Edwin, 265
langrage, 25, 44, 65
Lapenotière, John Richards, 146–9, 157–60
Launceston, Cornwall, 158
Lavenu, Jean Baptiste, 154
Le Hoche (French prize renamed *Donegal*), 128
Le Tourneur, Laurent, 56
Leadenhall Street, London, 172
Lee column, 38, 39, 40, 53, 54, 56, 58, 92, 93, 101
Leeds Intelligencer, 55
Leeward Islands, 3
Leicester Place Theatre, Westminster, 191–2
Lestock, Richard, 108n
Letellier, Jean-Marie, 153–4, 155
Leviathan, HMS (74), 10, 42, 84, 86, 131, 132, 134, 137, 143, 300
Lewis, Matthew, 196
Lincoln, George Pretyman Tomline, Bishop of, 232
Lincolnshire Regiment of Foot, 223
Lion (French 74), 2
lions, 242, 265
Lisbon, Portugal, 147–8, 170
Lithodipyra, 258
Liverpool, Merseyside, 269–78
Liverpool, Robert Jenkinson, 2nd Earl, 246–7
Livery Companies, 217
Lizard, Cornwall, 149, 151
Lloyd, Robert, 87, 92
Lloyd's of London, 272
Lloyd's Coffee House, London, 201
Lloyd's List, 152
Loch Etive, Argyllshire, 252–3
Lock, James, 248

INDEX

London, England
  fog in, 159–60
  illuminations in, 171–5
  monuments in, 242–3, 246–7, 261–6, 268, 275
  Nelson's funeral (1806), 205–36
  theatre in, 174–5, 184–200
London Bridge, 213
London Chronicle, 20
London Docks, 214
London Gazette, 72, 142–3, 170
London Zoological Society, 265
Lord Walsingham (English packet), 147n
Lorne Iron Furnace, Argyllshire, 253
Lough, John Graham, 264, 294
Lucas, Jean-Jacques-Étienne, 58–9, 63–6, 77, 85, 88, 89, 91, 115, 288–9
Ludgate Hill, London, 172, 211, 221, 225, 231, 246
Ludgate Street, London, 212

Macdonald, Lydia, 16
Mack von Leiberich, Karl, 168
Maclise, Daniel, 245–6
Macquin, Denis, 226–7
Madras, India, 15, 18
Magnanime (French 74), 2
Magon de Médine, Charles, 86, 118
Magrath, George, 37
Majestueux (French 120), 2
Malcolm, Pulteney, 136, 150, 151
Maldon, Essex, 158
Malmesbury, James Harris, 1st Earl, 171
Malta, HMS (80), 12
Mansfield, Charles John Moore, 116
Mansion House, London, 172
Marcus Aurelius, Roman Emperor, 277
Maritime Museum, Greenwich, 284
Marochetti, Carlo, 265
Marryat, Frederick, 92n, 228
Mars, HMS (74), 32, 40, 53–4, 85, 105
Marsden, William, 160, 171, 207, 219
Martin, James, 28–9
Martinique, 1, 2, 43–4, 290
Mary and Ellen (English merchantman), 151
Marylebone, Westminster, 174
Maurice, James Wilkes, 3–10, 285
McCrea, Robert Coutart, 93–4, 100, 115
McDonald, William, 77

McGonagall, William, 253
Meeting of Wellington and Blücher, The (Maclise), 246
Melpomene, HMS (frigate 38), 127
Melville, Herman, 276
Merchant Taylors' Company, 216
Merton Place, Surrey, 168
Minotaur, HMS (74), 83, 114, 116
Miss in her Teens (Garrick), 40
Missiessy, Édouard-Thomas de Burgues, comte de, 1, 2, 6
Mitchell, Robert, 258–9
Molyneux St George, William, 87
Monarca (Spanish 74), 47, 53, 56, 86, 120–21, 134, 137, 139
Moniteur universel, Le, 15, 16, 44
Mont Blanc (French 74), 59, 83, 89, 152–4
Monthly Mirror, 186, 187, 194, 198
Montreal, Quebec, 258–9
Montserrat, 2
Moorfields, London, 223, 233
Moorsom, Robert, 54–5, 110, 215
Morlaix, France, 285
Morning Advertiser, 212
Morning Chronicle, 171, 174, 198, 199, 221, 223, 224, 228, 235–6
Morning Herald, 198, 241
Morning Post, 12, 18, 20, 225, 231, 233, 248
Morpeth, Northumberland, 292
Morton, Thomas, 40
Moule, Thomas, 263
Mr Shrapnel's Jeweller, Charing Cross, 248
Mrs Salmon's Waxworks, Fleet Street, 241–2, 247
Munich, Bavaria, 20
Murat, Adrien, 155
Mylne, Robert, 241, 242, 248–9

Nagle, Edmund, 235
Naiad, HMS (frigate 38), 38, 110, 111, 113
Namur, HMS (74), 152–3
Napoleon I, Emperor of the French, 1–2, 166–7
  Battle of Austerlitz (1805), 219
  Battle of Waterloo (1815), 165, 167, 179, 296

INDEX

Napoleon I – *cont.*
   Diamond Rock campaign (1805), 2–3
   England invasion plan (1803–5), 1–2, 13–20, 201, 285
   Hanover invasion (1803), 17, 18
   imperial eagle icons, 48, 165
   St Helena, exile on (1815–21), 291, 300
   surrender (1815), 296
   Villeneuve's death (1806), 289–92
Napoleon III, Emperor of the French, 254
Nautilus, HMS (sloop 18), 148
Naval Chronicle, 10, 43, 286, 292
Naval General Service Medal, 70
Naval History of Great Britain (James), 112
Naval Hospital, Greenwich, 203
Naval Officer, The (Marryat), 92n
Naval Victory and Triumph of Lord Nelson (Rossi), 198–9
Navy Coffee House, Westminster, 172
Navy Office, Westminster, 172
Nelson Monument, Merseyside, 269–78
Nelson, Edmund, 106
Nelson, Horatia, 31, 74, 229
Nelson, Horatio, 1st Viscount, 25–7, 30, 31, 37, 42, 54, 58, 112–13
   Battle of Cape St Vincent (1797), 106, 172, 214
   Battle of Copenhagen (1801), 172
   Battle of Santa Cruz (1797), 25, 37, 197
   Battle of the Nile (1798), *see* Battle of the Nile
   carbines, views on, 65
   Collingwood, comparisons with, 140, 141
   death (1805), 25–7, 54, 57, 58, 67, 72–4, 84, 105
   decorations, 38, 209, 214
   funeral (1806), 205–36
   Hamilton, relationship with, 31, 74, 107, 168–9
   illumination commemorations, 171–83
   monuments to, 242–3, 246–7, 251–67, 268–78
   news of death, 157, 160, 165–83
   paintings of, 243–6
   remains, transport of, 106–9, 203–5
   sartorial advice, 37
   signals, 42, 61–2, 111–12
   Styles and Titles, 233–4
   theatrical representations, 174–5, 185–200
   tomb, 241–2, 248–50
Nelson, William, 1st Earl, 204–5, 241, 283
Nelson's Column, Trafalgar Square, 262–6, 268
Nelson's Farewell, 191
Nelson's Glory (Dibdin), 174–5, 186–7, 196–7
Neptune, 28, 207, 247, 255, 260, 261, 263
Neptune, HMS (98), 28, 53, 63, 86, 91, 124, 129, 142, 299
Neptuno (Spanish 80), 83, 84, 114, 116–17, 125, 135
Netherlands, 13, 14, 19
Nevis, 2
Newbury, Berkshire, 15
Newcastle, Tyne and Wear, 181, 294, 295
Newcastle Street, Westminster, 221
Newtown Limavady, Ulster, 183
Nicholas, Paul Harris, 28, 39, 53, 140
Nike (Goddess of Victory), 225
Norfolk, England, 259
North Gloucestershire Regiment, 28th, 223
North-West Passage, 32
Northcote, William, 33, 34–5, 36, 69, 74–5
Northesk, William Carnegie, 7th Earl, 79, 181
Northumberland, HMS (74), 300
Norwich, Norfolk, 177, 259
Nott, John, 43–4
Nova Scotia graving dock, Liverpool, 271

O'Connell Street, Dublin, 257, 266
O'Meara, Barry, 291–2
Ocean, HMS (98), 166, 293
Okehampton, Devon, 158
Old Bailey, London, 212
Operation Humpty Dumpty (1966), 266
Oporto, Portugal, 148
Order of the Crescent, 38, 234

Orion, HMS (74), 83, 92, 114–15, 132, 133, 140, 251
Ostend, Belgium, 14, 18
Ottoman Empire, 38, 209, 234
Otway, Thomas, 186
Ouessant (Ushant), France, 149
Overton, Edward, 78, 105
Overton, Hampshire, 159
Owen, John, 47
Oxford Street, Westminster, 160, 173, 174

Paget, Arthur, 290*n*
Paget, Clarence, 259–60
Painted Hall, Greenwich Hospital, 207–10, 214
Palace of Westminster, 245–6
Pall Mall, Westminster, 160, 166, 206–7, 248
Palmer, Alex, 71–2
Palmer, John, 72
Palmerston, Henry John Temple, 3rd Viscount, 254
Panzetta, Joseph, 255
Parker, Peter, 215, 228
Parrott, Thomas, 129
Pasco, John, 30, 31, 42, 61
Patriotic Fund, 147, 201–2, 262
Patterdale, Cumberland, 178–81
Peace of Amiens (1802–3), 292
Peak District, 253
Pendennis Castle, Cornwall, 151
Penrith, Cumberland, 179
Percy, Henry, 165
Pérez Galdós, Benito, 32, 130
Pernot, Charles, 77, 138
Petit, Jean Louis, 35, 37
Phantasmagoria, 192
Philibert, Pierre, 127
Phoebe, HMS (frigate 36), 39, 114, 117, 120, 139
Phoenix, HMS (frigate 36), 153
Piccadilly, Westminster, 160, 165
Pickle, HMS (schooner 10), 39, 68*n*, 110, 111, 146–51, 157–60, 181
pickpockets, 183, 221, 236
Pillet, René-Martin, 297
Pistrucci, Benedetto, 262–3
Pitt the Elder, William, 247

Pitt the Younger, William, 20, 165
Plas Llanfair, Anglesey, 259–60
Playa de Santa María, Cadiz, 101
Plume of Triumph, 209, 214
Plunkett, Edward, 91
Pluton (French 74), 7, 53, 77, 124, 126, 138
Plymouth, Devon, 49, 59, 141, 150, 156, 157, 251, 271, 288, 296, 297, 298
point-blank range, 43
Poland, 19
Pollard, John, 67
Polyphemus, HMS (64), 92
Ponsonby, William Francis Spencer, 220
Poor Jack (Dibdin), 185, 186
Popham, Home, 42, 61–2, 246
Portland Bill, Dorset, 180
Portland stone, 251, 257, 260, 264, 277
Portsdown Hill, Hampshire, 251, 253–4
Portsmouth, Hampshire, 15, 131, 150, 251, 284, 285, 296, 297
Portugal, 147–8, 170
post-traumatic stress disorder, 144
pots à feu, 78
Prigny, Mathieu, 120, 121, 123
Prince, HMS (98), 93–5, 111, 114, 120, 130, 132–3, 141, 142
Prince of Wales, HMS (98), 285
Príncipe de Asturias (Spanish 112), 53, 54, 55, 56, 292
prison hulks, 293–6
prisoners, 90, 102, 129–34, 288, 296–300
  Liverpool monument and, 275–6
  recaptures by, 121–8
  wounded, 102, 119–20, 129, 130, 134
Privy Council, 224
prizes, 11, 12, 29–30, 61, 75, 85, 88, 90, 94, 100, 112–34, 283–4
  abandonment of, 92, 129–34, 139
  alcohol stores, 119–20, 137
  donation of, 251
  recaptures of, 121–7
  wrecking of, 92, 114–16, 122–3, 137, 139
prostitution, 189
Protestantism, 40

Prothée (prison hulk), 297–8
Prussia, 254
Psyche (French privateer), 15
Public Ledger & Daily Advertiser, 242
Puercas Rocks, 122
Puerto de Santa María, Spain, 126, 135, 136
Purbrook, Hampshire, 254
Purcell, Henry, 39

Queen's Royal Regiment of Foot, 223
Quiot, Casimir, 94

Railton, William, 263–4
Ram, William, 66, 72, 102
Ramsgate, Kent, 15
Rathbone Place, Westminster, 174
Ratto di Proserpina, Il (von Winter), 197–8
Rayner, Thomas, 71
Rayo (Spanish 100), 84, 124, 126, 139
Reading, Berkshire, 288
Redoutable (French 74), 25–7, 58, 59, 61, 63, 65, 66, 68, 71, 77, 78, 288
  prize, taking as, 85, 88, 91, 115–16, 143
Reeves, Thomas, 116
Régiment de Ligne, 16ème, 138
Régiment de Ligne, 4ème, 48
Régiment de Ligne, 67ème, 154
Régiment de Ligne, 82ème, 7
Rennes, France, 285–8
Revenge, HMS (74), 27, 32, 51, 55, 76, 104, 110, 130, 215
Révolutionnaire, HMS (frigate 40), 153
Reynolds, Frederic, 189
Rhine River, 20
Richards, Jacob, 205
Río Guadalete, 136
Riordan, Mortley, 7
River Fencibles, 208, 214, 216
Rivers Jr, William, 68–9, 103–4
Rivers Sr, William, 63, 68
Roach Abbey limestone, 264
Roberts, Andrew, 287
Robinson, Hercules, 27, 101, 142
Robinson, James, 53, 85
Robinson, William, 32, 51, 55, 130

Rochefort, France, 1, 2, 6, 284, 300
Rochefort squadron, 151–7
Rodie, Thomas, 272
Rogers, John, 15
Romeo and Juliet (Shakespeare), 196
Romney, Francis, 153
Roscoe, William, 273–4, 276
Rosily, François, 138–9
Roskruge, Francis, 104
Rossi, Signor, 198–9
Rota, Spain, 126, 135
Rotely, Lewis, 60, 64, 67, 70, 107, 108
Rotherhithe, Surrey, 217, 300
Rouquet, James, 201
Royal Academy of Arts, 243, 253–4, 255
Royal Amphitheatre, Dublin, 194
Royal Cornwall Gazette, 155
Royal Gallery, Palace of Westminster, 245–6
Royal Marines, 28, 64, 68, 70, 108
Royal Naval College, Greenwich, 255
Royal Sovereign, HMS (100), 38, 39, 44, 46, 49–57, 58, 63, 76, 92, 113, 134, 295
Royalty Theatre, Goodman's Fields, 191
'Rule Britannia' (Arne), 39, 176, 177, 184, 185, 196–7, 260
Russian Empire, 19, 20, 48, 141, 254
Rutherford, William, 101

Sackville Street, Dublin, 257
Sadler's Wells, Islington, 192–5
Saffron Walden, Essex, 200
Sailor's Word Book (Smyth), 108*n*
Saint-Cloud, Paris, 289
Saint-Malo, France, 13
Salisbury, Wiltshire, 159
Salmon, John, 88
Salvador del Mundo, HMS (112), 157
San Agustín (Spanish 74), 59, 82, 84, 132, 133, 134
San Francisco de Asis (Spanish 74), 59, 84, 124, 135
San Ildefonso (Spanish 74), 54, 87, 139
San Josef (Spanish 112), 214, 225
San Juan Nepomuceno (Spanish 74), 53, 85, 139
San Justo (Spanish 74), 51, 53

INDEX

San Leandro (Spanish 64), 51, 53
San Lúcar, Spain, 126, 136, 137, 138
San Nicolás (Spanish 84), 106
San Rafael (Spanish 80), 6, 11–12
San Sebastián lighthouse, Cadiz, 122, 124
Sancti Petri rocks, Cadiz, 114, 119, 124
Santa Ana (Spanish 112), 48, 49–50, 57, 58, 76, 114, 117, 125
Santa Catalina, Cadiz, 122, 127
Santa Cruz de Tenerife, 25, 37, 197
Santa Margarita, HMS (frigate 36), 152, 153
Santísima Trinidad (Spanish 140), 30, 32, 51, 79, 85, 86, 90, 111
  prize, taking as, 114, 225, 286–7
  sinking of, 129, 131
  Victory, firing on, 59, 60, 61, 64, 157
Santo Domingo, 252
Saul (Handel), 177, 219, 222
Saunders, William, 244
Schirmer, Friedrich, 191–2
Scipion (French 74), 12, 83, 89, 152–4
Scotland, 181–2, 255–7
Scots Greys, 223
Scots Magazine, 182
Scott, Alexander, 66, 73, 205, 209, 215, 219, 245
Scott, John, 38, 59, 66
Scout, HMS (brig sloop 16), 127
Sea Fencibles, 158, 252
Selsey Bill, West Sussex, 284
Senhouse, Humphrey, 64, 80, 91, 94, 100, 112, 124
Servaux, Pierre, 50, 114
Seven Years War (1756–63), 133
Seymour, John, 121, 123–4
Seymour, Joseph, 80
Shades Tavern, Swansea, 64
Shambles sandbank, 180
She Wou'd and She Wou'd Not (Cibber), 185
Sheerness, Kent, 73, 205, 299, 300
Sheffield, Catherine, 247
Sheridan, Richard Brinsley, 262
Shoreditch, Middlesex, 15
Shoveller, William, 134, 144
Shrewsbury, Shropshire, 177
Sicily, 234

Siege of Belgrade, The (Storace and Cobb), 184
Siege of Gibraltar (Dibdin), 195
Sievier, Robert, 263
signals, 30, 42, 61–2, 82–4, 111–12
Silhouette, Jean Baptiste, 154
silk stockings, 37, 52, 134
Silliman, Benjamin, 171
Simmonds, Joseph, 49
Simmons, James, 176
Sirène (French frigate 44), 7
Sirius, HMS (frigate 36), 38, 113
Sketch for a Monument to Lord Nelson (West), 255
Skinners' Company, 216
slavery, 4, 235, 268–76
Smith, James, 261–2, 275
Smith, Neil, 68
Smith, Thomas, 70
Smith, William, 69
Smiton, Alexander, 182
Smyth, William Henry, 108*n*
Sneinton, Nottinghamshire, 200
Society of Arts and Sciences, 247
Soho Mint, Handsworth, 206
Solana, Francisco Solano, 6th Marquis, 102
Somerset House, Westminster, 217
de Soto, Diego, 117
South Carolina, United States, 73
Southampton, Hampshire, 176
Southampton Street, Westminster, 221
Spain, 1, 5–6, 11–13, 19, 20–21, 40, 99–103, 122–7
Spartiate, HMS (74), 83, 113, 214
Spear, Richard, 120, 122, 123
Spedillo, Gaetano, 205
Spencer-Stanhope, Walter, 166
Spencer, Robert, 167
Spithead, Hampshire, 203, 205
Spratt, James, 27, 134, 144–5
St Andrew's Chapel, Westminster Abbey, 248
St Bride's church, London, 217
St Clement Danes, London, 220, 235
St Croix, 273
St Dunstan's Church, London, 212
St George's Chapel, Windsor, 249
St Helena, 291, 300

St James's Palace, Westminster, 232
St James's Park, Westminster, 160, 222
St James's Street, Westminster, 248
St Katharine's Dock, London, 216
St Kitts, 2
St Lucia, 7
St Mary, Azores, 73
St Nicholas's Square, Newcastle, 295
St Omers, France, 13
St Paul's Cathedral, London, 106, 172, 200, 202, 241
   Nelson monument, 242–3, 246–7
   Nelson's funeral (1806), 210–14, 216, 219–20, 223, 224, 227, 230–36
   Nelson's tomb, 241–2, 248–50
   Wellington's tomb, 278
St Paul's Coffee House, London, 211
St Vincent, 273
Staines, Surrey, 159
Star, 142, 170, 232, 287
Stationers' Company, 216
Staunton, John, 272
Stevens, George Alexander, 185
Stevens, William Bagshaw, 270
Stevenson, Robert Louis, 257
stink pots, 78
Storace, Stephen, 184
Storm, The (Stevens), 185
Strachan, Richard, 151–7, 181, 202, 283, 288
Strand, Westminster, 160, 172, 173, 191, 217, 220, 226
striking the colours, 11–12, 80, 85, 87, 88–9, 91–2
Suffren (French 74), 2
Sullivan, Jeremiah, 71
Sumatra, 15
Sun Street, Shoreditch, 15
Sun, 13, 169, 198, 199, 242
Superb, HMS (74), 149, 150, 151, 252
surgeons, 33–7, 68–79, 144
Surrey Chapel, Southwark, 202
Surrey, England, 159
Swansea, Wales, 60, 64
Swiftsure (French 74), 47, 79, 101, 114, 117, 139, 294–5
Swiftsure, HMS (74), 10, 28, 93–4, 100, 101, 115–16, 203, 298

Sykes, John, 148, 157–8, 160

Taft, William, 70
Taylor, George Ledwell, 261
Taylor, Simon, 268
Téméraire, HMS (98), 42, 51, 54, 63, 64, 85, 88, 91, 94, 141–3, 299–300
   casualties, 92
   prize crews, 85, 114, 115
   towing of, 113
   wounded on, 134
Temple Bar, London, 220, 221, 226, 229
Temple of the Muses, Finsbury Square, 233
Tenerife, 25, 37, 197
Terrant, William, 76
Tewkesbury, Gloucestershire, 177
Theatre Royal, Covent Garden, 174, 185–7, 189–91, 196
Theatre Royal, Drury Lane, 184, 187–9, 191
Theatre Royal, Southampton, 176
Thémis (French frigate 40), 125
Thétis (French frigate 40), 2
Thistlethwayte, Evelyn, 254
Thomas, Edmund Fanning, 120
Thornhill, James, 208
Thornton, Thomas, 177
Thornville Royal, Yorkshire, 177
Thorpe, William, 125, 135
Thunderer, HMS (74), 114, 117, 125
Times, The, 59, 169, 211, 265, 287–8
Tiverton, Devon, 283
de Tocqueville, Charles, 154
Tomlinson, Robert, 158
Tonnant, HMS (80), 31, 33, 41, 56–7, 76, 86, 88, 94, 113, 117, 134
Touffet, Claude, 154
Toulon, France, 1, 2, 10, 77, 290, 292–3
tourniquets, 34, 35, 36, 37, 134
Tower of London, 214, 242
Trafalgar Square, Westminster, 227, 261, 262–6, 268
Trelawny, Edward John, 149–50
Trewinnard, Joshua, 173
Trewman's Exeter Flying Post, 157
Trinidad and Tobago, 10
Truro, Cornwall, 158

INDEX

Tufton, Alfred, 16
Turk's Head, London, 214
Turnbull, William, 59
Turner, Colin, 72
Turner, Joseph Mallord William, 300
Tyler, Charles, 41, 56
Tyson, John, 203, 205

Ullswater, Cumberland, 178
Ulm campaign (1805), 20, 141, 168, 171
Union Stairs, London, 214
United Kingdom
   Napoleon's invasion plan (1803–5), 1–2, 13–20, 201, 289
   news of victory, 146–60, 165–83
United States, 73, 167
   War of Independence (1775–83), 60, 193, 243
de Uriarte, Francisco Javier, 130
Ushant (Ouessant), France, 149

Valdés, Cayetano, 84, 125, 135
de Vargas, José Ramón, 87
Venice Preserv'd (Otway), 186
Vernon, Edward, 31
Verona, Italy, 171
Victory, HMS (100), 10, 25–7, 57, 58–76, 77, 84, 90, 102, 115, 143, 173, 269
   anchoring, 112–13
   casualties on, 92
   Chatham docking, 205–6
   clothing on, 37
   figurehead, 68
   food on, 41
   gun decks, 32, 33
   Nelson's death, 25–7, 54, 57, 58, 67, 72–4, 84, 105
   Nelson's funeral, 215, 224, 226, 229, 234
   Nelson's remains, 106–9, 203–4
   prisoners on, 90
   prize system on, 30
   restorations of, 284
   signals, 42, 61–2, 111–12
   surgery on, 26, 37, 68–76
Victory and Death of Lord Nelson, The (Cumberland), 187–9

Vienna, Austria, 20, 140–41
Vigo, Spain, 19
Village, The (Halloran), 40
Ville de Paris, HMS (110), 292–3
Villeneuve, Pierre-Charles, 1, 2, 5–7, 10, 19, 191, 269, 288–92
   Battle of Cape Finisterre (1805), 11, 19, 285
   Battle of Diamond Rock (1805), 1, 7–10
   Battle of Trafalgar (1805), 48, 62, 80, 82–6, 101, 191
   death (1806), 289–92
   imprisonment (1805), 288
Vimereux, France, 18
Voltaire, 282
Vreedenhoop, Demerara, 272

Wakefield, Yorkshire, 55
Wales, 60, 64, 177, 259–60
Walker, Henry, 120–21, 137, 139
Wallington, Hampshire, 254
Wapping, Middlesex, 214
Watson, Chatto, 220
Watson, Joshua Rowley, 252
Watson, William, 216, 220, 229
waxworks, 241–2, 247
Weather column, 38, 40, 54, 62, 63, 79, 82, 92
Weekly Dispatch, 18
Wellington, Arthur Wellesley, 1st Duke, 277–8, 296
Wells, William, 70
Wemyss, James, 78
West, Benjamin, 243–4, 245, 255
West Harptree, Somerset, 201
West India Association, 272
West Indies, *see* Caribbean
Westburgh, William, 68
Westmacott, Richard, 258, 268, 274
Westminster Abbey, 106–7, 232, 246
Westmorland marble, 274
Weymouth, Dorset, 180
Whim (slave ship), 270
Whipple, Thomas, 59, 72
Whitby, Henry, 168–9
Whitby, Yorkshire, 55
White, William, 78

Whitehall, Westminster, 159, 211, 218, 222, 224, 226, 227, 230
Whitford, Richard, 235
Wigton, Cumberland, 178
Wilberforce, William, 269
Wild Islanders, The (Russell), 196
Wilkins, William, 257, 259
William IV, King, 224, 230, 261
Williams, Edward, 244
Williams, John, 229
Willmot, William, 62, 63
Wiltshire, England, 159
Wincanton, Somerset, 297
Winchester, Hampshire, 176
'wind of a ball' deaths, 59
Windham, William, 235
Windsor Castle, Berkshire, 249
Windward Islands, 3
Woelfl, Joseph, 198
Wolsey, Thomas, 249–50
Wood, Robert, 200
Woodyates, Dorset, 159
Woolocombe, Roger, 7
Woolwich, Kent, 193
  Arsenal, 264, 291
Wordsworth, Dorothy, 178–9, 180
Wordsworth, John, 180
Wordsworth, William, 178–81
World Ship Trust, 284
Worshipful Companies, 216, 217
wounded, 102, 119–20, 129, 130, 134
Wright, Patience, 247
Wroughton, Richard, 184
Wyatt, James, 233, 274
Wyatt, Matthew Cotes, 274, 275

yellow fever, 10
York Herald, 177
Young, Robert Benjamin, 74, 147
Young, William, 157–8

Zorg (slave ship), 273